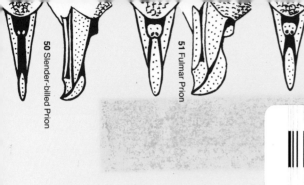

50 Slender-billed Prion

51 Fulmar Prion

52 Fairy Prion

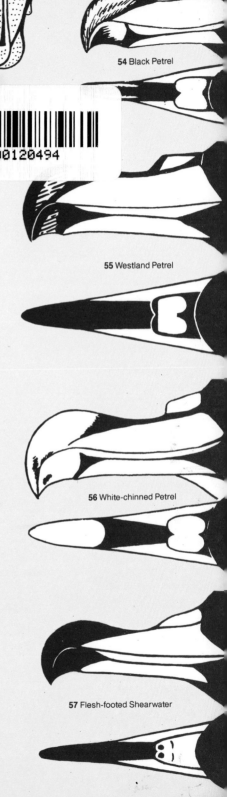

54 Black Petrel

55 Westland Petrel

56 White-chinned Petrel

57 Flesh-footed Shearwater

D0120494

Sea-bird bill profiles: albatrosses, petrels, shearwaters

Use these life-size bill profiles together with the field information for the accurate identification of dead birds washed up on the beach.

• Compare the bill shape of your specimen with the drawings.

• Take precise measurements (using calipers) of *culmen length* and *bill width* (see diagram). If you think the bird is rare or unusual, take it to the museum.

Culmen length

Bill Width

• Prion identification is very difficult. Our drawings are guides to average specimens only. Prion bills vary greatly. Some are virtually impossible to identify because species and racial clines are probably operating. Take all difficult prions to the museum.

47 Broad-billed Prion
Length 31.5-38 mm
Width 18-25 mm

48 Lesser Broad-billed Prion
Length 26.5-34 mm
Width 12.5-20.5 mm

49 Antarctic Prion
Length 25-30 mm
Width 12-16 mm

50 Slender-billed Prion
Length 23-27.5 mm
Width 9-12 mm

51 Fulmar Prion
Length 19-25 mm
Width 10-14.7 mm

52 Fairy Prion
Length 19.5-26 mm
Width 10-12.5 mm

Simpson & Day

FIELD GUIDE
to the
Birds of Australia

A BOOK OF IDENTIFICATION

VIKING O'NEIL

Contents

Viking O'Neil
Penguin Books Australia Ltd
487 Maroondah Highway, PO Box 257
Ringwood, Victoria 3134, Australia
Penguin Books Ltd
Harmondsworth, Middlesex, England
Viking Penguin Inc.
40 West 23rd Street, New York, N.Y., U.S.A.
Penguin Books Canada Limited
2801 John Street, Markham, Ontario, Canada L3R 1B4
Penguin Books (N.Z.) Ltd
182-190 Wairau Road, Auckland 10, New Zealand

First published by Lloyd O'Neil Pty Ltd in 1984 as
The Birds of Australia
Second edition 1986
First published in this format by Penguin Books Australia Ltd
as *Field Guide to the Birds of Australia* 1989

10 9 8 7 6 5 4 3 2

© Ken Simpson, Nicolas Day and Peter Trusler, 1984
© Form, concept, design: Penguin Books Australia Ltd, 1984
Copyright in individual contributions and illustrations remains the
property of the contributing writers or illustrators or artists
as acknowledged within the preliminary pages of the work.

All rights reserved. Without limiting the rights under
copyright reserved above, no part of this publication may
be reproduced, stored in or introduced into a retrieval system,
or transmitted, in any form or by any means (electronic,
mechanical, photocopying, recording or otherwise) without
the prior written permission of both the copyright owner
and the above publisher of this book.

Produced by Viking O'Neil
56 Claremont Street, South Yarra, Victoria 3141, Australia
A division of Penguin Books Australia Ltd

Designed by Zoë Gent-Murphy
Printed and bound in Hong Kong through
Bookbuilders Limited

National Library of Australia
Cataloguing-in-Publication data

Simpson, Ken, 1938-
 Field guide to the birds of Australia.

 Includes index.
 ISBN 0 670 90072 9.

 1. Birds – Australia – Identification. I. Day,
Nicolas, 1955-

 598.2994

Introduction

Use this book in conjunction with other major identification texts; Peter Slater (1970, 1974, 1986), J. D. Macdonald (1973), Reader's Digest Services (1976, 1986), Graham Pizzey (1980, 1987). We also thank the many authors of prior bird books: we have used them with respect.

The language we have used is as plain as we could make it. Each bird species is given in the sequence used by the 'senior bird-watchers' in the country, i.e. the Royal Australasian Ornithologists Union (RAOU) (1975) *Checklist of the Birds of Australia, Part 1, Non-Passerines,* and (1975) *Interim List of Australian Songbirds, Passerines.* Common (vernacular) names used in this book basically follow the list, also by the RAOU, entitled 'Recommended English Names for Australian Birds', supplement to *The Emu,* Vol. 77 (1978). Latin (genus and species) names have been brought up to date.

We have added a few recently reported species which are not yet on the official Australian list, slotting them in where we considered it appropriate. We have also retained several which have virtually been discredited. No harm is done if you learn their appearances, but double-check before claiming that you have seen one of them.

The numbers on our maps are those that are given in *The Atlas of Australian Birds* (RAOU)*. The numbers are there if you want to participate in research and census schemes – we urge you to do so (see page 283). We stress, our maps are not the RAOU *Atlas* maps. *Blakers, M., Davies, S. J. J. F. & P. N. Reilly (1984), *The Atlas of Australian Birds,* Melbourne University Press, Melbourne.

We thank all the contributors. The contribution of each writer is listed on page 352. At different times during the book's preparation and in a variety of ways, assistance of great value was given by Gael Coutts, Colin Critchell, Jeff Davies, David Eades, Rene Gordon, Christina Herd, Ed McNab, Luke Naismith, Richard Pope, Hilton Potgeiter, Wayne Roffey, Cecilia Scanlan, Chris Sewell and Bob Swindley. Finally, we wish to thank Lloyd O'Neil and his company.

Ken Simpson
Nicolas Day
July 1988

The publishers would like to thank the following organisations and their staff for their professional advice and assistance with specimens:
The Museum of Victoria (Belinda Gillies, Alan McEvey, Les Christidis)
South Australian Museum (Shane Parker)
Fisheries and Wildlife Division, Ministry for Conservation
(Ron Brown, Andrew Corrick, Peter Menkhorst, Ian Norman, Don White)
Royal Melbourne Zoological Gardens (Roy Dunn, Mervyn Jenkins)
Sir Colin MacKenzie Zoological Park, Healesville (Neil Morley)
Zoology Department, Monash University (Margaret Davies)
Victorian Ornithological Research Group (Marc Gottsch)
Royal Australasian Ornithologists Union (Margaret Blakers)
Bird Observers Club (Alma Mitchell)
Andrew Wegener Australian Wildlife Lectures (Andrew Wegener)
Australasian Wader Study Group.

Writers

Tom Aumann
David Baker-Gabb
Kevin Bartram
Simon Bennett
Ron Brown
Margaret Cameron
Mike Carter
Andrew Corrick
Stephen Debus
Denise Deerson
Xenia Dennett
Peter Fell
Kate Fitzherbert
Cliff Frith
Geoff Gayner
Belinda Gillies
Marc Gottsch
Murray Grant
John Hatch
Victor Hurley
Jack Hyett
Andrew Isles
Angela Jessop
Jaroslav Klapste
Peter Klapste
Tess Kloot
Brett Lane
Alan Lill
Gordon McCarthy
Ellen McCulloch
Peter Mason
Peter Menkhorst
Clive Minton
Mick Murliss
Richard Noske
David Paton
Paul Peake
Trevor Pescott
Des Quinn
Pat Rich
Bruce Robertson
Len Robinson
Tony Robinson
Ken Simpson
Lance Williams
John Woinarski
Richard Zann

Editor
Ken Simpson

Illustrator
Nicolas Day

Art Director
Peter Trusler

Field Consultants
Kevin Bartram
Len Robinson

Publisher's Editor
Robyn Carter

Publisher's Reader
Walter Boles

Designer
Zoë Gent-Murphy

Designer's Assistant
Heather Jones

Typesetter
Tricia Randle

Contents Illustrator
Jeremy Boot

Contributing Illustrators
Black and white:
Kevin Bartram
Alistair Coutts
Nicolas Day
Annette Dowd
Graham Milledge
Alison Titchen
Peter Trusler

How to use this book to identify a bird

Step 1   Key to Families (pages 6-15)
By using the illustrations and text in the **Key to Families** try to work out which Family your bird belongs to. For example: does it look like a gull, a kingfisher, or an owl?

Step 2   Field Information (pages 16-271)
● When you think you know which Family your bird belongs to, turn to the **Field Information** section. The appropriate pages are indicated in bold type in the **Key to Families**.

● Look for your bird on the colour plate(s). The number beside the illustration refers to the species. All the field information for that species appears on the facing page, under the same number. Read the text carefully, then check the map (see map legend below) to make sure the bird you have observed is likely to be found in the area you have seen it. Remember, the maps are only a general guide to distribution. If you require a more detailed map reference see *The Atlas of Australian Birds* (Royal Australasian Ornithologists Union) under the RAOU number given.

● If all the information provided corresponds with what you have seen, then you have probably identified your bird correctly. You may wish to record it in the ticking boxes beside the map. If not, re-check the colour plate(s) for a similar species or go back to the **Key to Families**.

Step 3   The Handbook (pages 272-341)
If you want to read more about the taxonomy, behaviour, feeding and breeding habits (see breeding bar legend below) of the bird, the second page reference in the **Key to Families** will refer you to this information.

The indexes of scientific and common names should be used if you know the name of the bird you wish to look up.

Legend for distribution maps

▨	Breeding
▧	Non-breeding and vagrant
▷	Offshore islands where birds have been recorded
→	Migration trends

Legend for breeding bars in The Handbook

▨	Main breeding season
▦	Casual breeding and breeding in response to unseasonable rainfall

Parts of a bird's body

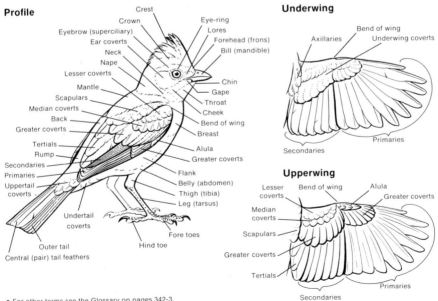

● For other terms see the Glossary on pages 342-3.

Preface to the Field Guide

In response to many requests we have produced this Third Edition as a smaller, more portable volume. As such, it is now truly a field guide. Included here are two new plates to replace those for the ibis, spoonbills and Black-necked Stork (p. 55), and for the chats (p. 245). There are 10 new line drawings, 315 map corrections and additions, and the text and index have been updated and revised.

Since 1984, a number of additional bird species have been positively identified as stragglers to the continent. One, the Laughing Gull, is detailed below. The other seabirds are Bareau's Petrel *Pterodroma baraui* from Reunion Island; an additional race (subspecies) of White-necked Petrel *Pterodroma externa externa* from Juan Fernandez Archipelago off Chile's coast; Bulwer's Petrel *Bulweria bulwerii* which occurs widely in both the Atlantic and Pacific oceans; and the Pink-footed Shearwater *Puffinus creatopus*, another eastern Pacific and Chilean species. A Northern Hemisphere duck, Northern Pintail *Anas acuta*, Gurney's Eagle *Aquila gurneyi* and Black-backed Wagtail *Motacilla lugens* complete the list of new species.

Bird distributions may change if the Australian climate slowly warms up in response to the 'Greenhouse Effect', as is predicted. The enormous job of identifying, understanding, cataloguing and conserving the nation's wild fauna, including birds, continues. You can fully participate by regularly, neatly and systematically recording your bird observations in Simpson & Day's *Birds of Australia Logbook* and by making your records available to research scientists and appropriate lay organisations (see this book, p. 283).

Your ideas and criticisms to improve this book will always be welcomed.

Ken Simpson and Nicolas Day

759 Gray's Grasshopper Warbler *Locustella fasciolata*

Resembles 532 Clamorous Reed-warbler. Dark rufous-brown above. Eyebrow pronounced, pale, extends above ear coverts. White to pale throat. Dark grey-brown chest, paler abdomen and vent. Tail long, round-tipped.
Size 17-19 cm. **Voice** loud; calls from a concealed position.
Habitat Bullrush (cumbungi) beds in Australia.
Hides low in vegetation cover. Two records Northern Territory only. Rare vagrant from northern Asia.
Reading McKean, J.L. 1984. The occurrence in Australia of Gray's Grasshopper Warbler *Locustella fasciolata*. *Australian Bird Watcher* 10 (5):171-172.

760 Laughing Gull *Larus atricilla*

Straggler to Aust. from E tropical Americas. Two birds at Cairns, N Qld, autumn 1988, are adult and 1st year, both in winter plumage. **Size** 38 cm approx. Smaller, darker than 280 Silver Gull. Appears long-winged in flight. Identify from 285 Franklin's Gull. (A) breeding adult (America); (B) adult winter plumage; (C) 1st year winter; (D) adult winter; (E) 1st year winter. Based on photos of Cairns birds. **Reading** Plumage details: Grant, P. J. (1982), *Gulls – A Guide to Identification*, T & A. D. Poyser, U.K.; Harrison, Peter (1987), *Seabirds of the World – A Photographic Guide*, Christopher Helm (Ltd), U.K.

Key to Families

Emus Family Dromaiidae   **16-17,** 284

Australia's national emblem and largest endemic bird. Flightless, fast-running, strong-legged, stands two metres high. Loose, grey, shaggy plumage.   Species: World 1; Australia 1.

Cassowaries Family Casuariidae   **16-17,** 284

Stocky and flightless, this large ratite has black, hair-like plumage, a helmeted head, a bright face and distinctive neck wattles.   Species: World 3; Australia 1.

Mihirungs (Extinct) Family Dromornithidae   275

Huge runners with heavy bills, hoof-like toes, tiny wings. Miocene-Pleistocene fossils. Not illustrated here.

Ostriches Family Struthionidae   **16-17,** 284

The plumage of the Ostrich is black and it is the world's largest living bird. Each foot has two toes — the only bird with less than three.   Species: World 1; Australia 1.

Grebes Family Podicipedidae   **18-19,** 285

Sharp-billed diving birds with legs far back on the body; feet have lobed toes. Grebes cannot walk well on land.
Species: World 17; Australia 3.

Penguins Family Spheniscidae   **20-21,** 285

Plump, small to large sea-birds with upright stance. Dense, waterproof plumage. Wings modified as flippers for sustained swimming, diving.   Species: World 17; Australia 11.

Albatrosses Family Diomedeidae   **22-27,** 285-286

Medium to very large, long-winged, gliding, oceanic sea-birds. Small tubular nostrils at side of large, hook-tipped bills; webbed feet.   Species: World 15; Australia 10.

Petrels, Shearwaters
Family Procellariidae   **28-39,** 286-288

Small to medium, long-winged, gliding, oceanic sea-birds. Tubular nostrils on top of stout, hooked bills; webbed feet.
Species: World approx. 60; Australia 41.

Storm-Petrels Family Oceanitidae   **40-41,** 288

Tiny, blackish or grey, long-legged petrels with rapid swooping flight. Feed by fluttering or pattering over wave surfaces. Species: World 18; Australia 7.

Diving-Petrels Family Pelecanoididae   **40-41,** 288

Tiny, dumpy, short-winged, resembling Northern Hemisphere auks. Fly between waves with rapid wing beats; dive and swim well. Species: World 5; Australia 2.

6

Pelicans Family Pelecanidae   42-43, 288-289

The large Australian Pelican has a spectacular long bill and loose pouch. All four toes are linked by webbing.
Species: World 8; Australia 1.

Gannets, Boobies Family Sulidae   42-43, 289

Stout-billed sea-birds which indulge in spectacular plunge-diving. Feet fully webbed. Gannets frequent colder seas; boobies more tropical seas.   Species: World 9; Australia 5.

Darters Family Anhingidae   44-45, 289

Darters lunge with snake-like necks and slender bills to spear fish under water. Resemble cormorants but larger, slimmer, broader-winged.   Species: World 2; Australia 1.

Cormorants, Shags Family Phalacrocoracidae   44-45, 289

Cormorants swim and dive for fish. Like darters, their feet are fully webbed. They often perch with outstretched wings.
Species: World 29-33; Australia 5.

Frigatebirds Family Fregatidae   46-47, 289

Large, dark sea-birds with long, hooked bills and long, deeply forked tails. Soar on long pointed wings over tropical seas. Feed on the wing.
Species: World 5; Australia 3.

Tropicbirds Family Phaethontidae   46-47, 289

Stout, white-plumaged sea-birds with two long, central tail streamers. Plunge-dive for food; strong direct flight; soar in updrafts.   Species: World 3; Australia 2.

Herons, Egrets, Bitterns Family Ardeidae   48-53, 290

Slender, long-legged, long-necked, aquatic birds with bills like daggers.   Species: World 64; Australia 14.

Storks Family Ciconiidae   54-55, 290

Large waterbirds with long, stout bills. During flight or soaring, their broad wings, extended neck and long trailing legs are distinctive.   Species: World 17; Australia 1.

Ibises, Spoonbills Family Plataleidae   54-55, 290

Diagnostic bills distinguish these from similarly built herons. They feed by touch: probing (ibises), sweeping through shallow water (spoonbills).   Species: World 28; Australia 5.

Flamingos (Extinct) Family Phoenicopteridae   275

Tall, long-limbed, filter-feeding, aquatic birds. Miocene-Pleistocene fossils. Not illustrated here.

Palaelodids (Extinct) Family Palaelodidae   · 275

Large, tall, probably straight-billed, aquatic birds. Miocene fossils. Not illustrated here.

Geese, Swans, Ducks   Family Anatidae   56-65, 291-292

Birds of the wetlands with dense waterproof plumage, webbed feet and flattened bills. Most fly strongly. Important game birds.   Species: World 148; Australia 23.

Osprey   Family Pandionidae   66-67, 293

A fishing hawk with broad wings, strong legs and talons to seize slippery prey. Nest is a large, conspicuous stick platform.   Species: World 1; Australia 1.

Kites, Goshawks, Eagles, Harriers   Famiy Accipitridae   66-75, 293-295

Birds of prey with short heads, broad wings, hooked bills and large talons. Females larger than males. Often seen soaring.
Species: World approx. 217; Australia 18.

Falcons   Family Falconidae   74-77, 295

Predatory birds with 'toothed' upper bill, a dark cap or tear-drop cheek mark, long pointed wings and swift flight.
Species: World 61; Australia 6.

Mound-builders (Megapodes) Family Megapodiidae   78-79, 296

Large, strong-legged, dark or spotted, ground birds. Some have bare heads and bright wattles. Eggs incubated in soil mounds.   Species: World 12; Australia 3.

Quails, Pheasants   Family Phasianidae   80-81, 296

Small and striped to large and long-tailed, bright ground birds.   Species: World approx. 213; Australia approx. 7.

Button-quails   Family Turnicidae   82-83, 297

Resemble true quails (Phasianidae) but lack a hind toe. Females larger, brighter and polyandrous — mate with several males each breeding season.   Species: World 16; Australia 7.

Plains-wanderer   Family Pedionomidae   82-83, 297

Like button-quails but have a hind toe. Weak, fluttering flight.   Species: World 1; Australia 1.

Rails, Crakes, Swamphens, Coots   Family Rallidae   84-89, 297-298

Small to large, long-toed, stout-billed, skulking, aquatic birds.   Species: World 132; Australia 16.

Cranes   Family Gruidae   90-91, 298

Tall, elegant, upright birds with red heads, grey bodies. Sharp bill longer than head. Elaborate dancing displays. Soaring flight.   Species: World 14; Australia 2.

Bustards   Family Otididae   90-91, 298

Stately, heavy, grassland-dwelling birds with long legs, pointed bills.   Species: World 23; Australia 1.

Jacanas (Lotusbirds)   Family Jacanidae   **92-93**, 300

Rail-like in appearance, jacanas are waders with specialised long toes and hind claws for running over floating freshwater plants.   Species: World 7; Australia 1.

Thick-knees (Stone Curlews)
Family Burhinidae   **92-93**, 300

Tall, large-eyed, plover-like, bush- and beach-dwelling waders. Both species are widespread but relatively uncommon.   Species: World 9; Australia 2.

Painted Snipe   Family Rostratulidae   **92-93**, 300

Long-billed, strikingly patterned waders. Female brighter. May 'freeze' when disturbed.   Species: World 2; Australia 1.

Oystercatchers
Family Haematopodidae   **92-93**, 300

Black or pied coastal waders.   Species: World 6; Australia 2.

**Lapwings, Plovers,
Dotterels**   Family Charadriidae   **94-99**, 300-301

Short-billed, round-headed, large-eyed, plain or camouflaged waders.   Species: World 65; Australia 16.

Stilts, Avocets   Family Recurvirostridae   **98-99**, 302

Medium-sized, distinctive waders with very long legs. Bills slender: straight (stilts), upturned (avocets). Often in large flocks. Yapping calls.   Species: World 6; Australia 3.

**Curlews, Sandpipers, Snipes,
Godwits**   Family Scolopacidae   **100-109**, 302-304

Large Family of usually long-billed, longish-legged, migratory waders. Smallest are the stints; largest the Eastern Curlew.   Species: World approx. 92; Australia approx. 43.

Phalaropes   Family Phalaropodidae   **110-111**, 304

Boldly marked, fast-flying waders. Feed by spinning when swimming.   Species: World 3; Australia 3.

Pratincoles   Family Glareolidae   **110-111**, 304

Fork-tailed, long-winged, brownish waders of inland and barren areas.   Species: World 16; Australia 2.

Skuas, Jaegers   Family Stercorariidae   **112-113**, 305

Piratical sea-birds with variable plumage, elongated central tail feathers and white wing flashes.   Species: World 5; Australia 5.

Gulls, Terns   Family Laridae   **114-123**, 306-309

Solid and medium-winged, gulls have white, grey and dark plumages, heavy bills, webbed feet. Terns and noddies are similar, but slender, thin-billed and narrow-winged. They stand horizontally. Some are crested. Dive into water for food or pick it off the surface.
Species: World approx. 85; Australia 28.

Pigeons, Doves
Family Columbidae   **124-131**, 310-311

Plump, plain or colourful, fast-flying fruit- or seed-eaters. Some have crests. Stout bill; some drink by sucking. Tail medium to long, square or pointed. Build frail stick nests.
Species: World approx. 290; Australia 25.

Cockatoos
Sub-Family Cacatuinae (see below)   **132-135**, 312-314

Medium to large parrots with prominent erectile crests. They have a complete orbital ring. Plumages range from black to white. Tail long, or short and square. Loud, often raucous voices. Feed on roots, seeds, blossom; some eat insects. Recent work has clarified the identification of corellas and black-cockatoos in Western Australia.

'True' Parrots   Family Psittacidae   **134-135**, 312-314

All parrots are 'true' parrots: stocky-bodied; medium-sized wings; stout, hooked bills; two toes forward and two back. In this book, all parrots are regarded as one Family with several well-defined Sub-Families (see above and below).
Species: World approx. 340; Australia 52.

Lorikeets   Sub-Family Loriinae   **136-137**, 312-314

Noisy, fast-flying, forest-dwelling parrots. They are small, with short, pointed tails, or medium-sized, with long pointed tails. Three Australian genera; all eat nectar, pollen and fruit.

Fig-Parrots
Sub-Family Opopsittinae   **136-137**, 312-314

The smallest Australian parrot. Tail is short, rather rounded. Predominantly green, the three isolated populations (races) may be identified from each other by facial markings.

'Long-tailed' Parrots
Sub-Family Polytelitinae   **138-139**, 312-314

Tails are long and graduated, each narrow tail feather with a fine tip. Wings are long and pointed. Fast-flying birds. Bills are small. Male and female plumages differ. Large flocks of a couple of the species may frequent grain crops in arid areas.

'Broad-tailed' Parrots
Sub-Family Platycercinae   **140-147**, 312-314

A 'grab-bag' of assorted parrots. Tails medium to long in proportion to body length and frequently fanned in display. Taxonomic fluctuations effect the total number regarded as 'full species' — rosellas, ringnecks, hooded parrots are all under consideration at present.

Parasitic Cuckoos,
Coucals   Family Cuculidae   **148-151**, 314-315

Slender, small to large, plain or barred, long-tailed birds with narrow wings, fast undulating flight and ventriloquial calls. All but the Pheasant Coucal are parasitic on other bird species.   Species: World 128; Australia 13.

Hawk Owls Family Strigidae   152-153, 315-316

Small to large nocturnal birds, usually with yellow irises and large eyes set in an indistinct facial disc. Females generally larger (except in Australia). Often heard giving monotonous territorial calls.   Species: World 123; Australia 5.

Barn Owls Family Tytonidae   154-155, 316

Small to large, slender-legged, nocturnal birds with all dark eyes set in a distinctive facial disc. Females larger. Usually silent. Hunt largely by listening for rodents, reptiles, large insects.   Species: World 10; Australia 5.

Frogmouths Family Podargidae   156-157, 316

Small to large nocturnal birds with weak feet, longish tails, rounded wings and massive, broad bills. Males larger. Plumage grey or brown. Resemble dead branch stubs while perched. Active in open forests and rainforests at late dusk.   Species: World 12; Australia 3.

Owlet-nightjars Family Aegothelidae   156-157, 317

Very small, delicate, grey, nocturnal birds. Small, broad bill edged by prominent bristles. Large, forward-facing eyes, weak feet, rounded wings and long, broad tail. Almost no reflective eye shine.   Species: World 8; Australia 1.

Nightjars Family Caprimulgidae   156-157, 317

Small to medium nocturnal birds with long tails, small broad bills and long pointed wings which, in flight, are stiff and irregular in movement. Very reflective eye shine in light. Normally roost by day on the ground. Nest amid leaf litter. Camouflaged plumage provides marvellous protection.   Species: World 67; Australia 3.

Swiftlets, Swifts Family Apodidae   158-159, 317

Quick-flying, dark-coloured insectivores with long, swept wings, square or forked tails, large eyes, a small bill but wide gape. Large swifts are migratory; resident swiftlets breed in caves.   Species: World 76; Australia 6.

Kingfishers Family Alcedinidae   160-163, 317-318

Usually brightly coloured, kingfishers have stout bodies, large heads, long heavy pointed bills and small feet. Fast, direct flight. Nest in holes in trees, banks, termite mounds.   Species: World 87; Australia 11.

Bee-eaters Family Meropidae   162-163, 318

Vocal, gregarious, migratory and brightly coloured birds. Bill long and down-curved; legs small. Hawk aerial insects. Nest in a burrow.   Species: World 24; Australia 1.

Rollers Family Coraciidae   162-163, 318

Known for their habit of rolling during aerial display flights. The Dollarbird has a red bill and stout body. When it hawks insects from exposed perches, white 'silver-dollar' wing spots become visible.   Species: World 17; Australia 1.

Pittas   Family Pittidae   164-165, 318

Plump, medium-sized, brightly coloured birds with short tails and long legs. Upright stance. White wing patches in flight. Secretive, ground-dwelling, in rainforests, tropical scrubs and mangroves. Usually located by loud, distinctive calls, often given while perched high.
Species: World 28; Australia 3

Lyrebirds   Family Menuridae   164-165, 319

Large, predominantly brown forest birds with long tails, legs and toes. They forage on the ground and fly only weakly. Breeding males have a loud, protracted song including much mimicry given during spectacular displays on prepared dancing mounds.   Species: World 2; Australia 2.

Scrub-birds   Family Atrichornithidae   164-165, 319

Considered to have close affinities with lyrebirds (Menuridae). Plumages are dark rufous and dark brown, with fine vermiculated patterns. Sexes differ. Birds are retiring, remain near ground, rarely fly. Loud, ventriloquial voice, containing much mimicry. The Noisy Scrub-bird is an endangered species.   Species: World 2; Australia 2.

Old World Larks   Family Alaudidae   166-167, 320

Small, streaked, grassland songbirds. Hind toe long, sharply clawed. Erectile head feathers as short crest. Endemic Bushlark and introduced Skylark both have aerial display flights. Identify them from Richard's Pipit (Motacillidae).
Species: World 75; Australia 2.

Swallows, Martins
Family Hirundinidae   166-167, 320

Small songbirds which hawk aerial insects. They have long, straight, pointed wings and either forked or square tails. Most are migratory or nomadic.   Species: World 75; Australia 6.

Old World Pipits,
Wagtails   Family Motacillidae   168-169, 320

Slender birds which often wag their long tails up and down. Pipits resemble larks (Alaudidae) but have yellow legs and *no* crest. The vagrant wagtails have pied plumages, plus yellow, green or grey.   Species: World 54; Australia 5.

Cuckoo-shrikes,
Trillers   Family Campephagidae   170-171, 321

Insectivorous, arboreal birds with slender bodies, long pointed wings and graduated tails. Plumages black, grey, brown and pied combinations; some have barrings. They have undulating flight and trilling voices.
Species: World 72; Australia 7.

Bulbuls   Family Pycnonotidae   172-173, 321

Generally small Old World birds. Brown to olive-green, often crested with decurved notched bills and distinctive head marks. Two introduced species; one survives about Sydney and Coffs Harbour, NSW.   Species: World 120; Australia 1.

Thrushes, Flycatchers and allies
Family Muscicapidae   172-193, 321-323

A varied group of small to medium-sized insectivorous birds, often taking their prey on the wing. Usually excellent songsters. Pronounced sexual differences in some. Some juveniles are spotted. A taxonomically complex group.
Species: World approx. 400; Australia 54-56.

Chowchillas, Whipbirds, Wedgebills, Quail-thrushes
Family Orthonychidae   · 194-197, 324

Four genera of rather secretive, long-tailed songbirds which live on or close to the ground, although in diverse habitats. Most are camouflaged; some are crested; some are mimics.
Species: World 11; Australia 10.

Babblers   Family Timaliidae   198-199, 324

Noisy, gregarious, mainly ground-feeding birds with plump brownish bodies, longish tails and pointed, down-curved bills. Territorial groups build several prominent dome-shaped stick nests for nesting and communal roosting.
Species: World approx. 255; Australia 4.

Old World Warblers   Family Sylviidae   200-203, 324

A Family whose membership often changes with the vagaries of taxonomists. Currently includes small, brownish, grass- and reed-dwelling, heavily streaked, strong-voiced song-birds. Some have aerial display flights.
Species: World approx. 400; Australia 8.

Fairy-wrens   Family Maluridae   202-209, 325

Three genera of small, cocked-tailed, insectivorous 'wrens' (warblers). Breeding males are brilliant; non-breeding and young males, and females are brown (fairy-wrens). Both sexes generally similar to the streak-plumaged grasswrens, and in the emu-wrens, which have modified tail feathers.
Species: World approx. 26; Australia approx. 18.

Bristlebirds, Scrubwrens, Gerygones, Thornbills
Family Acanthizidae   210-221, 326

Large Family of small to tiny dull birds. Active and with pleasant voices, they are mainly ground-dwelling or foliage-foraging insectivores. All build dome-shaped, sometimes pendant, nests. Only females incubate.
Species: World approx. 59; Australia approx. 41.

Sittellas   Family Neosittidae   222-223, 327

These birds climb on tree-trunks and branches. They are small, social, grey and black-and-white with orange to white wing bars, slightly upturned bills, yellow legs and feet. One variable species.   Species: World 1; Australia 1.

Treecreepers   Family Climacteridae   222-223, 327

These birds climb up tree-trunks and branches; some also hop on the ground. They are small and brownish with pale fawn wing bars, slightly down-curved bills, strong legs, long toes. Sexes are different.   Species: World 6; Australia 6.

Honeyeaters
Family Meliphagidae   224-243, 328-331

Honeyeaters have brush-tipped tongues, decurved bills (1-3 cm long), are mainly dull green or brown with patches of brighter plumage or skin around face, and are slim (10-15 cm long)   Species: World 173; Australia 66.

Chats   Family Ephthianuridae   244-245, 331

Bright males and similarly coloured but duller females and juveniles, typify these often nomadic and flocking small birds of the inland plains and coastal salt marshes.
Species: World 5; Australia 5.

Sunbirds   Family Nectariniidae   246-247, 331

Small, brightly coloured, slender-billed, quick-flying, nectar and insect feeders. At times are like honeyeaters and humming-birds in behaviour and flight mannerisms. Build pendulous nests with side entrances.   Species: World 118; Australia 1.

Flowerpeckers   Family Dicaeidae   246-247, 332

Tiny, short-billed and short-tailed, Mistletoebirds spread the parasitic plant on which they largely depend for food.
Species: World 58; Australia 1.

Pardalotes   Family Pardalotidae   246-247, 332-333

Tiny birds restricted to Australia. Mostly spotted and colourful with short tails, and short, broad bills. Feed on insects on tree foliage; breed in hollows or burrows, sometimes in colonies.   Species: World 5; Australia 5.

White-eyes   Family Zosteropidae   248-249, 333

Small greenish or yellowish birds with divided, extensible brush-tipped tongues. Most have a white eye-ring of tiny feathers. Migratory and nomadic. Build small, suspended, cup-shaped nests. Piping calls.   Species: World 80; Australia 3.

True Finches   Family Fringillidae   250-251, 334

Small to large seed-eaters with stout conical bills for cracking seeds and nuts. Plumages vary from camouflaged to brilliantly coloured. The nest is cup-shaped. Two species introduced into Australia.   Species: World 440; Australia 2.

Old World Sparrows
Family Passeridae   250-251, 334

Small, compact, brown-plumaged seed-eaters with 12 tail feathers and thick conical bills. Sexes rather similar. They build roofed, spherical nests. Often classified with weavers (Ploceidae).   Species: World 37; Australia 2.

Weavers, Waxbills, Grass-Finches, Mannikins
Family Ploceidae   250-257, 334-336

Two groups of small, colourful seed-eaters. Weavers construct beautifully woven grass nests with roofs. Estrildids are long-tailed and smaller with peculiar palate patterns. Their nests are bottle-shaped.   Species: World 120; Australia 22.

Starlings, Mynahs   Family Sturnidae   258-259, 336

Solid, sharp-beaked, dark-plumaged (iridescent in two species), strong-legged birds. They are vocal, aggressive, nomadic or migratory colonists.
Species: World 110; Australia 3.

Orioles, Figbirds   Family Oriolidae   258-259, 336

Both sexes of Australian orioles and Figbird females are similar, resembling the duller streaked females of some brighter foreign species.   Species: World 27-34; Australia 3.

Drongos   Family Dicruridae   258-259, 336

Gleaming black, fish-tailed and red-eyed, the Spangled Drongo is distinctive.   Species: World 20; Australia 1.

Bowerbirds   Family Ptilonorhynchidae   260-261, 337

Males have bright crests, capes or iridescent plumage; females are drab and camouflaged. Males clear courts or construct bowers.
Species: World 17; Australia 8.

Birds of Paradise
Family Paradisaeidae   262-263, 338

Adult sexes are different. Males are spectacular in colour and feathering; females and immature males are drab and camouflaged. Rainforest birds. Mainly fruit-eaters.
Species: World 43; Australia 4.

Australian Mud-nesters
Family Corcoracidae   264-265, 339

Large black, or small grey birds which live in sociable groups, build solid mud nests and assist each other in breeding.   Species: World 2; Australia 2.

Magpie-larks   Family Grallinidae   264-265, 339

Black and white (plover-like), long-legged, vocal, mud-nest building birds. Pairs often seen on roadsides. Flocks in winter.   Species: World 2; Australia 1.

Woodswallows   Family Artamidae   264-265, 339-340

Small, robust, mostly nomadic songbirds with bluish, black-tipped bills. Distinctive 'batwing' shape (in flight) rotate tails (when perched); may huddle together.
Species: World 10; Australia 6.

Butcherbirds,
Currawongs   Family Cracticidae   266-269, 340

Solid, arboreal, strong-flying birds. Black, or black, grey and white. Large, robust, hooked bills; loud voices, harsh and/or melodious.   Species: World 10; Australia 8.

Ravens, Crows   Family Corvidae   270-271, 341

Uniform, glossy black birds with minor physical differences. They have stout, rather long bills. Plumage is often reflective. Calls are 'cawing'.   Species: World 102; Australia 6.

Field Information

Emu, Cassowary, Ostrich

1 Emu *Dromaius novaehollandiae*

Distinctive. General body plumage dark brown to grey-brown. Feathers have shaft and aftershaft; plumage long, thick, drooping, soft and appears shaggy. Skin of head and throat blue. Long legs and feet dark grey-brown; three toes. Body plumage of breeding female darkens; thick black feathers cover head and neck. **Size** stands up to 2 m. **Chick** crown spotted; body downy with dark brown to black body stripes. **1st year** grey to buff plumage. **Imm.** similar to adult but smaller. Three races recognised; *novaehollandiae* — whitish ruff in breeding plumage (SE Aust.); *woodwardi* — slender and paler (N Aust.); *rothschildi* — darker race, no white ruff during breeding (SW Aust.). **Habitat** varies widely; arid inland plains to tropical woodlands; not rainforests. Flightless. Runs with a bouncy, swaying motion. May be solitary, in family groups, or in flocks of hundreds.

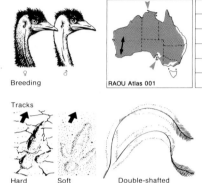

Breeding

RAOU Atlas 001

Tracks

Hard Surface   Soft Surface   Double-shafted feather

2 Southern Cassowary *Casuarius casuarius*

Distinctive. **Female** slightly larger and more brightly coloured. Tall, greyish casque (helmet) on both sexes. Skin on head pale blue, becoming darker down neck. Two long red-to-crimson free-swinging fleshy wattles originate at front of neck. Body black. Feathers coarse and hair-like with shafts and aftershafts. Short stout green-grey legs; feet same colour; three toes; inner toe-nail an elongated spike up to 120 mm. **Size** stands up to 2 m. **Chick** downy; striped yellow and black to about 3 months. **1st year** brown-bodied with head and neck pattern of adult but duller. **Imm.** similar but body plumage blacker with increase in age and size. Aust. race is *johnsonii*. **Habitat** restricted to tropical rainforests, preferring stream banks and clearings.

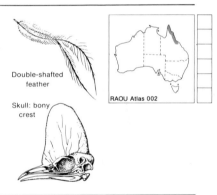

Double-shafted feather

Skull: bony crest

RAOU Atlas 002

3 Ostrich *Struthio camelus**

Distinctive. **Male** plumage black, long, soft and loosely webbed. Bill broad and flat. Head, neck and upper legs grey. White plumes in wings and tail. Lower legs and feet grey-brown; two toes – the only bird with fewer than three. Breeding males develop reddish colour on gape, edge of upper mandible and feet. A red, protrusible hemi-penis may be apparent at times. **Female** lighter brown body plumage with off-white plumes. **Size** stands up to 2.4 m; world's largest living bird. **1st year** brownish; black stripes on head and neck. **Imm.** mottled brown and grey plumage, darkening with age. Race *australis* often mentioned but precise genetic composition not known. **Habitat** open mulga woodlands and sandhills. Flightless. Runs with vestigial wings held out, at speeds up to 55 km/h.

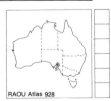

RAOU Atlas 928

*Introduced

1

3 ♂

3 ♀

Chicks

1

Chick

2 ♂

2 ♀

Chicks

Chick

4 Great Crested Grebe *Podiceps cristatus*

Distinctive. Dagger-like bill. Eye red. Black line from
gape to eye. Cheeks and throat white. Has pointed black
ear tufts on dark brown head. Neck encircled with
rufous, black-tipped ruff. Silky-white underparts gleam
snow-white in sunlight. In flight, conspicuous white
margins on dark grey wings. **Non-breeding** ruff and tufts
greatly reduced or absent in winter. **Size** to 50 cm.
 Downy young dark brown with white stripes on head and
body. **1st year** retains some stripes on head. **Imm.** without
ear tufts or ruff; many resemble wintering adult. Race
in Aust. is *australis*. **Voice** barking and rattling.
Habitat pairs in breeding season on freshwater lakes with
aquatic and marginal vegetation. Gregarious at other
times, on fresh or saline waters — lakes, lagoons, estuaries,
bays. Winter flocks may appear unexpectedly. Dives for
food and to escape from danger; average duration less than
30 seconds.

Diving

Hatchling

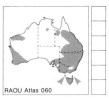

RAOU Atlas 060

5 Hoary-headed Grebe *Poliocephalus poliocephalus*

Bill dark, tipped cream. Eye pale. Head black with white
plumes. Back dark grey, occasionally brownish. Breast
pale buff. Underparts silky white. **Non-breeding** pale grey
body. Head without, or with only a few white facial
plumes. **Size** 25-30 cm. **Imm.** like winter adults.
Voice normally silent; soft churrings near a nest.
Habitat lakes, swamps; frequently on brackish water or on
sea off estuaries. Frequently seen to fly away from danger
or observer. Has a long, splashing take off from water
surface; flies low and fast with quick wing beats; dives for
food.

Head shaking

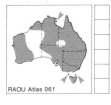

RAOU Atlas 062

Courtship behaviour

6 Australasian Grebe *Tachybaptus novaehollandiae*

Bill dark, tipped cream. Eye yellow. Head and neck
black. Bare skin forms a pale yellow face spot. Richly
coloured chestnut stripe extends back on to side of
neck. Back dark brown. Underparts silver-grey.
Non-breeding/Imm. duller; facial spot whitens; may be
barely visible. These, and Hoary-headed Grebes in
breeding plumage, may easily be confused with one
another. **Size** 25-27 cm; fractionally smaller than
Hoary-headed Grebe. **Juv.** face striped black and white.
Voice shrill and chittering. **Habitat** generally on
fresh water; may join Hoary-headed Grebes in mixed
flocks during winter but less gregarious. This species is
more likely to dive than to flee danger (or bird-watcher)
by flying.

Hatchlings

5

6

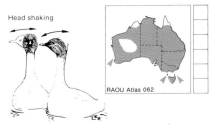

RAOU Atlas 061

4: **Great Crested Grebe**

Courtship behaviour

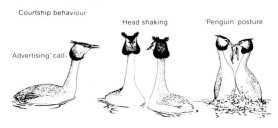

'Advertising' call

Head shaking

'Penguin' posture

4

6

5

4
Breeding

4
Non-breeding

4 Imm

5
Breeding

5
Non-breeding

6
Breeding

6
Non-breeding

6 Juv.

N. Day.

7 King Penguin *Aptenodytes patagonica*

Distinctive. Steel-blue on back. Prominent ear patch orange (adult), to pale (juv./imm.). **Size** 80-92 cm.

8 Gentoo Penguin *Pygoscelis papua*

Distinctive. Bill, feet orange. White patches over eyes just meet on crown. Head speckled white. **Size** 71-76 cm.

9 Chinstrap Penguin *Pygoscelis antarctica*

Distinctive. Bill black. White face; black line slanting under chin diagnostic. **Size** 69-77 cm.

10 Adelie Penguin *Pygoscelis adeliae*

Distinctive. White eye-ring diagnostic. **Size** 60-79 cm. **Juv./Imm.** chin whitish; black about eye.

11 Magellanic Penguin *Spheniscus magellanicus*

Distinctive. Two white bands of about equal width, each *above* similar blackish bands on throat and breast, diagnostic. **Size** 68-72 cm.

12 Royal Penguin *Eudyptes schlegeli*

Golden frontal crest; white to grey face diagnostic. **Size** 65-76 cm. **1st to 4 years** crest shorter.

Imm: 1-2 yrs

13 Rockhopper Penguin *Eudyptes chrysocome*

Distinctive. Position of front end of lateral eye-stripe/crest diagnostic. Dull black cheeks. **Size** 45-60 cm. **1st year** eye-stripe not defined; chin whitish; dark bill, horn-tipped. Race *mosleyi* visits Aust. regularly; *filholi* one record.

14 Fiordland Penguin *Eudyptes pachyrhynchus*

Distinctive. Back bluish. White streaked, dull blackish cheeks. Position of each end of lateral eye-stripe/crest diagnostic. **Size** 54-71 cm. **1st year to imm.** eye-stripe defined; chin whitish.

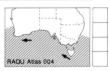

15 Erect-crested Penguin *Eudyptes sclateri*

Distinctive. Shape and position of front end of lateral eye-stripe/crest diagnostic. Cheeks glossy black. **Size** 67-74 cm. **1st year** chin, throat pale; eye-stripe defined.

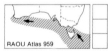

16 Snares Penguin *Eudyptes robustus*

Position of front end of lateral eye-stripe/crest diagnostic. Cheeks glossy black. **Size** 67-74 cm. **1st year** eye-stripe defined.

17 Little Penguin *Eudyptula minor novaehollandiae*

Smallest penguin. Greyish face; back dark blue. Trailing edge of flipper white. **Size** 32-34 cm. **1st year** chin, throat greyish. Bill blackish.

Metal flipper band

9

11

7
Imm.

16

10

8

15

12

13

13
Imm.
1st yr

14
Moulting

17

17
Chick

14
Imm.
1-2 yrs

18 Wandering Albatross *Diomedea exulans*

Note: plumage varies widely; amount of white developed by an individual depends on its sex, age (generally whiter with age) and population characteristics at its breeding island. **Male** powerful pink bill, tipped yellow. White above and below, including crown. White upperparts; breast has varying densities of fine black wavy lines (vermiculations). Tail white, sometimes tipped black. Outer wing and trailing edge black. Underwing white, extreme tips *always* black; pattern constant, little variation with sex or age. Legs, webbed feet pale flesh. **Female** like male, but *always* has brown speckles or striations on crown. **Size** 80-135 cm; wingspan 260-350 cm. **Imm.** (and some darker breeding adults) widely varying (see diagrams). Upperparts with varying black chequered patterns. Upperwing shows increasing white with age, spreading outward from body along *centre* of wings, typically with white patches. Tail white, black terminal band. **Juv.** completely chocolate-brown except for white face and virtually white underwing. Tail black. Body becomes paler, until most of brown replaced by white. A dark to pale brown collar and breast band are last traces of juv. plumage. **Voice** croaking, guttural cackles; bill clappering. **Habitat** oceanic, coastal seas. Habitually follows ships, fishing boats. Most common great albatross in Aust. seas. 'Domed' crown, 'humped' back give 'angular' appearance. Identify from Royal Albatross and from much smaller Australasian Gannet.

Aging:
Imm. (top)
to
Adult (bottom)

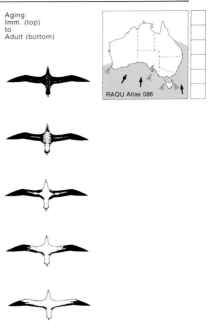

RAOU Atlas 086

19 Royal Albatross *Diomedea epomophora*

Note: white develops along the leading edge of the upper wing only in race *epomophora*. Where the white merges with black tips and along trailing edge, it appears as a dusting or speckling, *not* chequering as in Wandering Albatross. Powerful bill flesh-coloured, less pink than Wanderer, usually longer. Crown less domed, forehead gently sloped. Diagnostic black cutting edge along upper bill visible at close range. Race *epomophora* 'Southern Royal Albatross'. **Breeding** wholly white above and below (no vermiculations). Underwing like Wandering Albatross. Tail wholly white. Old adults resemble the whitest 'Wanderers'. Legs, feet fleshy-white. Race *sanfordi* 'Northern Royal Albatross' smaller than *epomophora*. Upper wing wholly black; pincer-like extensions on to the back formed by black tips to long scapular feathers. Underwing has broader black mark along outer wing adjacent to the carpal — *diagnostic* of this race. **Size** 76-130 cm; wingspan 305-350 cm. **Imm.** both races resemble adult *sanfordi* but females of *epomophora* have a sprinkling of white along leading edge of inner upperwing. **Juv.** both races generally similar to adult *sanfordi* but few black flecks on crown, back, rump. Tail has narrow black sub-terminal band or spots. **Voice** coarse croakings, guttural sound; bill clappering.
Habitat oceanic, more so than Wanderer. Attends fishing boats; less inclined to follow ships. More 'rounded', less 'angular' appearance than Wanderer. Identify from Wanderer and much smaller Australasian Gannet. Check underwing of White-capped Albatross; backs of all mollymawks for *sanfordi*.

Aging:
Imm. (top)
to
Adult (bottom)

Race *sanfordi*:

Race *sanfordi*:

Race *epomophora*

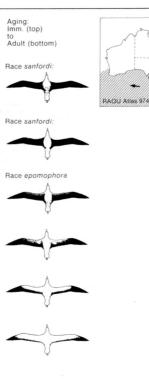

RAOU Atlas 974

19
Race *sanfordi*

19
Race *epomophora*

18

18

18

19
epomophora
Juv.

18 Juv.

18

18

19
Race *epomophora*

19
Race *sanfordi*

18
Juv.

18

18

19
Race *epomophora*

18
Juv.

18

19
Race *sanfordi*
Juv.

N.D.

20 Black-browed Albatross *Diomedea melanophrys*

Race *melanophrys:* Bill yellow-orange. Head white except black brow. Iris black. Rump, underparts white. Upperwing, mantle, tail black. Underwing white; has broad black leading edge, occupying a third or less of wing breadth, widening at 'elbow' and past the carpal joint. Primaries, secondaries black. Legs flesh-white. **Sub-adult** more black on underwing. Bill browner, tipped black. **Juv./Imm.** bill blackish-brown, *or* dull yellow at base with a black tip. Usually grey on collar, sometimes extending to crown with increasing age. Underwing changes from all dark with pale grey centre, to a white centre. Race *impavida:* Like Black-browed adult but has pale honey-coloured iris; more black in eyebrow. Underwing has black streaks on axillaries, and on carpal to primary covert region. **Juv.** like *melanophrys* juv. but iris dark honey. **Size** 85 cm; wingspan 240 cm. **Habitat** oceanic, coastal; follows ships.

Bill base

from above

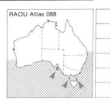

RAOU Atlas 088

21 Buller's Albatross *Diomedea bulleri*

Bill like Grey-headed Albatross, but yellow, broader along top ridge of bill (culmen). Hood dark grey with white cap. Underwing has narrower black borders than Black-browed, which are parallel to leading edges. Black primaries with white bases, secondaries black. Feet flesh-pink. **Size** 80 cm; wingspan 220 cm. **Juv.** like adult; bill dark horn-brown, darker on sides, tip. **Habitat** oceanic, coastal.

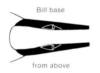

Bill base

from above

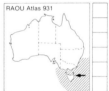

RAOU Atlas 931

22 Grey-headed Albatross *Diomedea chrysostoma*

Yellow along top ridge (culmen) of black bill; small pink mark on bill tip. Yellow or pink *also* on basal edge of lower bill to half-way along its length. Uniform pearl-grey hood, slightly paler cap. Black eye-ring. Otherwise like Black-browed adult, including underwing. **Sub-adult/Imm.** like adult; bill duller. Head varies from white with grey nape, to grey with white cheeks, front and crown. Underwing has broad black edges. At sea, identify from sub-adult Black-browed Albatross by black (*not* pale) bill, combined with white centre in black-edged underwing. **Size** 85 cm; wingspan 240 cm. **Juv.** head dark grey; *may* have white throat, cheeks. Bill black with very faint colour areas; tip black. Underwing dark, pale grey in centre. **Habitat** oceanic.

Bill base

from above

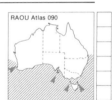

RAOU Atlas 090

23 Yellow-nosed Albatross *Diomedea chlororhynchos*

Race *bassi:* Smallest mollymawk. Bill long, slender, black; yellow only on top ridge (culmen), pink tip. Head white, *sometimes* with grey cheeks. Underwing like Buller's Albatross, but primaries black; black along leading edge of wing narrower. Feet whitish blue-grey. Race *chlororhynchos:* Probably also occurs off Aust. Like *bassi* but grey hood with a white cap. **Size** 75 cm; wingspan 200 cm. **Juv.** bill black; yellow being faint or absent. Head white. **Habitat** coastal, oceanic.

Bill base

from above

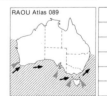

RAOU Atlas 089

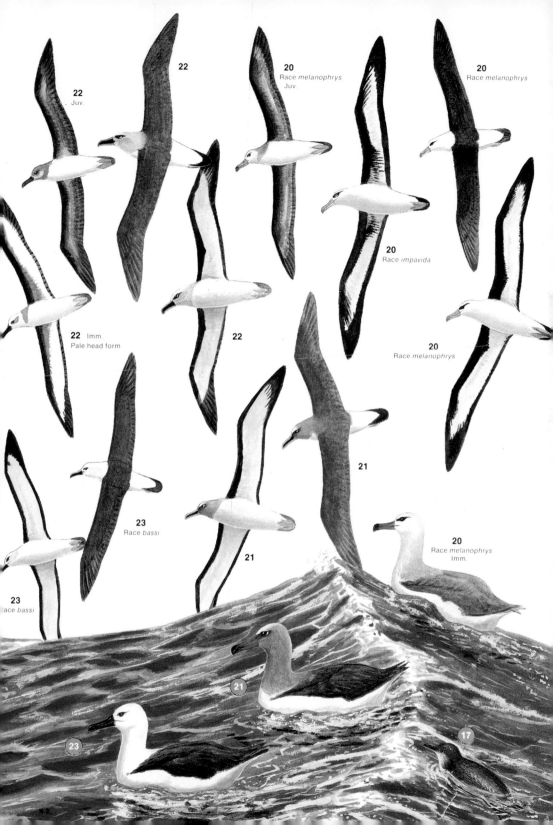

22
Juv.

22

22
Imm.
Pale head form

22

22

20
Race *melanophrys*
Juv.

20
Race *melanophrys*

20
Race *impavida*

20
Race *melanophrys*

21

23
Race *bassi*

21

21

23
ace *bassi*

20
Race *melanophrys*
Imm.

21

23

17

24 Shy Albatross *Diomedea cauta*

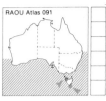

RAOU Atlas 091

Largest mollymawk. Three races. Race *cauta:* Bill grey on sides, with yellow tinge and tips. Cap white. Black line from eye to bill. Head either white, grey-cheeked, *or* grey-hooded, cut off by a white collar. Mantle grey. Wings, tail grey-black. Rump, underparts, underwing white except for thin black borders. Primaries white at base, black outer half. Small, black triangle at leading base of wing. Feet pale blue-grey. **Imm.** bill greyer, small black spot at tip. Head white *or* with a strong collar. **Juv.** head moults progressively from all-grey with white cheeks, frons and cap; to collared appearance. Bill grey, whole tip black. Underwing with slightly broader borders. Primaries about two-thirds black.
Race *salvini:* Like nominate but has yellower bill, with small black spot on lower tip. Head, neck grey, forming a hood. Cap white. Underwing like nominate but primaries all black; only a faint ghosting of white at their bases. **Imm./Juv.** bill like imm./juv. of nominate. Head similar to nominate, normally greyer. Sometimes only pale frons, lores and throat. **Imm.** collar like nominate; underwing like adult *salvini.*
Race *eremita:* Bill bright yellow, small black spot on lower tip. Head all leaden-grey; cap slightly paler. Underwing like *salvini.* Feet bright orange-pink. **Juv.** bill olive-brown, with black tip; plumage like adult; grey sometimes extends over upper breast.
Size 95-100 cm; wingspan 240-260 cm. **Habitat** oceanic, coastal. Race *cauta* common; *salvini* uncommon; *eremita* few Aust. records.

25 Sooty Albatross *Phoebetria fusca*

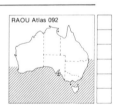

RAOU Atlas 092

Small albatross. Chocolate-brown; wings, face blacker. Eye-ring white, black in front. Bill black with a yellow line (sulcus). Tail very long, wedge-shaped. Pale shafts to primaries. Legs, feet pale grey with flesh tones. **Size** 85-90 cm; wingspan 185-215 cm. **Juv.** like adults but buffy scales on neck, collar, mantle and breast. Shafts black. **Habitat** oceanic. Graceful flight on long, narrow wings.

26 Light-mantled Sooty Albatross
Phoebetria palpebrata

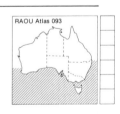

RAOU Atlas 093

Like Sooty Albatross but has a frosty grey mantle, belly and rump which contrast with a black face and wings. Bill has a blue line (sulcus). Legs, feet pale grey with flesh tones. **Size** 85-90 cm; wingspan 185-215 cm. **Juv.** like adult but has buffy scales on back, neck and breast. **Habitat** oceanic. Flight like Sooty Albatross.

Comparison of Amsterdam Albatross with Wandering Albatross and Royal Albatross

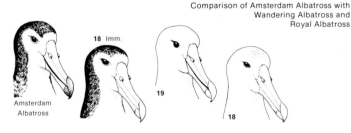

Amsterdam Albatross · 18 Imm. · 19 · 18

24
Race *cauta*

24
Race *salvini*

25
Juv.

26
Juv.

25

26

24
Race *cauta*

24
Race *cauta*

24
Race *salvini*

26

24
Race *salvini* Juv.

24
Race *eremita* Juv.

26

24
Race *cauta* Juv.

24
Race *eremita*

27 Southern Giant-Petrel *Macronectes giganteus*

Albatross-sized petrel with a bulbous bill. **Dark morph** (adults rare in Aust.; juvs common). Bill horn. tipped green. Nostrils extend far along bill. Brown or grey eyes. Dark brown body. White head. White mottling down neck and leading edge of wing to carpal. Tail medium length with a shallow wedge. Feet fleshy-grey. **Juv./Imm.** all dark; face whitens with age. Sometimes green tip on bill duller. **White morph** white, a few spots on body and wings. **Size** 85-90 cm; wingspan 200-220 cm. **Habitat** oceans, bays. Follows ships, scavenging. Identify from Sooty Albatross by short, less pointed tail, pale bill; Wandering Albatross juv. is larger and has white underwing.

Head markings

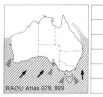

28 Northern Giant-Petrel *Macronectes halli*

Identical to Southern Giant-Petrel except bill tipped reddish-brown. Iris grey or grey brown. White about bill and face, mottled at borders. Eye, throat, rest of head dark. *No* white leading edge of wing. *No* white phase. **Juv.** all dark. Bill often duller red than adult. **Size** and **Habitat** like Southern.

Flight profile

Head markings

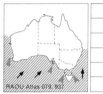

29 Southern Fulmar *Fulmarus glacialoides*

Pink bill; black tip; blue nostrils. Eye dark. Face, underparts white. Silver-grey from behind eye to tail. Primaries and their coverts black; large white primary patch; covert bases grey. Secondaries black. Underwing white; edge of primaries to carpal black, thin grey trailing edge. Feet blue, webs pink. **Size** 50 cm. **Habitat** oceans. Flight stiff-winged; quick flapping then gliding. Varying numbers reach Aust.

Head profile

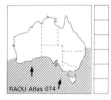

30 Antarctic Petrel *Thalassoica antàrctica*

Like Cape Petrel, but browner or greyer, with a broad unbroken white stripe through centre of wings; all dark mantle and rump. Bill longer than Cape; brown on sides. Feet greyish-flesh. **Size** 45 cm. **Habitat** oceans. Flight stiff-winged; quick flapping then gliding. Vagrant.

Head profile

RAOU Atlas 949

31 Cape Petrel *Daption capense*

Black and white petrel. Soft parts black. Race *capense:* Blackish head, hind neck, upperback. Lower back and rump white, spotted black. Upperwing black with two large separate white patches, one at primary bases, the other at secondary bases. Throat white, mottled black. Underparts white. Underwing white, edged black. Race *australis* (doubtful): Black more extensive on back and wings; many intermediate individuals. **Size** 35-45 cm. **Habitat** oceans, bays, follows boats. Flight stiff-winged; quick fluttering, flapping and then gliding.

Head profile

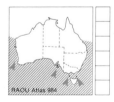

32 Snow Petrel *Pagodroma nivea*

All white. Short, stout black bill. Eyes, legs black. Long wings. Slightly wedge-shaped tail when fanned. **Habitat** oceans. Flight erratic; gliding and fluttering. Rare vagrant.

Head profile

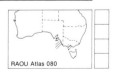

RAOU Atlas 080

29

30

27 Juv

31

32

31
Race australis

31

27 White morph

27 Dark morph

28 Juv

28

29

31

33 Great-winged Petrel *Pterodroma macroptera*

Dark brown. Reflective dark underwing. Pale face
(race *gouldii*); darker (race *macroptera*). **Size** 41 cm.
Habitat oceanic. Wheeling flight, wings held forward.

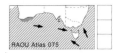

34 White-headed Petrel *Pterodroma lessonii*

Whitish head, black eye patch. White below. Dark
reflective underwing; white basal leading edge. **Size** 43 cm.

Underwing pattern

35 Providence Petrel *Pterodroma solandri*

Brown head, grey body. White primary bases separated
from black-tipped white greater coverts. **Size** 40 cm.

36 Kermadec Petrel *Pterodroma neglecta*

Upperwing pattern

Dark morph all dark underwing like Providence, with white
basal leading edge. **Pale morph** white head and body.
Variable intermediate phases. **Size** 38 cm. **Habitat** oceanic.

37 Herald Petrel *Pterodroma arminjoniana*

Colour phases like Kermadec, but white stripe through
centre of underwing; smaller. **Size** 36 cm. **Habitat** oceanic.
Flight arcing and wheeling, typical of other *Pterodromas*.

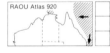

38 Tahiti Petrel *Pterodroma rostrata*

Bulbous bill. Brown, white belly. **Size** 38 cm.
Habitat oceanic.

Underwing pattern

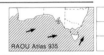

39 Kerguelen Petrel *Pterodroma brevirostris*

Dark grey. Large head. Stiff wings. Dark reflective
underwing, white basal leading edge. **Size** 33 cm.

40 Soft-plumaged Petrel *Pterodroma mollis*

Like White-headed Petrel but much smaller, with darker
head and tail, sometimes collared. **Size** 33 cm.

41 Mottled Petrel *Pterodroma inexpectata*

White below; grey belly. Underwing white, primaries
tipped black. Black from base of primaries to carpal. Broad
line extends into central median coverts. **Size** 33 cm.
Habitat oceanic.

Head pattern

42 Gould's Petrel *Pterodroma leucoptera*

Dark head. Pale below. Underwing white; primaries,
secondaries mostly black. Primaries to carpal edge black.
Line extends from carpal into central median coverts.
Size 29 cm. **Habitat** oceanic.

Head pattern

43 Black-winged Petrel *Pterodroma nigripennis*

Like Gould's but head pale grey with black eye patch.
Underwing borders broader. **Size** 29 cm. **Habitat** oceanic.
Typical flight of 'cookalarias' (includes Gould's, Cook's)
is rapid and strong, wheeling in great arcs.

Head pattern

30

39

35

35

33

40

40

45
White-necked Petrel

37

34

37

33

41

43

43

36
Pale morph

36
Pale morph

36
Dark morph

41

38

42

42

N. Day.

44 Cook's Petrel *Pterodroma cookii*

Pale grey from cap to mantle. Dark upperwings.
Underparts, underwing white, a narrow black line along
trailing edge to primary/carpal region into centre of
secondary median coverts. Size 28 cm. Habitat oceanic. Rare.

45 White-necked Petrel *Pterodroma externa*

Race *cervicalis:* Black cap on white head. Broad white
collar. Blue-grey above, broad black 'M' on wings.
Underparts, underwings as Cook's; black margins a little
broader. Size 40 cm. Habitat oceanic. Rare.

Underwing
pattern

46 Blue Petrel *Halobaena caerulea*

Bill slender, black. Blue line on lower bill. Frons white.
Cap black. Blue-grey above, faint 'M' across wings. Dark
tail band; *white* tail tip. White below. Size 28 cm.
Habitat oceanic. Long-winged graceful flight.

47 Broad-billed Prion *Pachyptila vittata*

Huge, bowed (boat-shaped) black bill; extensive exposed
lamellae; small nail. Blue line on lower bill. Head, frons
dark grey. Thin white eyebrow. Large dark collar. Blue-
grey above; strong 'M' marking. White below. Narrow
black tail tip. Undertail barred grey and white, black
centred. Feet blue; webs yellow. Size 27 cm; folded wing
19-23 cm. Habitat oceanic. Rare. Glides, banks; flutters on
surface.

Head pattern

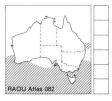

48 Lesser Broad-billed Prion *Pachyptila salvini*

Like Broad-billed; bill generally smaller, narrower;
distinctly bowed; sides bluish; less lamellae but obvious;
nail small. Head *paler;* frons *paler* grey. Size 26 cm; folded
wing 17-21 cm. Habitat oceanic.

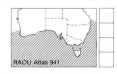

49 Antarctic (Dove) Prion *Pachyptila desolata*

Identical at sea to Lesser Broad-billed. In hand, bill
generally narrower; *larger* nail; sides usually straight;
little lamellae. Size 26 cm. Habitat oceanic.

Head pattern

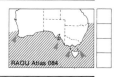

50 Slender-billed Prion *Pachyptila belcheri*

Like Antarctic Prion (some individuals indistinguishable
at sea) but bill *thinner* (no lamellae). Frons white;
eyebrow broad. The prion with greyest back. Faint 'M'
marking. Size 25 cm. Habitat oceanic.

Head pattern

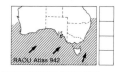

51 Fulmar Prion *Pachyptila crassirostris*

As Fairy Prion; bill more robust. Aust. record suspect.

52 Fairy Prion *Pachyptila turtur*

Bill short; nail large. Eyebrow faint. 'Bluest' prion (except
Fulmar Prion); bold black 'M' on wings. Tail band *twice
as broad* as Antarctic Prion. Undertail broadly tipped
black; *no* central black. Size 25 cm. Habitat oceans, coastal
breeding islands.

Head pattern

N. Day.

53 **Grey Petrel** *Procellaria cinerea*

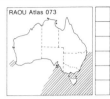

RAOU Atlas 073

Bill greenish or greyish-flesh coloured. Grey upperparts; darker on wings, crown and tail; often appears uniformly dark. Dark crown extends well below eye. Throat, breast and belly white. Undertail coverts, underwings dark. Prominent wedge-shaped tail. Legs like bill. **Size** 50 cm. **Habitat** oceanic. High, wheeling flight with much gliding and shallow dives, and submerged swimming. Often described as duck-like in flight. Generally solitary or in small flocks; known to follow ships.

54 **Black Petrel** *Procellaria parkinsoni*

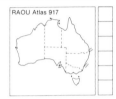

RAOU Atlas 917

Dark-tipped pale bill; otherwise completely black, including feet. In practice, very difficult species to identify. Distinguished from Flesh-footed Shearwater by heavier bill and black rather than pale feet; from Great-winged Petrel (both races) by relatively short, pale bill and lack of face colour; from White-chinned Petrel (both races) by dark bill tip and lack of chin colour. Most problems occur with the closely related Westland Petrel from which it can only really be differentiated by its smaller size. **Size** 46 cm. **Habitat** oceanic. Buoyant flight and dives.

55 **Westland Petrel** *Procellaria westlandica*

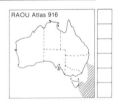

RAOU Atlas 916

Dark-tipped pale bill. Otherwise completely black, including feet. In all respects a larger version of the Black Petrel from which it cannot be readily distinguished. Differentiate from similar species by using same criteria as for the Black Petrel. Its greater size differentiates it further from the Great-winged Petrel but makes confusion with the White-chinned Petrel more likely. **Size** 53 cm. **Habitat** oceanic.

56 **White-chinned Petrel** *Procellaria aequinoctialis*

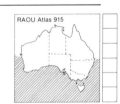

RAOU Atlas 915

All dark except for a rather variable white chin patch. This feature is not always prominent and thus confusion with Black and Westland Petrels is possible. The conspicuously large all pale bill, distinguishes it from these species. Distinguished from Flesh-footed Shearwater by black *not* pale feet; from Great-winged Petrel (both races) by bill colour and body size. A South Atlantic race *conspicillata* (illustrated) is relatively rare (only a small breeding population on Tristan da Cunha) and may be wholly sedentary. These birds have extensive white on face and chin giving a dramatic spectacled appearance. Local race *aequinoctialis* might be confused with juvenile Giant Petrels but much smaller size and complete *absence* of white in plumage *except* on the chin should differentiate it. **Size** 56 cm. **Habitat** oceanic. Generally solitary or in small groups. Known to be aggressive when feeding and a regular ship follower. Flight like that of a small albatross with slow, deliberate wing beats and glides.

53

53

55

54

33
Great-winged Petrel

25
Sooty Albatross

28
Northern Giant Petrel
Imm.

56
Race *aequinoctialis*

60
Sooty Shearwater

56
Race *conspicillata*

N.K.T.Day.

57 Flesh-footed Shearwater *Puffinus carneipes*

Large chocolate-brown shearwater. Bill horn, tipped black. Underwing dark; reflective coverts and primaries. Feet flesh-pink; do *not* trail beyond tail. **Size** 47-48 cm. **Habitat** oceanic, coastal. In flight holds wings straight; tail rounded.

Pink-footed Shearwater

possible visitor

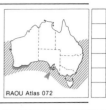

RAOU Atlas 072

58 Wedge-tailed Shearwater *Puffinus pacificus*

Smaller than Flesh-footed Shearwater. Bill leaden-grey, tipped black; looks pale at a distance. **Dark morph** all dark; paler non-reflective centres to underwings. Tail long, wedge-shaped. Legs flesh-white. **Light morph** paler above; faint 'M' marking. Throat to vent white. Underwing white, except black primaries and secondaries; some grey blotching on axilla and leading edge. **Size** 45-47 cm. **Habitat** oceanic, coastal. In flight holds wings well forward, glides low over water.

Light phase: flight posture

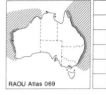

RAOU Atlas 069

59 Buller's Shearwater *Puffinus bulleri*

Bill blue-black. Cap black, contrasts with blue-grey upperparts which have a strong 'M' marking. Underparts, underwing white. Narrow black trailing edge to underwing. Tail slightly wedge-shaped. Feet pink. **Size** 45-46 cm. **Habitat** oceanic, coastal. Gliding graceful flight.

Cory's Shearwater

possible visitor

RAOU Atlas 975

60 Sooty Shearwater *Puffinus griseus*

All dark. Wedge-tailed Shearwater size. Dark grey, large, long bill. Underwing may vary: (a) greyish centre, streaked black; (b) white on primary coverts extends down wing through median coverts; some black streaking; (c) mostly white, faint streaking. Tail short, rounded. Feet trail. Outside surface of legs black, inside surface flesh-pink. **Size** 45-47 cm. **Habitat** coastal, oceanic. Flies with rapid wing beat and gliding. In summer, southern birds are visibly in heavy wing moult; gaps appear in wings.

Wing moult

RAOU Atlas 070

61 Short-tailed Shearwater *Puffinus tenuirostris*

Like Sooty but much smaller; shorter-billed. Usually has darker underwing than Sooty; variable gradings: (a) all dark silvery-grey; (b) grey; white central streak, faint black streaks; not usually white on primary medians or greater coverts; (c) all white in centre (rare). Short, rounded tail. Feet trail. **Size** 41-43 cm. **Habitat** coastal, oceanic. Flight like Sooty but more rapid. From January to April birds do *not* moult on wings; no gaps appear.

Juv.

RAOU Atlas 071

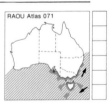

62 Streaked Shearwater *Calonectris leucomelas*

Largest of Aust. shearwaters. Very large dark-tipped, pale bill. Head white; black streaks on crown vary in amount. Black nape. Upperparts grey-brown with paler scalloping; an indistinct 'M' across back. White tips to uppertail coverts. Underparts white; underwing white but black primaries and secondaries; variably streaked on axilla and leading edge. Tail rounded. Feet pink. **Size** 50 cm. **Habitat** coastal, oceanic. Straight-winged, glides like an albatross.

Gliding

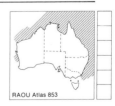

RAOU Atlas 853

63 Manx Shearwater *Puffinus puffinus*

Nominate race smaller than Short-tailed Shearwater. Bill larger and more robust than Fluttering or Hutton's Shearwater. Upperparts black. Underparts from throat to tail white. Underwing including axillaries white, but primaries black. Thin black leading edge. Legs light pink but outer surfaces black. **Size** 36-40 cm. **Habitat** coastal, oceanic. One Aust. record. Flies like Short-tailed Shearwater but faster wing beats.

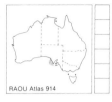

RAOU Atlas 914

64 Fluttering Shearwater *Puffinus gavia*

Most are slightly smaller than Hutton's Shearwater. Black above, including slight collar, ear coverts and below eye. Underwing white, but dark axillaries tipped white. Central shafts of feathers on leading edge of wing dark; appears streaked (a variable feature). Undertail coverts white. **Size** 31-36 cm. **Habitat** nearly always coastal, occasionally oceanic. Flies with rapid, whirring wing beats close to the sea, banks only in strong wind. Note: some *gavia* and *huttoni* are so similar that they may not be distinguished at sea.

Undertail pattern

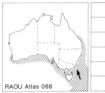

RAOU Atlas 068

65 Hutton's Shearwater *Puffinis huttoni*

Like Manx Shearwater, but smaller. In body size and bill length, most are larger than Fluttering Shearwater. Collar usually very prominent; at sea gives a hooded effect. Underwing varies: (a) grey with faint white centre and dark streaking, or (b) extensive white centre, strongly streaked; axillaries black. Undertail coverts vary from heavily flecked black to white. Sides of undertail usually flecked. **Size** 35-38 cm. **Habitat** prefers coast, also oceanic. Flies like Fluttering Shearwater.

Undertail pattern

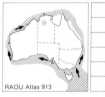

RAOU Atlas 913

66 Little Shearwater *Puffinis assimilis*

Smaller than Fluttering Shearwater. Bill very short. Eye-ring, ear coverts white. Underwing white except for black outer half of primaries and thin leading edge. Feet blue. **Size** 25-30 cm. **Habitat** coastal, oceanic. Fastest wing beats of any shearwater.

Head pattern

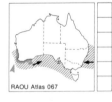

RAOU Atlas 067

67 Audubon's Shearwater *Puffinus lherminieri*

Like Fluttering Shearwater, with a shorter bill, longer tail. Underwing like Little Shearwater, but broader black margins. Undertail coverts black. **Size** 30-35 cm. **Habitat** oceanic, coastal. Vagrant. Several recent sightings. Glides close to the water.

Undertail pattern

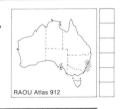

RAOU Atlas 912

64 Fluttering Shearwater
Underwing pattern

65 Hutton's Shearwater
Underwing pattern

68 Wilson's Storm-Petrel *Oceanites oceanicus*

Rump pattern

Sooty-black; white rump. Wings rounded; pale greyish crescent on greater upperwing coverts. **Size** 15-19 cm. **Habitat** oceanic. In flight, long legs and yellow webbed feet project beyond square tail.

RAOU Atlas 063

69 Grey-backed Storm-Petrel *Oceanites nereis*

Head to chest brown-black. Pale ashy-grey back; paler grey rump, tail. Upperwings dark grey; pale grey upper coverts; black primaries. Underwing white, except thin leading edge. Wide black band on square tail. White belly, underwings. **Size** 16 cm. **Habitat** oceanic.

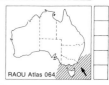
RAOU Atlas 064

70 White-faced Storm-Petrel *Pelagodroma marina*

White frons, eyebrow. Dark grey crown; broad eye-stripe. Grey shoulders, back. Rump pale grey. Black primaries. White below. Underwing white, dark-bordered. Square dark tail. **Size** 20 cm. **Habitat** oceanic. Yellow webbed feet project in flight.

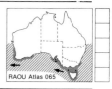
RAOU Atlas 065

71 Black-bellied Storm-Petrel *Fregetta tropica*

Pale form

Black above. Throat usually white. Grey on greater upperwing coverts. Black 'V' on chest leads to narrow central stripe; some lack this but breast 'V' usually present. Rest of underparts white; underwing white, bordered black. White rump. **Size** 20 cm. **Habitat** oceanic. Feet project beyond square black tail.

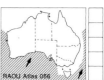
RAOU Atlas 066

72 White-bellied Storm-Petrel *Fregetta grallaria*

Like Black-bellied but black chest cuts straight off from white belly. Black throat. Some have dark rump, *or* streaked, dusky or dark underparts. Shorter legs than Black-bellied. **Size** 20 cm. **Habitat** oceanic. Feet do *not* extend beyond square tail.

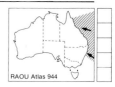
RAOU Atlas 944

73 Matsudaira's Storm-Petrel *Oceanodroma matsudairae*

Sooty-brown. Forked tail. Long wings; paler crescents on coverts; quill bases show as white patches. **Size** 24 cm. **Habitat** oceanic.

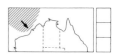

74 Leach's Storm-Petrel *Oceanodroma leucorhoa*

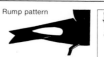
Rump pattern

Brownish-black. Rump usually white (can be black) with complete or broken black line. Paler grey-brown greater upperwing coverts. Deeply forked tail. **Size** 20 cm. **Habitat** oceanic.

RAOU Atlas 911

75 Common Diving-Petrel *Pelecanoides urinator*

Bill

Tiny, dumpy petrel. Bill sides parallel. Black above; white below; silvery underwing. **Size** 20-25 cm. **Habitat** oceanic. Quail-like flight, neck out.

Oblique view

RAOU Atlas 085

76 South Georgian Diving-Petrel
Pelecanoides georgicus

Bill

Like Common Diving-Petrel. Bill sides rounded. Some have white scapular bands. **Size** 18-21 cm. **Habitat** oceanic.

Oblique view

RAOU Atlas 910

77 **Australian Pelican** *Pelecanus conspicillatus*

A large black and white bird with a long pink bill and large throat pouch. Primaries, shoulders, rump and tail black; rest white, including centre of upperwing and undertail coverts. Head sometimes diffuse grey. Legs grey. **Size** 160-180 cm. **Voice** grunting. **Habitat** large areas of fresh and salt water. Flies gracefully; swims in flocks.

Dorsal flight

Standing   Swimming

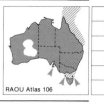

RAOU Atlas 106

78 **Australasian Gannet** *Morus serrator*

Bill grey; edges of bill plates (sheaths) and borders black. Black stripe down centre of throat. Black line through gape. Eye-ring dark blue; iris grey. Head buff-yellow. Rest of body white, with black primaries, secondaries. Black centre to tail (edges white). Black feet with green lines along toes. **Size** 90-95 cm. **Juv.** uniform grey-brown including hood. Spotted white above. White below. **Imm.** patchy brown; head, upperparts spotted white. Older birds have patchy black feathers on wings and mantle, sometimes tail is all black. **Habitat** oceans, bays.

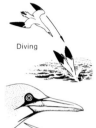

Diving

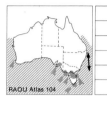

RAOU Atlas 104

79 **Cape Gannet** *Morus capensis*

Like Australasian Gannet, but *always* has a black tail, a longer black stripe down centre of throat, a brighter blue eye-ring and white eyes, broader, blacker margins around face and on bill. **Size** 85-90 cm. **Juv./Imm.** probably indistinguishable from juv./imm. Australasian Gannet. **Habitat** oceans, bays; one resident in Port Phillip Bay, Vic.

80 **Red-footed Booby** *Sula sula*

White morph blue-grey bill, eye-ring. Pink mask. Yellow head. White body. Black primaries, secondaries. Red legs. **Dark morph** all brown. **Intermediate morph** brown with white rump, tail and abdomen. **Size** 75 cm. **Juv./Imm.** brown, mottled white. Bill black, may be tinted dull blue. Legs, feet dark grey, becoming red. **Habitat** oceans; the most pelagic booby.

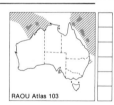

RAOU Atlas 103

81 **Masked Booby** *Sula dactylatra*

Largest booby. **Male** yellow bill. Black mask. Yellow eye. Body white with black primaries, secondaries. Tail black. Legs grey. **Female** green base to bill. **Size** 80-85 cm. **Juv./Imm.** head, neck brown; white collar. Upperparts grey-brown, tipped white. Narrow white rump. Underwing white with band running from carpal to axillaries. Plumage whitens with age: upperparts whiten from rump; white wing bar forms on upperwing; collar becomes more extensive. Identify from young gannets by more contrasting head pattern; darker mask; longer tail; also a dumpier bird. **Habitat** oceans, reefs.

Facial pattern

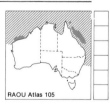

RAOU Atlas 105

82 **Brown Booby** *Sula leucogaster*

Male yellow bill; bluish base. Upperparts, breast dark brown. Belly to vent white. Underwing white with broad dark brown borders. Legs yellow. **Female** bill all yellow. **Size** 75 cm. **Juv./Imm.** belly, underwing dull brown, contrasting with otherwise dark brown pattern of adults. **Habitat** oceans, reefs.

Body pattern

RAOU Atlas 102

82 ♀

82
Juv.

81 ♂

Abbott's
Booby ♂

81
Juv.

♀ **81**

Abbott's
Booby ♀

82 ♂

78
Juv.

78
Sub-adult

78

79

80
White morph

80
White morph

80
Juv.

77

80
Intermediate morph

80
Dark morph

78

80
Intermediate morph

80
Dark morph

N. Day.

83 Darter *Anhinga melanogaster*

Long pointed bill. Snake-shaped neck. Long rounded tail.
Male dark grey to glossy black with a white stripe bordered
by black, from bill to first bend in neck. Wings iridescent
with cream streaks. **Female** grey-brown above; pale grey
below; also has white neck stripe. **Size** 90 cm.
Juv./Imm. like female, but stripe less distinct and body paler.
Voice clicking sounds. **Habitat** lakes, rivers, swamps; rarely
coastal. Often immerses in water up to neck. Holds wings
out 'to dry' when perched. In flight, cream upperwing
streaks form a wing bar; soars.

Drying
wings

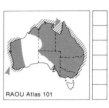

RAOU Atlas 101

84 Black-faced Shag *Leucocarbo fuscescens*

Non-breeding black bill, facial skin, cap (*no* white over
eyes), back of neck, wings, tail and thigh patch to legs.
Black-edged feathers glossed green. Eye aqua-green. White
below. **Breeding** short white nuptial plumes on hind-neck,
rump, thighs. **Size** 65 cm. **Imm.** browner above; face paler
grey; eye brown. **Voice** grunts, hissing. **Habitat** rocky sea
coasts. At various times shags and cormorants spread wings
out when perched.

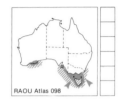

RAOU Atlas 098

85 Pied Cormorant *Phalacrocorax varius*

Like Black-faced Shag but larger. Longer, dark horn bill.
Orange facial and throat skin. Blue eye-ring. Side of neck
all white. Belly sometimes rusty. **Size** 70-75 cm.
Juv./Imm. browner; face duller. **Voice** grunts.
Habitat prefers large areas of water, coastal or inland lakes,
rivers. Regularly flies in 'V' formation.

'V' flight

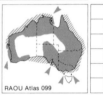

RAOU Atlas 099

86 Little Pied Cormorant *Phalacrocorax melanoleucos*

Small version of the Pied Cormorant. Short, yellow bill
with black borders; *no* bare throat skin. Face blackish.
White goes *over* eye to bill base. A short crest of black
feathers before bill. Side of neck *divided* black and white.
No black leg stripe. **Size** 50-55 cm. **Juv./Imm.** black
feathers above eye and on thighs. **Voice** short croak.
Habitat most aquatic habitats. Flies separately, *not* in 'V'
formation.

Typical cormorant foot

RAOU Atlas 100

87 Great (Black) Cormorant *Phalacrocorax carbo*

The largest Aust. cormorant. All black with yellow facial
skin and throat pouch. **Breeding** white nuptial plumes on
neck, plus white chin and thigh patch, otherwise black.
Size 80-85 cm. **Juv./Imm.** dirty blackish-brown; facial skin
duller. **Voice** croaks, grunts, hisses. **Habitat** most aquatic
habitats. Flies in 'V' formation.

Flight line

RAOU Atlas 096

88 Little Black Cormorant *Phalacrocorax sulcirostris*

Small, slender black cormorant. All black (including dark
slender bill) except for glossy green back. More bronzed
when breeding. **Size** 60-65 cm. **Voice** male makes ticking
sounds. **Habitat** most aquatic habitats. Flies in 'V'
formation. Congregates in larger flocks than do other
cormorants.

Feeding flock

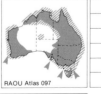

RAOU Atlas 097

89 Christmas Frigatebird *Fregata andrewsi*

Male black. Red throat pouch which expands into a
balloon during courtship (as in all other male frigatebirds).
White abdominal patch. Brown wing panels.
Female similar to Least Frigatebird female, but white on
belly leads to abdomen, and conspicuous black 'spur'
markings on upper breast. **Size** 89-100 cm. **Juv.** difficult to
separate from other juv. frigatebirds. **Habitat** tropical NW
seas. Once recorded in Darwin. Breeds on Christmas Is.

RAOU Atlas 909

90 Great Frigatebird *Fregata minor*

Male black. Red throat pouch. **Female** white chest; pale
grey throat. Brown wing bars. Eye-ring, feet reddish.
Size 86-100 cm. **Juv./Imm.** begins with tawny-coloured
head, gradually gets darker all over (males) or gets a black
cap (female). **Habitat** tropical seas.

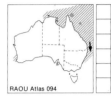

RAOU Atlas 094

91 Least Frigatebird *Fregata ariel*

Male black. Red throat pouch. Thin white markings from
flanks on to wings. **Female** like female Great Frigatebird,
but with a black throat, white collar, and markings on
underwings. **Size** 71-81 cm. **Juv./Imm.** difficult to
distinguish from other juv. frigatebirds. **Habitat** tropical
seas. For further information on frigatebird plumages see:
Harrison P. (1983), *Seabirds: an Identification Guide*,
A. H. & A. W. Reed, Sydney, pp. 307-317.

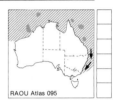

RAOU Atlas 095

92 Red-tailed Tropicbird *Phaethon rubricauda*

Race *westralis* (tropical, temperate seas off WA):
Breeding white, often tinted pink. Pointed, stout, tern-like,
scarlet to orange-yellow bill. Black crescent-shaped patch
before and through eye. Black primary shafts; broader
black marks on tertiary feathers. White tail with two long
(40-43 cm), red, central tail streamers. Legs black. Race
roseotincta (E Aust. seas): Larger. **Size** 86-90 cm.
Juv./Imm. bill black. Lacks tail streamers. White body
with upper body to tail, and upper, inner wings, barred
black. **Voice** clamorous rattles, screams. **Habitat** tropical,
subtropical seas. Soars, glides, hovers, flies high and fast,
dives into sea; swims with tail feathers cocked up.

Imm.

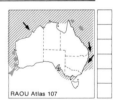

RAOU Atlas 107

93 White-tailed Tropicbird *Phaethon lepturus*

Race *fulvus* ('Golden Bosunbird', northern seas off WA):
Breeding brilliant white, often tinted apricot-yellow. Bill
yellow to orange. Black crescent-shaped patch before and
through eye. Black central wing bar; primary bases long
(40 cm); central tail streamers white. Legs blue-grey to off-
white; webs black. Race *dorotheae* (E Aust. seas — vagrant):
Small; white. **Size** 72.5 cm. **Juv./Imm.** numerous, narrow,
black, crescent-shaped, dorsal barrings from crown to
rump and on upper, inner wings. Dark tail margins; *no*
white tail streamers or gold tint. **Voice** harsh rattles,
screams. **Habitat** tropical, subtropical seas. Flight like Red-
tailed but quicker, more graceful, pigeon-like.

Imm.

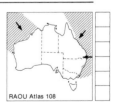

RAOU Atlas 108

89 ♀

91 ♀

90 ♀

89 ♂

91
Juv.

90
Juv.

91 ♂

♂ 90

♂ 91

92

93

92

93

94 Great-billed Heron *Ardea sumatrana*

Bill long, stout and dark brown; paler at base of lower mandible. Entire plumage bronzy-brown with nuchal crest, hackles on foreneck and lanceolate plumes on back. Belly creamy-brown. Legs dark grey. **Size** 100-110 cm. **Juv.** more rusty brown; no crest, hackles or plumes. **Voice** penetrating (and to the inexperienced), frightening calls including loud guttural roars and groans given by day and night. **Habitat** mangrove-fringed tidal channels of tropical Aust.; occasionally recorded upstream along major rivers.

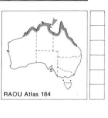

RAOU Atlas 184

95 Pacific (White-necked) Heron *Ardea pacifica*

Bill dark grey. Head and neck white except for a line of brown and back spots down the foreneck. Back and wings sooty-black with a bluish sheen. Maroon lanceolate plumes on back and upper breast. Prominent white patch on shoulder of wing. Breast and belly grey-brown, streaked white. Legs dark grey. **Non-breeding** plumes reduced or absent. **Size** 76-107 cm. **Juv.** neck has greyish wash; the foreneck is more heavily spotted and lanceolate plumes are absent. The white shoulder patch, visible both at rest and in flight (looks like headlights on flying bird), distinguishes this from juv. of much smaller Pied Heron. **Voice** harsh croaks. **Habitat** moist pasture, floodwaters and shallows of freshwater wetlands.

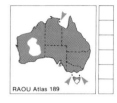

RAOU Atlas 189

96 White-faced Heron *Ardea novaehollandiae*

Bill dark brown, paler at base of lower mandible. Face to just behind the eye, white. Upperparts and wings grey. Belly paler grey. Flight feathers dark grey. Pale chestnut hackles on lower neck. Lanceolate plumes on back. Legs yellow. **Non-breeding** plumes and hackles reduced or absent. **Size** 60-70 cm. **Juv.** face grey or with white only on chin. Dull brown wash on plumage, particularly on belly. **Voice** harsh croaks. **Habitat** pasture, farm dams, parkland, most wetlands including intertidal flats. Often perches on trees and posts.

96 Adult

96 Imm.

102 Grey phase

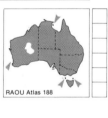

RAOU Atlas 188

97 Pied Heron *Ardea picata*

Bill yellow. Head and nuchal plumes dark blue-grey. Neck white. Body and wings dark blue-grey. Both blue-grey and white hackles frill the lower neck and there are lanceolate plumes on the back. Legs yellow. **Non-breeding** plumes and hackles reduced. **Size** 45-50 cm. **Juv.** both head and nuchal crest white; hackles and plumes absent; back tinged brown. Belly grey-brown streaked with white. **Voice** harsh croaks. **Habitat** near coastal swamps, rubbish tips, sewage-works and intertidal flats.

Roosting

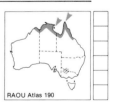

RAOU Atlas 190

97

96

94
Juv.

96
Juv.

95
Juv.

95

94

96
Juv.

96
Breeding

95
Breeding

97
Juv.

97
Breeding

N. Cox

98 Cattle Egret *Ardea ibis*

Bill yellow or pinkish-yellow. Long loose rusty-brown plumes on head. Neck, breast and back rusty-brown; remaining plumage white. Legs greenish-grey. Bill, face and legs may become red briefly prior to egg laying. **Non-breeding** plumage snowy white. Rusty plumes are progressively acquired from mid-August and traces may remain until May. Short stocky appearance, rounded forehead and prominent feathers under the lower mandible distinguish it from other egrets. **Size** 46-54 cm. **Voice** harsh croaks. **Habitat** pasture; among stock; occasionally shallows of wetlands.

Feeding amongst cattle

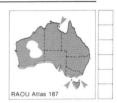

RAOU Atlas 977

99 Great Egret *Ardea alba*

Bill usually black; facial skin green. Body and wings white as are the long lacy scapular plumes. Legs dark grey or black; slightly paler on tibia. **Non-breeding** bill usually yellow; facial skin yellow; plumes fewer or absent. Distinguished from other egrets, particularly the Intermediate Egret, by long bill and low flat forehead, long neck with prominent kink (neck = 1.5 times length of body). **Size** 90-103 cm. **Voice** harsh croaks. **Habitat** floodwaters, rivers, shallows of wetlands, intertidal mud-flats. Legs extend well beyond tail in flight.

Stalking

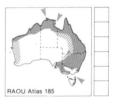

RAOU Atlas 187

100 Little Egret *Ardea garzetta*

Bill black; facial skin orange. Entire plumage white; two long thin nuchal plumes; lacy plumes on upper breast, wing and mantle. Legs black; soles of feet yellow. **Non-breeding** facial skin yellow; plumes few or absent. Small size, black bill, yellow soles and slender build distinguish it from other egrets. **Size** 55-65 cm. **Voice** harsh croaks. **Habitat** floodwaters, rivers, shallows of wetlands and intertidal flats.

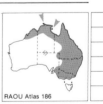

RAOU Atlas 185

101 Intermediate Egret *Ardea intermedia*

Bill orange or red; facial skin green. Plumage white with long lacy plumes arising from the upper breast and scapulars. Tibia red; tarsus black. **Non-breeding** bill orange-yellow; face yellow. Few or no plumes. Legs black. Distinguished from the Great Egret by proportionately shorter and thicker bill; higher forehead; shorter, thicker and less-kinked neck (neck = length of body). Legs appear shorter in flight. **Size** 56-70 cm. **Voice** harsh croaks. **Habitat** shallows of wetlands, intertidal mud-flats.

99 96 101

RAOU Atlas 186

102 Eastern Reef Egret *Ardea sacra*

White morph: stalking

Bill comparatively long and thick. Two colour morphs. **Grey morph** bill grey, plumage dark sooty-grey except for some white on throat. Hackles on lower neck; lanceolate plumes on back. Legs yellowish-grey. Most common in south. Distinguished from White-faced Heron by darker plumage and *no* white on face. **White morph** bill pale horn to yellow. Entire plumage white; legs yellow. Legs shorter and thicker than other egrets. **Size** 58-75 cm. **Voice** harsh croaks. **Habitat** intertidal zone including rock and coral reefs, mangroves, mud-flats.

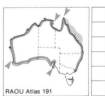

RAOU Atlas 191

99
Breeding

101
Breeding

100
Breeding

98
Breeding

102
White morph

101 Non-breeding

99 Breeding

100 Non-breeding

102
Grey morph

101
Non-breeding

98 Non-breeding

99
Non-breeding

98

102
White morph

98
Non-breeding

100
Non-breeding

102
Grey morph

103 Striated Heron *Ardeola striatus*

Five Aust. races have in common: glossy black crown, nuchal crest; body darker above than below; metallic sheen on back; throat, foreneck streaked black and dark brown. Races are *macrorhynchus*, E Aust., dark-olive above, dusky-brown below; *litteri*, NE Aust. and PNG, dark grey-green; *stagnatilis*, N Aust., browny-grey; *cinereus*, NW Aust., pale grey; *rogersi*, WA, rufous. **Size** to 49 cm. **Voice** variety of sharp calls. **Habitat** mangroves, intertidal flats. Crouches low with neck extended or retracted; adopts head-up posture of bitterns when disturbed.

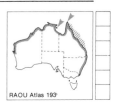

RAOU Atlas 193¹

104 Rufous Night Heron *Nycticorax caledonicus*

Breeding bill, crown black; two slender white nuchal plumes. Upperparts, wings rufous; belly white. **Non-breeding** lacks plumes. **Size** to 59 cm. **Juv.** mottled and streaked brown on white. **Voice** deep croaks. **Habitat** swamps, intertidal flats, estuaries, rivers, creeks. Feeds nocturnally; roosts in trees close to water by day.

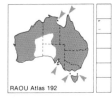

Imm.

Dorsal flight

RAOU Atlas 192

105 Little Bittern *Ixobrychus minutus*

Male crown, back, tail black; hind-neck deep reddish-brown. Wing black; large pale-buff wing patches. Breast, flanks white, streaked dark and light brown. Belly, undertail white. **Female** black replaced by brown; underside more heavily streaked; wing patch brown-buff. **Size** to 30 cm. **Juv.** browner and streaked overall. Wing patch not obvious. **Voice** deep repetitive croaks. **Habitat** reedbeds, dense vegetation of freshwater swamps, watercourses. Very secretive.

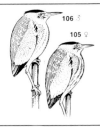

106 ♂

105 ♀

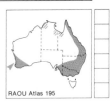

RAOU Atlas 195

106 Yellow Bittern *Ixobrychus sinensis*

Like male Little Bittern but *no* black on back; differs from female Little Bittern by black wings, less obvious wing patches. **Juv.** heavily streaked. **Size** to 30 cm. **Habitat** as for Little Bittern. Only one Aust. record.

105

106

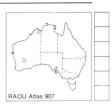

RAOU Atlas 907

107 Black Bittern *Ixobrychus flavicollis*

Male bill black above, yellow below. Upperparts sooty-black; side of neck yellow. Underparts white; prominent brown and black streaks down neck. Dark brown blotches on breast, belly. **Female** upperparts brown, *not* black. **Size** to 66 cm. **Juv.** like female; buff feather edges. **Voice** deep repetitive notes. **Habitat** mangroves, streamside vegetation including small creeks in forests.

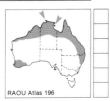

RAOU Atlas 196

108 Australasian Bittern *Botaurus poiciloptilus*

Adults/Juv. similar. Upperparts brown; mottled cream and buff; more so on wing coverts. Brown stripe down side of neck edges the white throat. Underside cream-buff, streaked and barred dark brown. **Size** to 72 cm. **Voice** male call low-pitched boom. **Habitat** reedbeds, swamps, streams, estuaries. Secretive, flies heavily when disturbed.

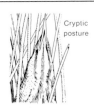

Cryptic posture

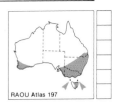

RAOU Atlas 197

108

104

104
Breeding

104
Juv.

103
Race *stagnatilus*

103
Juv.

103
Race *cinereus*

107

105

103 Race *macrorhynchus*

105
Juv.

♂ **105**

106
Juv.

108

107 ♂

107
Juv.

109 Black-necked Stork *Ephippiorhynchus asiaticus*

Black, thick, straight bill. Head. neck, tail, broad wing-stripe glossy black. Body, remainder of wings, white. Very long red legs. **Size** 112-115 cm; stands to 120 cm; wingspan to 200 cm. **Juv.** dull brown. **Voice** not adequately described; clappers with bill. **Habitat** river pools, swamps, intertidal flats. Soars expertly with neck extended and legs trailing; at height check Australian Pelican.

 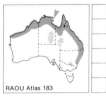

RAOU Atlas 183

110 Glossy Ibis *Plegadis falcinellus*

Bill olive-brown. Reddish-brown body; back and wings have purple-green sheen which changes with light and distance; may appear black. Legs variable, olive to dark brown. **Size** 50-53 cm. **Juv.** duller; white and brown streaks on head, upper neck. **Voice** soft calls. **Habitat** freshwater wetlands, pasture. Distinctive; in flight check Little Black Cormorant.

Nestling
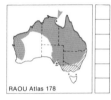

RAOU Atlas 178

111 Sacred Ibis *Threskiornis aethiopica*

Black bill and naked skin on head, upper neck. Body, wings white; often stained dirty brown. Black inner secondary plumes give appearance of black tail. Wings tipped black. Legs reddish-brown. **Size** 65-70 cm. **Juv.** head duskier; bill shorter. **Voice** harsh croaks. **Habitat** all but most saline of wetlands and pasture. In flight note head, white body and wings; soars. Roosts in trees, mangroves. Feeds along muddy coasts.

Breeding colony
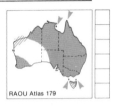

RAOU Atlas 179

112 Straw-necked Ibis *Threskiornis spinicollis*

Bare head, bill, upper neck black. Back, tail and wings black with metallic sheen. Belly, neck white; yellow straw-like breast plumes not visible at distance. Legs black. **Size** 65-70 cm. **Juv.** bill shorter. **Voice** drawn-out croaks. **Habitat** shallow freshwater wetlands and pasture, rarely intertidal flats. In flight note white body and black wings. Soars in thermals; flies directly in 'V' formation.

'V' flight
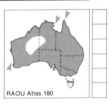

RAOU Atlas 180

113 Royal Spoonbill *Platalea regia*

Bill black, distinctive. Black skin on head to just behind eye. Small patches of red on forehead and yellow above each eye. White erectile nuchal plumes. Body, wings white. Legs black. **Non-breeding** lacks plumes, coloured patches on face. **Size** 70-76 cm. **Habitat** shallows of fresh and saltwater wetlands including intertidal flats. Feeds by sweeping submerged bill from side to side.

Bill from side

Bill from above
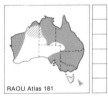

RAOU Atlas 181

114 Yellow-billed Spoonbill *Platalea flavipes*

Bill yellow, distinctive. Grey facial skin edged black. Body creamy-white except for black lace-like plumes on inner secondaries. Hackles on upper breast. Legs yellow. **Non-breeding** face yellow, without black edge. Hackles, plumes reduced or absent. **Imm.** birds show black markings on tertials. **Size** 80-90 cm. **Voice** soft calls: bill clattering. **Habitat** shallows of freshwater wetlands, occasionally on dry pasture. Often roosts in trees.

Bill from side

Bill from above
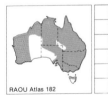

RAOU Atlas 182

88 Little Black Cormorant

111

♂ **109**

110

112

113

111
Juv.

112
Juv.

114

112

110
Imm.

111

112

110

111

109
Imm.

♀ **109**

113
Non-breeding

113
Breeding

111
Stained Plumage

114
Non-breeding

Nicolas Day.

115 **Magpie Goose** *Anseranas semipalmata*

Head black with distinct knob in older birds. Hooked bill. Face skin yellow to flesh in colour. Neck to upper breast black. Mantle, upperwing coverts, rump and belly white. Upperwing black with white coverts. Underwing black with white wing linings. Tail black. Legs long and yellow. Partly webbed toes. **Size** 71-92 cm; wingspan 150-160 cm approx. Distinguished from all other species by pied plumage and long yellow legs; from Black Swan in flight by short neck, lack of white flight feathers. **Imm.** as adult but white parts mottled grey or brown. **Habitat** rush and sedge-dominated swamps, flood plains.

Gosling

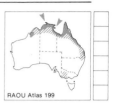
RAOU Atlas 199

116 **Wandering Whistling-Duck** *Dendrocygna arcuata*

Blackish crown and hind neck contrasting with uniform buff face and foreneck. Bill black. Upperparts brownish-black, feathers edged chestnut. Shoulders chestnut. Undertail white. Flank plumes white, edged chestnut. Legs and feet black. Race in Aust. and New Guinea is *australis*. **Size** 54-60 cm. Distinguished from Plumed Whistling-Duck by darker body plumage and shorter flank plumes. **Imm.** similar to adults but duller. **Voice** distinctive; shrill and whistling. **Habitat** deep vegetated lagoons and swamps, flooded grasslands. In flight has short rounded wings, trailing legs.

Duckling

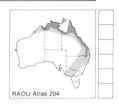
RAOU Atlas 204

117 **Plumed Whistling-Duck** *Dendrocygna eytoni*

Pale brown on crown and hind neck. Face and foreneck whitish-buff. Bill pink. Upperparts brown, feathers of upper back edged yellow. Wings above brown; paler below. Breast pale chestnut, finely barred in black. Long buff flank plumes, edged black. Abdomen pale buff. Tail and rump darker brown with upper tail coverts buff, spotted darker brown. **Size** 42-60 cm. Conclusively identified by the long flank plumes which extend over back. **Imm.** paler than adults; indistinct breast markings. **Habitat** tropical grasslands.

Duckling

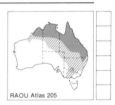
RAOU Atlas 205

118 **Black Swan** *Cygnus atratus*

Very large black bird with long slender neck and white tipped wings. Bill orange and dark red with white bar near tip, nail whitish. Legs and feet black. **Female** slightly smaller; bill and iris paler. **Size** 106-142 cm; wingspan 160-200 cm approx. **Imm.** grey-brown with paler feather edgings; white flight feathers tipped black. **Voice** musical trumpeting calls. **Habitat** large expanses of open water, fresh through to salt, with abundant aquatic vegetation; pasture, crops and mud-flats. Frequently heard flying overhead at night.

Feeding
Roosting
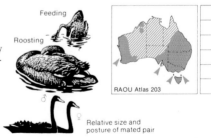
♂
♀
Relative size and posture of mated pair

RAOU Atlas 203

119 **Mute Swan** *Cygnus olor**

Huge, entirely white swan with loud musical wing beat. **Female** smaller. Bill orange with black knob at base, larger in breeding males. Legs and feet black. **Size** 127-156 cm; wingspan 220-240 cm approx. **Imm.** grey-brown (except for white 'Polish' phase) with grey knobless bill. **Habitat** rivers and ornamental lakes.

RAOU Atlas 906

*Introduced

120 Freckled Duck *Stictonetta naevosa*

Duckling

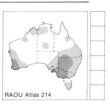

RAOU Atlas 214

Uniformly coloured with large (crested) head and dish-shaped bill. **Male** uniform dark brown to black head covered in small white or buff freckles. Bill slate to dark grey; red to orange base when breeding. Body dark brown with uniform freckling. Abdomen to undertail paler with white freckles. Upperwing dark brown; coverts freckled. Underwing light brown; white wing linings mottled pale brown. Distinguished from **Pacific Black Duck** in flight by hunched appearance and lack of bright white underwings. **Female** paler; obscure freckling. **Size** M 52-59, F 48-54 cm. **Imm.** pale brown; deep buff freckles. **Habitat** breeds in heavily vegetated permanent fresh swamps; disperses to fresh and saline permanent open lakes, especially during drought. Usually seen loafing in daytime on fallen trees or sand spits in small or large groups. Distinctive 'peaked' appearance to back of head often visible on roosting birds.

121 Cape Barren Goose *Cereopsis novaehollandiae*

Gosling

RAOU Atlas 198

Distinctive. Pale grey with small head and short triangular-shaped bill. Pale grey head with white crown. Bill black with prominent greenish cere. Body pale grey, dark spots on scapulars and wing coverts. Legs pink to deep red; feet black. In flight black wing tips, undertail coverts and tail are diagnostic. **Size** 75-100 cm. **Imm.** paler cere; duller body. **Habitat** breeds on small offshore islands with tussocks, grassland and scrub. Disperses to open improved pasture on breeding and other islands, also mainland.

122 Australian Shelduck *Tadorna tadornoides*

Duckling

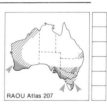

RAOU Atlas 207

Large-bodied, brightly-coloured duck with small head and bill. **Male** head and neck black, tinged green. White ring around base of neck and occasionally around black bill. Upperparts mainly black; underparts dark brown with cinnamon breast. Upperwing coverts white; primaries black; large green speculum. White underwing linings with black flight feathers. Legs, feet dark grey. **Male eclipse** yellowish-brown breast with less defined neck ring. In flight large white panel on forewing contrasts with dark body. **Female** eye-ring and base of bill white, sometimes merged; chestnut breast. **Size** M 59-72, F 56-68 cm. **Imm.** white flecking on front of head; white areas of plumage flecked grey; otherwise body duller. Unlike other Aust. ducks, often flies in long lines or 'V' formation when travelling. **Habitat** large open brackish or fresh lakes; pastures and open woodlands.

123 Radjah Shelduck *Tadorna radjah*

Duckling

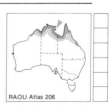

RAOU Atlas 206

Striking white duck with chestnut breast band. Head pure white with pink bill. Body white except for dark back, black rump and tail. Undertail and flanks black. White upperwing coverts; black primaries. Legs, feet pink. Black wing-tips visible in flight. The Aust. race is *rufitergum*. **Size** M 50-56, F 49-61 cm. **Imm.** white areas flecked grey-brown. **Voice** very vocal, often utters harsh rattling call whilst flying through thick timber. **Habitat** coastal wetlands and rivers; mud-flats, paperbark swamps.

121

121

121
Imm.

122 ♂

122 ♂

122 ♂

♀ 122

♀ 122

123

123

123

123

120

120

120

♀ 120

120 ♂
Breeding

♂ 120
Non-breeding

124 Pacific Black Duck *Anas superciliosa*

Crown blackish, face white to buff with two black stripes. Body plumage dark brown. Upperwing has purplish-green speculum. Legs, feet yellow-green. Distinguished from Freckled Duck and Mallard in flight by dark body plumage contrasting with white wing linings and dark-striped pale face. Aust. race is *rogersi*. **Size** 47-60 cm. **Habitat** usually deep, permanent, heavily vegetated swamps, but also more open waters.

Duckling

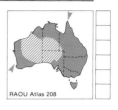
RAOU Atlas 208

125 Mallard *Anas platyrhynchos**

Male green head and white neck ring. White underparts. Legs, feet orange. In eclipse, as female but bill dull green. **Female** mottled and streaked dusky-brown; distinguished from Pacific Black Duck by lighter plumage, pale (not bright) underwing and lack of striped face pattern. Introduced; many domestic forms. Hybridises with Pacific Black Duck. **Size** 52-68 cm. **Habitat** mainly lakes in town parks, dams and larger lakes.

Domestic varieties

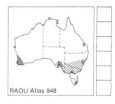
RAOU Atlas 948

126 Grey Teal *Anas gibberifrons*

Mottled grey-brown duck. In good light, a white throat and paler face distinguish it from darker female Chestnut Teal; from other species by narrow white wing-stripe and thin white wedge down centre of underwing. Aust. race is *gracilis*. **Size** 37-48 cm. **Imm.** paler. **Habitat** any available water, including floodwaters, tanks and dams. More coastal during dry periods.

Duckling

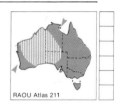
RAOU Atlas 211

127 Chestnut Teal *Anas castanea*

Male dark iridescent green head, chestnut underparts and distinctive white patch on flank. Can be confused with male Aust. Shoveler unless lack of white face crescent and smaller bill is noticed. Eclipse, if occurring, probably not distinguishable from imm. male. **Female** similar to Grey Teal but darker, lacking the pale throat. **Size** 38-48 cm. **Imm. male** duller, more blotchy body plumage, dark patchy head pattern. **Habitat** breeds in brackish to fresh coastal swamps. Disperses to fresh water, tidal mud-flats and inlets.

Duckling

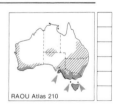
RAOU Atlas 210

128 Australasian Shoveller *Anas rhynchotis*

Heavy spatulate black bill and low sloping forehead diagnostic. **Male** head blue-grey with vertical white crescent. Body plumage similar to male Chestnut Teal. Upperwing coverts pale blue-grey. Legs, feet bright orange. In eclipse, duller. **Female** mottled brown with paler chestnut underparts and blue forewing duller. Aust. race is *rhynchotis*. **Size** 46-53 cm. **Habitat** permanent, heavily vegetated swamps, floodwaters. Only Aust. duck with noisy whirring flight.

Duckling

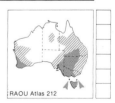
RAOU Atlas 212

129 Northern Shoveller *Anas clypeata*

Male differs from the Australasian Shoveller by the uniform green head, pure white breast and sides of back. **Female** white edging to tail *not* brown as in Australasian Shoveller. **Size** 46-55 cm. **Habitat** mainly vegetated freshwater swamps. Vagrant.

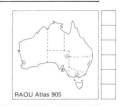
RAOU Atlas 905

*Introduced

130 Garganey *Anas querquedula*

Grey Teal-sized duck with striking blue-grey forewing. **Male** rich brown head, neck and breast with prominent white stripe over eye. Upperparts blackish-brown with long drooping black and white scapulars. Underparts white with fine black wavy lines. In eclipse, similar to female, but forewing blue-grey. **Female** distinguished from Grey Teal by dark crown and eye-stripe contrasting with pale face. Belly white and forewing pale grey. **Size** 38-41 cm. **Voice** a distinctive harsh rattling call. **Habitat** shallow swamps with dense cover. A long-distance migrant from N Hem. to N Aust. Rare.

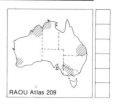

RAOU Atlas 209

131 Pink-eared Duck *Malacorhynchus membranaceus*

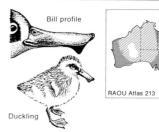

Bill profile

Distinguished by striking 'zebra' striped plumage and large, square-ended spatulate bill. Head has large brown eye patch on white, finely-barred face. Small pink patch behind eye. Bill grey with skin flaps either side of tip. Upperparts brown. Underparts white, barred dark brown. Undertail buff. Upperwing brown with white trailing edge. Underwing linings white, finely-barred brown. Rump has distinctive white crescent. Tail brown with white tip. **Size** 36-45 cm. **Imm.** paler, with less distinct pink ear patch. **Voice** can be located in mixed flocks of ducks by distinctive chirruping call. **Habitat** breeds inland, on temporary floodwaters; in periods of drought occurs on more permanent open waters including sewage farms near the coast.

Duckling

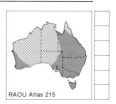

RAOU Atlas 213

132 Hardhead *Aythya australis*

Male large rounded head rich dark brown. Bill black with blue bar near tip. Eye white. Rest of body plumage as head, except for white, mottled brown lower breast. Undertail coverts white. Upperwing brown with broad white bar across secondaries. Underwing white, bordered dark brown. Diagnostic, broad, white wing bar in flight. **Female** paler; iris brown. **Size** 42-49 cm. **Imm.** uniform yellow-brown; eye dark. **Voice** nasal 'mow'. **Habitat** deep vegetated swamps and other large open waters when not breeding. Diving habits, sloping 'stern' (which can obscure the white undertail), and large head can lead to confusion of this species with Blue-billed Duck.

Duckling

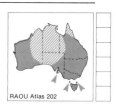

RAOU Atlas 215

133 Maned (Wood) Duck *Chenonetta jubata*

Duckling

Land-dwelling duck of fine goose-like proportions with dark head and pale body. **Male** head and neck brown with short dark mane. Bill small blackish. Body mainly grey with speckled brown breast and black lower belly and undertail. Upperwing diagnostic pale grey forewing contrasting with black wing-tips. Noticeable white panel along rear edge of secondaries. **Female** whitish line above and below eye; grey-brown body plumage with white lower belly and undertail. **Size** 44-50 cm. **Imm.** lighter than adults. **Voice** a distinctive drawn-out mournful 'now' with a rising inflection. **Habitat** lightly timbered areas near water with access to short pasture or herbage; inland tanks and dams. Often perches in trees.

RAOU Atlas 202

132 ♂

133 ♂

133 ♀

130 ♂

130 ♀

133 ♂

130 ♂

131

131

132 ♀

132
Imm.

132 ♂

130 ♂

131

132 ♀

131

130 ♀

♂ 133

♀ 133

N.Day

·134 Cotton Pygmy-Goose
Nettapus coromandelianus

Duckling

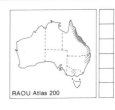
RAOU Atlas 200

A tiny duck with white face and neck. White on primaries (male) and thin white trailing edge to wing (female) distinguish this species from Green Pygmy-Goose in flight. **Male** basically white. Short black bill. Upperparts blackish, glossed green. Underparts white; narrow black breast band. **Female** more dusky with noticeable white eyebrow and dark line through eye. Aust. race *albipennis* is slightly larger than the Asiatic race *coromandelianus*. **Size** M 35-38, F 33-38 cm. **Imm.** as female but lacks green gloss. **Habitat** deep lagoons, swamps and dams particularly with waterlilies and other floating vegetation. A surface feeder; not known to dive.

135 Green Pygmy-Goose *Nettapus pulchellus*

Duckling

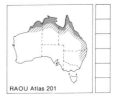
RAOU Atlas 201

Distinguished in flight from Cotton Pygmy-Goose by large white wing panels on rear edge of wing next to body. **Male** head, neck and upperparts blackish, glossed green with bright white face patch. Underparts off-white. **Female** duller, flanks and neck have more grey-brown mottling than Cotton Pygmy-Goose and the white eyebrow is more obscure. **Size** M 30-36, F 30-34 cm. **Imm.** as female. **Voice** male has a distinctive shrill 'pee-whit' call. **Habitat** as for Cotton Pygmy-Goose but will also utilise shallow, spike-rush dominated swamps in the wet season. Tends to dive on occasion, unlike Cotton Pygmy-Goose.

136 Blue-billed Duck *Oxyura australis*

Duckling

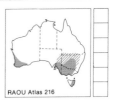
RAOU Atlas 216

Dark, compact diving duck with short 'dished' bill. **Male** head black. Bright blue bill. Body deep chestnut. Tail black with stiff, pointed feathers, usually carried below the water surface but sometimes erected and fanned. Eclipse plumage becomes duller and feathers are broadly edged pale brown. Bill is then slate-grey. **Female** head dark brown, paler on throat and below eye. Bill dark grey. Body finely barred and freckled buffish. Paler below. **Size** 35-44 cm. **Imm.** paler, barring more distinct. Distinguished in all plumages from the Musk Duck by 'dished', *not* triangular bill, also by more rounded head and smaller size; from Hardhead by *lack* of white undertail and broad white wing bar. **Habitat** deep freshwater marshes with dense vegetation; more open waters in non-breeding season. Flight rapid and low on short narrow wings. Floats higher than Musk Duck.

♀ with duckling

137 Musk Duck *Biziura lobata*

Swimming

Diving

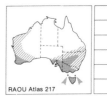
RAOU Atlas 217

A powerful, bizarre-looking duck that often swims partially submerged. **Male** large. Heavy thickset head. Stout, dark-grey triangular bill with a large black lobe of skin hanging below. **Female** smaller. Very small bill lobe. **Size** M 60-73, F 47-60 cm. **Imm.** as female but tip of lower mandible yellow. **Habitat** permanent swamps with dense vegetation. Large open lakes, inlets and bays. When disturbed thrashes across water in a cloud of spray; not often seen in flight. Spectacular splashing displays by courting males. An expert diver.

134 ♂

134 ♀

135 ♀

135 ♂

136

137 ♂

137 ♂
Displaying

134 ♀

134 ♂

135 ♂

135 ♀

♀ 136

♂ 136

136
Imm.

137 ♂

♀ 137

N. Day

138 Osprey *Pandion haliaetus*

Dark brown upperparts; white head and underparts.
Brown streak through eye and down sides of neck. Band
of brown mottling across chest. Barring underwings and
tail. **Female** larger. **Size** F 60-66, M 50-55 cm. **1st year** rufous
markings on upperparts; heavier chest band than adults.
Voice plaintive whistles. **Habitat** mangroves, rivers and
estuaries, inshore seas, coastal islands. Soars on long,
angled, bowed wings. Patrols over water, hovers, plunges
feet-first. Identify from imm. White-bellied Sea-Eagle.

Gliding head-on

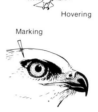
Ventral pattern

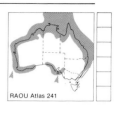
RAOU Atlas 241

139 Black-shouldered Kite *Elanus notatus*

Body white with grey and white wings; prominent black
shoulders. **Male** slightly smaller. **Size** F 35-38, M 33-36 cm.
Juv. spotted brown to golden-tan on head, neck, breast
and back. **Voice** harsh 'kar'; quiet 'chep'. **Habitat** hunts
from perches in open woodlands or by hovering over tall
grasses. Often a dawn and dusk hunter; hovers with faster
wing beats than Letter-winged Kite; soars with elevated
wings. Perches singly or in family groups in top branches
of dead trees.

Hovering

Marking

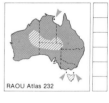
RAOU Atlas 232

140 Letter-winged Kite *Elanus scriptus*

Large eyes surrounded by black patch give an owl-like
appearance. Body white with prominent black bar along
undersides of grey and white wings. **Male** slightly smaller.
Size F 35-38, M 33-36 cm. **1st year** white with mottled
brown to tan-orange on head, back, breast. **Voice** harsh
'kar-kar' or 'chip-chip'. **Habitat** desert grasslands and
timbered watercourses. Depends on rodent plagues for
prey; hunts at night — the only Aust. hawk to do so;
roosts communally in daylight. Soars with elevated
wings; wing beat slower than Black-shouldered Kite;
hovers. Identify from Barn Owl, Eastern Grass Owl at
night.

No marking

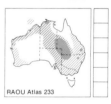
RAOU Atlas 233

141 Pacific Baza *Aviceda subcristata*

Slate-grey upperparts and chest. Short crest. Belly whitish
with bold dark bars. Thighs and vent pale rufous.
Underwings have pale rufous lining; boldly barred
'fingers'. **Female** slightly larger. **Size** F 43-46, M 35-40 cm.
1st year much browner upperparts. Race *njikena*, NT and
Kimberleys, WA, smaller and darker. **Voice** shrill double
whistle, rising and falling; quieter whistles and trills.
Habitat coastal and sub-coastal closed and open forests;
urban trees. Flight buoyant, leisurely; hovers around tree
canopy; hangs from foliage with beating wings. Soars on
flat or slightly drooped wings; performs undulating diving
display flight with wings held in a stiff 'V'.

Gliding head-on

Juv.

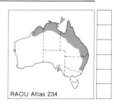
RAOU Atlas 234

142 Black Kite *Milvus migrans*

Uniformly dark brown, appearing black in strong light.
Pale shoulder bar. **Male** slightly smaller. **Size** F 50-55,
M 47-52 cm; wingspan 120 cm. **1st year** paler than adults;
upperwing surfaces lightly mottled. **Voice** plaintive
descending 'see-err', and whistles 'si-i-i-i-'. **Habitat** open
plains, timbered watercourses, rubbish dumps, abattoirs,
cattle yards. Identify from dark phase of Little Eagle.
Birds soar effortlessly with frequent twistings of forked
tail. Resembles Square-tailed Kite, but in flight wings
held flat, not in a 'V'; wings without pale patches.

Gliding head-on

1st yr

Adult
Underwing pattern

RAOU Atlas 229

143 Square-tailed Kite *Lophoictinia isura*

Slender, very long-winged. Dark brown upperparts. White
crown, face; pale eye. Pale shoulder bar. Underparts
rufous with dark streaks. Underwings have rufous lining,
pale 'bulls-eye' and boldly barred fingers. Tail long,
square-cut. **Female** slightly larger. **Size** F 55-56, M 50-51 cm;
wingspan to 130 cm. **1st year** head, underparts rich rufous;
less streaked. **Voice** hoarse yelp; weak twitter (chatter).
Habitat open forests, riverine woodlands, scrubs,
heathlands. Solitary; soars low over or through tree
canopy on raised wings. Identify from Black Kite, also
light phase of Black-breasted Buzzard.

Gliding head-on

Underwing pattern

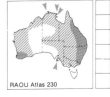

RAOU Atlas 230

144 Black-breasted Buzzard
Hamirostra melanosternon

Robust; short-tailed. **Adult** mostly blackish above
and below. Rufous nape, shoulder mottling, thighs and
vent. Prominent white 'bulls-eye' in broad wings. Pale
tail. **2-3 year** birds paler. Head and underparts light brown;
'bulls-eyes' less distinct. **Female** larger. **Size** F 55-61, M 51-
53 cm; wingspan to 150 cm. **1st year** rich rufous; dark
wing-tips, indistinct 'bulls-eyes'; pale tail. **Voice** short,
sharp calls: hoarse yelp, thin whistle, harsh sounds.
Habitat arid scrub, riverine and tropical woodlands. Soars
high on raised, back-swept wings. Identify from dark
morph of Little Eagle.

Gliding head-on

2-3 yr.

Adult
Underwing pattern

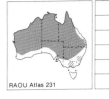

RAOU Atlas 231

145 Brahminy Kite *Milvus indus*

Distinctive. Head, neck, breast white; body, upper surface
of flight feathers chestnut. **Male** slightly smaller. **Size** F 48-
51, M 45-49 cm; wingspan to 125 cm. **1st year** browner and
mottled, resembling Whistling Kite but tail is shorter. **Voice**
plaintive 'pee-ah-ah-ah'. **Habitat** coastal mud-flats, mangroves,
harbours, offshore islands. Identify imm. from Osprey.

Gliding head-on

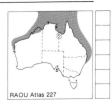

RAOU Atlas 227

146 Whistling Kite *Milvus sphenurus*

Head, underparts light brown with pale streaks. Darker
outer primaries and pale inner primaries; dark
secondaries. Long rounded tail. **Male** slightly smaller.
Size F 52-59, M 51-54 cm; wingspan to 120 cm. **1st
year** brown back spotted with white. **Voice** long
descending 'seeo' followed by an upward staccato 'si-si-si-si-
si'. **Habitat** soars over open woodlands, plains, streams,
swamps, sea shores. Identify from Little Eagle.

Gliding head-on

146

153 Underwing pattern

RAOU Atlas 228

142

142
1st yr

142
1st yr

142

143

143
1st yr

143

143

146
1st yr

146

146
1st yr

146

145

145
1st yr

145

145
1st yr

144
Dark phase

144
1st yr

144
1st yr

144
Dark phase

147 Brown Goshawk *Accipiter fasciatus*

Head grey. Eye bright yellow. Body slate-grey or dark brown above; rufous collar across nape. Underparts finely barred rufous and white. Wings rounded; slate-grey or dark brown above, buff and rufous below; wing-tips darker. Tail long, rounded; slate-grey or dark brown above; light grey with darker barring below. Legs long, yellow; rufous feathering about thighs. **Male** smaller. **Size** F 45-55, M 38-45 cm. **1st year** head streaked chocolate, rufous and white. Eyes yellow. *No* rufous collar. Body dark brown above; off-white with bold chocolate streaking below. Wings dark brown above; off-white with chocolate barring below. Tail long, rounded; dark brown above; light grey with darker barring below. Two races: the widely distributed *fasciatus* and the smaller, paler *didimus*, restricted to the far north. **Voice** rapid, shrill chatter (female generally lower-pitched). **Habitat** most timbered types.

Gliding head-on

Foot: toe proportions

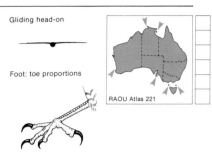

RAOU Atlas 221

148 Collared Sparrowhawk *Accipiter cirrhocephalus*

Adult/Imm. similarly plumaged to their Brown Goshawk counterpart. **Female** approximates male Brown Goshawk in size. Collared Sparrowhawk is distinguished by squarer tail, finer legs and toes. **Male** smaller. **Size** F 35-38, M 29-33. Two races: the widely distributed *cirrhocephalus* and the smaller, more rufous *quaesitandus*, restricted to the far north. **Voice** very rapid, shrill chatter. **Habitat** most terrestrial types.

Gliding head-on

Foot: toe proportions

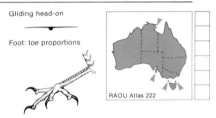

RAOU Atlas 222

149 Grey (White) Goshawk *Accipiter novaehollandiae*

Two colour morphs. **Grey morph** head grey; eye dark red. Body grey above; white below, with fine grey chest barrings. Wings rounded; grey above; white below with darker wing-tips. Tail long, rounded; grey above; white below with grey barring. Legs yellow. **1st year** similar but broader chest barring, and often buff-washed areas. **White morph** all plumage pure white in adult and imm. **Male** smaller. **Size** F 50-55, M 38-42 cm. White morph predominates in Kimberleys, WA, coastal Vic., and in Tas., where grey morph does not occur. **Voice** rapid, shrill chatter, also repeated rising shrill whistle. **Habitat** various forest types, especially coastal closed forests.

Gliding head-on

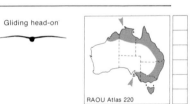

RAOU Atlas 220

150 Red Goshawk *Erythrotriorchis radiatus*

Head rufous, streaked black and white; much white on face and throat. Eye yellow. Body rufous above, with bold dark markings; male paler below, with fine black streaking. Wings long, rounded, fingered at tips. Upperwings rufous, streaked with black above; much lighter below, with rufous underwing coverts and darker barring on flight feathers. Tail long, broad; barred grey and rufous-brown above and below. Legs powerful, yellow. **Male** smaller. **Size** F 57-61, M 46-51 cm. **Voice** loud, harsh chatter. **Habitat** coastal and sub-coastal forests and tropical woodlands. Rare and often confused with other rufous-coloured raptors. Identify from imm. harriers, Brown Goshawk, Black-breasted Buzzard, Little Eagle.

Gliding head-on

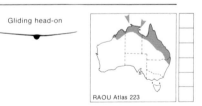

RAOU Atlas 223

149
White morph

149
Grey morph

149 ♂
Grey morph

Imm. ♀ **149**
White morph

♂ **149**

150

149 ♀
Imm.
Grey morph

e-eared Honeyeater

150

148 ♀

♂ **148**

148 ♂
Imm.

147 ♀
Imm.

♀ **148**
Imm.

♂ **148**

147 ♂

658
New Holland Honeyeater

♂ **147**
Imm.

♀ **147**

151 White-bellied Sea-Eagle *Haliaeetus leucogaster*

White, with grey back, rump, wings and base of tail. Bare whitish legs. **Female** larger. **Size** F 80-85, M 75-77 cm; wingspan 190 cm approx. **1st year** brown with lighter markings; paler on head and rump. Whitish 'bulls-eye' in wings. Tail whitish, shading to light brown at the tip. Tail short; rounded or wedge-shaped. Birds become lighter with age. **Voice** deep goose-like honking or cackling. **Habitat** large rivers, fresh and saline lakes, reservoirs, estuaries, coastal seas, islands. Wings broad and rounded, held stiffly upswept when soaring. Identify imm. from Wedge-tailed Eagle, Black-breasted Buzzard; adult from Australian Pelican

Gliding head-on

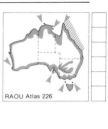

RAOU Atlas 226

Ventral pattern

152 Wedge-tailed Eagle *Aquila audax*

Sooty-black with tawny hackles on nape. Pale brown wing coverts and undertail coverts. Feathered legs. Tail long and wedge-shaped. **Female** larger. **Size** F 89-104, M 87-91 cm; wingspan 210 cm approx. **End of 1st year to 4th or 5th year** usually paler than adults. Dark brown with golden-brown nape, uppertail coverts and wing coverts. Whitish undertail coverts. Birds become darker with age. **Voice** feeble yelps and squeals. **Habitat** most types except closed forest. Soars on long, fingered, upswept wings. Identify from Black-breasted Buzzard; imm. White-bellied Sea-Eagle.

Gliding head-on

RAOU Atlas 224

Adult at nest

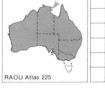

153 Little Eagle *Hieraaetus morphnoides*

Light morph head buff to pale rufous with blackish streaks on cheeks. Blackish crown feathers extending into a short crest. Upperparts brown, paler on nape and scapulars, with a distinct pale band across the wing. Underparts white with fine black streaks and a buff to rufous wash, especially on breast. Underwing has rufous leading edge and white oblique band contrasting with grey-barred secondaries and black-tipped outer primaries. Tail barred, rather short and square-cut. Legs feathered. **Dark morph** head and underparts light brown with black streaks. Leading edge and oblique band on underwing dark brown. **Female** larger. **Size** F 50-55, M 45-48 cm. **1st year light morph** head and underparts richer rufous, less streaked. **1st year dark morph** more rufous-brown than adults; less streaked. **Voice** loud, excited, high-pitched whistle, usually of two or three notes uttered rapidly. Also a series of mellow or plaintive piping notes. **Habitat** most open forest, woodland and scrub types; open agricultural country. Compact in flight; wings slightly drooped when gliding, held level to slightly raised when soaring. Identify from Whistling Kite, Square-tailed Kite.

Gliding head-on

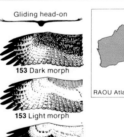

153 Dark morph

153 Light morph

146 Underwing pattern

RAOU Atlas 225

153 Erect 'crest'

Note: An adult Gurney's Eagle *Aquila gurneyi* present on Boigu Is., Torres Strait, February 1987 – a new species for Australia. This is an eagle ranging from the Moluccan area to Papua New Guinea; distinguish from 152 Wedge-tailed Eagle. A rare bird even in New Guinea.

153
Light morph

153
Light morph: 1st yr

153
Dark morph

153
Light morph: 1st yr

153
morph

153
Dark morph: 1st yr

152

152

152

152

152
Imm : 1-4 yrs

151
Imm : 1st yr

151

151
Juv.

151

151

154 Spotted Harrier *Circus assimilis*

Upperparts blue-grey. Wings with prominent black tips.
Face and underparts chestnut with numerous white spots.
Tail prominently barred and slightly wedge-shaped. Long
yellow legs. **Male** much smaller. **Size** F 58-61, M 50-55 cm.
1st year dark brown and buff above; pale buff with brown
streaks below. **2nd year** like adults but white streaks (not
spots) below. **Habitat** hunts low over open grassland, crops
and windbreaks. Soars with wings elevated.

Gliding head-on

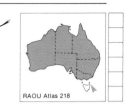

RAOU Atlas 218

155 Swamp (Marsh) Harrier *Circus approximans*

Adults/Imm. dark brown above; prominent white rump
(uppertail coverts). Tail and wings barred. Long yellow legs.
Male slightly smaller. Off-white to buff underparts.
Female rufous underparts. **Size** F 55-61, M 50-57 cm.
1st year darker brown; rump brownish; no bars on wings.
Voice high-pitched 'seee-uh' during aerial food transfer
between birds; loud 'kee-a' during courtship flights.
Habitat hunts low over tall grass, reeds, rushes, crops. Soars
with elevated wings; performs courtship dives high above swamps.

Gliding head-on

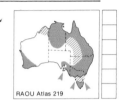

RAOU Atlas 219

[156 New Guinea Pied Harrier *Circus spilonotus*]

Male black and silver-grey above. Rump white. White
below, streaked on breast. Colour morphs occur. **Size** F 48-53,
M 47-51 cm. This bird is a race of the (New Guinea) Spotted Marsh
Harrier and is thus *Circus spilonotus spilothorax* formerly regarded as a
distinct New Guinea species. Vagrant. One recent record, Darwin, NT.

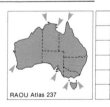

157 Black Falcon *Falco subniger*

Dark brown to sooty-black, with pale chin and face; dark
streak below eye. Heavy-shouldered. Tail usually square-
cut. Legs short. **Male** smaller. **Size** F 52-56, M 45-54 cm. **1st
year** darker than adults, with faint narrow bars under
wings and tail. **Voice** chatters and screeches. **Habitat**
woodland, scrub, shrubland and grassland types in arid
and semi-arid zones. Glides on slightly drooped wings.
Flight swift when hunting, otherwise leisurely.

Gliding head-on

Posture on ground

RAOU Atlas 238

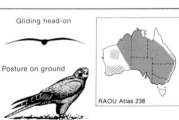

158 Peregrine Falcon *Falco peregrinus*

Heavily built and compact. Head and cheeks black,
upperparts blue-grey, underparts cream with dark barring
on belly. Race *submelanogenys* of SW of WA is smaller
and darker. **Male** smaller. **Size** F 45-50, M 35-42 cm.
1st year upperparts tinged brown; underparts buff with heavy
dark streaks. **Voice** hoarse chatter and whining sounds.
Habitat most land types, especially cliffs and rocky
outcrops; rocky coastal islands. Flight powerful. Wings
held stiffly outstretched when soaring; trailing edge
usually straight. Identify from Australian Hobby.

Gliding head-on

Stooping

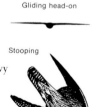

RAOU Atlas 237

158 ♀

158 1st yr ♂

159
Australian Hobby

158 1st yr ♀

158 ♂

157

157 1st yr

157

157

161
Brown Falcon
Dark morph

157

154 1st yr

155 1st yr

154

156

154

155

155

154
2nd yr

155

154

155 1st yr

154 1st yr

159 Australian Hobby *Falco longipennis*

Slender and long-winged. Cap and 'mask' black, forehead and half-collar whitish. Upperparts blue-grey; underparts rufous, streaked darker. Race *murchisonianus*, of arid zone, is paler. **Female** larger. **Size** F 34-35.5, M 30-32 cm. **1st year** upperparts tinged brown. **Voice** rapid shrill chatter, also loud chuckling call. **Habitat** most open forest, woodland and scrub types, also urban areas. In flight, silhouette *may* resemble White-throated Needletail, Oriental Cuckoo.

Gliding head-on

Aerial feeding

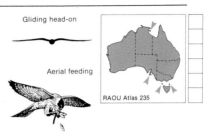

RAOU Atlas 235

160 Grey Falcon *Falco hypoleucos*

Grey above with black streak under eye, black wing-tips. White below with fine dark streaks. Tail grey, faintly barred as are the wings. **Female** larger. **Size** F 41-43, M 33-36 cm. **1st year** darker with heavier streaks on underparts. **Voice** chattering and clucking sounds. **Habitat** woodland and scrub types in arid zone. Heavy-shouldered, Peregrine-like in flight. Rare. Identify from *Elanus* kites; Grey Goshawk.

Gliding head-on

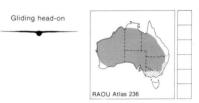

RAOU Atlas 236

161 Brown Falcon *Falco berigora*

Brown above, with dark marks below and behind eye. Underparts either whitish with dark streaks and brown thighs, or blotched brown and white, or wholly dark brown. Underwings barred. Tail rounded. Legs long. Five races: *berigora, tasmanica, centralia, occidentalis, melvillensis*. Birds from central Aust. are usually paler, and those from the tropical north are often very dark. **Female** larger. **Size** F 48-51, M 41-45 cm. **1st year** usually darker underparts; broad buff collar; incomplete barring of tail. **Voice** raucous cackles and screeches. **Habitat** most land surface types except closed forest. Glides on raised wings, flight usually heavy and slow. Hovers 'unsteadily'.

Gliding head-on

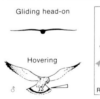

Hovering

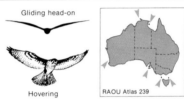

RAOU Atlas 239

162 Australian Kestrel *Falco cenchroides*

Male grey head, pale rufous back and wings. Whitish underparts with fine dark streaks. Grey tail. **Female/1st year** head and tail pale rufous. **Size** F 33-35.5, M 30-33 cm. **Voice** shrill, excited chatter. **Habitat** most land surface types except forests. Slender, hovers with body horizontal, showing black band near tail-tip.

Gliding head-on

Hovering

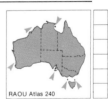

RAOU Atlas 240

158
Peregrine Falcon
1st yr

159

158
Peregrine Falcon

160

♂ **162**

159

161
Race *tasmanica*

160

160 ♂
Imm.

♀ **162**

♀ **160**

159

159
Imm.

162
Imm.

♂ **161**
Race *berigora*

♂ **161**
Race *tasmanica*

162 ♂

♀ **161** Imm.
Race *berigora*

♀ **161**
Race *centralia*

N. Day

163 Orange-footed Scrubfowl *Megapodius reinwardt*

Bill reddish-brown. Short, pointed, brown nuchal crest.
Dark chestnut-brown above. Neck, underparts slate-grey.
Legs orange. **Size** 40-60 cm. **Voice** loud crows, gurgles;
often many birds call at once. **Habitat** rainforests,
monsoon forests, dense vegetation bordering water.

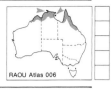

RAOU Atlas 006

164 Malleefowl *Leipoa ocellata*

Bill dark grey. Crown, nape blackish-brown. Head, neck,
breast, mantle leaden-grey. Large ear hole. Black streak
down central breast. Throat white, streaked black.
Upperparts white barred, blotched brown, black and grey.
Underparts light fawn. Large feet; legs dark grey.
Size 60 cm. **Voice** booming (territorial); sharp grunt
(alarm); soft lowing call (communication). **Habitat** dry
inland scrub, mallee.

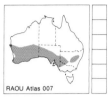

Flight

Front view

RAOU Atlas 007

165 Australian Brush-turkey *Alectura lathami*

Race *lathami*: **Breeding male** bill black. Bare red skin on
head, neck, crown and nape (with sparse black hair-like
feathers). Large yellow collar/wattle. Body dull black;
underpart feathers edged dull white. Legs brown.
Female smaller neck band; no wattle. Race *purpureicollis*
has purplish-white collar (C. York Pen., Qld). **Size** 70 cm.
Voice harsh grunts. **Habitat** rainforests and wet open
forests; also some dry inland areas.

Perched

Flight

RAOU Atlas 008

166 Stubble Quail *Coturnix pectoralis*

Male bill grey. Eye red. Grey-brown above with obvious
cream streaks and dark brown, buff and grey
vermiculations. Throat orange. Cream below; strong black
and cream streaking on chest and flanks. Legs pale flesh.
Female/Juv. throat white, tinged brown below **Size** 18 cm.
Voice high whistle 'titch-u-wip'. **Habitat** grasslands. In
flight, a large brown quail with white streaks.

Hatchling

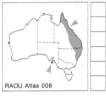

RAOU Atlas 009

167 Swamp Quail *Coturnix ypsilophora*

Probably same species as Brown; larger. Eye pale
yellow. **Size** 20 cm.

Confined to Tas.

168 Brown Quail *Coturnix australis*

Male large. Bill black. Eye red to yellow. Chestnut to
grey-brown with faint white streaks and black barring.
Legs orange-yellow. **Female/Juv.** paler below. **Size** 18 cm.
Voice 'f-whip' and 'be-quick, be-quick'. **Habitat** dense
grassland, often near forest. In flight, a rich brown quail,
streaks hard to see.

Hatchling

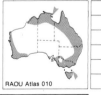

RAOU Atlas 010

169 King Quail *Coturnix chinensis*

Male very small. Bill black. Eye red. Cap, wings brown
with faint white streaks and blackish bars. Sides of face,
chest and flanks slate-blue. White crescent from eye across
upper chest, bordered black. Throat black. Chestnut belly
to vent. Legs yellow. **Female/Juv.** dark brown, faintly
streaked, with throat white. Eye brown. **Size** 13 cm.
Voice two to three descending notes. **Habitat** dense
grassland, often swampy. In flight a very small, all-dark
quail.

Hatchling

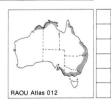

RAOU Atlas 012

163

164

165

169 ♀

169 ♂

169 ♀

♀ 169

168

167

168

♂ 166

166 ♀

166 ♂

170 Peafowl *Pavo cristatus**

Male blue with fan-shaped crest. Long uppertail coverts ('tail') have green spots with bronze reflections and blue spots surrounded by brown near tips. **Female** body chestnut brown, with a metallic blue sheen. 'Tail' shorter than male. **Size** M 180-200 (including 'tail'), F 90-100 cm. **Voice** 'kee-ow kee-ow'. **Habitat** introduced to Rottnest Island (WA). Also introduced but not established on other islands. Semi-feral populations exist.

Courtship display

RAOU Atlas 903

171 Feral Chicken *Gallus gallus**

Male many colour variations. Large comb on head. Long, drooping red and green tail. **Female** smaller comb. **Size** 43-75 cm. **Voice** male 'cock a doodle-do'; also clucking. **Habitat** introduced to thick scrub on some Great Barrier Reef islands.

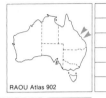

RAOU Atlas 902

172 Common Pheasant *Phasianus colchicus**

Male red facial skin. Blue head. White collar. Body reddish-golden, spotted black below. **Female** brown with buff and blackish mottles. No wattles. Tail shorter. **Size** 76-89 cm. **Voice** 'korrk-koh'. **Habitat** scrub, rank grasslands. Introduced on various islands.

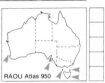

RAOU Atlas 950

173 California Quail *Lophortyx californicus**

Male long black crest. Black and white striped head. Brown nape, upperparts. Black collar finely spotted white. Grey chest. Blackish below, spotted and streaked white. **Female** duller. **Size** 24 cm. **Voice** 'ut-ut'; 'cu-ca-cow'; other calls. **Habitat** introduced on King Island (Bass Strait) in grasslands.

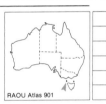

RAOU Atlas 901

— Chukar Partridge *Alectoris chukar**

Plump partridge. Grey-white face, throat surrounded by black line. Bill, eye-ring, legs red. Brown-grey above and on chest. Flanks barred black, white, chestnut. **Size** 33 cm. **Voice** loud wails, drummings. **Habitat** allegedly released for sporting reasons in Gulgong district, NSW. Runs, flies noisily if pressed, then glides. Not on Aust. list yet.

— Common Turkey *Meleagris gallopavo**

Dark brown to blue-black, speckled, slightly iridescent plumage. **Male** naked rear neck purple and white. Fleshy red wattle and throat. **Female** smaller; duller; little head decoration. **Size** M 95-125, F 90-110 cm. **Voice** coarse 'gobbling'; clucks, yelps. **Habitat** feral populations on King and Flinders Islands, Bass Strait. Not on Aust. list yet.

— Helmeted Guinea Fowl *Numida meleagris**

Plump, upright fowl. Grey-black body with fine, white spots. Bluish skin on sides of face, neck. Bony red-brown helmet (casque). **Size** 60 cm. **Voice** squeaking wail. **Habitat** feral populations on Heron and other Great Barrier Reef islands, Qld. Not on Aust. list yet.

* Introduced

173 ♀

♂ 173

171 ♂

♀ 171

172 ♂

♀ 172

170 ♂

170 ♀

172 ♂

174 Red-backed Button-quail *Turnix maculosa*

Slender bill. Eye pale. **Female** chestnut on hind neck, upper back. Wing coverts yellow, spotted black. **Male** duller, smaller; little or no chestnut on back. **Size** F 16, M 15 cm. **Habitat** moist grasslands.

RAOU Atlas 013

175 Painted Button-quail *Turnix varia*

Female eye red. Crown, face, breast flecked white. Chestnut shoulder; thin white streaking above. **Male** duller, smaller. **Size** F 20, M 19 cm. **Habitat** grassy forests, woodlands.

Hatchling

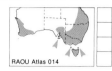

RAOU Atlas 014

176 Chestnut-backed Button-quail *Turnix castanota*

Stout bill. Eye yellow. Breast grey-buff with fine whitish streaks. **Female** larger; back cinnamon, mottled black or chestnut, also fine white streaks; contrasts with plain cinnamon rump, tail. **Male** duller. **Size** F 18, M 17 cm. **Habitat** grassy woodlands.

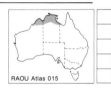

RAOU Atlas 015

177 Buff-breasted Button-quail *Turnix olivei*

Similar to Chestnut-backed except bill heavier; breast plain buff. **Female** larger. **Male** duller. **Size** F 20, M 19 cm. **Habitat** grassy woodlands.

RAOU Atlas 016

178 Black-breasted Button-quail *Turnix melanogaster*

Eye white. **Female** larger; black head; breast scalloped with bold white spots. **Male** paler; less black on head. **Size** F 20, M 19 cm. **Habitat** rainforests, lantana thickets.

RAOU Atlas 017

179 Little Button-quail *Turnix velox*

Female heavy grey-blue bill. Eye yellowish or white. Flanks whitish. Brownish above, faintly streaked white. Rump, tail reddish-buff, whitish sides. **Male** dark scales on side of neck. **Size** F15, M14 cm. **Habitat** dry to arid woodlands, grasslands.

RAOU Atlas 018

180 Red-chested Button-quail *Turnix pyrrhothorax*

Female like Little Button-quail but darker above. Throat, breast, flanks orange-buff. **Male** duller; black scallops on side of neck. **Size** F 15, M 14 cm. **Habitat** grasslands.

RAOU Atlas 019

181 Plains-wanderer *Pedionomus torquatus*

Bill long, thin; long, narrow nasal apertures. Iris very pale yellow. Plumage soft. Wing rounded, soft. Legs, feet yellow to greenish-yellow; legs longer than button-quails'. Toes long; hind toes short, prominent. **Female** larger; usually sandy-red feathers with narrow black lines. Chestnut patch on breast; collar of black and white feathers. Breast, upper abdomen with small black crescents. **Male** paler; buff and white; collar inconspicuous. **Size** F 17-18, M 15-17 cm. **Juv.** like male. **Voice** repetitive 'oom'. **Habitat** native grasslands, old stubble. Runs crouched, may spread wings; stands erect; crouches motionless; seldom flies. Rare.

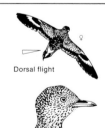

Dorsal flight

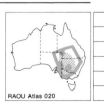

RAOU Atlas 020

♀ 175 175 ♂ 175 ♀

176 ♀ 176 ♀

178 ♂

177 ♀ 178 ♀

179 ♂ ♀ 179

♀ 179 180 ♀

174 ♀

♀ 180 180 ♂

♀ 174 174 ♂ ♀ 181

182 Buff-banded Rail *Gallirallus philippensis*

Race *australis:* Bill brown, shorter than Lewin's. Front of
eyebrow white. Chestnut eye-stripe and nape. Throat grey.
Upperparts, cap, wings brown; blackish feathers, edged
with white spots. Upper chest to underparts black with
white bars. Buffy-orange mid-chest band. Legs pink-
brown. Race *yorki:* Smaller with narrower darker breast
band. **Size** 29-33 cm. **Nestling** sooty-black. **Juv.** duller.
Voice squeaky 'sswit sswit'; loud throaty croaks; at nest a
low clucking. **Habitat** grassy, reedy or thickly vegetated
areas usually close to water.

Nestling

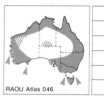

RAOU Atlas 046

183 Lewin's Rail *Dryolimnas pectoralis*

Much smaller than Buff-banded Rail. Bill long, black-
tipped, basal two-thirds reddish. Chestnut cap, black
streaked. Eyebrow and nape chestnut. Throat, chest olive-
grey. Black feathers of upperparts margined olive-brown.
Belly to undertail black, barred white. Undertail has two
lateral streaks of white. Feet flesh-coloured. **Size** 21-
23.5 cm. **Nestling** sooty-black. **Juv.** black head; white bars
duller. **Voice** wide variety of soft clicks, crowings, low
groanings. **Habitat** like Buff-banded Rail; prefers coastal
regions.

Flight

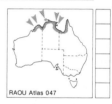

RAOU Atlas 045

184 Chestnut Rail *Eulabeornis castaneoventris*

Swamphen-sized. Bill green but tip horn. Head grey.
Throat pink-grey. Neck, all of upperparts olive-chestnut.
Glossy pink-chestnut underparts. Grey thighs. Legs olive-
yellow. **Male** larger. **Size** 44-52 cm. **Nestling/Juv.** not yet
described. **Voice** raucous 'wack, waka, wah-wah' often and
rhythmically repeated. Also grunting notes.
Habitat mangroves.

Calling

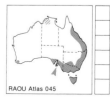

RAOU Atlas 047

185 Red-legged Crake *Rallina fasciata*

Smaller than Buff-banded Rail and Red-necked Crake
which it resembles. Bill reddish or brown; base red. Head,
neck, breast rich rufous. All upperparts olive and chestnut
with white barring on wings. Mid-chest to vent black,
barred white. Legs red. **Size** 19-24 cm. **Juv.** brown
instead of chestnut; duller white barrings. Legs brownish.
Voice unknown. **Habitat** wet areas in open country, scrub
and forest. Asian vagrant.

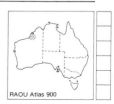

RAOU Atlas 900

186 Red-necked Crake *Rallina tricolor*

Bill green. Head, neck and chest rich chestnut; throat
buffy. Upperparts dark slate-grey. Abdomen, lower flanks,
vent and undertail sooty-black with dull rufous cross bars.
Size 27-28 cm. **Juv.** bill duller; duller chestnut and olive
upperparts. Duller bars below. **Voice** loud and descending
'raak, rah-rah-rah'; 'kih'; 'toh, toh' or 'plop-plop-plop'
often heard in wet season; grunts like piglets.
Habitat rainforest near water.

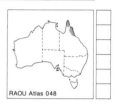

RAOU Atlas 048

183 Nestling

183 Juv.

183

185

182

184

186

187 Corncrake *Crex crex*

Larger than Australian Crake. Bill pale brown, short and stubby. Iris hazel. Eyebrow before and behind eye, and throat grey. Buffy eye-stripe. Cap, hind neck and upperparts black; feathers edged buff-grey. Chest buff-grey; flanks and undertail with brown bars; whitish vent. Wings bright chestnut. Legs pale brown. **Size** 25.5-26.5 cm. **Voice** 'rerp rerp'. **Habitat** meadows, lush vegetation, crops.

Flight

RAOU Atlas 899

188 Baillon's Crake *Porzana pusilla*

Smallest of Aust. crakes. Bill olive-brown. Eye red. Cap, hind neck ochre-brown, streaked black. Eyebrow light blue-grey. Eye-stripe ochre-brown. Upperparts ochre-brown, streaked black; wings have faint white spots on feather edges. Underparts light blue-grey, paler on throat, breast and abdomen. Flanks and undertail coverts barred black and white. Legs olive-brown. **Size** 15-16 cm. **Nestling** greenish-black. **Juv.** browner below, duller bars on underparts. **Voice** 'chutt, krekk' also a trill when alarmed. **Habitat** well vegetated, freshwater to brackish swamps. Often walks over water weed.

Undertail pattern

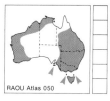

RAOU Atlas 050

189 Australian (Spotted) Crake *Porzana fluminea*

Largest of Aust. *Porzana* species. Bill olive-green, orange-red at base. Eye red. Cap, neck and upperparts dark olive-brown, streaked black and finely spotted white. Lores black. Face, chest pale slate-grey. Lower flanks black, barred white. Undertail coverts white. Legs olive-green. **Size** 19-21 cm. **Nestling** sooty-black. **Juv.** bill may have a little red at base is dull yellow. Upperparts brownish; buff feather edges. All underparts brown with white tips to feathers; abdomen, flanks have dull brown bars on white. **Voice** many calls; 'doo-ik'; high pitched 'chatter-chatter'; 'kirrik-kirrik-kirrik'; also whine. **Habitat** well-vegetated swamps, estuaries and lagoons.

Undertail pattern

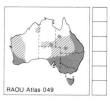

RAOU Atlas 049

190 Spotless Crake *Porzana tabuensis*

Slightly smaller than Australian Crake. Bill black. Iris red. Dark slate-grey head, chin and underparts. Rest of upperparts chocolate-brown. Barred undertail. Legs red. **Size** 18-19 cm. **Juv.** duller brown; iris black. **Voice** a sharp 'kikk, blop-blop-blop' like engine starting; 'krroo'. **Habitat** reedy and grassy freshwater swamps.

Undertail pattern

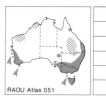

RAOU Atlas 051

191 White-browed Crake *Poliolimnas cinereus*

Small, similar to Spotless Crake. Bill olive-yellow, base red. Cap, lores and eye-stripe blackish. Eyebrow, stripe below dark eye-stripe, and throat, all white. Upperparts black with olive-brown feather margins. Cheeks, upper breast and upper flanks grey. Abdomen white; lower flanks and undertail coverts sandy-buff. Legs olive-green. **Size** 18-19 cm. **Juv.** facial markings duller; cap brown; neck buff. **Voice** various 'nasal' squealing notes. **Habitat** well-vegetated swamps, often walking onto lilypads like a Jacana.

Undertail pattern

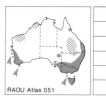

RAOU Atlas 052

187

188 Juv.

188

190 Juv.

190

189 Juv.

189

191 Juv.

191

N. Day

192 Bush-hen *Amaurornis olivacea*

Bill green. Small frontal shield orange. Iris brown. Cap to mantle olive-brown; browner towards tail. Sides of head to abdomen pale slate-grey. Vent dull pink-chestnut. Legs yellow. **Size** 25-26 cm. **Nestling** black; at 5-6 weeks brown with black head. **Juv.** paler; bill all green. **Voice** long, repeated 'nee-u', followed by a shuddering sound. Also clicks and grunts, and a single note repeated.
Habitat swamps, flooded grasslands, rainforest fringes.

RAOU Atlas 053

193 Tasmanian Native-hen *Gallinula mortierii*

Swamphen-sized. Bill yellow. Iris ruby-red. Upperparts olive-brown, browner on wings. Underparts slate-grey. White patch on flank. Tail, abdomen black. Legs yellow. **Size** 43-45 cm. **Nestling** black down; white spot on flanks. **Juv.** paler. **Voice** frequent 'see-saw'; alarm call; loud scream; low-pitched grunts. **Habitat** grassy regions, usually near water.

Calling

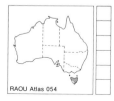

RAOU Atlas 054

194 Black-tailed Native-hen *Gallinula ventralis*

Moorhen-sized. Bill green; base of lower mandible orange. Iris yellow. Upperparts olive-brown. Tail black. Throat to breast blue-grey. Abdomen, undertail coverts black; flanks with pear-shaped spots. **Size** 32-36 cm. **Nestling** green, black down. **Juv.** paler; spots duller. **Voice** sharp alarm call; very quiet single cackle. **Habitat** close to water, often in open, sheltering in nearby bushes.

Running tail down

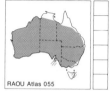

RAOU Atlas 055

195 Dusky Moorhen *Gallinula tenebrosa*

Slightly smaller than Swamphen. Bill, frontal shield red, tip yellow. Iris olive. Body slate-grey. Wings, rump browner. Tail black. White sides to undertail coverts. Legs yellow, scarlet and olive. **Size** 35-38 cm. **Nestling** black with white tips to chin and throat. Skin on cap bluish. Frontal shield red. **Juv.** paler; bill green, horn or black. Legs green. **Voice** many shrill notes. **Habitat** fresh water, usually near reeds.

Flight

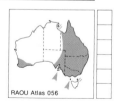

Juv.

RAOU Atlas 056

196 Purple Swamphen *Porphyrio porphyrio*

Race *melanotus:* Brick-red bill and frontal shield. Red eyes. Head, upperparts black. Underparts, wings deep blue to purple-black. White undertail coverts. Legs red. Race *bellus* of SW Aust. is paler blue on the underparts. **Size** 44-48 cm. **Nestling** black. Bill grey-white, black tip. Legs grey, becoming redder with age. **Juv.** plumage, iris, bill all browner. **Voice** harsh screaming noise 'hee-ow'. **Habitat** swamps, marshy paddocks.

Flight

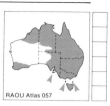

RAOU Atlas 057

197 Eurasian Coot *Fulica atra*

Slightly smaller than Moorhen. Bill, frontal shield white. Eyes red. Body dark slate-grey. Legs black. **Size** 32-39 cm. **Nestling** black down with yellow hair-like tips; bill cream. **Voice** various shrill notes. **Habitat** swamps, open lakes.

Flight

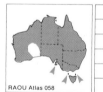

RAOU Atlas 058

198 Brolga *Grus rubicundus*

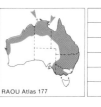

Trumpeting

Stately long-legged grey crane with 'bustle' of secondary feathers falling over rump. Head bare; skin on front of crown pale grey. Scarlet on rear of head and nape. Black 'haired' dewlap under chin. Eye yellow. Ear coverts grey. Neck, back silver-grey; back often with brown wash. Wings grey with black primaries. Underparts grey. Legs dark grey-brown to black. **Female** slightly smaller. **Size** stands up to 1.4 m; **Chick** downy; grey with paler markings. **Imm.** skin of face and nape fleshy-pink. **Voice** whooping trumpet uttered in flight and on ground; also harsh croaks. **Habitat** often pairs or parties in shallow swamps, wetlands, pastoral lands. Flies with neck, legs extended; shallow wing beats with upward flick. Dancing displays of leaps, bows, high steps and loud trumpeting calls are performed by both sexes. Brolgas often soar in thermals.

RAOU Atlas 177

199 Sarus Crane *Grus antigone*

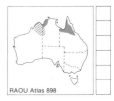

Stately long-legged grey crane with 'bustle' of secondary feathers falling over rump. Head, upper neck bare. Scarlet skin on face and upper neck distinguish it from the Brolga. Crown grey. Eye red. *No* dewlap under chin. Back, wings grey. Some white feathers in 'bustle'. Underparts grey. Legs, feet pink. Race in Aust. is *sharpei*. **Size** stands up to 1.5 m. **Imm.** skin on head, upper neck pale rufous. **Voice** whooping trumpet uttered in flight and on ground; also harsh croaks. **Habitat** often pairs or parties in shallow swamps, wetlands, pastoral lands. Mixed flocks of Brolgas and Sarus Cranes have been recorded so observe carefully. Flies with neck and legs extended. Dancing displays of leaps, bows, high steps and loud trumpeting calls are performed by both sexes.

RAOU Atlas 898

200 Kori (Australian) Bustard *Ardeotis kori*

Flight

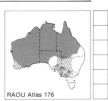

Male crown black. White eyebrow. Neck white and finely vermiculated. Black breast band. Back, wings, tail brown, finely marked with buff. Upperwing coverts black and white. Underparts white to grey. Legs, feet pale yellow to grey or olive; has three toes. **Female** narrow brown crown. Neck, breast off-white to grey. Breast band thinner, often not visible. Less black and white on wing. **Size** M stands up to 1 m. F stands up to 0.7 m. **Chick** downy; striped buff and brown. **Voice** males have guttural roar, uttered during display. Harsh barking cry when alarmed; otherwise mainly silent. **Habitat** open grasslands, grassy woodlands, pastoral land, crops. Stately erect posture, head usually tilted upwards. Often stands motionless for extended periods when being observed. Flight slow, powerful; neck, legs extended. Breeding display of males very spectacular: white throat-sac extends to the ground and swings as male steps from side to side, tail raised over back exposing white undertail coverts.

RAOU Atlas 176

Cryptic posture

199

198

198
Dancing

199

198

198
Imm

♂ 200

200 ♀

198
Chick

200
Chick

200 Imm

N. Day

201 Comb-crested Jacana *Irediparra gallinacea*

Hatchling

Forehead, comb red. Bill green-yellow, tipped brown. Cheeks golden-yellow. Crown, hind neck, breast band black. Brown upperparts. Belly, neck white. Long, dull green legs; extremely long toes. **Size** 23 cm. **Imm.** comb small; crown brown; breast white. **Voice** squeaky 'pee pee pee'; shrill alarm call. **Habitat** swamps, lakes, lagoons. Walks on floating plants.

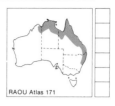

RAOU Atlas 171

202 Pheasant-tailed Jacana *Hydrophasianus chirurgus*

Breeding

Non-breeding neck pale golden bordered by line of black, becoming brown. Upperparts dark olive-brown; underparts white. **Breeding** (unlikely to be seen in Aust.). **Size** 31 cm. **Habitat** open swampy areas. Aust. record is in doubt.

203 Bush Thick-knee *Burhinus grallarius*

Small black bill. Forehead buff; pale buff eyebrow. Large yellow eye. Black eye-stripe through neck. Black streaking on grey-brown upperparts; buff-white underparts. Whitish shoulder patch. **Size** 55 cm. **Voice** mournful, wailing 'wee loo' usually at night. **Habitat** open woodlands, sometimes near beaches. Singly or pairs. Active at night. 'Skulking' habits; 'rigid' movements. Formerly called Southern Stone Curlew.

Dorsal flight

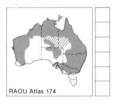

RAOU Atlas 174

204 Beach Thick-knee *Esacus magnirostris*

Large bill with yellow base, black tip. Large yellow eye. Broad black eye patch; white bands above and below. Upperparts brown; darker shoulder. White wing patches. Throat, breast grey; underparts white. Legs olive-yellow. **Size** 55 cm. **Voice** repeated, mournful, wailing 'wee loo'; higher, harsher than Bush Thick-knee. **Habitat** reefs, beaches, coastal mud-flats. Formerly called Beach Stone Curlew.

Flight

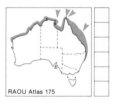

RAOU Atlas 175

205 Painted Snipe *Rostratula benghalensis*

Hatchling

Long, drooped, pinkish bill. **Female** chestnut-black hood. White eye patch, crown stripe. Curved white collar. Delicate black, green, grey and buff patterns above. **Male/Imm.** smaller, duller; more buff. Eye patch, crown stripe buff. Wings prominently spotted. **Size** F 25 cm, M 22 cm. **Voice** booming in display. **Habitat** marsh with moderate cover. Likely to 'freeze' when approached. Flight fast; rail-like.

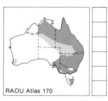

RAOU Atlas 170

206 Pied Oystercatcher *Haematopus ostralegus*

Race *longirostris:* Black with white belly, vent, rump and half wing-stripe. Bright red eye, eye-ring and bill. Pink legs. **Size** 48 cm. **Juv.** duller bill, eyes; grey legs. **Voice** double 'per-peep'; during display rapid 'pee-pee-pee-pee'. **Habitat** coastal; prefers beaches, estuaries.

Hatchling

RAOU Atlas 130

207 Sooty Oystercatcher *Haematopus fuliginosus*

Race *fuliginosus:* All black. Red eye, eye-ring and bill. Pink legs. Race *opthalmicus* (N Aust.) has broader red eye-ring. **Size** 48 cm. **Voice** like Pied. **Habitat** coastal; prefers rocky coastline; occasionally estuaries.

Hatchling

RAOU Atlas 131

201

201
Imm.

202
Non-breeding

205 ♂

205 ♀

205 ♀

203

204

206

206
Juv.

206

207
Race *fuliginosus*

207
Race *opthalmicu*

208 Masked Lapwing (Plover) *Vanellus miles*

Brown above; white below. Prominent yellow facial wattles; wing spurs. Black crown; flight feathers. Race *miles* (N Aust.): Wattle extends behind eye. Race *novaehollandiae* 'Spur-winged Plover' (SE Aust.): Smaller, rounded wattle; black hind neck and sides of breast. Hybrids occur. **Size** 35 cm. **Voice** loud 'kerr-kick-ki-ki-ki'; single 'kek'. **Habitat** grasslands, mud-flats.

Hatchling

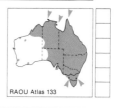

RAOU Atlas 133

209 Banded Lapwing (Plover) *Vanellus tricolor*

Brown above; white below. Red lore wattle. Yellow bill and eye-ring. White line behind eye. Black crown, side of neck, breast band. White wing-stripe. **Size** 25 cm. **Voice** crying 'er chill cher'. **Habitat** open grasslands, bare plains.

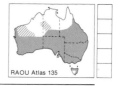

RAOU Atlas 135

210 Grey Plover *Pluvialis squatarola*

Larger, greyer than Lesser Golden Plover. Large head. **Non-breeding** bill black, longer, bulkier than Lesser. Small, pale eyebrow. Mottled grey back. In flight axillaries (armpit) black. Underparts white. White wing bar, rump. White tail, barred black. Legs dark grey. **Breeding** marbled silver and dark grey above. Black belly; white vent. **Size** 28 cm. **Habitat** like Lesser Golden Plover.

Ventral flight

RAOU Atlas 136

211 Lesser Golden Plover *Pluvialis dominica*

Race *fulva:* **Non-breeding** bill black. Eye large. Broad eyebrow, buff to whitish. Golden-buff to cream spots over dark upperparts to tail. Breast golden-brown to cream. Axillaries, underwing dark grey. Indistinct wing bar. White underparts. Legs dark grey-black. **Breeding** bright golden above with dark mottling. Black from throat to undertail coverts; divided from upperparts by a white line from eyebrow to flanks, which continues as white bars to sides of undertail coverts. **Size** 25 cm. **Voice** 'too weet'. **Habitat** beaches, mud-flats, sometimes inland.

Ventral flight

RAOU Atlas 137

212 Golden Plover *Pluvialis apricaria*

Like Lesser Golden Plover race *fulva,* except underwing white; slightly larger. **Size** 27 cm. **Habitat** like Lesser Golden Plover. Vagrant?

Ventral flight

213 Red-kneed Dotterel *Erythrogonys cinctus*

Hatchling

Brown above; white below. Hood, nape, breast band black. White throat. Flanks chestnut, edged white. Trailing edge of wings white. Legs brown-grey; red knees. **Size** 18 cm. **Imm.** brown instead of black; no breast band. **Voice** 'chet chet'. **Habitat** edges of swamps.

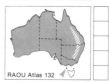

RAOU Atlas 132

214 Hooded Plover (Dotterel) *Charadrius rubricollis*

Hatchling

Red bill has black tip. Red eye-ring. Black head, white collar. Lower neck, side of breast black; pale grey-brown above. Broad white wing bar. Tail, rump black, edged white. **Size** 19-21 cm. **Imm.** head pale; darker about eye. **Voice** short, piping calls. **Habitat** ocean beaches, sometimes coastal lakes. Inland salt lakes in WA.

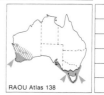

RAOU Atlas 138

208
Race *miles*

208
Race *miles*

208
Race *novaehollandiae*

209

209

211
Breeding

210
Breeding

210
Non-breeding

211
Non-breeding

210
Non-breeding

212
Non-breeding

211
Non-breeding

213

213
Imm.

213

214

223
Black-fronted Dotterel
Imm.

214
Imm.

214

215 Ringed Plover *Charadrius hiaticula*

Breeding grey-brown above; white below. Orange bill has black tip. Orange eye-ring. Black band through eye, with black band above white forehead. Eyebrow black above but white *behind* eye. White collar, black breast band. White wing bar. Legs orange. **Non-breeding** areas of black duller; white eyebrow complete. Breast band incomplete. **Size** 18 cm. **Voice** 'too-li' or 'coo-eep'. **Habitat** shores, marshes. Rare migrant.

Breeding

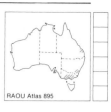
RAOU Atlas 895

216 Little Ringed Plover *Charadrius dubius*

Race *dubius*: Like Ringed Plover but smaller, browner. Bill black. Eye-ring yellow. *Lacks* white wing bar. Legs orange. **Size** 15 cm. **Voice** 'pee-oo'. **Habitat** shores, marshes. Rare migrant.

Breeding

RAOU Atlas 851

217 Mongolian Plover *Charadrius mongolus*

Non-breeding small, black bill. Lores dark brown. Dark eye patch. Dark brown-grey above; white below. Faint grey breast band. **Breeding** chestnut-red nape and breast. Throat white, cut off from breast by a slender black line. Distinctive black eye patch and edge to white forehead. Narrow white wing bar. Legs greyish. **Size** 19-20 cm. **Voice** 'drit drit'. **Habitat** shores, marshes, rarely inland.

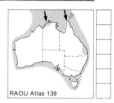
RAOU Atlas 139

218 Double-banded Plover *Charadrius bicinctus*

Breeding grey-brown above; white below. Bill short, slender, black. Forehead, eyebrow white. Upper chest-band black; lower band broader, chestnut. White wing bar. Legs yellow-grey or grey-green. **Non-breeding** tinged buff; browner than Mongolian and Large Sand Plovers. **Size** 18-19 cm. **Voice** loud, staccato 'pit-pit'; rapid trill. **Habitat** beaches, mud-flats, grasslands, bare ground.

Head pattern
Juv.

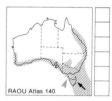
RAOU Atlas 140

219 Large Sand Plover *Charadrius leschenaultii*

Non-breeding like Mongolian. Bill longer, heavier. Face paler; lores often incompletely marked grey-brown. Uniform pale grey-brown above; white below. Broader wing bar. Legs dusky-greenish. **Breeding** narrow chestnut chest band. **Size** 20-23 cm. **Voice** 'chweep-chweep'. **Habitat** like Mongolian.

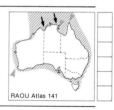
RAOU Atlas 141

220 Caspian Plover *Charadrius asiaticus*

Like Oriental Plover except underwing white; smaller; shorter legs. **Size** 21 cm. **Habitat** like Oriental Plover. Vagrant.

Underwing pattern

RAOU Atlas 894

221 Oriental Plover *Charadrius veredus*

Slender, long-legged plover. **Non-breeding** fine black bill. Buffy-white eyebrow, throat. Uniform grey-brown upperparts, tail and faint chest band. No wing bar. White below. Legs dusky-olive. **Breeding** white head; faint brown cap, ear coverts. Chestnut breast separated from white belly by black line. **Size** 22-25 cm. **Voice** nasal 'chit-chit'; 'chrreep'. **Habitat** dry inland plains, occasionally coastal.

Underwing pattern

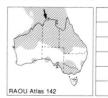
RAOU Atlas 142

216
Non-breeding

215
Non-breeding

215

216

217
Breeding

217
Non-breeding

217
Non-breeding

218
Breeding

218
Non-breeding

218
Non-breeding

219
Non-breeding

218
Non-breeding

219
Breeding

221
Breeding

219
Non-breeding

220
Non-breeding

221
Non-breeding

221
Non-breeding

222 Red-capped Plover *Charadrius ruficapillus*

Hatchling

Small plover with white underparts. **Male** distinctive rufous crown and nape, bordered black. Black eye-stripe; white forehead. Underparts brown. White wing bar. Black line through rump. **Female** similar, crown duller; black markings indistinct. **Size** 15 cm. **Imm.** duller than female. **Voice** a sharp "twink'. **Habitat** seashores, estuaries, inland lake margins, marshes. Favours sandy areas.

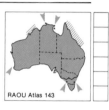
RAOU Atlas 143

223 Black-fronted Plover *Elseyornis melanops*

Hatchling

Small plover with brown upperparts, pale streaks and chestnut shoulder patch. Bill bright red, tipped black. Face white; black forehead and black eye-line. Underparts white. Broad black 'V' on chest. **Size** 16 cm. **Imm.** *no* black on chest. **Voice** metallic 'pink'. **Habitat** margins of freshwater lakes, farm dams; rarely in tidal areas. Nomadic. Flight jerky, reveals broad white wing bars.

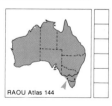
RAOU Atlas 144

224 Inland Dotterel *Peltohyas australis*

Cryptic posture

Bill short, black. Upperparts yellowish-buff, streaked dark grey-brown. Forehead, face, upper breast white-buff. Black bar across crown to below large eye. Black mark behind eye joins a black collar, which extends to a 'V' on chest. Rich chestnut inverted 'V', below black 'V', separates white abdomen from lower breast and dark buff flank. Legs buffy-grey. **Size** 20 cm. **Imm./Non-breeding** may lack black markings. **Voice** mostly silent. **Habitat** ploughed ground, open sparse plains and gibber. Well camouflaged.

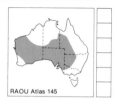
RAOU Atlas 145

225 Black-winged Stilt *Himantopus himantopus*

Imm. Ventral flight

Adult
Dorsal flight

Race *leucocephalus:* White; black nape, back, wings. Long, fine, black bill. Red eye. Long coral-pink legs trail in flight. **Size** 36-38 cm. **Imm.** face, wings, back grey-brown. **Voice** yelps. **Habitat** fresh and salt water marshes.

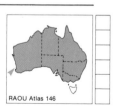
RAOU Atlas 146

226 Banded Stilt *Cladorhynchus leucocephalus*

Imm. Ventral flight

Adult
Dorsal flight

White; prominent red-brown breast band above deep brown mid-belly patch. Long, fine black bill. Eye dark brown. Wings brown-black; white trailing edge in flight. Legs flesh-pink; shorter than Black-winged Stilt. **Size** 36-45 cm. **Imm.** white breast, belly; wings brownish; legs greyish. **Voice** single or double 'yook'; 'chogga'. **Habitat** fresh and salt water marshes, marine mud-flats. Large ephemeral lakes. Often in dense flocks, frequently swims; legs trail in flight.

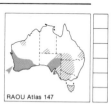
RAOU Atlas 147

227 Red-necked Avocet *Recurvirostra novaehollandiae*

Adult

Dorsal flight

Body white. Head, neck chestnut. Long, black bill *upcurved* (more steeply in male). Black wing bar, wing-tips, and stripes down side of back are distinctive in flight. Long pale blue-grey legs trail in flight. Partly-webbed feet. **Size** 40-46 cm. **Imm.** paler; grey on scapulars. **Voice** yelps, wheezes; musical 'toot toot'. **Habitat** salt lakes, mud-flats, marshes, shallow inland waters. Gregarious, often swims.

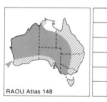
RAOU Atlas 148

226   227   225

227   226   225

226
Imm.

225
Imm.

223
Displaying

222

224

223

222
Imm.

222 ♂

228 Ruddy Turnstone *Arenaria interpres*

Distinctive, thickset, black and white wader (especially in flight). Short, wedged-shaped bill. Short orange legs. **Non-breeding** dark brown above and breast band. **Breeding** chestnut upperparts; pied head; black breast band. **Size** 21-25 cm. **Voice** loud rattle. **Habitat** rocky shores.

Juv.

RAOU Atlas 129

229 European Curlew *Numenius arquata*

Like Eastern Curlew but shorter bill. *No* eyebrow or crown stripe. White lower back and rump. Tail barred. **Size** 54-58 cm. Vagrant.

RAOU Atlas 893

230 Eastern Curlew *Numenius madagascariensis*

Large wader. Very long down-curved black bill; pink at base. Pale eyebrow. Streaked dark brown and buff above, including rump. Slightly paler below. **Size** 53-61 cm. **Voice** mournful 'karr-er'; higher 'kerlee-kerlee'. **Habitat** estuaries, mud-flats, mangroves, sandpits.

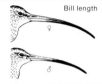

RAOU Atlas 149

231 Whimbrel *Numenius phaeopus*

Race *variegatus*: Like Eastern Curlew but smaller. Bill much shorter. Paler eye-stripe, crown stripe. White lower-back, rump. Race *hudsonicus* (rare) brown rump. **Size** 38-43 cm. **Voice** shrill chattering 'tee-tee-tee'. **Habitat** as Eastern Curlew, occasionally inland.

Race *hudsonicus*

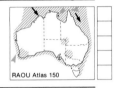
RAOU Atlas 150

232 Little Curlew *Numenius minutus*

Like Lesser Golden Plover; slightly larger. Long down-curved grey bill; lower-base pink. **Size** 31-36 cm. **Voice** flute-like double whistle. **Habitat** open plains, grasslands, sometimes mud-flats.

RAOU Atlas 151

233 Upland Sandpiper *Bartramia longicauda*

Generally upright stance; 'plover-like'. Long tail, neck. Buffy coloured, heavily dark-streaked. Bill short, tip slightly down-curved; yellowish base. Small head; dark crown. Large, brown eye; white eye-ring. Rump, tail dark-centred, edged white. Underwing barred. Legs, feet yellowish. **Size** 28-32 cm. One old record.

Underwing pattern

RAOU Atlas 892

234 Wood Sandpiper *Tringa glareola*

Sharp-tailed Sandpiper-sized. Medium, straight, black bill. Longish neck. Back and dark wings spotted white. White rump; tail thinly barred black. Pale, plain underwing. Yellow-greenish legs. **Size** 20-23 cm. **Juv.** wing spots golden. **Voice** loud, rapid, four-note whistle. **Habitat** fresh water; marsh with light cover. Jerky movements. High zigzag flight.

Underwing pattern

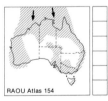
RAOU Atlas 154

235 Green Sandpiper *Tringa ochropus*

Like Common Sandpiper. In flight diagnostic pattern of uniform dark brown upperparts (appearing blackish; no wing bar) contrasts with brilliant white rump. Uppertail broadly barred black. Underwing blackish. **Size** 23 cm. **Habitat** usually fresh water, especially ditches. Vagrant.

Flight

228
Breeding

228
Breeding

228
Non-breeding

229

230

231
Race *variegatus*

232

230

233

231

232

233

234
Juv.

234

234

235

235

236 Grey-tailed Tattler *Tringa brevipes*

Bill straight, grey with nasal groove. White eyebrow.
Light grey above. Grey breast; white below. Legs
yellowish. **Breeding** thinly barred brown-grey below.
Size 26 cm. **Voice** fluty 'troo-eet'; 'weet-eet'.
Habitat estuaries, rocky coasts, reefs.

237 Wandering Tattler *Tringa incana*

Like Grey-tailed. In hand, *deep* section of nasal groove
longer. Eyebrow less distinct. Darker above.
Breeding underparts boldly barred brown-grey. **Size** 27 cm.
Voice trill 6-10 notes 'whee-wee-wee'. **Habitat** reefs, rocks.

238 Common Sandpiper *Actitis hypoleucos*

White eyebrow, shoulder mark. Brown; finely scaled black
above and on breast sides. White below. **Size** 20 cm.
Habitat banks, rocks near water. Bobs head, tail. Low jerky
flight, shows broad white wing bar; dark centre to rump.

239 Greenshank *Tringa nebularia*

Bill slightly upturned, black, bluish base. Upperparts
grey. Forehead, underparts white; underwing barred.
White on rump extends up back in wedge. Long green
legs trail in flight. **Size** 31-35 cm. **Voice** ringing 'tew-tew'.
Habitat coastal, inland lakes. Nervous. Bobs head.

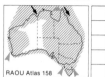

240 Spotted Greenshank *Tringa guttifer*

Like Greenshank. Bill stouter; yellowish base. Underwing
white. Legs short, barely trail in flight. **Breeding** obvious
spotting across breast. **Size** 30 cm. **Voice** loud piercing
'keyew'. **Habitat** as Greenshank.

241 Redshank *Tringa totanus*

Like Greenshank but browner above. Red bill base, legs.
Upperwing with a broad white trailing edge. **Size** 28 cm.
Voice loud 'then-hu-hu'. **Habitat** as Greenshank. Rare
migrant.

242 Lesser Yellowlegs *Tringa flavipes*

Like Wood Sandpiper but larger with long, slender,
straight bill and long neck. Legs bright yellow or orange;
trail in flight. **Size** 27 cm. **Voice** soft, high 'ti-di-ti', 'ti-
dup'. **Habitat** as Greenshank. Vagrant.

243 Marsh Sandpiper *Tringa stagnatilis*

Like a tiny, paler Greenshank. Bill straight, needle-like.
Forehead, underparts white. Legs greenish; trail in flight.
Size 20-23 cm. **Voice** soft 'tee-oo'. **Habitat** as Greenshank,
prefers fresh water.

244 Terek Sandpiper *Xenus cinereus*

Grey above; white below. Long slightly upturned bill.
Thin white trailing edge to wings. Yellow to orange legs.
Size 22-23 cm. **Voice** fluty trill 'weeta-weeta-weeta'; rapid
'tee-tee-tee'. **Habitat** coastal mud-flats, occasionally inland.

236

236
Non-breeding

237
Non-breeding

238

238

239

239
Non-breeding

240
Non-breeding

241

242

241
Non-breeding

243

242
Non-breeding

244

243
Non-breeding

244
Non-breeding

N. Day.

245 **Latham's Snipe** *Gallinago hardwickii*

Long bill; brown base. Crown dark brown with cream centre. Dark eye-stripe, cheek stripe. Rest of face pale cream. Mottled black, brown, buff. Belly white; flanks barred. **Size** 24-26 cm. **Voice** rasping 'shik'. **Habitat** wet grasslands; open and wooded swamps. Well camouflaged. Often flies late dusk.

Tail pattern

16-18 feathers

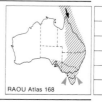

RAOU Atlas 168

246 **Pin-tailed Snipe** *Gallinago stenura*

Smaller than Latham's. Barring on the back indistinct; shorter wings. **Size** 23-25 cm. **Voice** abrupt 'charp'. **Habitat** as Latham's. Rare migrant to N Aust.

24-28 feathers

RAOU Atlas 852

247 **Swinhoe's Snipe** *Gallinago megala*

Like Latham's; shorter wings. **Size** 24-26 cm. **Voice** short 'shrek'. **Habitat** as Latham's. Migrant to N Aust.

20-24 feathers

RAOU Atlas 169

248 **Asian Dowitcher** *Limnodromus semipalmatus*

Great Knot-sized; leg length like godwits. Long, straight black bill; 'swollen' tip. Plumage like Bar-tailed Godwit. White tips to secondaries. **Size** 25-35 cm. **Voice** single yelp. **Habitat** coastal flats, occasionally inland. Rare migrant.

Breeding

RAOU Atlas 939

249 **Black-tailed Godwit** *Limosa limosa*

Long, straight bill; pink base. Uniform grey-brown; white below. White rump, wing bar, underwing. Black flight feathers, borders to underwing and tail. **Breeding** russet head, belly. **Size** 36-43 cm. **Habitat** tidal flats, occasionally inland.

Bill length ♂

♀

RAOU Atlas 152

250 **Bar-tailed Godwit** *Limosa lapponica*

Bill long, slightly upturned; pink base. White rump; tail barred grey-brown. Upperparts, underwing finely barred and mottled grey-brown. **Breeding male** head, belly rich chestnut-red. **Size** 38-45 cm. **Habitat** tidal flats, rarely inland.

Bill length ♂

♀

RAOU Atlas 153

251 **Hudsonian Godwit** *Limosa haemastica*

Like Black-tailed Godwit. Bill slightly upturned. Underwing almost all black. Wing bar less distinct than Black-tailed. Less white in rump. **Size** 45 cm. **Habitat** as other godwits. Vagrant.

♂

Non-breeding

252 **Red Knot** *Calidris canutus*

Robust, straight, 3 cm bill. Dumpy. **Non-breeding** upperparts uniform grey; white below. **Breeding** rust-red. **Size** 25 cm. **Voice** throaty 'knut' or 'kloot kloot'. **Habitat** tidal mud-flats, rarely inland.

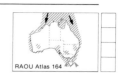

RAOU Atlas 164

253 **Great Knot** *Calidris tenuirostris*

Like Red Knot but larger, much longer bill (4-5 cm); heavily streaked above. **Breeding** head, neck striped black. Black breast spotted white. **Size** 28 cm. **Voice** occasional 'nyut-nyut'. **Habitat** as Red Knot.

RAOU Atlas 165

246

245

247

245

251
Non-breeding

249
Non-breeding

249
Breeding

249
Non-breeding

250
Non-breeding

250
Juv.

250
Breeding

250
Non-breeding

248
Non-breeding

248
Non-breeding

253
Breeding

253
Non-breeding

253
Non-breeding

252
Juv.

252
Non-breeding

252
Breeding

252
Non-breeding

254 Sharp-tailed Sandpiper *Calidris acuminata*

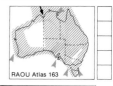

Straight black bill; dull olive base. Chestnut crown. Back feathers have black centres, buff edges. Black through rump. Indistinct wing bar. Dark streaked and speckled breast and flanks to undertail sides. White belly. Olive legs. **Voice** 'wit-wit'. **Habitat** inland waters, coastal.

263 Curlew Sandpiper

RAOU Atlas 163

255 Pectoral Sandpiper *Calidris melanotos*

Like Sharp-tailed, but smaller head, bill longer; base yellow. Streaked 'V' on breast distinct from white belly. Crown brown, streaked dark, *not* chestnut. Legs yellow. **Voice** reedy, rasping 'krrrt'. **Habitat** prefers inland swamps.

RAOU Atlas 978

256 Cox's Sandpiper *Calidris paramelanotos*

Like Pectoral, but bill long, down-curved, black, shorter than Curlew Sandpiper. Small head. Breast *not* strongly demarcated. Line on rump thinner. Streaks on undertail coverts. Legs olive; same length or shorter than Pectoral Sandpiper. **Breeding** heavy dark bars below. **Voice** like Pectoral, shriller. **Habitat** like Curlew Sandpiper. Extremely rare; recently described.

257 Baird's Sandpiper *Calidris bairdii*

Feathers above black, scaled buff. Wings project well past tail at rest. Rump dark. Legs dark olive. **Breeding** deeper buff. **Size** 18 cm. Vagrant.

RAOU Atlas 890

258 White-rumped Sandpiper *Calidris fuscicollis*

Like Baird's; white rump. **Size** 19 cm. Vagrant.

RAOU Atlas 849

259 Western Sandpiper *Calidris mauri*

Like Red-necked Stint. Bill slightly longer, down-curved. Feet semi-webbed. **Breeding** crown, nape, cheeks rusty; breast, flanks finely chevroned. **Juv.** rufous scapulars. **Size** 17 cm. Unsubstantiated sightings so far in Aust.

260 Little Stint *Calidris minuta*

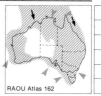

Non-breeding as Red-necked. **Breeding** back feathers have black centres, chestnut edges. Breast orange with a band of dark streaks. White throat. Cream 'V' on mantle. **Juv.** streaked black and chestnut above. White 'V' on mantle. **Voice** 'tit'. **Size** 14 cm. **Habitat** as Red-necked. Rare migrant.

RAOU Atlas 857

261 Red-necked Stint *Calidris ruficollis*

Non-breeding short, black bill. Grey-brown above; white below; thin black line through rump. Obvious white wing bar. **Breeding** back feathers have black centres, chestnut edges. Head, neck, breast pink-chestnut. Legs black. **Size** 15 cm. **Voice** 'chit, chit'; high pitched trill. **Habitat** coastal, inland shores.

263 Curlew Sandpiper

RAOU Atlas 162

262 Long-toed Stint *Calidris subminuta*

Stint-sized 'Sharp-tail'. Long, yellow legs trail in flight. **Breeding** upperparts edged chestnut. **Size** 15 cm. **Voice** rapid 'chre-chre-chre'. **Habitat** inland swamps, rarely coast.

Alert posture

RAOU Atlas 965

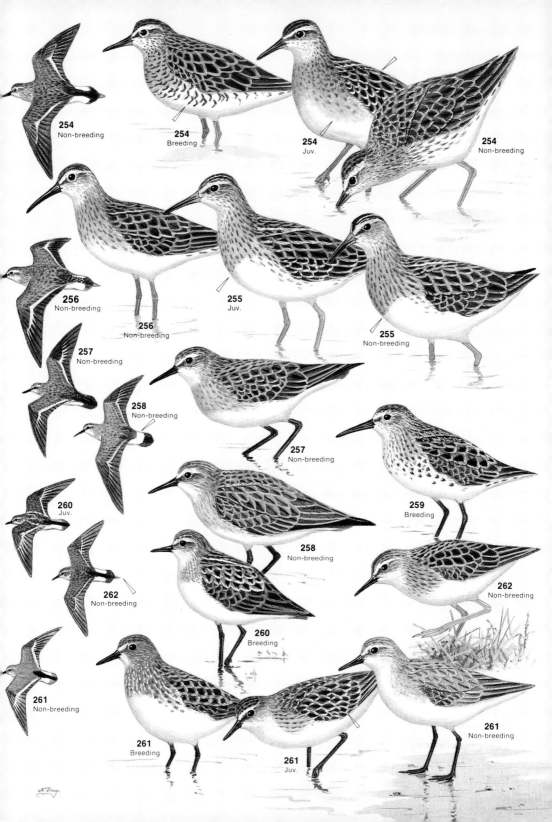

254
Non-breeding

254
Breeding

254
Juv.

254
Non-breeding

256
Non-breeding

256
Non-breeding

255
Juv.

255
Non-breeding

257
Non-breeding

258
Non-breeding

257
Non-breeding

259
Breeding

260
Juv.

258
Non-breeding

262
Non-breeding

262
Non-breeding

260
Breeding

261
Non-breeding

261
Breeding

261
Juv.

261
Non-breeding

N. Day.

263 Curlew Sandpiper *Calidris ferruginea*

Bill long, black, down-curved. **Non-breeding** grey-brown above. Broad white wing bar; white rump. White below. Legs black. **Breeding** copper-red below, barred black. **Size** 21 cm. **Voice** loud 'chirrup'. **Habitat** coastal, inland mud-flats.

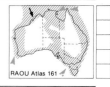
RAOU Atlas 161

264 Dunlin *Calidris alpina*

Like Curlew Sandpiper; smaller. Black centre to rump. **Non-breeding** grey-brown above; white below. Broad white wing bar in flight. **Breeding** chestnut above; black belly. **Size** 20 cm. **Voice** nasal 'tree'. **Habitat** as Curlew Sandpiper. Vagrant.

RAOU Atlas 888

265 Sanderling *Calidris alba*

Larger than Red-necked Stint; longer bill. **Non-breeding** white face, underparts. Silver-grey back. In flight broad white wing bar, blackish forewing. Lacks hind toe. **Breeding** chestnut face, breast. **Size** 20 cm. **Habitat** beaches, rarely inland.

Juv.

RAOU Atlas 166

266 Buff-breasted Sandpiper *Tryngites subruficollis*

Medium-sized sandpiper; 'plover-like' stance. **Non-breeding** small round head. Short straight black bill. All buff-brown above (includes rump, breast) with dark spots. No wing bar. Buff underparts. Underwing white with a dark bar on greater primary coverts. Legs long, yellow-orange. **Size** 21 cm. **Voice** harsh 'krik'; 'tik'. **Habitat** grass near water. Vagrant.

Underwing pattern

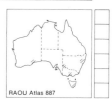
RAOU Atlas 887

267 Broad-billed Sandpiper *Limicola falcinellus*

Slightly larger than stint with long, black bill, heavy at base, drooped at tip. **Non-breeding** crown streaked black; *double* white eyebrow. Dark shoulder patch and line through rump. Slender white wing bar. Legs dark olive. **Breeding** upperpart feathers black centred, buff or rufous edges. **Size** 18 cm. **Voice** trilling. **Habitat** coastal mud-flats, occasionally inland.

Head from above
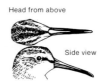
Side view

RAOU Atlas 167

268 Ruff (Reeve) *Philomachus pugnax*

Much larger than Sharp-tailed Sandpiper. Small head; long neck; long legs. **Non-breeding** bill straight. Dark brown and buff above (colour variable); scaly look. Head, neck, light grey-brown, streaked darker. Breast light greyish-brown. Whitish below. In flight, white oval patches on sides of dark rump. Legs green, yellow, to red. **Breeding male** develops erectile ruff, ear tufts of various colours. **Breeding female** darker barring above. **Size** M 30, F 23-27 cm. **Voice** 'tu-whit' when flushed. **Habitat** inland wetlands; rarely coast. Rare migrant.

Breeding

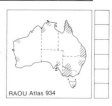
RAOU Atlas 934

269 Stilt Sandpiper *Micropalama himantopus*

Superficially like Curlew Sandpiper but larger. Long yellowish legs; *no* wing bar. **Breeding** blackish upperparts, pale fringes. Chestnut ear coverts and nape. Underparts heavily barred black. **Size** 21 cm. **Voice** 'too too'. **Habitat** swamps. Vagrant.

263
Breeding

263
Non-breeding

263
Non-breeding

263
Juv.

264
Non-breeding

264
Non-breeding

264
Breeding

265
Non-breeding

265
Non-breeding

265
Breeding

267
Breeding

267
Non-breeding

267
Non-breeding

269

266

266

268 ♀
Non-breeding

269

268
Non-breeding

♂ **268**
Non-breeding

270 Red-necked Phalarope *Phalaropus lobatus*

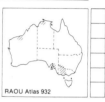

Non-breeding bill black, needle-like. Broad black eye patch. Slender neck. Dusky-grey above, striped white. White below. White wing bars and 'braces' in flight. Black line through rump. Feet lobed. **Breeding female** broad bright rufous neck stripe. Rest of head black. White throat. Blackish above with buff streaks. **Breeding male** much duller. **Size** 17-20 cm. **Voice** 'chek' or 'chik-chik-chik'. **Habitat** oceans, bays, swamps, lakes. Mostly swims for food, bobs head, spins around in circles. Rare migrant.

RAOU Atlas 932

271 Wilson's Phalarope *Phalaropus tricolor*

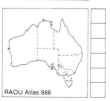

Bill much longer, even more needle-like than Red-necked Phalarope. **Non-breeding** uniform pale grey above; forehead, eyebrow, underparts white. Grey curving eye-stripe. Tail grey. White rump. Greenish legs. Superficially similar to Marsh Sandpiper; distinguish by shorter, finer bill; shorter legs; lobed feet; lack of white on lower back. **Breeding female** broad black eye-stripe extends down sides of neck to red-brown shoulder, back stripes. Crown, back of neck grey; buffy lower neck. **Breeding male** much duller. White nape spot. **Size** 22-25 cm. **Voice** low-pitched honking. **Habitat** lagoons, lakes, mud-flats, swamps. Feeds by swimming. Occasionally spins. Few Aust. records.

RAOU Atlas 886

272 Grey Phalarope *Phalaropus fulicarius*

Shorter, stouter bill than other phalaropes, tipped black; often yellowish at base (adults). **Non-breeding** grey above; white below. Large black eye patch. Uniform grey upperparts; black line through rump. White wing bar. Feet lobed. **Breeding female** forehead, crown black. Face white. Black above, scaled buff. Entire underparts red-brown. **Breeding male** duller, paler. **Size** 19-22 cm. **Voice** shrill 'twit'. **Habitat** oceans, bays, lakes, swamps. Vagrant.

273 Oriental Pratincole *Glareola maldivarum*

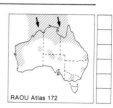

Non-breeding upperparts olive-brown. Bill black; red at gape. Throat buff, edged with broken line of black streaks. Breast dusky grey. White rump. Tail white, dark-tipped, shallow fork. Underparts whitish. In flight swallow-like, showing chestnut underwing coverts and trailing edge black. Legs short, black. **Breeding** bill, gape brighter red. Throat light buff; bordered black. **Size** 23 cm. **Voice** tern-like 'chik chik'; soft 'towheet-towheet'. **Habitat** open plains, bare ground around swamps, claypans. Hawks insects; sometimes in huge flocks.

Dorsal flight

RAOU Atlas 172

274 Australian Pratincole *Stiltia isabella*

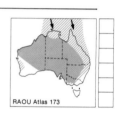

Very slender; long wings. Bill red with black tip. Golden buff above and on upperwing coverts; grey on back. Primaries black. Dark chestnut on flanks to legs. Square tail white, with triangular black sub-terminal mark. Wings project well beyond tail when perched. Legs very long, grey. **Juv.** bill duller. **Size** 22-24 cm. **Habitat** open plains of semi-arid regions; winters on coast in N Aust.

Dorsal flight

RAOU Atlas 173

273
Breeding

273
Breeding

274

273
Breeding

274

274
Juv.

273
Non-breeding

270 Non-breeding

272
Non-breeding

243
Non-breeding

270 ♀
Breeding

272
Breeding ♀

271
Breeding ♀

271
Non-breeding

270
Non-breeding

243
Non-breeding

272
Non-breeding

271
Non-breeding

275 Great Skua *Catharacta skua*

Race *lonnbergi*: Large, stocky, gull-like. Bill black. Short
tail. Chocolate-brown, flecked buff; boldly streaked buff
on back. Dark brown wings with broad white primary
bases. Legs black. **Size** 61-66 cm. **Juv.** reddish tinge to
upper body. **Habitat** coastal, oceanic. Flight direct,
powerful flapping and gliding. All skuas are piratic.

Wing moult

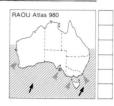

RAOU Atlas 980

276 South Polar Skua *Catharacta maccormicki*

Like Great Skua but smaller. **Light morph** light grey-brown
body; pale collar contrasts with dark upperparts. **Dark
morph** dark brown to blackish; nape sometimes paler; paler
around bill. **Size** 55 cm. **Juv.** bill base, legs blue. Chin,
throat paler. **Habitat** oceanic. Few records.

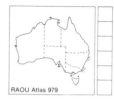

Dark
morph

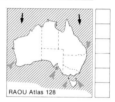

RAOU Atlas 979

277 Arctic Jaeger *Stercorarius parasiticus*

Small skua. Small head with two long, pointed, central
tail streamers. Slender wings. **Light morph breeding** bill,
cap black. Collar, throat, upper breast buff. Brown breast
band. Belly white. Upperparts, wings brown-grey, little
contrast with trailing edge. Underwing dark grey. Bases of
primaries white. Tail black, white base. Legs black. **Light
morph non-breeding** head paler. Black and white barring
on flanks, upper and undertail coverts. Often *lacks* tail
streamers. **Light morph Juv.** like non-breeding. Bill base
paler. Legs black and blue. Brown above, barred buff and
rufous. Underwing coverts barred brown, rufous and
white. Short pointed tail streamers. **Dark morph breeding**
dark brown; cap black; yellow collar, cheeks. **Dark morph
non-breeding** white bars on rump. **Dark morph Juv.** faint
buff to rufous bars below. **Size** 40-45 cm. **Habitat** oceanic,
coastal, often in bays. All jaegers are piratic.

Juv.

Underwing pattern

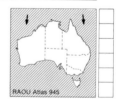

RAOU Atlas 128

Often stands on floating
debris at sea.

278 Pomarine Jaeger *Stercorarius pomarinus*

Like Arctic but larger. Head, bill bigger; body bulkier;
twisted when fully grown. All plumages as Arctic Jaeger
but wing flashes usually larger; non-breeding birds
but wing flashes usually larger; non-breeding birds
have broader white bars on rump. **Size** 45-50 cm.
Juv. upperparts brownish; faint to pale barring; *no* rufous
bars. Underwing coverts with brown and white bars.
Central tail streamers short, rounded. Legs black and
blue. **Habitat** more oceanic than Arctic.

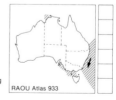

RAOU Atlas 945

279 Long-tailed Jaeger *Stercorarius longicauda*

Like Arctic but body smaller; slender wings; tern-like
flight. Long tail with double-length streamers 'pin-like'
near tips. Bill sheath blue to horn. Upperparts pale blue-
grey, *not* brown; contrasting black secondaries and
primaries (usually no white in wing). Legs black to black
and blue. **Non-breeding** pale head. Barred flanks, tail coverts.
Juv. greyish to dark brown above (no rufous), scaled buff-
white. Rump, flanks, underwing coverts barred grey and
white. White crescents on primary bases. Short central tail
feathers *rounded*. **Size** 40-45 cm. **Habitat** oceanic.

Non-breeding
Underwing pattern

RAOU Atlas 933

277
Light morph
Breeding

277
Dark morph

275

277
Light morph
Non-breeding

301
Crested Tern

278
Non-breeding

275

276
Light morph

276
Light morph

278
Juv.

279
Breeding

278
Dark morph
Breeding

278
Light morph
Breeding

279
Juv.

58
Wedge-tailed Shearwater

279
Juv.

277
Juv.

280 Silver Gull *Larus novaehollandiae*

Body white. Soft parts red. Iris white. Mantle grey.
Upperwings, inner primaries grey. Outer wing region from
carpal white, with black sub-terminal band through
primaries, white-tipped; three white mirrors (spots).
Size 41 cm. **Juv.** soft parts dark. Faint brown ear patch.
Upperparts mottled brown. Sub-terminal tail band
brownish. **Habitat** coastal, inland waters.

Imm. Swimming
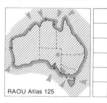
RAOU Atlas 125

281 Pacific Gull *Larus pacificus*

Thick yellow bill; both mandibles tipped red. Eye pale.
Body white. Black mantle and wings with white trailing
edge; black outer primaries. Tail white; thin black sub-
terminal band. Legs yellow. **Size** 63 cm. **Juv.** dark soft parts.
Body dark brown, slightly mottled. Tail black, tip white.
Imm. (1st-3rd year) whiter on body; blacker on back and
wings; matures in four years. **Habitat** coastal.

Imm: 3 yrs
Plumage varies

RAOU Atlas 126

282 Kelp Gull *Larus dominicanus*

Like Pacific Gull but finer bill. Red spot on lower bill.
White tips and mirrors (spots) on primaries. Broader
trailing edge. Tail white. Legs olive-yellow. **Size** 57 cm.
Juv. like Pacific juv., but paler, with black band on
secondaries. Ages like Pacific. **Habitat** coastal.

Imm: 2 yrs
Plumage varies
RAOU Atlas 981

283 Lesser Black-backed Gull *Larus fuscus*

Like Kelp Gull. See: Grant P. J. (1981), *Gulls: A Guide to
Identification*, T. & A. D. Poyser, Calton, UK. Recent
N Aust. record unlikely.

Adult

284 Black-tailed (Japanese) Gull *Larus crassirostris*

Breeding bill lemon, tipped red with a black sub-terminal
band. Eye honey. Body white. Slate-grey back and
upperwings. White trailing edge ends at central primaries;
rest of primaries black. Tail white with black sub-terminal
band. **Non-breeding** grey markings on head. Legs olive-
brown. **Size** 47 cm. **Imm.** greyer head extending to flanks.
Broad tail band. **Juv.** bill flesh-pink, tip black. Vagrant.

Juv.
Breeding adult
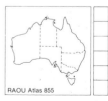
RAOU Atlas 855

285 Franklin's Gull *Larus pipixcan*

Breeding black hood. White eyelids. Black bill, tipped red.
Upperwings, back slate-grey; white trailing edge curves
behind black outer band on white-tipped primaries. *New*
underpart feathers have pink tinge. Tail white, with pale
grey centre. Legs red. **Non-breeding** black *hind* crown to
eyes; streaked crown; white frons, throat. Blackish legs.
Size 35 cm. **Imm.** like non-breeding; outer primaries black;
black sub-terminal tail band. Vagrant.

Juv.
Breeding adult
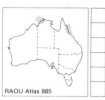
RAOU Atlas 885

286 Sabine's Gull *Xema sabini*

Breeding black hood. Black bill, tipped yellow. *Forked*
white tail. Upperwing has grey shoulder, black outer
primaries with white tips and white triangular trailing
edge. **Non-breeding/Imm.** white head; dark nape. **Juv.** eye
to mantle and shoulders scaly grey-brown. Tail tip black.
Size 34 cm. Vagrant.

Juv.
Breeding adult
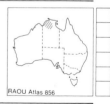
RAOU Atlas 856

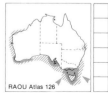

114

281 Imm: 1st yr

282 Juv.

281 Imm: 2nd yr

281

282

281 Juv.

281

282 Juv.

282

284 Imm.

285 Non-breeding

280

284 Non-breeding

286 Non-breeding

280 Juv.

280 Juv.

280

280 Imm.

280

287 Whiskered (Marsh) Tern *Chlidonias hybrida*

Large head on chunky body. Short tail has slight fork.
Long legs. **Breeding** short, thick, crimson bill; cap black;
cheek white. Pearl-grey above. Black belly, white vent.
Non-breeding as breeding; bill dusky red. Forehead, crown
white; some streaking at rear of black cap. Underparts white.
Size 25.5-27 cm. **Juv.** like non-breeding adult but bill
blackish; crown has more black; mantle variegated: dusky
and buff; faint shoulder bars. **Habitat** lakes, estuaries.

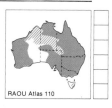

288 White-winged (Black) Tern *Chlidonias leucoptera*

Small head, body. Short red bill. Short, almost square
tail. **Breeding** head, mantle, breast, belly black.
Upperwing mid-grey; whitish shoulder bars. Underwing
coverts black, primaries grey. **Non-breeding** bill black;
black on crown extends in a lobe to ear coverts behind and
below eye. Central nape black, may be streaked white;
white mask. Upperparts mid-grey. Rump, underparts
white. Dusky shoulder bar. Underwing white, trailing
edge grey. **Size** 22-24 cm. **Juv.** like non-breeding adult but
contrasting blackish mantle, back. **Habitat** lakes, estuaries.

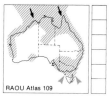

289 Black Tern *Chlidonias nigra*

Like White-winged Tern but long slender bill; longer
wings and tail (which is obviously forked). **Breeding** bill
black; very like White-winged except mid-grey mantle,
back, tail, wing coverts. **Non-breeding** like White-winged;
look for blackish droop extending from mantle on to
breast sides, and white underwing coverts (beware
moulting White-winged). **Size** 24-25.5 cm. **Juv.** darkest of
Chlidonias at this age; upperwing, mantle, back dark
grey; brownish fringes to latter. **Habitat** lakes, estuaries,
oceans. Very rare in Aust.

290 Caspian Tern *Sterna caspia*

The largest tern. Massive red bill. **Breeding** bill has dusky
sub-terminal mark. Cap black. Pale grey above; white
below. Primaries entirely blackish below. **Non-
breeding** black eye, ear coverts. Forehead, crown white;
fine black streaks increasing to nape. **Size** 50-56 cm.
Juv. like non-breeding adult but bill paler; forehead to
nape grey-buff; streaked black. Mantle variegated: dusky
and buff. **Habitat** coastal, inland watercourses.

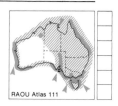

291 Gull-billed Tern *Sterna nilotica*

Race *macrotarsa*: Very pale, chunky tern; slightly forked
tail. Short, thick, black bill. Long black legs.
Breeding cap black. Upperparts whitish-grey; underparts
white. Underwing white with thick blackish trailing edge
to most of primaries. **Non-breeding** black ear coverts; rest
of head white; usually has faint, dark crown streaks.
Size 35-43 cm. **Juv.** like non-breeding adult but crown
greyish-brown, finely streaked and darker than adult.
Mantle variegated: dusky and pale buff. Race *affinis*:
Smaller; darker above contrasting with whiteness of head
and white underparts; an uncommon non-breeding
summer visitor to N Aust. **Habitat** coastal flats, inland
lakes, ploughed and fallowed fields.

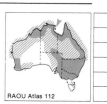

287
Non-breeding

288
Breeding

288
Non-breeding

287
Breeding

289
Breeding

287
Juv.

289
Non-breeding

288
Juv.

290
Breeding

290
Non-breeding

291
Breeding

291
Race *macrotarsa*

291
Race *affinis*

291

291
Non-breeding

290
Non-breeding

292 Common Tern *Sterna hirundo*

Race *longipennis:* **Breeding** black, mid-length bill. Cap to bill black. Belly, upperparts mid-grey; rest white. Tail streamers shorter than folded wings. Underwing *opaque* against light, with black trailing edge on outer half of wings. Brown, mid-length legs. Other races vary: black-tipped, red bill; red legs. **Non-breeding** black bill. Frons, underparts white. Black shoulder bar. Rump, tail pale greyish, *no* contrast with back. Tail shorter. **Size** 37 cm. **Voice** 'ki-ork'; 'kik-kik-kik'. **Habitat** oceans, bays. Race *longipennis* common; race *hirundo* rare. Other races not confirmed in Aust.

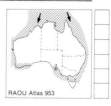

RAOU Atlas 953

293 Arctic Tern *Sterna paradisaea*

Like Common; smaller body. In flight, head projects less past long slender wings. Contrasting white rump. Shorter bill. Crown more domed. Shorter legs. **Breeding** bill red. Tail streamers project past primaries (longer in Roseate). Legs red. In flight, under primaries strongly *translucent* against light, with a strongly defined black trailing edge of constant width. **Non-breeding** bill blackish. Top of crown, frons white; head black at rear. Legs darker. **Size** 36 cm. **Habitat** oceans, coastal. Rare.

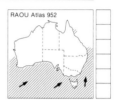

RAOU Atlas 952

294 Roseate Tern *Sterna dougallii*

Much smaller body than other Aust. 'commic' terns. Wings, long legs red. **Breeding** bill very long, slender, slightly drooped; varies from red with black tip, to black with red base. Cap black. Upperparts, tail pale grey. When developed, tail streamers longer than other 'commic' terns. White below; new plumage has soft pink tinge. Underwing white. **Non-breeding/Imm.** black bill. Forehead like Common. Underparts white. Upperwing slender, black wing bar; outer primaries black due to suspended moult. Legs blackish. **Size** 32 cm. **Juv.** crown feathers edged silver. Scapulars banded black, white edges. Tail short; feathers blotched black sub-terminally. **Voice** 'chew-ich'; grating 'aach'. **Habitat** oceanic.

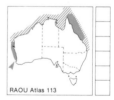

RAOU Atlas 113

295 White-fronted Tern *Sterna striata*

Largest 'commic' tern. **Breeding** bill, cap black; separated by white frons. Upperparts pale grey; *no* rump contrast. Underwing white. Folded primaries show a white line along upper edge. Underparts white. Tail white, a little longer than primaries. Legs dusky-red. **Non-breeding** forehead like non-breeding Common Tern. **Size** 39 cm. **Juv.** upperparts, central tail feathers boldly barred blackish. Upperwing has broad black triangle on shoulder. Dark outer primaries; the rest whitish. **Voice** 'kech kech'; 'kee-ech-kee-ech'. **Habitat** oceanic.

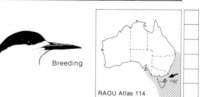

Breeding

RAOU Atlas 114

296 Black-naped Tern *Sterna sumatrana*

Bill black. Head, underparts, tail white. Thin black line from eye front on to nape. Upperparts pale grey. Tail deeply forked. Legs black. **Size** 31 cm. **Juv.** bill base dusky yellow. Distinguish from juv. Roseate by grey nape and whitish-grey bases to dark-fringed upperpart feathers; bulkier body, shorter legs. **Habitat** coastal, oceanic.

294 Juv.

296 Juv.

Head pattern

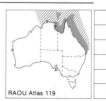

RAOU Atlas 119

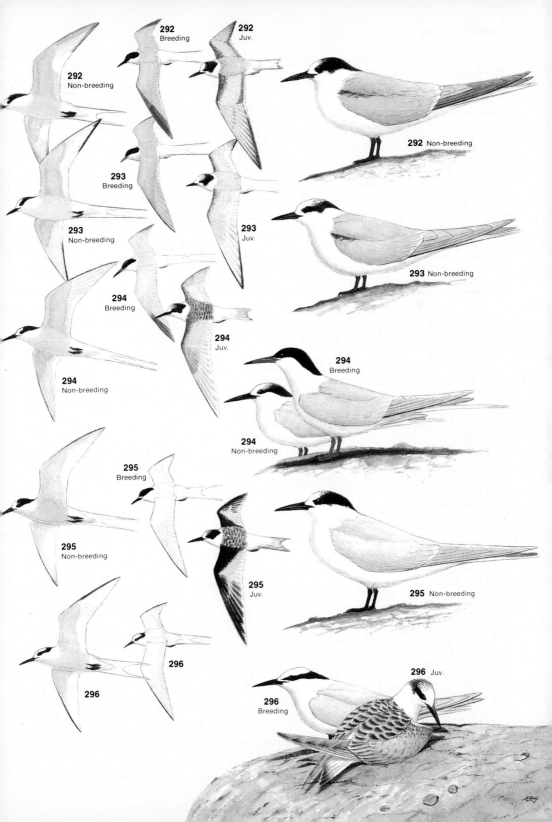

292 Non-breeding

292 Breeding

292 Juv.

292 Non-breeding

293 Breeding

293 Non-breeding

293 Juv.

293 Non-breeding

294 Breeding

294 Non-breeding

294 Juv.

294 Breeding

294 Non-breeding

295 Breeding

295 Non-breeding

295 Juv.

295 Non-breeding

296

296

296 Juv.

296 Breeding

297 Sooty Tern *Sterna fuscata*

Broad, triangular, white forehead patch. Upperparts
black. Tail deeply forked, outer tail feathers white.
Underparts white; faint grey on belly when breeding.
Underwing white; primaries, secondaries black. Size 40-
46 cm. Juv. dark brown upperparts; feathers tipped pale
buffish to white. Underwing coverts pale grey; vent white.
Tail short. Habitat oceans, islands.

Breeding

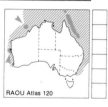

RAOU Atlas 120

298 Bridled Tern *Sterna anaethetus*

Like Sooty Tern but has less white on forecrown. White
extends as an eyebrow past the eye. Back dark grey-brown.
Underparts slightly darker grey when breeding.
Underwing like Sooty but primary bases slightly silvery-
grey. Size 36-42 cm. Juv. cap strongly streaked white. Lores
white with a black mark in front of eye. Upperparts
grey-brown, buffy-tipped. Underparts white; underwing
same as adult. Tail shorter, less deeply forked.
Habitat oceans, coasts, islands.

Breeding

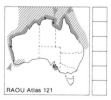

RAOU Atlas 121

299 Little Tern *Sterna albifrons*

Race *sinensis:* Very small grey and white tern with long,
narrow wings; rapid wing beats. Smaller head, flatter
crown, noticeably longer legs and body more slender than
Fairy Tern. **Breeding** bill mid-yellow, *usually* black tip.
Triangular white forehead from bill to above eye. Black
line through lores. Rest of cap black. Pale grey
upperparts contrast with forked white tail. Upperwing
pale grey, contrasting with blackish outer three or four
primaries. **Non-breeding** bill black. Lores to rear of crown
white; black band remains from eye to nape. Upperwing
has a dusty-greyish shoulder bar. Outer primaries slightly
darker than remaining wing; these wear (abrade) to black.
Legs blackish-brown. Size 20-23 cm. Juv. bill black,
brownish base. Cap streaked dusky and buff; dark ear
patch. Upperparts grey with dark sub-terminal feather
bands and buffish fringes. Darker, broader shoulder bar
than non-breeding birds. Secondaries grey, tipped white.
Habitat coasts, sometimes inland watercourses.

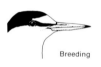

Breeding

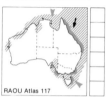

RAOU Atlas 117

300 Fairy Tern *Sterna nereis*

Like Little Tern but larger head with more rounded
profile. Also has noticeably bulkier body, giving round-
bellied appearance, and shorter, thicker legs. **Breeding** like
Little Tern but bill all bright orange. Larger white
forehead area. Lores white with black patch in front of
eye. Pearl-grey upperparts give *less* contrast with whitish
tail. Legs bright orange. **Non-breeding** bill dusky orange-
brown, blackish at tip and often at base of upper bill.
White *only* on forehead. Upperwing as breeding adult but
outer primaries *less* contrasting; *no* dark shoulder bar.
Size 22-24 cm. Juv. like juv. Little Tern but generally
darker and *no* dark wing bar. Outer wing dark greyish,
grading to pale grey inner wing, secondaries whitish (grey
in Little Tern). Habitat coasts, occasionally inland
watercourses.

Breeding

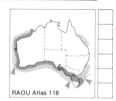

RAOU Atlas 118

298

297

297
Juv.

298
Juv.

298

297

297

298
Juv

300
Breeding

300
Non-breeding

299
Non-breeding

299
Breeding

299
Breeding

292
Common Tern
Non-breeding

300
Juv.

299
Juv.

299
Non-breeding

300
Breeding

300
Non-breeding

N. Day.

301 Crested Tern *Sterna bergii*

Breeding bill lemon-yellow; sometimes orange-yellow. Frons white. Cap black; short, shaggy crest on nape. **Non-breeding** forecrown black, scalloped white; rest of cap black. **Size** 43-48 cm. **Juv.** bill greenish-yellow; as non-breeding but cap black, extends as collar to throat sides. Upperparts variegated: dark grey and white. Black shoulder.

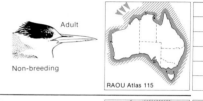

RAOU Atlas 115

302 Lesser Crested Tern *Sterna bengalensis*

Breeding like Crested Tern but smaller. Smaller bright orange bill; paler grey upperparts. Front black to bill. **Non-breeding** upper crown white. **Juv.** bill dull orange. Variegated and paler than Crested. Shoulder bar paler grey; forehead, crown whiter. Feet, legs *often* dull orange. **Voice** like Crested, shriller. **Habitat** estuaries, seas, islands.

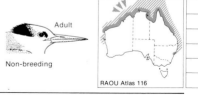

RAOU Atlas 116

303 Common Noddy *Anous stolidus*

Largest noddy. Bill shorter, thicker than other noddies. Indistinct white crown. Black line through lores. Rest of bird brown. Tail long, wedged, with shallow central notch. Underwing grey-brown, edges blacker. **Size** 37-41 cm. **Juv.** like adult; upperparts have fine pale fringing; duller, poorly defined greyish-brown cap. **Voice** purring and 'kraa, kraa'. **Habitat** seas, islands. Glides low to sea, wings forward, slow wing beats.

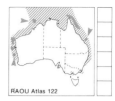

RAOU Atlas 122

304 Lesser Noddy *Anous tenuirostris*

Like Black Noddy but shorter bill; head greyer, contrasts less with white cap. Frons grey. **Juv.** cap may be whiter. **Size** 30-34 cm. **Voice** rattling alarm; purring call. **Habitat** oceans, coastal islands.

RAOU Atlas 124

305 Black (White-capped) Noddy *Anous minutus*

Smaller than Common Noddy. Longer, finer bill. Frons black. Distinguish in flight from Common Noddy by white cap, blackish body, black underwing, short tail with wider fork. **Juv.** like adult. **Size** 35-38 cm. **Voice** 'kirr'; cackling 'krik-krik-krik'. **Habitat** oceans, coastal.

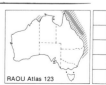

RAOU Atlas 123

306 Grey Ternlet *Procelsterna albivittata*

Small. Shape similar to Black Noddy. **Pale phase** pale grey; head, underparts whitish. Upperwing pale grey; dark grey trailing edge. Underwing white, trailing edge darker. **Dark phase** dark grey overall. Face, cap white; underwing grey. Long legs, black with yellow webs. **Size** 25-30 cm. **Juv.** brownish wash on upperparts. **Habitat** oceans. Feeds by bouncing on the water like storm-petrel.

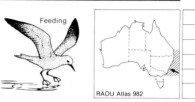

RAOU Atlas 982

307 White Tern *Gygis alba*

White with black eye, primary shafts and upturned bill. Almost transparent wings. Tail short. Legs blue. **Size** 28-33 cm. **Juv.** dusky ear coverts, nape and mantle. **Habitat** oceans.

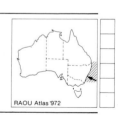

RAOU Atlas 972

297
Sooty Tern
Juv.

305

307

303

304

288
White-winged Tern
Non-breeding

306

303

304
Juv.

304

307
Juv.

306

305

302
Juv.

301
Juv.

302
Breeding

301
Non-breeding

301

301
Breeding

302
Non-breeding

308 Banded Fruit-Dove *Ptilinopus cinctus*

Head, neck white. Breast band, upperparts black. Rump, belly mid-grey. Tail black; broad grey tip. **Size** 33-35.5 cm. **Juv.** pale grey head, tail. **Voice** strong, low, repeated cooing. **Habitat** forested gullies of rocky escarpments, woodlands.

RAOU Atlas 024

309 Superb Fruit-Dove *Ptilinopus superbus*

Male crown purple. Cheeks pale green. Throat, breast blue-grey. Hind neck, collar orange. Upperparts green, spotted black; tail tip white. Black breast band; belly white. Green barred flanks. **Female** dull blue crown; *lacks* black breast band and orange on neck. **Size** 22-24 cm. **Juv.** as female, *lacks* crown patch. **Voice** five to six clear, deep whoops. **Habitat** rainforests, adjacent mangroves; eucalypt forests, scrublands with native fruits.

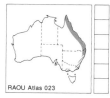

RAOU Atlas 023

310 Rose-crowned Fruit-Dove *Ptilinopus regina*

Male crown rose, edged yellow. Rest of head and breast blue, spotted white. Upperparts green-grey. Tail tip yellow. Abdomen orange. **Female** duller. Race *ewingii*: Crown paler, rose-pink; throat yellower. **Size** 22-24.5 cm. **Juv.** mostly green, *lacks* rose crown. **Voice** 'woo-hoo' repeated, becoming faster, ending in rapid 'hoo-hoo-hoo'. **Habitat** rainforests, monsoon and paperbark forests, eucalypt woodlands, vine groves, fruit trees.

RAOU Atlas 021

311 Wompoo Fruit-Dove *Ptilinopus magnificus*

Dorsal view

Head, neck light blue-grey. Eye red. Back, upperparts green; wing bar golden. Breast plum-purple; abdomen yellow. Races *keri* (Cairns-Atherton area) and *assimilis* (C. York Pen.) smaller than *magnificus* (south of Rockhampton). **Size** 35-55 cm. **Juv.** purple breast blotched green. **Voice** deep, carrying 'wallock-a-woo'; softer 'book-a-roo, book'. **Habitat** rainforests.

RAOU Atlas 025

312 Torresian Imperial-Pigeon *Ducula bicolor*

White; black eye. Primaries, end of tail, blackish. Belly scaled black. **Size** 38-44 cm. **Voice** deep 'coo woo'. **Habitat** coastal rainforests, mangroves, islands.

Ventral flight

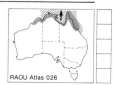

RAOU Atlas 026

313 Black-collared Fruit-Pigeon *Ducula mullerii*

Crown pink. Broad black collar. Mantle, sides of chest glossy claret. Silver-grey throat band between black collar and dark mauve-pink underparts. Wings, back, tail dark grey. Broad silver-grey mid-tail band. **Size** 43 cm. **Voice** little known. **Habitat** tree-lined creeks, low-lying woodlands.

Ventral view

314 Topknot Pigeon *Lopholaimus antarcticus*

Grey; black primaries. Long swept-back crest; grey in front; rusty behind. Black tail with pale grey central band. **Size** 40-46 cm. **Voice** occasional sharp screech. **Habitat** rainforests, adjacent woodlands or forests; palms; groves; fruit trees.

Ventral flight

RAOU Atlas 027

315 White-headed Pigeon *Columba leucomela*

Head, breast white; often with buff or grey wash. Back, wings, tail black with glossy margins to the feathers. Lower breast, abdomen, undertail grey. **Female** generally has some grey mottling to head and breast. Crown darker. **Size** 38-42 cm. **Juv.** crown, sides of head grey to brown; underparts mottled grey-brown. **Voice** low, mournful, repeated and ventriloquial 'oom coo'. **Habitat** rainforests and scrubs, occasionally in regrowth forest or isolated trees.

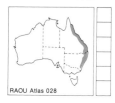

RAOU Atlas 028

316 Feral Pigeon *Columba livia**

Plumage immensely variable but with the basic pattern of blue-grey with glossy sheen on neck; wings black with a chequered pattern, or two black wing bars. **Size** 33 cm. **Voice** deep moaning 'cooo'; display call 'racketty-coo' or 'co-coo-coo-coo'. **Habitat** mainly urban areas, city buildings, crop margins along roads, railways. Flocks of racing pigeons may be seen.

Display flight

Perching

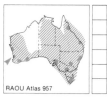

RAOU Atlas 957

317 Spotted Turtle-Dove *Streptopelia chinensis**

Head grey, tinged pink. Nape and back of neck black, spotted white. Wing, back and tail mottled dark and light brown. Underparts pinkish-fawn. Tail long. Undertail grey; outer feathers tipped white. Race *tigrina* differs from *chinensis* by having wing coverts streaked black, undertail coverts white, and feathers on front of wings lighter grey. **Size** 31.5 cm. **Juv.** lacks nape pattern. **Voice** mellow, musical 'coo', 'coocoo, croo' 'coo-coo-croo-coor'. **Habitat** cities; suburban gardens, parks; established grain-growing areas of coastal, eastern Australia. Raises and lowers tail on alighting.

Display flight

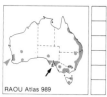

RAOU Atlas 989

318 Laughing Turtle-Dove *Streptopelia senegalensis**

Head, neck mauve-pink. Back brown with mauve-pink tinge. Broad black-spotted buffish band on lower throat. Breast mauve-pink, shading to white on abdomen. Shoulder, wings, lower back, and uppertail coverts slaty blue-grey. Outer tail tipped white. **Size** 25.5 cm. **Juv.** duller; without blue-grey on wings. **Voice** musical, laughing or bubbling 'coo coo coo'; 'coo oo coo'. **Habitat** city and suburban areas of Perth and surrounding region; Kalgoorlie and Esperence, WA.

Display flight

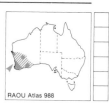

RAOU Atlas 988

319 Brown Cuckoo-Dove *Macropygia amboinensis*

Dark copper-brown upperparts; iridescent on neck. Lighter cinnamon-brown underparts. **Female** chestnut on crown, dark mottling on throat and breast. Tail long. **Size** 38-43 cm. **Juv.** crown chestnut. Neck and upper breast finely barred black. Wings mottled brown and chestnut. **Voice** 'whoop-a-whoop', last note rising in tone and longer. **Habitat** rainforests, forest margins, regrowth thickets.

Feeding

RAOU Atlas 029

* Introduced

319 ♀

319 ♂

315 ♂

315 ♀

316

316

316

316

316

316

692 ♂
House Sparrow

316

693
Tree Sparrow

317
Juv.

318
Juv.

318

317

N. Day.

320 Peaceful Dove *Geopelia placida*

Race *tranquilla*: Forehead, throat blue-grey. Crown grey-brown, fine black streaks. Back, wings, grey-brown, buff-toned; breast blue-grey; *all* are barred black. Races *placida* darker, smaller; *clelandi* paler. **Size** 21-23 cm. **Juv.** browner. **Voice** carrying 'woodle-woo', and 'woo-luk'; softer cooing. **Habitat** lightly timbered country near water.

Tail pattern

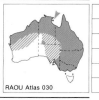

RAOU Atlas 030

321 Diamond Dove *Geopelia cuneata*

Red eye-ring. Blue-grey; smoky-brown back, wings. Fine white wing spots. **Female** browner. **Size** 19-20 cm. **Juv.** browner with buff marks, appears banded. **Voice** soft, mournful; cooing. **Habitat** watercourses in woodlands, hills.

Tail pattern

RAOU Atlas 031

322 Bar-shouldered Dove *Geopelia humeralis*

Race *humeralis*: Hind neck, mantle bronze, scalloped black. Throat, upper breast blue-grey. Upperparts dark grey-brown, scalloped black. Wings in flight chestnut. Clinal colour changes occur. **Size** 26.5-30 cm. **Juv.** duller. **Voice** 'cukoo-woop'; coos. **Habitat** scrubby bush, mangroves, eucalypt woodlands.

Tail pattern

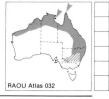

RAOU Atlas 032

323 Emerald Ground-Dove *Chalcophaps indica*

Race *chrysochlora*: Bill, legs reddish. Dull purple-brown head, neck and underparts, tinged wine-red. Wings emerald. White shoulder patch. **Female** shoulder grey. Race *longirostris*: Larger, less wine-red; female has white shoulder. Race *melvillensis* (Melville Is., NT): Paler. **Size** 23-25.5 cm. **Juv.** head, wings, underparts marked black. **Voice** low, repeated cooing. **Habitat** rainforests and wet eucalypt forests, mangroves.

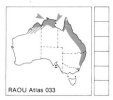

RAOU Atlas 033

324 Common Bronzewing *Phaps chalcoptera*

Male forehead cream; crown, sides of nape purple-brown. White line under eye. Back brown, feathers pale-edged. Metallic sheen on wings, back. Breast pink-brown. **Female** forehead grey; breast grey-buff. Races are clinal: *chalcoptera*, *murchisoni* and *consobrina*. **Size** 28-35 cm. **Imm.** duller. **Voice** resonant, deep, repeated 'oom'. **Habitat** dry forest, woodlands, mallee, heath, coastal scrub.

Back view

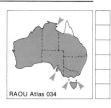

RAOU Atlas 034

325 Brush Bronzewing *Phaps elegans*

Eye-stripe, throat, back of neck, shoulder, rich chestnut. Crown buff. Back, wings, chestnut to brown with metallic feathers, tipped white. Breast blue-grey; darker below. **Female** dark grey-brown upperparts, *not* chestnut. **Size** 25-33 cm. **Imm.** like female, duller. **Voice** repeated, muffled 'oom'. **Habitat** woodlands, heathlands; some mallee areas.

Back view ♂

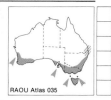

RAOU Atlas 035

326 Flock Bronzewing *Phaps histrionica*

Head black. Frons, chin, ear-mark white. Back, wings rich sandy-brown. White upper-chest bar. Grey underparts. **Female/Imm.** duller. Head brown; white areas less distinct. **Size** 27-30 cm. **Voice** usually silent. **Habitat** grassy plains, near water.

Flight

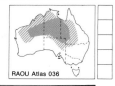

RAOU Atlas 036

320

321

322

323 Juv.

321
Juv.

323

♀ 326

♂ 326

325 ♀

325 ♂

324 ♀

324 ♂

N. Day

327 Crested Pigeon *Geophaps lophotes*

Eye, eye-ring red. Grey body. Black crest is upright, long, slender. Brown wings have conspicuous black bars, iridescent green to purple patch. Abdomen brown. Tail tip white. Race *whitlocki* (central and northern WA): Narrower black wing bars; less white on tail tip. **Size** 31-35 cm. **Imm.** duller. **Voice** explosive 'whoop'; low 'coo'. **Habitat** lightly wooded grasslands near water; roadsides; stubble; rail yards in grain-crop areas.

Tail flick on alighting

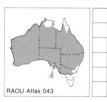

RAOU Atlas 043

328 Squatter Pigeon *Geophaps scripta*

Crown, upperparts brown. Face black with white marks about eye, neck, chin, throat. Wings brown; pale feather margins give a mottled effect. Breast blue-grey with deep white 'V' below. **Size** 26-32 cm. **Voice** low 'coo'. **Habitat** grassy plains; open woodlands.

Crest erect

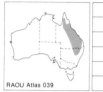

RAOU Atlas 039

329 Partridge Pigeon *Geophaps smithii*

Heavy black bill. Crown, neck, back, wings, tail dull brown. Bare skin on face red or yellow, edged white. Throat white. Breast pinkish-brown; purplish-grey breast patch is scalloped black with deep white 'V' below. **Size** 25-28 cm. **Imm.** upperparts finely flecked chestnut. **Voice** low-pitched 'coo'. **Habitat** grassy woodlands; open areas near water.

Crest erect

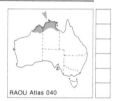

RAOU Atlas 040

330 Rock-Pigeon
Petrophassa albipennis and *P. rufipennis*

Dark brown with light scalloping. White-quilled *P. albipennis:* Throat black, spotted white. Outer primary bases show as a white patch in flight. Generally redder than Chestnut-quilled *P. rufipennis:* Head, face, neck spotted grey. Throat white. Chestnut wing patch in flight. **Size** 28-32 cm. **Voice** loud 'coo-corook' or low 'coo'. **Habitat** sandstone escarpments, gullies (west Arnhem Land, NT).

Wing pattern

Variable white patch

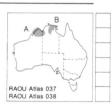

RAOU Atlas 037
RAOU Atlas 038

A = *P. albipennis*
B = *P. rufipennis*

331 Spinifex Pigeon *Geophaps plumifera*

Thin, erect crest. Crown red-brown. Frons blue-grey; bare skin on eye red. Chin and face stripe white; throat black. Back, uppertail, tail, wings rich red-brown; wing coverts barred black and grey; wing patch metallic bronze-green. Breast red-brown with narrow black and grey bar. Race *ferruginea:* Abdomen *also* red-brown. Race *leucogaster:* Lower breast, abdomen white; flanks brown, back dark brown. **Size** 20.5-22.5 cm. **Voice** soft, high 'ooar'; deep 'coo-rrr'. **Habitat** spinifex grasslands, rocky, hilly land; near water.

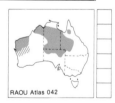

RAOU Atlas 042

332 Wonga Pigeon *Leucosarcia melanoleuca*

Generally a series of grey shades. White frons. Upper breast has broad white 'V'. Lower breast, abdomen, flanks, undertail white, boldly marked black. **Size** 36-38.5 cm. **Voice** resonant; high 'coo-coo' repeated monotonously. **Habitat** coastal, dense forests and scrubs; rainforests.

Ventral pattern

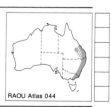

RAOU Atlas 044

Note: 330 Rock-Pigeon is now regarded as two distinct species: Chestnut-quilled Rock Pigeon *Petrophassa rufipennis* and White-quilled Rock Pigeon *P. albipennis*. The latter has two colour morphs.

331
Race *leucogaster*

330
Chestnut-quilled Rock-Pigeon

330
White-quilled Rock-Pigeon reddish morph

330
White-quilled Rock-Pigeon

331
Race *ferruginea*

330
Chestnut-quilled Rock Pigeon

327

329

329
Yellow-faced morph

332

328
Nth Qld morph

328

333 Palm Cockatoo *Probosciger aterrimus*

Distinctive. The *only* wholly dark cockatoo. Massive pointed bill, smaller in female. **Size** 60 cm. **Voice** disyllabic call when perched; wailing flight call; harsh screeching alarm. **Habitat** closed tropical forest; also adjacent savannah woodlands. Broad wings; deep, slow wing beat. Prominent crest is raised in display and when calling.

Ventral flight

RAOU Atlas 263

334 Red-tailed Black-Cockatoo
Calyptorhynchus banksii

Rounded helmet-like crest and massive bill are diagnostic. **Male** sooty-black; red panels in tail. **Female** duller, spotted and barred yellow. Bill whitish. Tail orange-yellow, barred black. **Size** 63 cm. **Imm.** resembles female but duller. **Voice** metallic, rolling, far-carrying 'creee creee'. **Habitat** coastal forest and woodlands in N Aust.; inland woodlands and open shrubland near water, open forest in SE Aust. Noisy flocks, often large. Buoyant flight.

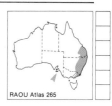

RAOU Atlas 264

335 Glossy Black-Cockatoo *Calyptorhynchus lathami*

Smallest black-cockatoo. **Male** similar to Red-tailed Black-Cockatoo but brownish-black with less red in tail, shorter crest and bulbous bill. **Female** has irregular yellow blotches on head and neck. Bill paler. Red panels in tail have black bars and yellow edges on inner webs. **Size** 48 cm. **Imm.** like female; brownish head. **Voice** soft, wailing 'tarr-red'. **Habitat** open forest and semi-arid woodland, especially in *Casuarina*. Buoyant flight.

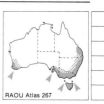

RAOU Atlas 265

336 Yellow-tailed Black-Cockatoo
Calyptorhynchus funereus

Yellow panels in tail. Yellow cheek patches. Most body feathers edged pale yellow. *C. latirostris* (SW Aust.) is smaller, browner; cheek and tail patches whitish *not* yellow. Identify from Long-billed Black-Cockatoo by differently shaped upper bill and different contact calls. **Size** 56-66 cm. **Voice** characteristic loud wail, 'kee-ow'. **Habitat** open forest, woodland, farmland, pine plantations; *C. latirostris*, drier sandplain woodlands, mallee. Flocks. Buoyant flight, slow wing beat; tail appears long.

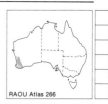

RAOU Atlas 267

337 Long-billed Black-Cockatoo
Calyptorhynchus baudinii

Bill length longer than white-tailed race *latirostris* of Yellow-tailed Black-Cockatoo. Otherwise smaller, browner. **Size** 56 cm. **Habitat** largely confined to karri and marri open forests; also surrounding farmland and wandoo woodlands.

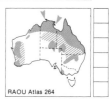

RAOU Atlas 266

338 Gang-gang Cockatoo *Callocephalon fimbriatum*

Male slate-grey, scarlet head and wispy crest. **Female/ Imm.** grey head and crest; feathers of underparts edged salmon-pink. **Size** 34 cm. **Voice** unmistakable 'creaky door' screech. **Habitat** tall open forest, open forest; moving in autumn and winter to woodland, farmland, suburban gardens. Quiet and inconspicuous when feeding. Flight erratic.

Feeding

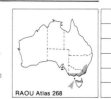

RAOU Atlas 268

Note: Former race *latirostris*, of 336 Yellow-tailed Black-Cockatoo, is now considered a full species, White-tailed Black-Cockatoo *Calyptorhynchus latirostris*.

334 ♂

335 ♂

333

337

336

335 ♀

♂ 335

334 ♂

♀ 334

337

♀ 338

♀ 338

336

338 ♂

♂ 338

339 Galah *Cacatua roseicapilla*

Distinctive. Crown, crest pale pink. Upperwings grey; rump whitish. Face, neck, underparts, including underwing coverts, salmon-pink to rose-red. **Size** 36 cm. **Imm.** duller; grey about face. **Voice** high-pitched 'chi-chi'. **Habitat** woodlands, open shrublands, grasslands, parks.

Erect crest

RAOU Atlas 273

340 Long-billed Corella *Cacatua tenuirostris*

White. Distinctive long upper mandible. Pink lores, forehead. Bluish bare skin around eye. Pink splashes on throat, sides of breast. Light yellow wash on underwings, tail. **Size** 38 cm. **Voice** high-pitched quavering three-note contact call (in flight). **Habitat** River Red Gum woodlands, farmlands. Large flocks feed on ground.

RAOU Atlas 272

341 Little Corella *Cacatua pastinator*

White. Short crest; small whitish bill. Bluish bare skin around eye; pink lores. Underwing, undertail sulphur-yellow. *No* pink on breast or cere. Race *pastinator* (SW Aust.): Elongated upper mandible. **Size** 37 cm. **Voice** like Long-billed Corella; higher-pitched, shorter duration, two notes. **Habitat** semi-arid and monsoonal woodlands and shrublands; semi-arid shrublands, spinifex, saltbush, farmlands. Near water; often vast, noisy flocks.

Races

pastinator   *gymnopis*
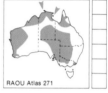
RAOU Atlas 271

342 Pink Cockatoo *Cacatua leadbeateri*

Upperparts white. Face, neck, underwings, underparts pink. Long crest, bright red and yellow bands. **Female** broader yellow band in crest. **Size** 35 cm. **Voice** distinctive; quavering, falsetto, two-note cry. **Habitat** mallee, mulga, *Callitris* and *Casuarina* associations. Usually small flocks; buoyant flight.

Crest pattern
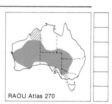
RAOU Atlas 270

343 Sulphur-crested Cockatoo *Cacatua galerita*

White. Sulphur-yellow forward-curving crest. Underwing, undertail washed yellow. **Size** 45 cm. **Voice** extremely loud, raucous screech. **Habitat** wide-ranging in temperate to tropical areas. Flight distinctive; uneven wing beat (flap, flap, glide) on stiff, broad, rounded wings.

Erect crest

RAOU Atlas 269

344 Eclectus Parrot *Eclectus roratus*

Plump, unmistakable. Sexual dimorphism extreme. **Male** bright green. Scarlet underwing coverts and sides of abdomen. Upper bill orange; lower bill black. **Female** scarlet. Bill black. Broad blue band across lower breast, mantle. **Size** 40 cm. **Voice** harsh screech. **Habitat** rainforests, adjacent savannah woodlands. In flight wings very broad, dark; tail short. Slow shallow wing beat but fast flight.

Ventral flight
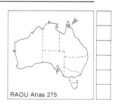
RAOU Atlas 275

345 Red-cheeked Parrot *Geoffroyus geoffroyi*

Male bright green. Bright red face, forehead; blue-violet crown. Blue underwing coverts. Upper bill red, lower bill grey. **Female** head brownish; all of bill grey. **Size** 23 cm. **Imm.** head greenish. **Voice** metallic 'honk honk', repeated rapidly. **Habitat** tropical rainforests. Noisy, active. Flight swift, direct, like Common Starling.

Flight
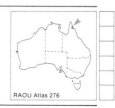
RAOU Atlas 276

Note: In SW Western Aust. a probable third species of Corella exists, the 'Bare-eyed Corella'. Research on this bird is continuing.

♂ **344**

344 ♀

345
Imm.

345 ♂

♀ **345**

341
Race *pastinator*

342

341

149
Grey Goshawk
White morph

342

341

343

340

339

340

343

339

N. Day.

346 Rainbow Lorikeet *Trichoglossus haematodus*

Dark blue head. Bill bright red. Yellow-green collar. Abdomen deep violet-blue. Underwing coverts orange. **Imm.** duller; bill brown. **Size** 28 cm. **Voice** continuous screeching, chattering. **Habitat** rainforests, open forests, woodlands, heaths, gardens.

Ventral flight

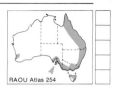

RAOU Atlas 254

347 Red-collared Lorikeet *Trichoglossus rubritorquis*

Ventral flight

Often regarded as race of Rainbow Lorikeet. Orange-red collar extending down side of breast. Abdomen blackish-blue. **Size** 28 cm. **Imm.** as Rainbow. Voice as Rainbow. **Habitat** tropical open forests.

RAOU Atlas 255

348 Scaly-breasted Lorikeet *Trichoglossus chlorolepidotus*

Only lorikeet with completely green head. Bill red. Yellow crescents on breast, flanks, thighs. Orange-red underwing. **Size** 23 cm. **Imm.** bill brown. **Habitat** coastal open forests, and modified habitat. Behaviour and calls resemble Rainbow Lorikeet's.

Ventral flight

RAOU Atlas 256

349 Varied Lorikeet *Psitteuteles versicolor*

Male bill bright orange-red. Bluish nape; yellow streaks on back, nape, shoulders. Crown, forehead, lores bright red. White naked skin around eye. Cheeks lime-yellow. Breast pale pink, yellow streaks. Green underwings. **Female** duller; olive-green crown. **Size** 19 cm. **Imm.** like female but green crown, brown bill. **Voice** less strident, higher-pitched than Rainbow. **Habitat** monsoonal woodlands, melaleuca swamps, streamsides, open forests.

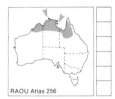

RAOU Atlas 256

350 Musk Lorikeet *Glossopsitta concinna*

Bright green. Bill black, tipped red. Scarlet forehead, lores, ear patches. Blue crown. **Size** 22 cm. **Imm.** bill all dark. **Voice** metallic screech. **Habitat** open forests, woodlands; agricultural, suburban lands. Avoids tall open forest.

Ventral flight

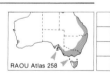

RAOU Atlas 258

351 Purple-crowned Lorikeet *Glossopsitta porphyrocephala*

Bill black. Upperparts bright green. Crown purple. Forehead, lores, ear patch yellow-orange. Throat, breast, abdomen pale blue-green. Crimson underwing. **Size** 16 cm. **Imm.** *no* purple on crown. **Voice** short sharp 'zit-zit-zit'. **Habitat** drier open forests, woodlands, mallee.

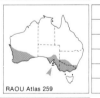

RAOU Atlas 259

352 Little Lorikeet *Glossopsitta pusilla*

Bright green. Bill black. Red face, forehead, throat. Green underwing. **Size** 16 cm. **Voice** a shrill 'zit' (in flight) repeated often. **Habitat** tall open forests, woodlands, orchards, parks, street trees.

RAOU Atlas 260

353 Double-eyed Fig-Parrot *Cyclopsitta diophthalma*

Smallest Aust. parrot. Bright green. Yellow sides to breast. Complex facial pattern varies with sex and race. **Female** *coxeni* (not illustrated) like its male; less red in cheek. **Size** 14 cm. **Voice** thin 'zeet-zeet' (in flight). **Habitat** rainforests, gardens with soft-fruit trees.

Underwing pattern

RAOU Atlas 261

Note: 347 Red-collared Lorikeet is now considered to be a race of 346 Rainbow Lorikeet.

♀ 353
Race *marshalli*

♂ 353
Race *marshalli*

352

♂ 353
Race *macleayana*

351

353 ♀
Race *macleayana*

349

♂ 353
Race *coxeni*

348

350

347

346

354 Australian King Parrot *Alisterus scapularis*

Distinctive. **Male** head, neck, underparts brilliant scarlet.
Back green; rump blue; tail blackish-blue. Green crescents
on abdomen and undertail coverts. Light green shoulder
stripes. **Female/Imm.** head and neck light green, usually
no light shoulder stripe; otherwise like male. **Size** 42 cm.
Voice loud 'carrak-carrak' in flight; male gives far-
carrying, piping whistle. **Habitat** moist, tall forest and
adjacent farmland. Orchards, parks and gardens in
autumn and winter. Small flocks. Strong but erratic
flight. Raids fruit trees.

Ventral flight

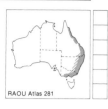

RAOU Atlas 281

355 Red-winged Parrot *Aprosmictus erythropterus*

Male brilliant light green head, neck, underparts. Bottle
green back, wings, tail. Deep blue lower back and rump.
Large scarlet shoulder patch. **Female/Imm.** uniform mid-
green with smaller shoulder patch. **Size** 32 cm.
Voice brassy 'crillik-crillik' in flight. **Habitat** subtropical
and semi-arid eucalypt and casuarina woodlands and
mulga shrublands. Strong, erratic, rocking flight with
deep wing beat; noisy, wary.

Ventral flight

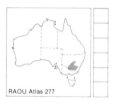

RAOU Atlas 280

356 Superb Parrot *Polytelis swainsonii*

Slender, long-tailed parrot. **Male** brilliant green. Canary-
yellow forehead, throat, cheeks. Broad scarlet border to
throat. **Female/Imm.** all green; blue on throat and cheeks.
Size 38 cm. **Voice** rolling 'currak-currak' in flight. Not as
harsh as Regent Parrot. **Habitat** riverine and flood-plain
open forest and woodland, particularly River Red Gum;
also stubble and roadsides. Small flocks.

Ventral flight

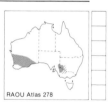

RAOU Atlas 277

357 Regent Parrot *Polytelis anthopeplus*

Lovely, slender, yellow and dark green parrot.
Male golden-yellow head, neck, underparts, shoulder
patch. Dark green back. Blue-black flight feathers and
tail. Red band across wing. **Female/Imm.** similar; greener,
particularly about head and neck. **Size** 39 cm. **Voice** loud,
harsh 'currak-currak' in flight. **Habitat** River Red Gum,
Black Box and casuarina woodlands, mallee and acacia
shrublands, adjacent farmlands. Pairs or small groups.
Flight graceful, swift, erratic; wings swept back.

Ventral flight

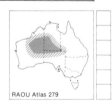

RAOU Atlas 278

358 Alexandra's Parrot *Polytelis alexandrae*

Male crown and sides of head pastel blue. Upperparts and
flight feathers light olive except for violet rump, light
green shoulder and purple greater coverts. Cheek, throat
rose-pink. Breast yellow-grey. Abdomen pinkish-mauve.
Female/Imm. duller. **Size** F 35, M 46 cm. **Voice** prolonged
clackering; 'queet-queet' alarm call. **Habitat** arid
shrublands, particularly mulga, Desert Oak and spinifex
country. Trees along watercourses. Pairs or small parties.
Flight undulating; very long tail conspicuous.

Ventral flight

RAOU Atlas 279

358 ♀

358 ♂

♀ 356

♂ 356

♂ 354

354 ♀

355 ♀

♂ 357

357 ♀

355 ♂

N. Day

359 **Cockatiel** *Leptolophus hollandicus*

Distinctive crest. **Male** grey-brown. Large, white shoulder patch. Lemon forehead, crest, face, throat, cheeks; orange ear patch. **Female/Imm.** paler yellow face; dull ear patch. Grey crest. Rump, upper tail barred pale yellow. **Size** 32 cm. **Voice** loud, rolling 'weero-weero'. **Habitat** semi-arid to arid habitats; usually near water; cereal crops. Flocks. Graceful flight; pointed wings, long tail, flashing white shoulders.

Flight patterns

RAOU Atlas 274

360 **Ground Parrot** *Pezoporus wallicus*

Bright green, barred and spotted yellow and black. Black streaks on forehead, crown. Frons red. Legs, toes long. **Size** 30 cm. **Imm.** frons grey. **Voice** distinctive, bell-like; heard at dusk and dawn. **Habitat** coastal, tableland heaths, sedgelands; also 'button-grass plains' (Tas.). Terrestrial; emerges at dusk. Flies swiftly away if flushed — yellow bars on long, green tail diagnostic. Flight snipe-like; plunges into dense cover, then runs.

Foot detail: claws

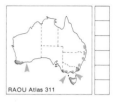
RAOU Atlas 311

361 **Night Parrot** *Pezoporus occidentalis*

Thick-set; short-tailed. Upperparts dull yellowish-green, mottled and barred black and dark brown. Underparts yellowish; primaries brown. *No* red frons. **Size** 23 cm. **Imm.** browner; more so on head, neck. **Voice** peculiar croaking alarm note; drawn out mournful whistle. **Habitat** inland plains, breakaways, samphire about salt lakes. By day hides in dense saltbush or spinifex; emerges at dusk. Extremely shy; difficult to flush. Flight quail-like, drops after short distance, runs to cover.

Foot detail: claws

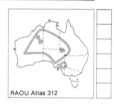
RAOU Atlas 312

362 **Budgerigar** *Melopsittacus undulatus*

Slender, bright green; yellow throat, forehead. Crown, neck, face with fine black bars. **Size** 18 cm. **Voice** continuous 'chirrup'; 'zitting' alarm call. **Habitat** arid and semi-arid woodlands, shrublands and grasslands. Pastures, grassy woodlands nearer coast in summer. Densely-packed, fast-wheeling flocks.

Allopreening

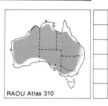
RAOU Atlas 310

363 **Swift Parrot** *Lathamus discolor*

Slender, narrow-tailed; lorikeet-like. **Male** bright green; red *around* bill base, throat, forehead. Lores, edges of red throat patch are yellow. Crown bluish-purple. Shoulders bright red; undertail coverts variably red. Greater coverts blue; red underwing coverts obvious in flight. **Female/Imm.** duller; less red. **Size** 24 cm. **Voice** high-pitched 'clink clink'. **Habitat** drier open forests, woodlands, parks, gardens. Swift, erratic flight.

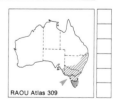
RAOU Atlas 309

364 **Red-capped Parrot** *Purpureicephalus spurius*

Forehead, crown dark red. Bill pale grey. Upper mandible elongated. Face, throat, rump lime-green. Upperparts dark green. Breast, upper abdomen purple. Lower abdomen, undertail coverts red. Undertail light blue. **Female** duller. **Size** 36 cm. **Imm.** *lacks* red on head. Violet-grey breast, abdomen. **Voice** harsh 'shrek shrek'. **Habitat** open forests, woodlands, orchards, parks, gardens. Undulating flight.

Feeding

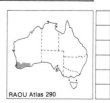
RAOU Atlas 290

364
Imm.

♂ **364**

♀ **359**

359 ♂

351
Purple-crowned

352
Little Lorikeet

363

350
Musk Lorikeet

349
Varied Lorikeet

363

362

361

360

361

360

N. Day

365 Green Rosella *Platycercus caledonicus*

Red band over bill. Dark green upperparts; bright yellow
head, underparts. Variable red wash on throat, breast,
undertail coverts. Blue cheeks, throat. **Size** 37 cm.
Imm. duller; greener. **Voice** loud 'cussick cussick' (in
flight); bell-like (perched). **Habitat** dense mountain
forests, farmlands, gardens.

RAOU Atlas 285

366 Crimson Rosella *Platycercus elegans*

Race *elegans*: Rich crimson and blue. **Imm.** crimson and
green. Race *flaveolus* 'Yellow Rosella': Crimson replaced
by yellow except for red frontal band. Race *adelaidae*
'Adelaide Rosella': Varying amounts of orange replace
yellow of *flaveolus* on head, neck, underparts. **Size** 35 cm.
Voice brassy 'kweek-kweek' (in flight); mellow piping
whistle (perched). **Habitat** Crimson: moist forests,
farmlands, parks. 'Yellow': floodplain open forest,
woodland adjacent farmland. 'Adelaide': watercourses,
adjacent timbered farmland. Seven races exist.

Race *flaveolus*

Ventral flight

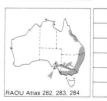

RAOU Atlas 282, 283, 284

367 Eastern Rosella *Platycercus eximius*

Red head, upper breast; white cheeks. Rump, abdomen,
inner-tail feathers pale to leaf-green. Outer-tail feathers
blue. **Size** 30 cm. **Voice** high-pitched 'clink-clink' (in
flight); piping 'pee pit-ee' or slow 'kwink-kwink'
(perched). **Habitat** woodlands, farmlands, with eucalypt
copses; parks, gardens. Hybridises with Pale-headed
Rosella.

Ventral flight

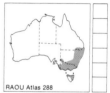

RAOU Atlas 288

368 Pale-headed Rosella *Platycercus adscitus*

White or pale yellow head and nape, diagnostic. White
and violet-blue cheeks. Lower back greenish; yellow
rump. Upper breast yellowish; lower breast pale blue.
Race *palliceps*: All white head; pale blue underparts.
Size 30 cm. **Voice** like Eastern Rosella. **Habitat** lowland
open forests, woodlands, semi-arid shrublands, farmlands.

Race *palliceps*

Ventral flight

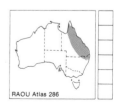

RAOU Atlas 286

369 Northern Rosella *Platycercus venustus*

Distinguished by black cap, white and violet cheeks.
Uppertail bluish-black. Rump, underparts yellow with
variable black scalloping. **Size** 29 cm. **Imm.** duller; red
specks on head. **Voice** like Eastern Rosella.
Habitat monsoonal eucalypt and melaleuca open forests,
woodlands. Usually in hills near water.

Ventral flight

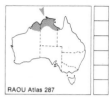

RAOU Atlas 287

370 Western Rosella *Platycercus icterotis*

Red head and underparts, and yellow cheeks, diagnostic.
Wings, rump, uppertail greenish-black, except deep blue
bend of wing. **Female** green head; breast, flanks have red
flecks; underwing stripe always present. **Size** 26 cm.
Imm. as female; lacks cheek patches. **Voice** soft 'clink-
clink'. **Habitat** open forests, woodlands, farmlands.

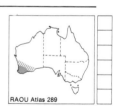

RAOU Atlas 289

Note: It is considered that 367 Eastern Rosella, 368 Pale-headed
Rosella, and 369 Northern Rosella are races of one species
Platycercus eximius, which *could* now be called the 'White-
cheeked Rosella'.

365
Imm.

365

366 Imm.
Race *elegans*

366
Race *elegans*

366
Race *adelaidae*

366
Imm.
Race *adelaidae*

366 Imm.
Race *flaveolus*

366
Race *flaveolus*

369

370
Imm.

368

367

70

368

370 ♂

367 ♂

367 ♀

371 Mallee Ringneck *Barnardius barnardi*

Blue and green head. Red frontal band. Hind neck, mantle blue-black. Collar yellow; some have yellow breast band. Upperwing coverts, rump green and turquoise. Primaries blue. Race *macgillivrayi* 'Cloncurry Parrot': Smaller, paler; *no* frontal band; yellow below. **Size** 35 cm. **Imm.** duller. **Voice** ringing. **Habitat** semi-arid woodlands, flood plains, farmlands.

Dorsal flight

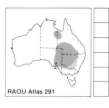
RAOU Atlas 291

372 Ringneck (Port Lincoln) *Barnardius zonarius*

Probably race of Mallee Ringneck. Race *zonarius:* Like Mallee Ringneck but black head, blue cheeks. *No* frontal band. Darker green above; yellow belly. Race *semitorquatus* 'Twenty-eight Parrot': Green below; red frontal band. **Size** 37 cm. **Voice** strident. Race *semitorquatus* calls 'twentee-eight'. **Habitat** tall, wet forest (SW Aust.) to mallee, mulga.

Dorsal flight

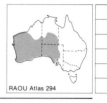
RAOU Atlas 294

373 Red-rumped Parrot *Psephotus haematonotus*

Male green. Rump red. Shoulder patch, abdomen yellow. **Female** dull olive-green; green rump. **Imm.** duller. **Size** 27 cm. **Voice** two-syllable whistle. **Habitat** open woodlands, Red Gums, grasslands, farms.

Ventral flight

RAOU Atlas 295

374 Mulga Parrot *Psephotus varius*

Male emerald green. Yellow frontal band, shoulder patch. Russet crown, abdomen, thighs, rump spot. **Female/Imm.** pale brown-olive, dull orange frontal band, nape, shoulder patch. **Size** 28 cm. **Voice** 3-4 flute-like notes. **Habitat** arid shrublands.

Dorsal flight

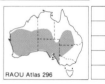
RAOU Atlas 296

375 Golden-shouldered Parrot *Psephotus chrysopterygius*

Male turquoise. Black crown. Yellow frons. Brown above; golden shoulder. Reddish vent. **Female/Imm.** light yellow-green. Pale blue-green cheeks. Lower underparts pale blue; some red on vent. **Size** 26 cm. **Voice** double whistle. **Habitat** savannah woodlands with termite mounds.

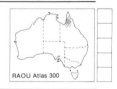
RAOU Atlas 300

376 Hooded Parrot *Psephotus dissimilis*

Like Golden-shouldered Parrot. Black hood to lower bill; shoulder patch larger, brighter.

Dorsal flight

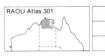
RAOU Atlas 301

377 Paradise Parrot *Psephotus pulcherrimus*

Extinct? **Male** brown above. Turquoise rump, underparts. Red frontal band, shoulder, abdomen, undertail coverts. **Female/Imm.** much duller. **Size** 27 cm. **Voice** unknown. **Habitat** grassy eucalypt woodlands with termite mounds.

RAOU Atlas 299

378 Blue Bonnet *Northiella haematogaster*

Brown, blue-faced parrot. Race *haematogaster:* Wing band blue; upperwing coverts olive-yellow; belly red; vent yellow. Race *haematorrhous:* Wing band green; upperwing coverts red; belly red. Race *narethae:* Smaller; two-tone blue on face; belly yellow; vent red. **Female/Imm.** duller. **Size** 26-30 cm. **Voice** harsh 'chack chack'; piping whistle. **Habitat** semi-arid woodlands.

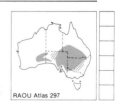
RAOU Atlas 297

Note: It is considered that 371 Mallee Ringneck is now a race of 372 Ringneck (formerly Port Lincoln Ringneck) *Barnardius zonarius.*

371
Race *macgillivrayi*

378
Race *haematorrhous*

378
Race *narethae*

378
Race *haematogaster*

372

371

372
Race *semitorquatus*

♀ **373**

373 ♂

♀ **374**

♂ **374**

♂ **373**

373 ♀

375 ♂

♀ **375**

377 ♂

♂ **376**

376 ♀

377 ♀

379 Bourke's Parrot *Neophema bourkii*

Distinctive pinkish-brown. **Male** whitish about eye, face.
Variable blue frontal band. Upperparts brown; wing
feathers edged yellowish-white. Salmon-pink below;
undertail pale blue. **Female/Imm.** dull; *lacks* frontal band.
Size 19 cm. **Voice** soft twitter. **Habitat** arid to semi-arid
scrublands, mainly mulga.

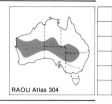

RAOU Atlas 304

380 Blue-winged Parrot *Neophema chrysostoma*

Male olive-green above. Yellow lores. Deep blue frontal
band but *not* over eye. Shoulder brilliant deep blue.
Green cheeks, underparts, merging to yellow abdomen,
which may be orange-centred. **Female/Imm.** dull;
indistinct frontal band. **Size** 21 cm. **Voice** tinkling (in
flight); sharp 'sit-sit' (alarm). **Habitat** open forests,
woodlands, grasslands, coastal heath, saltmarshes.

Flight

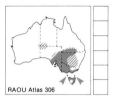

RAOU Atlas 306

381 Elegant Parrot *Neophema elegans*

Male like Blue-winged, but olive-yellow above; brighter
yellow rump, uppertail coverts, outer tail. Less of *two-
toned* blue in wing. Blues of frontal band extend *above,
behind* eye. **Female/Imm.** dull; *lacks* frontal band.
Size 22 cm. **Voice** sharp (in flight); soft (feeding).
Habitat open country; semi-arid scrublands.

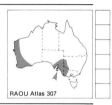

RAOU Atlas 307

382 Rock Parrot *Neophema petrophila*

Dullest *Neophema*. **Male** dark olive above; yellowish-olive
below. Frontal band deep blue, pale-edged; some blue
about eye. Bright yellow undertail coverts.
Female/Imm. dull. **Imm.** *lacks* frontal band. **Size** 22 cm.
Voice double 'sit-tee' (in flight). **Habitat** coastal dunes,
saltmarsh, rocky islands.

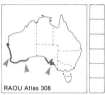

RAOU Atlas 308

383 Orange-bellied Parrot *Neophema chrysogaster*

Male rich grass-green above. Broad blue frontal band to
eye. Deep violet-blue in wing. Face, throat, breast
greenish-yellow; yellow abdomen with variable orange
centre. **Female/Imm.** duller. **Imm.** olive head, neck, breast.
Size 21 cm. **Voice** diagnostic 'buzz-buzz' (alarm).
Habitat breeds in open-forest copses in heath. Winters in
coastal saltmarsh, dunes, damp grasslands.

Feeding

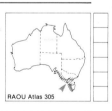

RAOU Atlas 305

384 Turquoise Parrot *Neophema pulchella*

Male distinctive. Bright green above. Turquoise blue
crown, face. *Two-tone* blue on shoulder. Deep blue flight
feathers. Upperwing patch chestnut-red. Upper breast has
orange tint. Yellow abdomen *may* have orange centre.
Female/Imm. duller; whitish lores; *no* red on shoulder.
Size 20 cm. **Voice** like Blue-winged. **Habitat** open forests.

at nest

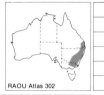

RAOU Atlas 302

385 Scarlet-chested Parrot *Neophema splendida*

Male brilliant. Green above. Yellow outer tail. Bright blue
face; darker on chin. Light blue shoulder. Breast scarlet;
bright yellow below. **Female/Imm.** breast greenish.
Crown, face *less* blue. Distinguish from female/imm.
Turquoise by blue lores; pale blue in wing. **Size** 20 cm.
Voice quiet twittering. **Habitat** mulga, mallee.

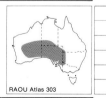

RAOU Atlas 303

♂ 379

385 ♀

385 ♂

384 ♀

♂ 384

383
Imm.

383

381

380

382

382
Imm.

386 Oriental Cuckoo *Cuculus saturatus*

Large cuckoo. Grey above; paler grey breast. Whitish belly, barred black. Eye-ring, bill base, legs bright yellow. Long, dark grey tail, spotted on edges, tipped white. Primaries grey, barred black. Underwing white, barred black; leading edge white. **Red morph female** upperparts chestnut; body barred black. **Size** 30-34 cm. **Voice** allegedly silent in Aust. **Habitat** forests. Summer migrant to N Aust.

386

159 Australian Hobby

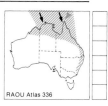

RAOU Atlas 336

387 Pallid Cuckoo *Cuculus pallidus*

Black bill. Yellow eye-ring. Dark grey eye-stripe; pale eyebrow, nape. Tail dark grey, notched white. Grey above; white below. **Size** 33 cm. **Juv.** boldly streaked dark brown and white all over. **Imm.** upperparts heavily mottled brown and chestnut. Underparts grey; buff breast, barred brown. **Voice** an ascending and accelerating series of hoarse, whistles 'too-too-too . . .'. **Habitat** open areas with trees.

Ventral flight

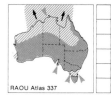

RAOU Atlas 337

388 Brush Cuckoo *Cuculus variolosus*

Grey-brown above. Grey eye-ring. Pale grey below, tinged buff. Tail square, tipped white, no notches above; shorter than Fan-tailed Cuckoo. Undertail broadly barred brown, thin whitish notching on inner web. **Size** 22-23 cm. **Juv./Imm.** rufous, barred dark brown above (including tail); paler below. **Voice** six or seven descending notes; mournful 'ther-er-wee' repeated. **Habitat** wet forests, brush.

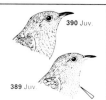

Ventral flight

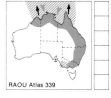

RAOU Atlas 339

389 Chestnut-breasted Cuckoo
Cuculus castaneiventris

Like Fan-tailed Cuckoo, but smaller. Darker above; brighter chestnut below. Undertail bands broader. **Size** 24 cm. **Juv./Imm.** like Fan-tailed juv. but pale cinnamon below. **Voice** like Fan-tailed. **Habitat** rainforest and its borders.

390 Juv.

389 Juv.

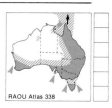

RAOU Atlas 340

390 Fan-tailed Cuckoo *Cuculus flabelliformis*

Dark grey above. Yellow eye-ring. Tail strongly notched white, wedge-shaped. Dull fawn-chestnut below. Undertail barred black and white. Distinguish from Brush Cuckoo by notched, wedge-shaped tail, larger size, often brighter underparts. NE Aust. birds brighter chestnut below and smaller. **Size** 24.5-28.5 cm. **Juv.** dark brown above, barred reddish-brown. Head streaked dark brown. Finely barred grey and brown below. Distinguish from juv. Brush by yellow eye-ring, tail shape. **Voice** mournful descending trill, repeated; other calls. **Habitat** forests, woodlands.

Ventral flight

RAOU Atlas 338

391 Black-eared Cuckoo *Chrysococcyx osculans*

Greyish above, with slight metallic sheen. Black eye-stripe, broadest behind eye. Whitish eyebrow, throat. Pale rump. Cream below. Tail grey, tipped white. Undertail barred black and cream. Distinguish from juv. Horsfield's Bronze-Cuckoo by *lack* of rufous on tail, *broader* black eye-stripe. **Size** 19-20 cm. **Juv./Imm.** duller brown eye-stripe. **Voice** descending 'feeeuw' singly or repeated; is lower, longer and more mournful than Horsfield's. **Habitat** inland low bushes to dry forest.

Juv.

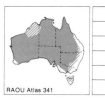

RAOU Atlas 341

Ventral flight

386
Red morph
Imm. ♀

386

387
Imm.

387

387
Juv.

388

389

390

390
Juv.

391

388
Juv.

N⸱Day.

392 Horsfield's Bronze-Cuckoo
Chrysococcyx basalis

Bronze-sheen above; cap duller. Brown eye-stripe; pale eyebrow. Tail edged rufous. Cream below with *incomplete* bronze bars. Undertail black and white, rusty centre. **Size** 17 cm. **Juv./Imm.** duller; sometimes *lacks* bars. Distinguish from Black-eared Cuckoo by rufous tail, size, less obvious eye-stripe. **Voice** descending whistle 'fee-ew'; shorter, higher than Black-eared. **Habitat** open country.

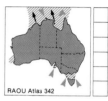

393 Shining Bronze-Cuckoo *Chrysococcyx lucidus*

Race *plagosus* 'Golden Bronze-Cuckoo': Copper cap. Metallic green upperparts. Sometimes pale spots on crown. Face, underparts white with complete bronze bars. *No* rufous in tail. Undertail black and white. **Juv.** duller; bars on flanks only. Race *lucidus* 'Shining Bronze-Cuckoo': Metallic green above; no head contrast; white flecks on forehead prominent; bars green. Bill broader than 'Golden Bronze'. **Size** 17-18 cm. **Voice** reverse of Horsfield's call: repeated 'few-ee'. **Habitat** forest.

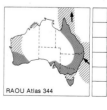

394 Little Bronze-Cuckoo *Chrysococcyx minutillus*

Male metallic green above. Red eye-ring, eyes. White eyebrow. White below; *complete* green bars. Three to four black bars on white outer tail feathers; inners rusty, black sub-terminally, white tipped. **Female** duller. Cream eye-ring; brown eyes. **Size** 16 cm. **Juv./Imm.** as female but duller; flank bars only. **Voice** high, short, accelerating and descending 'see-see . . .'. **Habitat** forests, mangroves. Hybridises with Gould's Bronze-Cuckoo.

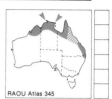

395 Gould's Bronze-Cuckoo *Chrysococcyx russatus*

Male like Little Bronze-Cuckoo but upperparts edged bronze. Side of chest pale to bright rust; bars bronze. Eyebrow buff. Rusty outer webs to tail. **Female** as female Little but rusty breast and tail. **Juv./Imm.** like female, duller, bars only on flanks. **Voice** and **Habitat** as Little.

396 Common Koel *Eudynamys scolopacea*

Male black; red eye; long tail. **Female** black cap. Brown spotted above, barred white. Throat buff. White below, barred brown. Eye red. **Size** 39-46 cm. **Juv./Imm.** like female; head mottled brown; eye brown. **Voice** 'koo-well' and 'wurra wurra'. **Habitat** forests, tall trees.

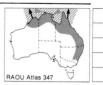

397 Channel-billed Cuckoo *Scythrops novaehollandiae*

Very large. Huge pale bill. Grey above with a long tail. White below, faintly barred black. **Size** 60 cm. **Juv.** head, neck pale buff. **Voice** bubbling trumpet. **Habitat** tall trees. Breeds in Aust.; winters in New Guinea, Indonesia.

398 Pheasant Coucal *Centropus phasianinus*

Breeding black head, underparts. Barred rufous, black and cream above. Long, pheasant-like tail. Short bill. **Non breeding** and **Juv./Imm.** duller; body all brown. **Size** 60-80 cm. **Voice** low bass 'coo-coo-coo-coo-coo-coo-coocal'. **Habitat** thick undergrowth, canefields.

Adult
Non-breeding

Note: It is considered that 395 Gould's Bronze-Cuckoo is a race of 394 Little Bronze-Cuckoo *Chrysococcyx minutillis*.

392

392

394 ♀

394 ♂

393
Race *plagosus*

393
Race *lucidus*

♂ 395

395 ♀

397

396 ♀

396 ♂

398

399 Rufous Owl *Ninox rufa*

Race *rufa:* Rufous colouration. Flat crown. Greenish-yellow eyes in indistinct facial mask. Upperparts very closely barred dark rufous-brown and buff. Underparts closely barred brownish-rufous and whitish. Race *meesi* (C. York Pen.): Smaller. Race *queenslandica* (Mackay area): Darker. **Size** 51 cm. **Juv.** head, underparts pure white, except distinct dark facial discs. **Voice** deep double-hoot, second note shorter. **Habitat** closed forests.

Juv.

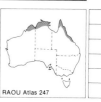

RAOU Atlas 247

400 Powerful Owl *Ninox strenua*

Smallish, dark yellow eyes. Short, broad head. Upperparts, tail, dark greyish-brown with indistinct off-white bars. Underparts whitish with dark greyish-brown chevrons. **Male** larger. **Size** 55 cm. **Juv.** white underparts and crown contrast with small dark streaks and dark eye patches. **Voice** slow, deep, resonant double-hoot; occasionally single. **Habitat** tall open forests. Slow deliberate flight on huge wings.

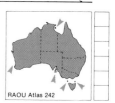

RAOU Atlas 248

401 Southern Boobook *Ninox novaeseelandiae*

Distinct, dark facial discs contrast sharply with surrounding pale borders. Eyes green-yellow. Upperparts dark chocolate-brown; upperwing coverts, scapulars spotted off-white. Underparts reddish-brown. Upper breast mottled buff becoming reddish-brown. White-streaked belly. **Size** 30 cm. **Juv.** crown whitish, streaked darker centrally; facial discs very distinct. Upperparts dark chocolate-brown, profusely spotted white and buff. Underparts downy white; tawny wash on upper breast. Great variation within and between races. Tas. birds smaller, darker; mantle spotted. Western, northern and central birds paler, more reddish; less clearly marked. NE rainforest birds smaller, darker, less spotted. **Voice** falsetto double-hoot; continuous hooting. **Habitat** woodlands, forests, scrublands. Delicate flight; rarely glides.

Ventral flight

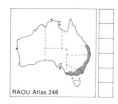

RAOU Atlas 242

402 Barking Owl *Ninox connivens*

Large, bright yellow eyes. Almost no facial mask. Upperparts brownish-grey, coarsely spotted white. Flight feathers, tail, barred lighter. Underparts white, streaked brownish-grey. **Male** larger. **Size** 40 cm. **Juv.** incomplete collar; flanks and breast have pattern like adults. Northern birds browner, darker, smaller. **Voice** explosive, dog-like, double-bark; wavering human-like scream; grating trill; various growls. **Habitat** forests, woodlands.

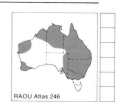

RAOU Atlas 246

403 Brown Hawk-Owl *Ninox scutulata*

Eyes yellow. Indistinct facial mask; whitish forehead, lores. Upperparts uniform dark brown. Underparts off-white, streaked brown. Pointed wings. Tail longish, dark brown, lighter bars. **Size** 29 cm. **Voice** musical double-hoot, second note brief, higher-pitched. **Habitat** forests, woodlands. One Aust. record, race *japonica*.

399

400

400
Juv.

402

402
Juv.

401
Pale race

401
Juv.

401

403

404 Barn Owl *Tyto alba*

Slim; upright posture. Small black eyes. Rounded heart-shaped mask: brown border, white disc, dark tear marks. Upperparts soft grey, patchily washed golden-fawn and marked with fine black, white-tipped spots. Underparts white, sparsely dark-flecked. Long, unfeathered lower legs protrude *just beyond tail* in flight. **Size** F 35, M 34 cm. **Voice** rasping screech. **Habitat** grasslands, farmlands, woodlands. May roost on ground; in caves.

Roosting

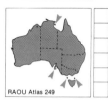

RAOU Atlas 249

405 Masked Owl *Tyto novaehollandiae*

Robust; crouched posture. Black eyes. Round, dark bordered mask. Dark chestnut near eyes. **Dark phase** chestnut disc; upperparts blackish-brown, washed rufous and speckled white; underparts pale rufous, coarsely dark-spotted. **Intermediate phase** off-white disc; upperparts blackish-brown, washed yellow and densely speckled white; underparts off-white, coarsely dark-spotted. **Light phase** white disc; upperparts pale grey, washed yellow, dark and white speckled; underparts white, sparsely grey-flecked. In S Aust., 'dark' females and 'intermediate' males predominate. In N Aust. smaller 'intermediate' females and 'light' males predominate. Legs feathered. Feet heavy. **Female** larger. **Size** F 47, M 37 cm. **Voice** deep, rasping screech; various twitterings. **Habitat** forests, woodlands, caves. Active in middle storey.

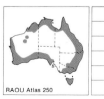

RAOU Atlas 250

406 Eastern Grass Owl *Tyto capensis*

Slim; upright posture. Very small, black eyes. Heart-shaped mask: brown and white border, white disc, dark tear marks. Upperparts dark brown, washed orange, white spotted. Underparts white, finely dark spotted; breast washed orange. Very long unfeathered lower legs protrude *well beyond tail* in flight. **Size** F 37, M 34 cm. **Voice** deep, soft screech; high-pitched trills. **Habitat** swampy heaths, grasslands. Usually roosts and always breeds on ground. In flight back appears bluish-grey.

Body feathers

404

406

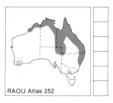

RAOU Atlas 252

407 Sooty Owl *Tyto tenebricosa*

Robust; crouched posture. Large, black eyes. Round mask: dark-grey border, grey disc, darkest near eyes. Upperparts and underparts dark brownish-grey, densely whitish-flecked. Belly paler grey, mottled whitish. Tail stumpy. Feathered legs. Heavy feet. **Female** larger. **Size** F 48, M 40 cm. **Voice** descending whistle; chirruping trills. **Habitat** closed and tall open forests, especially gullies. Active in canopy.

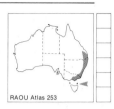

RAOU Atlas 253

408 Lesser Sooty Owl *Tyto multipunctata*

Much smaller than Sooty Owl. Robust; crouched posture. Large, black eyes. Disc whitish near border. Upperparts coarsely and densely spotted. Breast washed dark grey. Underparts greyish-white, barred blackish-grey. **Size** F 37, M 33 cm. **Voice** higher-pitched than Sooty Owl. **Habitat** similar to Sooty Owl.

408

405
Light phase

404

404

407
Light form

406

♂ 405
Race *kimberlyi*

405 ♀
Race *castanops*

406

409 Tawny Frogmouth *Podargus strigoides*

Broad, grey bill, edged by grey plumes. Gape, eye yellow.
Flat crown. Pale grey eyebrow. Grey to reddish-brown above
with grey patches, streaked black. Underparts paler. Tail
short, ungraduated. Five races: northern birds smaller; grey
and red morphs exist. **Size** 34-46 cm. **Nestling** head, back
speckled grey down; underparts paler. **Juv.** sides of breast
streaked. **Voice** a constant 'oo-oom . . .'. **Habitat** woodlands.

Ventral flight

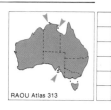
RAOU Atlas 313

410 Papuan Frogmouth *Podargus papuensis*

Like Tawny Frogmouth but larger; bigger head. Cream
eyebrow. Red eye. Grey to rufous with black-edged white
or grey marbling; paler below. Graduated long tail.
Size 45-54 cm. **Nestling** downy fawn. **Voice** ooms; clacks by
snapping of bill. **Habitat** forests.

RAOU Atlas 316

411 Marbled Frogmouth *Podargus ocellatus*

Race *plumiferus* 'Plumed Frogmouth': Tawny
Frogmouth-sized. Rounded crown (in profile). Long,
banded facial plumes. Bright orange eye. Buff to white
eyebrow prominent. Deep rufous-brown to greyish above,
delicately marbled cream, black-bordered. Underparts
have black streaks and white spots on feather tips. Long
graduated tail. Race *marmoratus* 'Marbled Frogmouth':
Longer tail. **Size** 40-48 cm. **Juv.** downy rufous-brown
above; downy fawn below. **Voice** high 'coo-lew'; low 'coo-
lew'; loud tocking, then laughing 'cor-cor-' followed by
six gobbles. **Habitat** rainforests with palms.

RAOU Atlas 314

412 Australian Owlet-nightjar *Aegotheles cristatus*

Bill black. Large brown eye; non-reflective to lights. Head
has wide black eye-stripes meeting behind and extending
to crown. Black collar. Upperparts, tail grey, finely barred
blackish. Paler underparts. Feet pink. Northern, central
birds lighter; rufous-washed. **Size** 21-24 cm. **Voice** grating,
strident churring. **Habitat** woodlands with tree hollows.

Dorsal flight

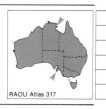
RAOU Atlas 317

413 White-throated Nightjar *Caprimulgus mystacalis*

Bill black. Eye brown; most highly reflective to lights of
all caprimulgids. Small white spots on primaries. Pointed
wings. Dark grey above with black, sandy and whitish
spots, patches, bars. Black throat; white patches at sides.
Underparts grade to cinnamon belly; dark-barred.
Size 33 cm. **Imm.** duller, redder. **Voice** accelerating 'kook-
kook...'. **Habitat** forests, woodlands.

Ventral flight

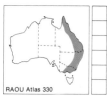
RAOU Atlas 330

414 Spotted Nightjar *Eurostopodus argus*

Like White-throated; smaller. All-white throat. Large
white wing spot. Rounded wings. **Size** 30 cm. **Imm.** paler,
duller. **Voice** few 'kook-kooks', then repeated faster.
Habitat open forests, woodlands, scrubs, deserts.

Ventral flight

RAOU Atlas 331

415 Large-tailed Nightjar *Caprimulgus macrurus*

Smaller, greyer nightjar with large white wing and tail-
tip spots. Throat as White-throated. Rounded wings.
Size 27 cm. **Voice** monotonous chopping. **Habitat** tropical
woodland margins.

Ventral flight

RAOU Atlas 332

411 Pale morph

410 Red morph

411

409 Red morph

409 Nestling

409

410

412

412 Red morph

415

13

414

416 Glossy Swiftlet *Collocalia esculenta*

Small. Shiny black-blue above, including rump; sometimes looks black. Chest black; belly white; intermediate area spotted. Underwing black. Tail rounded with a shallow notch. Upperparts *and* underparts must be seen to distinguish from White-rumped Swiftlet with pale belly. **Size** 9-11.5 cm. **Voice** soft twittering. **Habitat** over coastal ranges and islands. Vagrant.

Ventral flight

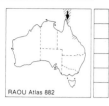

RAOU Atlas 882

417 White-rumped Swiftlet *Aerodramus spodiopygia*

Small. Dark grey above; slightly glossy on wings. Rump pale grey. Tail black. Chest grey; belly, vent slightly paler. In strong light can look whitish. Tail rounded with a shallow notch. A form breeding at Chillago (NE Qld) darker above; paler belly. **Size** 11 cm. **Voice** chips and twitters. Uses clicks in caves for echo location. **Habitat** aerial, over coastal ranges and islands. Breeds in caves.

417

449 Tree Martin
Dorsal flight

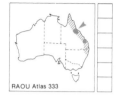

RAOU Atlas 333

418 Uniform Swiftlet *Aerodramus vanikorensis*

All grey-brown; upperparts darker with faint metallic sheen; rump slightly paler. Throat, undertail paler than belly. Tail shape like other swiftlets. In the field *inseparable* from similar New Guinea and Asian swifts. **Size** 12 cm. **Voice** soft twittering. **Habitat** over coastal ranges and islands. One specimen recorded in Aust. Unidentified completely dark swiftlets have been seen occasionally. Note: if completely dark swiftlets are seen, then notes on subtle body colour changes, shape, flight actions and calls should be taken for *future* reference.

Ventral flight

RAOU Atlas 881

419 White-throated Needletail *Hirundapus caudacutus*

Race *caudacutus*: Largest Aust. swift. Body all dark with white throat, vent, flanks. Frons pale grey. Edges of tertiary feathers white. Back, rump, brown. Rest of upperparts have a glossy green sheen. Wings swept back (curved, anchor-shaped). Tail black, rounded. **Size** 20 cm. **Voice** twittering, chattering. **Habitat** aerial, mainly in E Aust., often associated with coastal and mountain regions. Flight long-winged, raking glides, slow turns. N Asian migrant. Previously called Spine-tailed Swift.

Perched

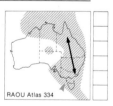

RAOU Atlas 334

420 Little Swift *Apus affinis*

Dark grey. Similar to Fork-tailed Swift with white rump and throat, but tail shorter, very shallowly forked, becoming square when fanned. Smaller, stockier; proportionately broader-winged than Fork-tailed. **Size** 15 cm. **Voice** shrill rattling trill. **Habitat** aerial, over open areas. Vagrant. Could prove to be more regular than single specimen suggests.

Ventral flight

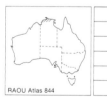

RAOU Atlas 844

421 Fork-tailed Swift *Apus pacificus*

All blackish. Pale throat. White rump. Body slimmer than White-throated Needletail. Tail is long and thin; deeply forked when fanned; fork invisible when tail closed. **Size** 17.5 cm. **Voice** twittering, buzzing. **Habitat** aerial, over a variety of habitats. N Asian migrant. Flight bat-like.

419

421

Ventral flight

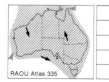

RAOU Atlas 335

422 Azure Kingfisher *Alcedo azurea*

Long black bill. Rufous spot before eye. Buff-white mark on side of neck. Upperparts violet-blue. Pale throat. Underparts rufous (variable). Legs bright orange. **Size** 18 cm. **Imm.** dull blue upperparts; pale underparts. **Voice** high-pitched whistle. **Habitat** rivers, creeks mangroves. Flight swift, low over water.

Diving sequence

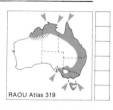

RAOU Atlas 319

423 Little Kingfisher *Alcedo pusilla*

Long black bill. White spot before eye and on side of neck. Upperparts blue. Underparts white. Legs black. **Size** 12 cm. **Imm.** duller; crown scalloped. **Voice** shrill whistle, higher than Azure Kingfisher. **Habitat** mangroves rivers, creeks.

422   423

RAOU Atlas 320

424 Laughing Kookaburra *Dacelo novaeguineae*

Largest kingfisher. Massive bill, black above, horn below. Large cream-white head; brown marks on crown. Brown eye-stripe. Back, wings brown; mottled blue on wings. **Male** often has blue patch on rump. Tail barred rufous-brown and black, margined white. **Female** brown rump; head more buff. Race *novaeguineae* larger than race *minor* of C. York Pen. **Size** 45 cm. **Imm.** duller, like female. **Voice** raucous 'laughter'. **Habitat** open forests, woodlands. Flight heavy, direct; raises tail on alighting.

Watching for prey

Dorsal pattern

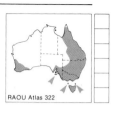

RAOU Atlas 322

425 Blue-winged Kookaburra *Dacelo leachii*

Large bill, dark above, horn below. Large cream-white head, streaked brown. Pale eye. *No* eye-stripe. Back brown; wings mostly blue. Rump blue; tail deep blue. **Female** tail rufous, barred dark blue. **Size** 40-45 cm. **Imm.** head paler; underparts scalloped brown. **Voice** harsh cackling scream. **Habitat** woodlands, open forests, paperbark swamps.

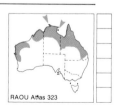

RAOU Atlas 323

426 Forest Kingfisher *Halcyon macleayii*

Head deep blue. White spot before eye. Bill black, with pale lower base. Broad black stripe from bill to ear coverts. Back, rump blue. Wings, tail rich blue. In flight distinguishing white spot on wing. **Female** blue back of neck. Race *incincta*: Greener on back; white wing spot smaller. Race *macleayii*: More blue on back; white wing spot larger. **Size** 20 cm. **Imm.** duller; forehead, shoulders scalloped white. Head spot, wing spot, underparts all buffish. **Voice** harsh trilling chatter, high-pitched whistle. **Habitat** coastal open forests, wooded swamps, mangroves, woodlands.

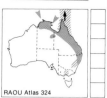

RAOU Atlas 324

427 Red-backed Kingfisher *Halcyon pyrrhopygia*

Bill black, with pale lower base. Crown streaked grey-green and white. Black eye-stripe, ear coverts, nape of neck. Collar white. Wings, tail blue-green. Lower back, rump, undertail coverts rufous-red. **Female** duller. **Size** 20 cm. **Imm.** speckled breast. **Voice** mournful; harsh alarm near nest. **Habitat** dry woodlands.

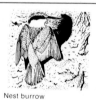

Nest burrow

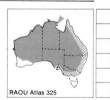

RAOU Atlas 325

160

Note: The generic name *Todiramphus* is proposed to replace generic name *Halcyon* in the future; would affect species 426, 427, 428 and 429.

♀
425

♂
425

♂
424

427

426

426

422

423

423
Imm.

N. Day.

428 Sacred Kingfisher *Halcyon sancta*

Head, back green. Black band through eye and ear coverts to back of neck. Buff spot before eye. White collar with buff tinge. Wings, rump, tail blue. Underparts white to buff. **Female** duller. **Size** 19-23.5 cm. **Imm.** speckled brown. **Voice** loud four-note call. Harsh alarm call near nest. **Habitat** eucalypt, paperbark forests; woodlands; mangroves.

426 Forest Kingfisher

428

Ventral flight

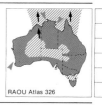

RAOU Atlas 326

429 Collared Kingfisher *Halcyon chloris*

Bill longer than Sacred Kingfisher. Green-blue on wings and tail. Head, back green. Black band through eye and ear coverts to back of neck. White spot before eye. White collar. Wings, tail blue. White underparts. **Female** duller. Aust. race *sordida*. **Size** 25-29 cm. **Imm.** speckled brown. **Voice** two-note call. **Habitat** mangroves, coastal areas.

Nesting in termite colony

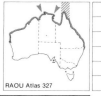

RAOU Atlas 327

430 Yellow-billed Kingfisher *Syma torotoro*

Bill yellow. Black ring around eye. **Male** rusty head. Back, wings green. Rump, tail blue. Underparts rufous. Black mark on side of neck. Legs yellow. **Female** large patch of black on rusty crown; larger black mark on neck; paler underparts. **Size** 18-21 cm. **Voice** loud, mournful trill. **Habitat** rainforest edges.

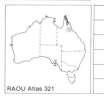

RAOU Atlas 321

431 Buff-breasted Paradise-Kingfisher
Tanysiptera sylvia

Bill orange-red. Crown, shoulders blue. Black band through eye, nape to upper back. Back, rump white. Tail blue with long white central feathers. Underparts rich rufous. Legs orange-red. **Size** 29-35 cm (includes all of tail). **Imm.** black bill; tail short and grey. **Voice** trilling call. **Habitat** lowland rainforests.

Tail flick

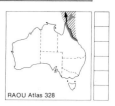

RAOU Atlas 328

432 Common Paradise-Kingfisher
Tanysiptera galatea

Bill red. Blue and black upperparts. White underparts. Blue and white tail with long blue central feathers, white rackets. **Size** 38 cm (includes all of tail). One Aust. record.

433 Rainbow Bee-eater *Merops ornatus*

Bill black. Rufous crown. Black eye-stripe, edged blue. Black band on yellow throat. Back light green. Tail black with extended central feathers, longer in male. **Size** 23-28 cm (includes all of tail). **Imm.** *no* black throat band. **Voice** high-pitched chitter. **Habitat** open country.

Leaving burrow

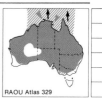

RAOU Atlas 329

434 Dollarbird *Eurystomus orientalis*

Bill, legs red. Upperparts brown. Blue throat. Wings green-blue. Tail blue. Conspicuous pale blue wing spots in flight. Aust. race is *pacificus*. **Size** 27-31 cm. **Imm.** brown-grey body. Bill, legs grey. **Voice** harsh. **Habitat** woodlands.

434 Perches prominently

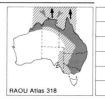

RAOU Atlas 318

434

433

433
Imm.

♂ 433

434

431

432

429 Imm.

429

♀ 430

♂ 430

428

428
Imm.

435 Red-bellied Pitta *Pitta erythrogaster*

Forehead, crown dark brown. Brown-red nape. Chest, rump, shoulders bright blue. Black line divides chest from red belly. Back, wings, tail blue-green. Note: pittas have dark underwings with white patch conspicuous in swift, direct flight. Legs dark grey. **Size** 16-19 cm. **Imm.** duller red below. **Voice** harsh 'kraa-kraa'. **Habitat** tropical closed forests, scrubs.

Flight

Bobbing

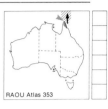

RAOU Atlas 353

436 Blue-winged Pitta *Pitta moluccensis*

Like Noisy Pitta but white throat; rufous-buff underparts. **Size** 17-19 cm. Vagrant from SE Asia.

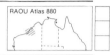

RAOU Atlas 880

437 Noisy Pitta *Pitta versicolor*

Head, throat black. Crown chestnut, black central stripe. Rich green above; shoulders, rump iridescent turquoise. Buff below; black central stripe extends to red vent. Short green tail. Long flesh-pink legs. **Size** 20 cm. **Imm.** similar, duller. **Voice** loud whistle 'walk-to-work'; a single high 'keow' alarm. **Habitat** rainforests, tropical and subtropical scrubs.

Flight

Perched

RAOU Atlas 352

438 Rainbow Pitta *Pitta iris*

Like Noisy Pitta but buffy underparts replaced by black. **Size** 18 cm. **Voice** like Noisy but softer. **Habitat** closed forests, thick scrub, occasionally mangrove edges.

Flight

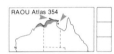

RAOU Atlas 354

439 Albert's Lyrebird *Menura alberti*

Like Superb Lyrebird; smaller. Rufous-brown above; buff-grey below. **Male** blackish-brown; broad grey outer tail. **Size** M 80-90, F 65-75 cm. **Voice** not unlike Superb. **Habitat** rainforests. Displays on platform of vine-stems.

Displaying

RAOU Atlas 351

440 Superb Lyrebird *Menura novaehollandiae*

Male dark brown above; grey-brown below. Long filamentous tail feathers, solid outer feathers patterned chestnut, white and black. Long legs; powerful feet dark grey. **Female/Imm.** smaller; shorter plain grey tail. **Size** M 80-98, F 74-84 cm. **Voice** loud, protracted and complex song with expert mimicry and loud alarm whistles. **Habitat** wet forests, temperate and subtropical rainforests. Male performs spectacular courtship display on earthern 'dancing' mounds.

Flight

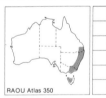

RAOU Atlas 350

441 Rufous Scrub-bird *Atrichornis rufescens*

Appears soft-plumaged. Rufous-brown with fine black bars. Throat whitish. **Male** chest blackish to abdomen sides. **Female** *no* black markings. **Size** 16 cm. **Juv.** unknown. **Voice** loud territorial song; softer notes; mimicry. **Habitat** dense, often secondary undergrowth in forests. Rare.

Breast markings

RAOU Atlas 355

442 Noisy Scrub-bird *Atrichornis clamosus*

Male dark brown above with fine black bars. Upper chest blackish, paler below. White throat extends down sides of breast. **Female** *no* black chest. **Size** 21 cm. **Juv.** no barring. **Habitat** low, thick, coastal vegetation. Very rare.

Breast markings

RAOU Atlas 356

435

♂ 441

442
Juv.

436

♂ 442

437

439 ♀

♂ 439

438

440 ♀   ♂ 440

443 Singing Bushlark *Mirafra javanica*

Colour variable. Distinct pale eyebrow. Brown body, dark brown streaks above. Breast speckled black. Rufous wing patch distinctive in flight. White-edged tail. Aust. race *horsfieldi*. **Size** 12-15 cm. **Imm.** paler. **Voice** melodious songs, including mimicry. **Habitat** grassland, crops.

Dorsal flight
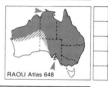
RAOU Atlas 648

444 Skylark *Alauda arvensis**

Buff eyebrow. Small crest. Larger, paler than Singing Bushlark. Darker above; lighter below; streaked breast and flanks. *No* rufous wing patch. White-edged tail. **Size** 17-19 cm. **Imm.** paler. **Juv.** no crest, shorter tail. **Voice** chirrup; musical warbling. **Habitat** grassland. Hovering aerial flight and dive.

Dorsal flight
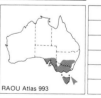
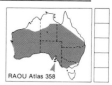
RAOU Atlas 993

445 White-backed Swallow *Cheramoeca leucosternum*

White crown, throat and back. Nape, body dull black. Deeply forked tail. **Size** 15 cm. **Imm.** similar. **Voice** single note in flight. **Habitat** prefers dry, sandy country. Flight more fluttering than *Hirundo* swallows.

Perched
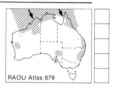
RAOU Atlas 358

446 Barn Swallow *Hirundo rustica*

Chestnut-red throat and forehead. Deeply forked tail. Glossy blue-black above; white below; blue-black breast band. Race *gutturalis* reaches Aust. **Size** 15 cm. **Imm.** duller; paler, narrower breast band; tail shorter. **Voice** twitter; pleasant warbling. **Habitat** open country, cultivated land, urban areas.

Perched
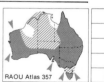
RAOU Atlas 879

447 Welcome Swallow *Hirundo neoxena*

Rufous-red throat and forehead. Forked tail. Blue-black above; dull white below; *no* black on breast. **Size** 15 cm. **Imm.** duller. **Juv.** smaller; cream gape prominent. **Voice** twittering chatter. **Habitat** all kinds, especially near water.

447
Perched
Pacific Swallow

RAOU Atlas 357

448 Red-rumped Swallow *Hirundo daurica*

Conspicuous rufous to chestnut rump. White to pale chestnut underparts, streaked. Browner, broader-winged than Barn Swallow; *no* dark chest bar. Deeply forked tail; longer tail streamers than Aust. swallows. **Size** 16-18 cm. **Habitat** open areas; woodlands. Asian vagrant.

Perched
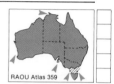

449 Tree Martin *Hirundo nigricans*

Appears black-headed. Glossy blue-black above. Square tail; 'dirty' white rump. **Size** 13 cm. **Imm.** browner; breast streaked brown. **Voice** pleasant twitter. **Habitat** open woodland.

450
449
Perched
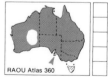
RAOU Atlas 359

450 Fairy Martin *Hirundo ariel*

Appears rufous-headed. Blue-black above; white streaks on back. Gleaming white rump. Square tail. Faint breast streaks. **Size** 12 cm. **Imm.** similar; duller. **Voice** distinct chirrup and sweet twittering. **Habitat** open country near water.

Nests
RAOU Atlas 360

* Introduced

Note: See 447 — Pacific Swallow *Hirundo tahitica* not yet officially identified in Australia.

451 Richard's Pipit *Anthus novaeseelandiae*

Brown bird with darker brown streaks above. Pale buff eyebrow stripe and below cheek. Slender bill. Underparts buff with brown spots and streaks on whitish breast. Unstreaked flanks. Long legs. Long white-edged tail. **Size** 17-18 cm. **Imm.** like adults. **Voice** chirrups; trilling calls in flight. **Habitat** open country. Wags tail up and down.

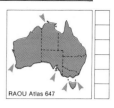

Tail wag
Dorsal flight
RAOU Atlas 647

452 Yellow Wagtail *Motacilla flava*

Two races recorded in Aust. but hardly distinguishable in non-breeding plumage. Eyebrow runs to base of bill, appears pointed (sharp). Back olive-green; greenish-yellow rump. Long black tail edged white; black legs. **Breeding** race *simillina* grey crown and ear coverts; underparts yellow; eyebrow white, broad and 'sharp'. Race *taivana* olive-green crown; yellow eyebrow. **Non-breeding** (both races) brown-grey upperparts; pale eyebrow; buffish underparts. **Size** 15-17 cm. **Juv.** white underparts. **Voice** shrill, trilling. **Habitat** salt works, paddocks, marshes.

Dorsal flight
Tail wag
RAOU Atlas 877

453 Yellow-headed (Citrine) Wagtail *Motacilla citreola*

Sexes different in breeding plumage. **Breeding male** bright yellow head; neck with black nape. **Breeding female/Non-breeding male and female** plumage similar, like non-breeding Yellow Wagtail, race *taivana*, but paler yellow on sides of head, more grey on back; white, double wing bars on dark wings; dark grey rump. **Size** 16-17 cm. **Juv.** soft grey upperparts; *no* olive and often *no* yellow in plumage. **Voice** louder, shriller than Yellow Wagtail. **Habitat** wet grasslands.

Dorsal flight
RAOU Atlas 876

454 Grey Wagtail *Motacilla cinerea*

Sexes different in breeding plumage. **Breeding male** black throat. **Breeding female/Non-breeding male and female** similar; grey upperparts; yellow underparts, brightest under tail. White eyebrow. Yellowish-green rump, uppertail coverts. Narrow, white wing band conspicuous in flight. Tail very long, black, edged white. Pale legs. **Size** 17-18 cm. **Juv.** buffish below; brown tinge above; speckled breast. Yellow only on tail coverts. **Voice** sharp 'tit' or 'chichit'. **Habitat** prefers higher altitudes near water but may be found anywhere.

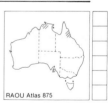

Dorsal flight
RAOU Atlas 875

455 White Wagtail *Motacilla alba*

Black and white bird with long black tail, edged white. White underparts; conspicuous white wing bars. **Size** 18 cm. Several sightings in WA. Specimen collected near Geraldton identified as race *ocularis*. One bird Gippsland Lakes, Vic., 1985 (race unknown).

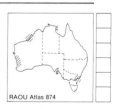

Dorsal flight
RAOU Atlas 874

Note: A Black-backed Wagtail *Motacilla lugens* (probably adult female) was present at Fraser Is., Queensland, May – September, 1987 — a new species for Australia; distinguish from 455 White Wagtail from which it was recently separated as a full species.

451

455
Breeding

♂ **454**
Breeding

454
Non-breeding

454
Non-breeding

452
Race *simillina*

452
Juv.

452
Non-breeding

452
Race *taivana*

453
Non-breeding

453 ♂
Breeding

453
Juv.

456 Black-faced Cuckoo-shrike *Coracina novaehollandiae*

Race *novaehollandiae:* Black face. Grey upperparts; paler below. Tail tipped white. Race *subpallidus* (coastal WA): Paler. **Size** 33 cm. **Juv./Imm.** broad black eye-stripe from bill to *behind* eye. Breast finely barred. **Voice** creaky 'kreeark'. **Habitat** open woodlands, forests. Undulating flight. Shuffles wings when lands. Check for White-bellied Cuckoo-shrike.

Wing shuffle

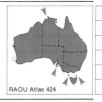

RAOU Atlas 424

457 Yellow-eyed Cuckoo-shrike *Coracina lineata*

Face dark; lores black; eye yellow. Dark grey above; wings darker. Breast to abdomen white, strongly barred black. **Size** 26-28 cm. **Juv.** whitish below. **Imm.** lighter barring below. **Habitat** rainforests, open forests. Pairs or large groups. Check for Oriental Cuckoo.

Ventral flight

386

457

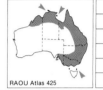

RAOU Atlas 428

458 White-bellied Cuckoo-shrike *Coracina papuensis*

Race *hypoleuca:* Black lores *to* eye. White below. Tail black, tipped white. Race *robusta* (E Aust.): Larger; sometimes has black face; sometimes has black head. Breasts vary from white to grey. **Size** 26-28 cm. **Imm.** underparts mottled grey-brown. **Voice** shrill 'kseak'. **Habitat** woodlands. Check for imm. Black-faced Cuckoo-shrike.

456

458

Ventral flight

RAOU Atlas 425

459 Cicadabird *Coracina tenuirostris*

Small cuckoo-shrike. **Male** blue grey. Flight, tail feathers black, edged grey. **Female** pale eyebrow. Browner above; buff below. Underparts finely barred. Like Varied Triller. Races *tenuirostris* widespread; *melvillensis* (NT). **Size** 24-26 cm. **Imm.** like female; more heavily barred. **Voice** cicada-like trill. **Habitat** forests, woodlands.

Juv.

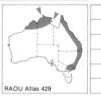

RAOU Atlas 429

460 Ground Cuckoo-shrike *Coracina maxima*

Largest cuckoo-shrike. Face dark grey; eye yellow. Silvery body. Wings, forked tail black. Rump, uppertail coverts, belly, flanks distinctively barred black. **Size** 33-37 cm. **Imm.** upperparts finely barred black. **Voice** distinctive, metallic. **Habitat** drier inland, open woodlands. A ground-feeder. Often in small family groups.

Ventral flight

On ground

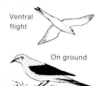

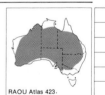

RAOU Atlas 423

461 White-winged Triller *Lalage tricolor*

Male breeding shoulder, edges of wing-feathers marked white. Light grey rump. Upperparts black; underparts white. **Male non-breeding** crown, back brown. **Female/Imm.** like non-breeding male except for buff wing, head markings. **Size** 18 cm. **Voice** trilling call. **Habitat** open country, woodlands.

Singing in flight ♂

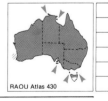

RAOU Atlas 430

462 Varied Triller *Lalage leucomela*

Male white eyebrow. Upperparts black; dark grey rump; white markings through wing. Underparts white, fine dark barring. Light cinnamon vent. **Female/Imm.** like male, browner above. Underparts grey-buff with barring; vent cinnamon. **Size** 19 cm. Three races: *leucomela* (east coast Aust.); *yorki* (C. York Pen.) cinnamon belly; *rufiventris* (NW Aust.) cinnamon breast. **Voice** distinctive trill. **Habitat** rainforests, woodlands.

Imm.

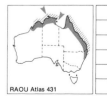

RAOU Atlas 431

456
Juv.

456

457
Imm.

457

458
Race *robusta*
Dark form

458
Juv.

460
Imm.

458
Race *hypoleuca*

460

♂ **459**

♀
459

♀
461

461 ♂
Breeding

♂
462

♀
462

461 ♂
Non-breeding

N.DAY

463 Red-whiskered Bulbul *Pycnonotus jocosus**

Head black. Tall pointed black crest. Black cheek line with red patch above. White throat. Olive to grey-brown above; greyish below. Undertail coverts red. Outer tail feathers with broad white tips. **Size** 20 cm. **Juv.** *no* red cheek; undertail coverts pink. **Voice** melodic whistles, chirps. **Habitat** introduced to urban areas, scrub fringes. Note: Red-vented Bulbul *Pycnonotus cafer* (introduced) now extinct in Melbourne, Vic. Black head, throat; scaled chest (see sketch opposite).

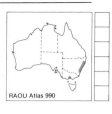

463
Red-vented Bulbul
RAOU Atlas 990

464 White's Thrush *Zoothera dauma*

Race *lunulata:* Tan above; white below. Heavy black scaly edges to body feathers (not abdomen). Pale wing bar in flight. Pale eye-ring; black eye. Dark bill. Grey-flesh legs. **Size** 26 cm. Race *cuneata* (Atherton Tablelands, Qld): Similar; larger (27 cm). Race *heinei* (lowlands of mid-central Qld): Probably a distinct species; smaller (25 cm); more rufous plumage especially on rump and tail; fainter scaling (hardly visible on rump); more white on tail tip. **Voice** high-pitched contact/alarm calls. Races *lunulata, cuneata* have pleasant soft complicated Blackbird-like warble; *heinei* has stronger, pleasant two-noted 'theea thooa'. **Habitat** usually fairly wet forest, dryer areas in winter.

Race *heinei*

Race *lunulata*

Underwing pattern

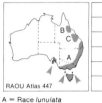

RAOU Atlas 447

A = Race *lunulata*
B = Race *cuneata*
C = Race *heinei*

465 Blackbird *Turdus merula**

Male black. Bill, eye-ring orange-yellow. **Female** dark brown above; rufous-brown below. Pale chin. Faintly streaked breast. **Size** 25 cm. **Juv.** streaked. **Voice** complicated, pleasant song; sharp alarm call. **Habitat** introduced; urban gardens, orchards; blackberries, forest edges.

Dorsal flight

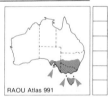

RAOU Atlas 991

466 Song Thrush *Turdus philomelos**

Grey-brown above. Cream cheeks, upper breast. Dark brown cheek streaks. Forward-pointing chevrons on chest. Dark bill; yellow below. White below. Legs yellow-brown. **Size** 23 cm. **Juv.** faint mottles on back. **Voice** superb, complicated song; high contact call. **Habitat** introduced; urban gardens, parks.

Singing

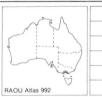

RAOU Atlas 992

467 Northern Scrub-robin *Drymodes superciliaris*

Olive-brown above. Face, underparts cream. Flanks buff. Black vertical eye-stripe. Wings black, two white wing bars. Rump rufous-brown. Tail tipped white. Legs pink. **Size** 22 cm. **Imm.** similar; softer colours. **Voice** four high descending notes; scolding call. **Habitat** forest floors.

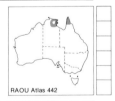

RAOU Atlas 442

468 Southern Scrub-robin *Drymodes brunneopygia*

Grey. White eye-ring; faint dark vertical eye-line. Wing feathers tipped white. Rump chestnut-brown. Tail dark grey, tipped white. **Size** 23 cm. **Juv.** browner above; paler, mottled underparts. **Voice** pleasant, loud whistles, typically 'clock-o-pee-er' but variable. **Habitat** mallee, scrubland.

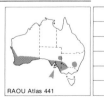

RAOU Atlas 441

463

465
Juv.

♀ **465**

♂ **465**

464
Race *lunulata*

466

466

467

468

469 Rose Robin *Petroica rosea*

Male breast rose-red. Deep grey throat, back. White frons, abdomen, under and outer tail. *No* wing bars.
Female/Imm. greyish-brown upperparts; throat, breast greyish-white with occasional pale rose wash. Wing bars whitish. Dark brown tail, outer-tail shafts white.
Size 11 cm. **Voice** male has characteristic calls; both sexes 'tick'. **Habitat** breeds in deep gullies of tall open forests and rainforests. An autumn-winter dispersal to more open forest. Singly or pairs; most acrobatic of *Petroica* genus. Often feeds in high canopy.

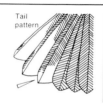
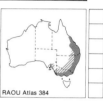

470 Pink Robin *Petroica rodinogaster*

Male breast, abdomen rose-pink. Throat, upper breast sooty-black. White frons. *No* white on wings or tail.
Female/Imm. darker brown upperparts; brownish-buff underparts. Two buff wing bars. *No* white in tail.
Size 12 cm. **Voice** rarely calls. **Habitat** breeds in dense gullies of tall open forest. An autumn-winter dispersal to more open forest. Singly or pairs; often perches low down in cover, motionless and silent, before darting down upon food.

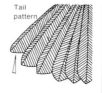
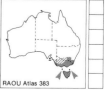

471 Flame Robin *Petroica phoenicea*

Male throat, breast, abdomen flame-red. Dark grey upperparts. White frons, wing bar, outer-tail shafts.
Female/Imm. upperparts brown; buff to white wing bars. Brown tail; outer-tail shafts white. Underparts lighter.
Size 14 cm. **Habitat** forages along the ground in series of short hops, runs and flights, preferring close-cropped pastoral land adjacent to woodland. Roosts in dense scrubs, citrus orchards. Nests in low open forest (coastal to alpine). Small flocks in autumn-winter dispersal. Upright stance; gives occasional flicks of wings and tail.

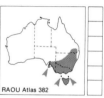

472 Scarlet Robin *Petroica multicolor*

Male scarlet breast; back, throat black. White on forehead, prominent wing bar, outer-tail shafts. **Female** pale red wash on breast. **Size** 13 cm. **Imm.** resembles duller female but initially lacks red. **Voice** male territorial song repeated. **Habitat** breeds in closed and tall open forest; an autumn-winter altitudinal dispersal to more open localities. Single or pairs.

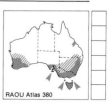

473 Red-capped Robin *Petroica goodenovii*

Male scarlet cap, breast. Back, throat dull black. Bold white wing bar, outer-tail shafts. **Female** forehead red-brown; grey-brown upperparts; darker brown wings, tail. Pale buff wing patch. Outer-tail shafts white. **Size** 12 cm. **Imm.** no red on frons; males may have slightly red-washed breast. **Juv.** brownish streaks and blotches. **Voice** male has characteristic calls; both sexes 'tick'. **Habitat** dryer scrub, woodlands. Autumn-winter dispersal. Single or pairs. Restless; flicks wings and tail while perched watchfully on stump or low branch; feeds mainly on ground.

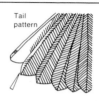
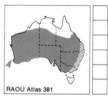

♀ 470

♀ 469

469 ♂

470 ♂

473 ♂

♂ 471

♀ 473

♀ 471

♀ 472

472 ♂

474 Hooded Robin *Melanodryas cucullata*

Male black hood. Bill black. Eye dark brown. Black above with white wing bars and bottom half of outer tail feathers white. Underparts white. Legs black. **Female/Imm.** head, back grey-brown; throat pale grey. Tail, wings darker with same markings as male. **Size** 16 cm. **Voice** piping whistles, trilling; usually quiet. **Habitat** dry forests, woodlands, mallee, scrublands.

Dorsal view

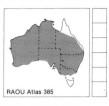

Tail pattern

RAOU Atlas 385

475 Dusky Robin *Melanodryas vittata*

Head, upperparts brown, darker on wings, tail. Eyes brown. Bill dark brown. Underparts pale brown. Pale edging below bend of wing, wing patch and tail. Legs dark brown. **Juv.** paler streaking above; darker mottling below. Race *kingi* (King Is., Tas.): Olive wash above; browner below. **Size** 16.5 cm. **Voice** low, penetrating 'choowee'. **Habitat** open forest woodlands, scrublands, usually close to cleared land.

Young at nest

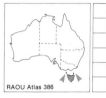

RAOU Atlas 386

476 Mangrove Robin *Eopsaltria pulverulenta*

Slaty-grey above; darker around eye and lores. Eyes dark brown. Bill black. Underparts white; grey wash to upper sides of breast. Tail blackish; bottom half of outer feathers white. Legs black. **Juv.** upperparts brown, streaked paler. Mottled buff breast. Three races: *cinereiceps*, *alligator* and *leucura* upperparts darkening from west to east respectively. **Size** 16 cm. **Voice** plaintive double whistle; melodious song; harsh 'chuk'. **Habitat** mangroves.

Tail pattern

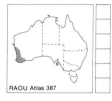

RAOU Atlas 388

477 White-breasted Robin *Eopsaltria georgiana*

Upperparts blue-grey. Paler eyebrow; darker on lores, wings, tail. Eyes dark brown. Bill black. Breast grey-washed; white below. Tips of outer tail white. Legs black. Smaller northern birds sooty-grey above. **Juv.** spotted brown above. **Size** 14.5 cm. **Voice** piping whistles 'wee-oh'; harsh chattering 'chit-chit'. **Habitat** southern birds: open forests, usually near streams. Northern birds: coastal scrubs or thickets.

Trunk perching:Typical of genus *Eopsaltria*

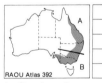

RAOU Atlas 387

478 Eastern Yellow Robin *Eopsaltria australis*

Up to five races described; two accepted. Head, back grey. Bill dark grey to black. Eye dark brown. Rump, uppertail coverts olive (southern birds) to bright yellow (northern birds). Upper throat whitish. Underparts yellow. Wings, tail brown-grey. Legs brownish-black. **Size** 15 cm. **Juv.** brown; mottled. **Voice** monotone piping; harsh 'chit'. **Habitat** wet open forests, woodlands, coastal thickets.

Juv.

RAOU Atlas 392

A = Race *chrysorrhoa*
B = Race *australis*

479 Western Yellow Robin *Eopsaltria griseogularis*

Like Eastern Yellow Robin but breast pale grey. Race *griseogularis* (SW of WA): Rump yellow. Race *rosinae* (Eyre Pen., SA): Rump olive-yellow. **Size** 15 cm. **Juv.** brown; mottled. **Voice** like Eastern Yellow Robin. **Habitat** open forests, woodlands, mallee, coastal scrubs.

478, 479
Wing bars in flight

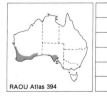

RAOU Atlas 394

475

474 ♂

474 ♀

477

478
Race *chrysorrhoa*

478
Race *australis*

479
Race *rosinae*

476

J. Day.

480 Yellow-legged Flycatcher *Microeca griseoceps*

Head, nape grey; pale brown wash on face, ear coverts.
Pale lores and thin eye-ring. Broad bill dark above, cream
below. Back, upperwing coverts yellowish-olive. Throat
dull white. Rest of underparts lemon-yellow with buff
wash on breast. Wings, tail brown, edged lemon-yellow.
Legs orange-yellow. **Juv.** dully spotted white. **Size** 12 cm.
Voice 'zzt-zzt-zzt'; also fine trilling song 'I-don't-ever-want-
to-see-you-again, again'. **Habitat** rainforests, adjacent forests.
Identify from Lemon-bellied Flycatcher, 'yellow robin'
group and Grey Whistler (race *griseiceps*).

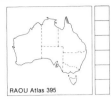

RAOU Atlas 395

481 Lemon-bellied Flycatcher *Microeca flavigaster*

Upperparts olive-brown, darker on wings and tail; yellow
wash on rump. Pale streak on lores. Broad bill dark
above, paler below. Throat white; rest of underparts
yellow; olive wash on breast. Minor race *terraereginae*
(Cape York Pen.) allegedly yellower. **Size** 12 cm. **Juv.** *lacks*
yellow below. Cream spotted above. **Voice** varied
melodious songs; 'choo-choo-suri-so-we-choo'.
Habitat woodlands, streamside vegetation, mangroves.
Identify from Grey Whistler (race *griseiceps*), Yellow-
legged Flycatcher and 'yellow robin' group.

Juv.
moulting

RAOU Atlas 379

482 Kimberley Flycatcher *Microeca tormenti*

Like Lemon-bellied Flycatcher, but underparts pale grey,
washed buff on breast. Broad, short bill wholly dark-
brown. Legs black. **Size** 12.5 cm. **Juv.** contrasting mottles,
spots. **Voice** like Lemon-bellied Flycatcher.
Habitat mangroves, river thickets. Identify from Jacky
Winter, Grey Whistler (race *simplex*) and juv. Lemon-
bellied Flycatcher.

RAOU Atlas 378

483 Jacky Winter *Microeca leucophaea*

Black bill. Narrow black line through eye; narrow whitish
eyebrow. Head, back grey-brown; darker on wings which
are edged white. Pale grey breast; underparts whitish. Tail
blackish-brown with white outer tail feathers. Legs black.
Races *leucophaea* (SE Aust.) darkest race; *assimilis*
(southern mallee, south and west area) black basal half to
outer tail feathers, *not* white; *barcoo* (central Aust.) palest
race; *pallida* (N Aust.) upperparts paler than *leucophaea*.
Size 13 cm. **Juv.** spotted white above. **Voice** sweet,
continuous, rapid 'jacky-jacky-winter-winter-winter'.
Habitat dry forests, woodlands, mallee, farmlands. Identify
from Kimberley Flycatcher. Perches on trees and vigorously
waves tail from side to side, emphasising its white edges.

Tail wag

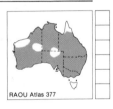

RAOU Atlas 377

Note: 482 Kimberley Flycatcher is now considered a race of 481
Lemon-bellied Flycatcher *Microeca flavigaster.*

494
Grey Whistler
Race *griseiceps*

494
Grey Whistler
Race *simplex*

480

483
Juv.

481

483

483

482

484 Pale-yellow Robin *Tregellasia capito*

Head olive-grey, darker on forehead; paler on ear coverts, nape. White lores and throat. Back, shoulder, rump olive. Wings, tail dark olive-brown, edged olive. Underparts pale yellow, washed olive on flanks. Legs pinkish. Race *nana* (Cooktown to Townsville, Qld) lores buff. **Size** 13 cm. **Juv.** browner above; feathers tipped cinnamon. **Voice** 'cheep'; monotonous whistles. **Habitat** rainforests.

Adult in nest

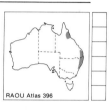
RAOU Atlas 396

485 White-faced Robin *Tregellasia leucops*

Distinctive white face, including sides of forehead, lores, eye-ring, upper throat. Rest of head olive-black. Back, shoulders, rump olive-green. Wings, tail olive-brown, edged olive. Underparts bright yellow; olive wash on breast. Legs pale yellow. **Size** 13 cm. **Juv.** browner above; duller below. **Voice** harsh 'chee-chee', like Pale-yellow Robin. **Habitat** rainforests. Aust. race is *albigularis*.

Face pattern

RAOU Atlas 397

486 White-browed Robin *Poecilodryas superciliosa*

Race *superciliosa* (Cape York Pen.): Upperparts uniformly dark brown. White eyebrow and patch below eye. Underparts white, washed light grey on breast. White wing patch; tail tipped white. Race *cerviniventris* 'Buff-sided Robin' (N and NW Aust.): Head darker; less white below eye. Buff flanks, undertail coverts. Flight feathers tipped white. **Size** 15 cm. **Voice** loud piping whistle; quieter whistles, harsh 'botta-chew'. **Habitat** race *superciliosa*: stream vegetation, rainforests, woodlands, vine scrub. Race *cerviniventris*: mangroves, swampy thickets, jungles, streamside vegetation.

Nest

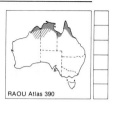
RAOU Atlas 390

487 Grey-headed Robin *Poecilodryas albispecularis*

Forehead, crown grey to nape; paler eyebrow. Bill black with yellow tip. Lores black. White line behind eye and white crescent below eye, lower face and throat. Blackish immediately behind eye-line, becoming brown on cheeks. Wings blackish-brown with two white wing bars. Rump to base of tail chestnut; rest of tail dark brown, tipped paler on outer tail feathers. Breast pale grey. Abdomen whitish; buff flanks. Legs flesh. **Juv.** brown above; head, underparts blotched rust. Bill pale brown. **Size** 17 cm. **Voice** piping whistle, often four notes long. **Habitat** rainforests, usually above 300 m.

Dorsal pattern

RAOU Atlas 389

Chick in nest

488 Crested Shrike-tit *Falcunculus frontatus*

Three races. **Male** race *frontatus* 'Eastern Shrike-tit' (SE Aust.): Distinctive crested head, black with two broad white bands and patch at base of robust bill. Back, rump olive-green. Throat black. Rest of underparts yellow. Wings, tail darker grey. Race *leucogaster* 'Western Shrike-tit' (SW of WA): Abdomen white; undertail coverts yellow. Yellower above. Race *whitei* 'Northern Shrike-tit' (N Aust.): Smaller; yellower overall. **Female** throat olive-green in each race. **Juv.** pale throat; back brown in each race. **Size** 15-19 cm. **Voice** 'knock-at-the-door'; repeated plaintive whistle. **Habitat** open forests, woodlands, mallee. Observer's attention may be drawn by tearing of bark.

Juv.

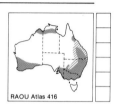
RAOU Atlas 416

488 ♂
Race *leucogaster*

488 ♂
Race *whitei*

488 ♀
Race *frontatus*

487

485

♂ 488
Race *frontatus*

484
Race *nana*

486

484

486
Race *cerviniventris*

489 Olive Whistler *Pachycephala olivacea*

Male head dark grey. Rest of upperparts dark olive-brown.
Bill blackish-brown. Throat white with broken grey
barrings. Underparts buff-brown with grey wash on
breast. **Female** similar but generally paler. Head more
olive-brown. Throat without barrings. Race
macphersoniana (Macpherson Ranges, Qld): Lighter
body colouration. **Size** 20.5 cm. **Voice** various two and
three-syllabic whistles; also territorial call 'jo-jo-jo'.
Habitat tall wet forest and rainforest, woodland and
alpine heaths. Northern populations in beech forest.

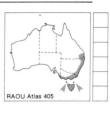

RAOU Atlas 405

490 Red-lored Whistler *Pachycephala rufogularis*

Slightly larger than Gilbert's Whistler. **Male** upperparts
brownish-grey. Orange lores and throat. Eye red.
Breast grey. Abdomen orange-buff. **Female** similar, except
paler overall, especially on lores and underparts.
Size 20.5 cm. **Voice** typical call is whistle followed by
sound like indrawn breath 'see-saw'. **Habitat** mallee, low
shrubland.

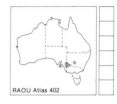

RAOU Atlas 402

491 Gilbert's Whistler *Pachycephala inornata*

Male upperparts brownish-grey with black lores. Eye red.
Throat and upper breast deep orange. Rest of breast and
abdomen pale grey. Undertail coverts buff-white.
Female uniform grey above; lighter grey below, with
breast darker. Eye red-brown. Race *gilberti* (SW Aust. to
Nullarbor Plain): Generally darker colouration. **Size** 19.5 cm.
Voice whistle 'poo-ee' rising at the end. Also repeated
'jock'. **Habitat** shrubby woodland, mallee.

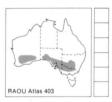

RAOU Atlas 403

492 Golden Whistler *Pachycephala pectoralis*

Male head black to nape and extending around upper
breast in a band. Throat white. Nape yellow extending
around to breast and abdomen. Back olive-green; wings
black, edged yellow-green. Tail black, or grey and black.
Female upperparts brownish-grey, sometimes with an
olive wash. Pale grey stripe on wings. Underparts grey-buff
to dull white. Some northern birds with lemon wash on
undertail coverts. **Size** 17 cm. **Voice** melodious, sometimes
with whip-crack ending 'wi-wi-wi-whit!' **Habitat** rainforests,
open forests, woodlands, mallee, coastal vegetation.

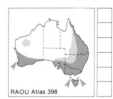

RAOU Atlas 398

493 Mangrove Golden Whistler
Pachycephala melanura

Male similar to, but slightly smaller than male Golden
Whistler. Yellow band of nape is broader, wings black,
edged yellow-grey and tail base sometimes yellow-green.
Female upperparts buff-grey with olive wash on back and
wings. Throat dull white. Rest of underparts yellow. Race
robusta (W Kimberleys, WA, to E Qld): Female tail black.
Size 15.5 cm. **Voice** like Golden Whistler.
Habitat mangroves and riverside or coastal forests.

RAOU Atlas 400

493 ♂

493 ♀

493 ♀
Race *robusta*

492 ♂

492
Imm.

♀ 492

491 ♂

491 ♀

♂ 490

490 ♀

489

494 Grey Whistler *Pachycephala simplex*

Two races. Race *simplex* (Arnhem Land, NT) 'Brown
Whistler': Upperparts grey-brown. Pale buff eyebrow.
Pale grey-buff band across faintly streaked upper breast.
Underparts white to buff-white. Race *griseiceps* Grey
Whistler (N Qld): Head grey. Back olive. Throat buff-white;
upper breast olive-buff merging with pale yellow of
lower breast and abdomen. Wings olive-brown with
small white 'flash' near bend of wing. Tail olive-
brown. **Size** 14.5 cm. **Voice** 'Brown': single note repeated
several times; also melodious song. Grey : a whistle 'dum
dum dee daa dum'. **Habitat** race *simplex:* mangroves, wet
forest. Race *griseiceps:* coastal rainforest and mangroves.

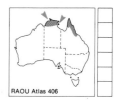

RAOU Atlas 406

495 Rufous Whistler *Pachycephala rufiventris*

Male head and back grey. Black from bill through eye and
extending down around upper breast in a band. Throat
white. Lower breast and abdomen deep buff. Wings and
tail blackish brown. **Female** upperparts olive-grey, darker
on wings and tail. Throat white, merging into pale buff
breast and abdomen, with dark streaking on throat and
breast, fainter on abdomen. Six races recognised with two
major patterns of variation, i.e. one of decreasing size
from south to north, and one of increasing darker
colouration from continental interior to coastal periphery:
race *falcata* (Melville Island and Arnhem Land, NT)
richly coloured but smaller than southern birds; *colletti*
(NW Aust./interior of NT) intermediate between *falcata*
and *pallida*; *pallida* (Normanton, Qld) palest race; *dulcior*
(Townsville to C. York Pen.) paler below than *rufiventris*;
rufiventris (southern Aust.) large and dark; *maudeae*
(central Aust.) paler than *rufiventris*. **Size** 17 cm.
Voice ringing, whipcrack-like 'ee-chong!', also 'joey-joey-
joey' repeated. **Habitat** mostly open forest, woodland,
mallee and scrub of arid inland; less common in wetter
tall forests.

♂
Singing

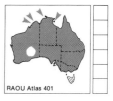

RAOU Atlas 401

♀

496 White-breasted Whistler *Pachycephala lanioides*

Feeding on crab

Male bill black; head black to nape and extending around
upper breast in a band. Nape rufous, with band extending
around below the black breast band. Throat, remainder of
breast and abdomen white. Back grey to grey-black. Wings
black, edged grey. Tail black. **Female** bill brownish. Dark
streaking on throat and breast. Upperparts grey-brown,
darker on wings and tail. Underparts buff, paler on
throat. Pale grey wash on breast. Three races recognised:
carnarvoni (Carnarvon to Eighty Mile Beach, WA) females
brownish above, buff below; *lanioides* (Broome to King
Sound, WA) females grey or olive above, paler below than
carnarvoni; fretorum (NE Kimberleys, WA, to Karumba,
Qld) smaller than *lanioides*, females greyer above, lighter
underneath than *lanioides*. **Size** 19.5 cm. **Voice** melodious
song, also whistles. **Habitat** mangroves; less common in
coastal rainforest.

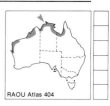

RAOU Atlas 404

494
Race *griseiceps*

480
Yellow-legged Flycatcher

494
Race *simplex*

495 ♂
Race *pallida*

495 ♂
Race *rufiventris*

495 ♀
Race *rufiventris*

496 ♂
Race *lanioides*

♀ **496**
Race *lanioides*

497 Little Shrike-thrush *Colluricincla megarhyncha*

Seven races described in Aust. E Aust. races olive-brown above; paler on face. Bill pinkish-brown. Underparts cinnamon, slightly streaked on upper breast and paler throat. Race *parvula* (NW Aust.): Light brown above. Bill blackish-brown. White lores and throat. Underparts cinnamon-buff. Faint streaking on throat, upper breast. **Size** 19 cm. **Voice** 'tu-ee, wot-wot-wot'; also harsh wheeze. **Habitat** E Aust. races: rainforest, coastal woodland, swamps, mangroves. Race *parvula:* mangroves, swamp thickets.

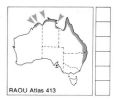

RAOU Atlas 413

498 Bower's Shrike-thrush *Colluricincla boweri*

Blue-grey head and back. Pale lores and throat. Cinnamon breast; paler on abdomen. Throat and breast darkly streaked. Wings and tail grey-brown. **Size** 20.5 cm. **Imm.** browner, duller; more heavily streaked. **Voice** melodious; quieter than other shrike-thrushes. **Habitat** rainforest above 300 m.

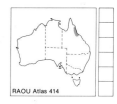

RAOU Atlas 414

499 Sandstone Shrike-thrush
Colluricincla woodwardi

Buff streak from bill to eye and on throat. Head dull grey. Back olive-brown. Breast, abdomen cinnamon. Grey wash on breast. Finely streaked throat and breast. Wings, tail olive-brown. Race *assimilis* (Kimberley region, WA): Larger; throat whiter; underparts darker. **Size** 24 cm. **Imm.** wing darker; breast paler. **Voice** rich, variable song. **Habitat** sandstone cliffy areas. Occurs almost entirely on the ground.

Singing

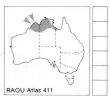

RAOU Atlas 411

500 Grey Shrike-thrush *Colluricincla harmonica*

Race *harmonica* (SE Aust.): **Male** head grey; white stripe from bill to eye. Back brown. Underparts light grey. Wings and tail grey. In NW Aust., upperparts plain grey-brown; underparts paler. **Female** white eye-ring and eye-stripe less distinct. Underside of bill paler, fine streaking on throat. Race *rufiventris* ('Western Shrike-thrush', central and W Aust.): Back and wings darker grey; undertail coverts cinnamon-buff. **Size** 24 cm. **Imm.** light brown eye-ring extends midway to bill. Strongly streaked throat and breast. **Voice** liquid melodious 'pip-pip-pip-ho-ee!'; harsh 'yorrick'. **Habitat** forest, woodland, scrub, mallee.

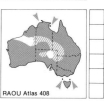

RAOU Atlas 408

501 Crested Bellbird *Oreoica gutturalis*

Male crown feathers can be raised into a crest. White forehead and throat encircled by a black band extending from crest through eye and down around breast. Eye orange. Back of head to nape grey. Back grey-brown. Underparts buff, richer colour on undertail coverts. Wings and tail grey-brown. **Female** lacks crest. Head grey with black crown. Eye red-brown. Throat, breast, back and wings grey, paling to white abdomen. **Size** 21.5 cm. **Voice** distinctive, ventriloquial. **Habitat** dry inland and sub-inland woodland and scrub.

Erect crest

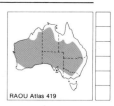

RAOU Atlas 419

497
Race *megarhyncha*

497
Race *parvula*

498
Juv.

498

499

500
North-west form

500 ♂

♀ **501**

♂ **501**

500
Imm.

500
Race *rufiventris*

502 Yellow-breasted Boatbill
Machaerirhynchus flaviventer

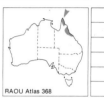

Head: ventral view

Male bill black, huge, 'boat-like' from below. Yellow eyebrow. Upperparts black; white shoulder, tail tips. Throat white; bright yellow below. **Female** like male; olive grey-brown above. More white on throat; dull yellow, scaled black-brown below. **Size** 11-12 cm. **Juv.** like female; duller yellow. **Voice** soft, like Brown Thornbill 'pee-dee-dee-dee-wit'. **Habitat** rainforests.

Wren-like posture

RAOU Atlas 368

503 Black-faced Monarch *Monarcha melanopsis*

Bill, legs blue. Black forehead joins black throat. Eye black; pale grey eye-ring. Upperparts, chest blue-grey. Wings, tail dark grey. Underparts rusty-rufous. **Size** 15-20 cm. **Juv.** *no* black in face. **Voice** whistling 'why-you-whichye-oo'; also creaks, chatters. **Habitat** forests.

RAOU Atlas 373

504 Black-winged Monarch *Monarcha frater*

Like Black-faced Monarch but light pearly-grey above; conspicuous black wings, tail. **Size** 18-19 cm. **Juv.** *less* black in face. **Voice** like Black-faced. **Habitat** rainforests, adjacent forests.

RAOU Atlas 374

505 Spectacled Monarch *Monarcha trivirgatus*

Bill, legs blue. Bill to ear coverts, throat black. Slaty-grey above. Tail black, tipped white. Cheeks, chest rusty-orange. Belly, vent white. **Size** 14-16 cm. **Juv.** paler grey above. Black face, underparts duller. Throat and forehead feathers tipped white. **Voice** harsh buzzing. **Habitat** wet forests, mangroves.

Incubating

RAOU Atlas 375

506 White-eared Monarch *Monarcha leucotis*

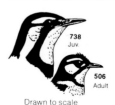
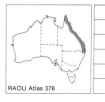

Bill, legs blue. Head, upperparts all black except for white on eyebrow, spot before bill, cheek, wing bars, rump, tail tips. Underparts pale grey. **Size** 13 cm. **Juv.** upperparts sooty grey-brown; buffy wash below. Head white; black crown, forehead streaks, ear coverts. **Voice** like bronze-cuckoo 'thee-ou'; also buzzings. **Habitat** rainforests.

738 Juv.

506 Adult

Drawn to scale

RAOU Atlas 376

507 Frilled Monarch *Arses lorealis*

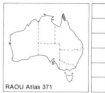

Foraging

Male bill blue. Eye-ring sky-blue; vertically-oval. Cap, chin black. Neck has erectile white frill. Upperparts black. Scapulars, back, underparts white. **Female** chin white, lores light grey. **Size** 14-17 cm. **Juv.** upperparts tinged brown. **Voice** scolding trills; a frog-like squawk. **Habitat** rainforests, adjacent forests.

RAOU Atlas 371

508 Pied Monarch *Arses kaupi*

Male like Frilled Monarch, but broad black chest band; white chin. Eye-ring blue-grey; rounded. **Female** head black. White nape tufts, throat, faintly scaled black. Chest band broader. **Size** 14-15 cm. **Juv.** brown-grey, *not* black; white head areas scaled dark. **Voice** ten or more soft, high, whistles; a continuous buzzing; a flycatcher 'creak'. **Habitat** rainforests, adjacent forests.

Foraging

RAOU Atlas 370

Note: Recent DNA studies suggest that the Magpie-larks are large Monarchs, closely related to 506 White-eared Monarch (see also p. 339).

503

503
Juv.

504
Juv.

504

506

505
Juv.

508 ♀

505

♂ 508

507 ♀

♂ 507

♀ 502

♂ 502

509 Broad-billed Flycatcher *Myiagra ruficollis*

Head: dorsal view

Bill more concave and broader between the nostrils than Satin or Leaden Flycatchers. **Male** like female Satin, but smaller, slightly darker and glossier above; has paler grey area around eye to frons. **Female** like female Leaden, but has grey area around eye to frons. **Size** 14-17 cm; same size as Leaden. **Juv.** whitish edges to tail and wing coverts; otherwise like female. **Voice** harsh 'shwek'; possibly harsher than Leaden and Satin; also repeated loud 'thee-ooo-uu' and whirrings. **Habitat** tropical mangroves, monsoon forests and adjacent woodlands.

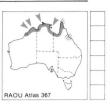

RAOU Atlas 367

510 Leaden Flycatcher *Myiagra rubecula*

Head: dorsal view

Male bill blue, tipped black; broad, but not concave as in Broad-billed. Eyes dark brown. Small erectile crest. Upperparts and upper chest blue-grey. Chest with a horizontal margin. Underparts white. Undertail grey. Legs black. **Female** like male but throat pale rust, belly white, undertail paler grey. **Size** 14-17 cm; smaller than Satin. **Juv.** like female but has white wing bars and edging to undertail feathers. **Voice** harsh rattles and buzzes; deep burp-like notes; whistling 'zoo-wee'. **Habitat** tall and medium open forests.

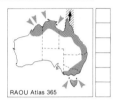

RAOU Atlas 365

511 Satin Flycatcher *Myiagra cyanoleuca*

Male like Leaden male. Glossy blue-black above and on chest. Chest with a larger extent of black than Leaden male; margin slightly curved towards the head. Undertail black. **Female** like Leaden female but glossier dark blue head; dark grey body. Throat bright chestnut. **Size** 15-18 cm; slightly larger than Leaden. **Juv.** like female but has white wing bars and edges to undertail. **Voice** louder than Leaden; churrings; strong carrying and repeated whistles. **Habitat** tall and medium open forests.

Incubating

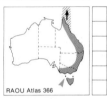

RAOU Atlas 366

512 Shining Flycatcher *Myiagra alecto*

Extreme sexual dimorphism. **Male** bill slender, shiny blue and black-tipped. Body entirely glossy black with intense blue sheen. Iris dark brown. **Female/Juv.** glossy blue and black cap with intense blue sheen. Orange-rufous upperparts. Underparts white from throat to tail. **Size** 15-18 cm; same size as Satin. **Voice** a considerable variety of clear whistles; harsh grating calls. **Habitat** tropical mangroves, forest streamside vegetation.

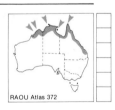

RAOU Atlas 372

513 Restless Flycatcher *Myiagra inquieta*

Largest *Myiagra*. Bill blue-black; iris dark brown. **Male** glossy blue-black from cap to tail. Chin and throat to undertail coverts white. Legs black. **Female** has pale-buff wash across breast. Race *nana* 'Paperback Flycatcher' of the northern part of NT and Kimberleys, WA, is smaller. **Size** 16.5-21 cm. **Voice** continuous whirring hisses whilst hovering; deep gratings; whistling song 'zoo-wee, zoo-wee'. **Habitat** open forests. Race *nana* prefers tropical melaleuca forests.

Hawking

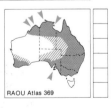

RAOU Atlas 369

Note: Race *nana* of 513 Restless Flycatcher is now considered a full species *Myiagra nana*, the Paperback Flycatcher.

512 ♂

♂ 510

512 ♀

♀ 510

509
Juv.

511 ♂

♀ 511

♀ 513

N.D.

514 Rufous Fantail *Rhipidura rufifrons*

Eye, bill, legs, dark brown. Eyebrow rufous. Rest of head, mantle, wings grey-brown. Throat white, bordered on upper chest by a black band. Rest of chest feathers black, scaled white. Underparts white. Lower back, tail base orange-rufous. Tail blackish with white tips. **Size** 15-16 cm. **Juv.** brown with rufous wash instead of rufous. **Voice** thin, ascending, high-pitched whistles; also a 'chip'. **Habitat** wet forested regions, occasionally more open forests. Very active; fans and waves long tail up and down and from side to side.

Ventral view

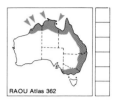
RAOU Atlas 362

515 Grey Fantail *Rhipidura fuliginosa*

Race *albicauda*

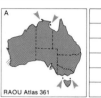

Six races. Race *alisteri:* Eye, bill, legs black. Mid-grey above with white eyebrow, ear mark, throat. Two white wing bars. White tail shafts and tips to all but the central feathers; pale grey inner webs; outer feather white. Upper breast sooty. Rest of underparts cream, some sooty spotting on chest. **Juv.** broader buffy wing bars, head markings. Race *preissi:* Like *alisteri* but breast grey. Race *albiscapa:* Like *alisteri* but broader breast band; tail less white; upperparts darker. Race *keasti:* Very dark above; pale buff below. White wing bars and tail edges reduced. Race *albicauda:* Tail distinctive, white except for central feathers. Broader wing bars; paler grey on breast, upperparts. Race *phasiana* 'Mangrove Fantail': Possibly a distinct species. Small, pallid. Large bill and short tail; small pale breast band; underparts paler cream. Tail pattern like *alisteri.* **Size** 15-17 cm. **Voice** races: *alisteri* a variety of rich, loud ascending whistling songs, also chattering; *albicauda* softer; has a more rapid 'trilling' song; *phasiana* softer; has a series of short twittering whistles. **Habitat** forests, woodlands; *phasiana* only in mangroves; *albicauda* confined to mulga. A very active fantail, flying up to catch insects and fanning tail constantly; tends to perch sideways.

Ventral view

'Wineglass' Fantail nest

Mangrove Fantail ventral view

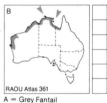
RAOU Atlas 361
A

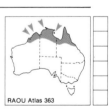
RAOU Atlas 361
B

A = Grey Fantail
B = Mangrove Fantail

516 Northern Fantail *Rhipidura rufiventris*

Large black bill. Eye brown. Legs black. Upperparts pale grey; brown wash on wings. White eyebrow; no ear mark. Throat white. Upper breast grey, streaked white; otherwise white below. Tail all grey, a third of the three outer-tail feathers broadly tipped white; outer feathers all white. **Size** 16-18.5 cm. **Juv.** throat, tail tips buff. **Voice** six-note song like gerygones. Also various 'chips', 'chunks'. **Habitat** open forests, edges of rainforests, mangroves. Only occasionally fans tail; tends to perch vertically; appears less active. Identify from Grey Fantail, Jacky Winter.

Ventral view

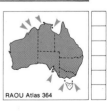
RAOU Atlas 363

517 Willie Wagtail *Rhipidura leucophrys*

Eye, bill, legs black. White eyebrow. Lower cheek stripe spotted white. Head, upperparts, upper chest and (long) tail glossy black; brown tinge to wings. Underparts otherwise white. **Size** 19-21.5 cm. **Juv.** upperparts have buff spotting on tips of black feathers. **Voice** scolding 'chick-a-chick-a-chick'. A chattering, musical 'sweet, pretty creature' song. **Habitat** everywhere except very wet forests. Runs on ground; wags tail around in a fan. Perches on livestock. Identify from Restless Flycatcher.

Eyebrow expanded

RAOU Atlas 364

Note: Race *phasiana* of 515 Grey Fantail is now considered a full species *Rhipidura phasiana*, the Mangrove Fantail.

516

516 Juv.

515

515
Juv.

514

514 Juv.

517

517 Juv.

518 Logrunner *Orthonyx temminckii*

Male crown rufous. Face grey. Upperparts rufous, mottled black. Rump rufous. Throat white with broad black edge. Shafts of tail feathers project, forming spine tips. **Female** throat orange. **Size** 17-20 cm. **Juv.** mottled brown. **Voice** rapid, excited 'weet weet'. **Habitat** floors of subtropical rainforests.

Juv.

RAOU Atlas 434

519 Chowchilla *Orthonyx spaldingii*

Male head black. Eye-ring pale. Upperparts dark brown. Throat and breast white. Tail feathers tipped with spines. **Female** throat, upper breast orange. **Size** 26-28 cm. **Juv.** browner, cinnamon mottling. **Voice** very vocal — parties may dominate dawn chorus with loud repeated 'chow-chilla' — 'chowry chook chook'. **Habitat** floors of tropical rainforests.

Juv.

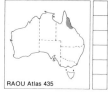
RAOU Atlas 435

520 Eastern Whipbird *Psophodes olivaceus*

A dark, crested bird with long, broad tail and ringing 'whip crack' call. Head and crest black. Upperparts dark olive-green. Bold white patches on sides of black throat. Breast black. Tail tipped white. Race *lateralis* (NE Qld): Browner below; dull tail tip. **Size** 25-30 cm. **Juv.** duller; first year birds *lack* white throat patches. **Voice** loud 'whipcrack' (male); sharp 'choo choo' (female response). Other harsh scolding notes. **Habitat** dense understories of rainforests, coastal scrubs, wet sclerophyll forests.

Juv.

RAOU Atlas 421

Imm.

521 Western Whipbird *Psophodes nigrogularis*

An elusive, olive-green bird with small crest and long, broad tail. Head and crest grey. Upperparts pale olive. Throat black, edged by white 'moustache'. Underparts olive-cream. Outer tail feathers tipped white. **Size** 20-25 cm. **Juv.** throat grey-brown, *no* white edge. **Voice** variety of harsh, grating calls; some likened to squeaking cartwheel. **Habitat** dense thickets of coastal heaths and mallee scrub.

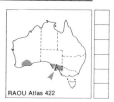
RAOU Atlas 422

522 Chirruping Wedgebill *Psophodes cristatus*

Distinctive. Crest and upperparts light brown. Underparts light grey; faint streaking on breast. Black, wedge-shaped bill. Long, white-tipped tail. **Size** 19-21 cm. **Juv.** pale bill; buff markings on wings. **Voice** 'tootsie cheer' (male); 'ee cheer' (female response) repeated monotonously with sparrow-like quality. **Habitat** semi-arid areas with low scrub, acacia woodlands, savannah.

Often in groups
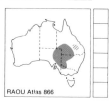
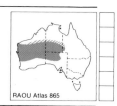
RAOU Atlas 866

523 Chiming Wedgebill *Psophodes occidentalis*

Almost identical, except for voice and distribution, to Chirruping Wedgebill. **Size** 19-22 cm. **Voice** descending chime 'why did you get drunk?' repeated monotonously with haunting quality. **Habitat** dense acacia, melaleuca, tea-tree scrub in arid areas.

RAOU Atlas 865

♂ 518

518 ♀

♀ 519

♂ 519

520

521

522

523

N. Day.

524 Spotted Quail-thrush *Cinclosoma punctatum*

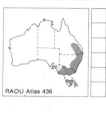

Juv.

Flight

Male white eyebrow. Face black. White patch on sides of black throat. Neck, breast grey. Broad black spots on back, flanks. Shoulder black, spotted white. Tail tipped white. **Female** paler; dull orange patch on side of buff-white throat. **Size** 25-28 cm. **Imm.** resembles female.
Voice thin high-pitched contact calls (the typical quail-thrush is very difficult to tune the human ear to); also loud double-whistle; occasional richer whistlings.
Habitat dry and wet sclerophyll forests but ideally on leaf-littered rocky ridges with short tussock grass. Occasionally perches in trees.

RAOU Atlas 436

525 Chestnut Quail-thrush *Cinclosoma castanotum*

Juv.

Male throat, face, upper breast black. White eyebrow. Broad white streak on sides of throat. Upper back grey-brown, becoming chestnut on lower back. Tail tipped white. **Female** paler; face brown; upper breast grey. **Size** M 22-26, F 17-23 cm. **Imm.** like female. **Voice** thin, high-pitched. Also rosella-like piping whistle. **Habitat** mallee and mulga scrub; inland desert heaths, woodlands.

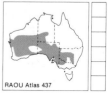

RAOU Atlas 437

526 Chestnut-breasted Quail-thrush
Cinclosoma castaneothorax

♀
A
Race
castaneothorax

♀
B
Race
marginatum

Race *castaneothorax*: **Male** upperparts warm cinnamon-brown; breast rich cinnamon-yellow *(not chestnut as name suggests)*. **Female** like female *cinnamomeum* but has rufous wash on grey breast. Race *marginatum* 'Western Quail-thrush': **Male** larger than nominate race. Upperparts rich chestnut. Breast reddish-brown. **Female** resembles female *castaneothorax*. **Size** 18-24 cm. **Imm.** all races generally like female. **Voice** thin, high-pitched ventriloquial notes; far-carrying whistles.
Habitat *castaneothorax* and *marginatum* favour low acacia-covered ridges.

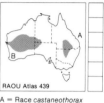

RAOU Atlas 439

A = Race *castaneothorax*
B = Race *marginatum*

527 Cinnamon Quail-thrush *Cinclosoma cinnamomeum*

♀
A
Race
cinnamomeum

Two races recognised. Nominate race is *cinnamomeum*:
Male white eyebrow; black face. Broad white streak down sides of black throat. Upperparts plain cinnamon-rufous. Buff-white patch on upper breast; broad black band below. Outer tail feathers black, tipped white.
Female duller; buff throat and eyebrow. Upper breast pale grey, *no* black below. **Imm.** males of race *cinnamomeum* may have indistinct breast band. Race *alisteri* 'Nullarbor Quail-thrush': **Male** face, throat, upper breast black. White eyebrow. Irregular white streak on sides of throat. Upperparts reddish-cinnamon. Outer tail feathers black, tipped white.
Female duller; face grey-brown; throat, upper breast grey.
Size 18-20 cm. **Imm.** resembles female but less clearly marked. **Voice** not well known. **Habitat** *cinnamomeum* on gibber plains, sparse vegetation along usually dry watercourses.
Race *alisteri* low vegetation associated with the Nullarbor Plain limestone outcroppings.

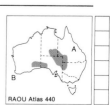

RAOU Atlas 440

A = Race *cinnamomeum*
B = Race *alisteri*

♀ 524

524 ♂

♀ 525

525 ♂

♀ 527
Race *alisteri*

527 ♂ Race *alisteri*

♀ 527
Race *cinnamomeum*

526 ♂
Race *marginatum*

♂ 527
ace *cinnamomeum*

526 ♂
Race *castaneothorax*

528 Grey-crowned Babbler
Pomatostomus temporalis

Largest and only babbler *without* dark crown. Head has
narrow grey crown, bordered by broad white eyebrow.
Dark brown eye-stripe. Eye pale yellow. Bill black, long
and down-curved. Upperparts greyish-brown; rump
darker. Throat, upper breast white, merging into grey
breast and rufous-brown belly. Wings dark brown;
chestnut patch in flight. Tail long, blackish-brown, broad
white tip. Legs black. Race *rubeculus* has reddish-brown
breast, darker brown underparts. **Size** 25-29 cm.
Imm. resembles adult; bill shorter; eye dark. **Voice** loud
'yahoo'; churring notes; cat-like meowing. **Habitat** drier,
more open forests, scrubby woodlands, trees bordering
roads, farmland with isolated trees. *Note:* in all babblers a
dark 'masked face', eye-stripe bordered by white eyebrows,
and white throat, gives a 'band of thieves' appearance to
any group of them.

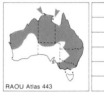

RAOU Atlas 443

Dorsal pattern

529 White-browed Babbler
Pomatostomus superciliosus

The plainest babbler. Crown dark brown; prominent
white eyebrow. Bill black, down-curved. Eye-stripe brown.
Upper back, wings greyish-brown; rump dark brown.
Throat, breast white, merging into grey-brown flanks and
belly. Tail blackish-brown tipped white. Legs dark grey.
Size 18-22 cm. **Imm.** bill shorter. **Voice** high-pitched chatter;
variety of churring, scolding notes. **Habitat** drier, more open
forests with shrubby understorey, mallee, mulga scrubs.
A very active, noisy and seemingly 'quarrelsome' bird.

Dorsal flight

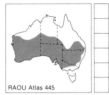

RAOU Atlas 445

530 Hall's Babbler *Pomatostomus halli*

Similar to White-browed Babbler but darker and more
definitely marked. Narrow, dark brown crown; broad
white eyebrow. Eye dark. Bill black, down-curved. Eye-
stripe dark, appears black. White throat, upper breast well
demarcated from dark brown underparts. Tail sooty-
brown, tipped white. Legs black. **Size** 23-25 cm.
Imm. duller. **Voice** excited high-pitched chatter; other
typical babbler calls. **Habitat** mainly ridges of dry acacia
scrubs; dry eucalypt woodlands.

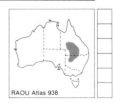

RAOU Atlas 938

531 Chestnut-crowned Babbler
Pomatostomus ruficeps

Rather 'dapper' appearance. Crown rich chestnut,
highlighted by narrow white eyebrow. Eye brown. Bill
dark, down-curved. Eye-stripe brown. Back mottled
greyish-brown. Two white wing bars identify this from
other babblers. Throat, breast white, grading into grey-
brown belly. Flanks dark brown. Tail blackish-brown,
tipped white. Legs dark grey. **Size** 20.5-23 cm. **Imm.** duller;
eyebrow has brown tinge. **Voice** harsh chatter; other
whistling calls. **Habitat** dry inland mulga, mallee scrubs,
more open arid woodlands; casuarina; acacia trees near
edges of salt lakes.

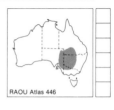

RAOU Atlas 446

531 Communal roosting nest

528
Race *rubeculus*

528

528
Juv.

529

529

530

531

N° Day.

532 Clamorous Reed-warbler *Acrocephalus stentoreus*

Race *australis:* Bill slender; dark above, pale below. Upperparts warm brown. Eyebrow, throat cream. Buffy-cream below. **Size** 17 cm. **Voice** clear, sweet 'crut-crut-crut, deet-deet-deet, crotchy-crotchy-crotchy' with variations and various scolding calls. **Habitat** dense vegetation near water.

Incubating

RAOU Atlas 524

533 Great Reed-warbler *Acrocephalus arundinaceus*

Race *orientalis:* Like Clamorous; bill deeper. **Non-breeding** fine streaks on throat and upper breast. **Size** 19 cm. **Voice** like Clamorous but much harsher, faster and lower. **Habitat** like Clamorous. Rare migrant.

Bill profile

532

533

RAOU Atlas 872

534 Tawny Grassbird *Megalurus timoriensis*

Race *alisteri:* Rufous crown unstreaked. Brown upperparts dark streaked. Whitish unstreaked underparts. Long brown tail. **Size** 19 cm. **Voice** descending wren-like reels; scolding calls. **Habitat** like Little Grassbird, also open grasslands.

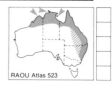

RAOU Atlas 523

535 Little Grassbird *Megalurus gramineus*

Crown, throat and brown upperparts distinctly streaked dark. Long graduated wing feathers, edged white. Underparts grey-brown. **Size** 14 cm. **Voice** distinct t-thee-thee. **Habitat** reeds, tussocks on swamps.

RAOU Atlas 522

536 Spinifexbird *Eremiornis carteri*

Rufous crown and nape. Upperparts rufous-brown, unstreaked. Whitish underparts. Long, graduated, dark tail, tipped buff. **Size** 15 cm. **Voice** pleasant warble. **Habitat** spinifex, dense grasses.

Tail cocked

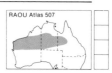

RAOU Atlas 507

537 Zitting Cisticola *Cisticola juncidus*

Race *leanyeri:* **Breeding male** head buff-brown, spotted black. Nape *unstreaked.* Upperparts like Golden-headed. Undertail pale grey, sub-terminal black spots. Tail always tipped white. **Female/Non-breeding male** like Golden-headed in same plumage. Other races exist. **Size** 10 cm. **Voice** monotonous insect-like 'tik-tik' and 'see-sick, see-sick'. **Habitat** rank grasslands.

Breeding

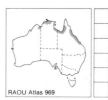

RAOU Atlas 969

538 Golden-headed Cisticola *Cisticola exilis*

Breeding male uniform golden crown, nape. Upperparts cinnamon-brown to rufous, streaked black. Underparts whitish. Dark undertail, tipped cinnamon. **Non-breeding female** crown browner, streaked black, tail longer, pointed. **Size** 10 cm. **Voice** 'churr, lik-lik'. **Habitat** long grasses.

Display flight

RAOU Atlas 525

539 Arctic Warbler *Phylloscopus borealis*

Dark olive upperparts. Yellowish-white, long, straight eyebrow. Whitish below. **Size** 12 cm. **Voice** distinctive loud 'twzee-et'. **Habitat** wooded areas, mangroves. One Aust. record, Scott Reef off NW Aust.

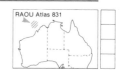

RAOU Atlas 831

200 Note: 759 Gray's Grasshopper Warbler (see p.5) would head this page if placed in its correct taxonomic position.

539

533

532

537 ♂
Breeding
Race *leanyeri*

536

♀ 538
Non-breeding

534

♂ 538
Breeding

535

N. Day.

540 Rufous Songlark *Cinclorhamphus mathewsi*

Pale white eyebrow. Streaky-brown upperparts. Rufous rump, uppertail coverts. Whitish underparts. Dark brown tail. **Male** breast may have fine spots. **Size** 16-19 cms. **Imm.** paler; dark spots on breast, throat. **Voice** melodious song (in flight or perched). **Habitat** parklands, hedges, lightly-timbered grasslands.

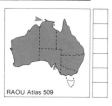

RAOU Atlas 509

541 Brown Songlark *Cinclorhamphus cruralis*

Male pale eyebrow. Black bill. Streaked brown upperparts; brownish-black underparts. Longish, pointed tail. **Female/Imm.** *much* smaller; paler. Pinkish-brown bill. Pale throat. Breast light buff, faintly streaked. Black-brown belly. **Size** M 23-25, F 18-23 cm. **Voice** loud, creaky. **Habitat** grasslands. Perches with crown, tail raised. Conspicuous song flight. Note different sex sizes.

Singing in flight

RAOU Atlas 508

542 Purple-crowned Fairy-wren *Malurus coronatus*

Male breeding frons and most of crown purple. Black, central crown patch. Face, nape, lores black. Back sandy-brown. Tail blue. Underparts buff-white. **Male eclipse** brown head, black eye patch. **Female** mainly buff. Chestnut face and ear coverts are diagnostic. Tail blue. Race *macgillivrayi* (Gulf of Carpentaria): **Male** darker above; white below. **Female/Imm.** crown, nape blue-grey; chestnut ear coverts. **Size** 16.5 cm. **Voice** high-pitched. **Habitat** mangroves, cane grass, pandanus near water.

Eclipse

RAOU Atlas 542

543 Superb Fairy-wren *Malurus cyaneus*

Male bill black. Crown, upper back, ear coverts bright blue. Breast, nape, lower back black. Tail dark blue. Underparts buffy-white. **Male eclipse** like female; tail shorter, blue. **Female** brown. Bill, lores, eyebrow reddish-brown. Tail brownish. **Size** 14 cm. **Voice** musical trill. **Habitat** open forests, swamps, coastal areas, rainforests; gardens.

Eclipse

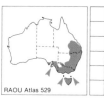

RAOU Atlas 529

544 Splendid Fairy-wren *Malurus splendens*

Male bill black. Forehead, ear coverts light blue. Rump blue. Tail broad, short. **Male eclipse** like female; bill black; tail dark blue. **Female** brown like Superb Fairy-wren female but slightly bluish tail. Race *callainus* 'Turquoise Fairy-wren': **Male** like race *splendens;* much lighter blue upperparts, belly; black rump. **Male eclipse** wing coverts, tail blue. **Female/Imm. male** like *splendens* female. Race *melanotus* 'Black-backed Fairy-wren': **Male** light blue ear coverts. Breast band narrower. Black rump. Tail blue. **Male eclipse** like female; wings, tail blue. **Female** brown like Superb Fairy-wren female; tail faintly dull blue. **Size** 14 cm. **Voice** resembles Superb Fairy-wren. **Habitat** race *splendens:* forest margins, dryer inland areas; often feeds higher in trees, shrubs than other wrens. Race *callainus:* dense mulga, mallee, saltbush. Race *melanotus:* mallee, porcupine grass.

A = Race *splendens*
B = Race *callainus*
C = Race *melanotus*

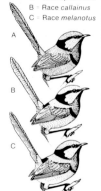

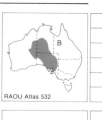

RAOU Atlas 532

RAOU Atlas 532

540

♂ 541

♀ 541

♀ 542

542 ♂
Breeding

♀ 543

♂ 543
Breeding

♂ 544
Breeding

544 ♀

544 ♂
Non-breeding

545 Variegated Fairy-wren *Malurus lamberti*

A = Race *lamberti*
B = Race *assimilis*
C = Race *amabilis*
D = Race *dulcis*
E = Race *rogersi*

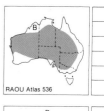

RAOU Atlas 536

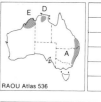

RAOU Atlas 536

RAOU Atlas 536

Five races. Race *lamberti* (nominate): **Male** bill black; iris dark brown; mid-blue crown and mantle; paler blue ear coverts. Frons, chest and neck black. Sides of chest dark blue. Wings brownish; shoulders chestnut. Rump black; tail blue with white tips; rest of underparts whitish. Legs dark brown. **Male eclipse** grey upperparts; white underparts black bill and white eye-ring; tail blue. **Female/Imm.** grey with red bill, lores and eye-ring; tail dull blue; legs reddish. Race *assimilis* 'Purple-backed Fairy-wren': Like *lamberti* but male has darker blue cap and mantle. Race *amabilis* 'Lovely Fairy-wren': **Male** like *lamberti*, but blue areas are light blue; ear coverts broader; tail darker, shorter with broader white tips. Wings dark with brown edges. **Female** bright blue upperparts; white eye-ring. Race *dulcis* 'Lavender-flanked Fairy-wren': **Male** like *assimilis*, but has purplish flanks. **Female** grey-blue with white eye-ring. Race *rogersi* 'Lavender-flanked Fairy-wren': Like *dulcis* but female has red eye-ring and bill. **Size** 14-15 cm. **Voice** like Superb Fairy-wren but faster, far more metallic. **Habitat** race *lamberti*: heathlands, open forests of coastal ranges in E Aust. Race *amabilis*: rainforest edges in NE Qld. Race *dulcis*: rocky escarpments, Arnhem Land NT. Race *rogersi*: escarpments, Kimberley Region, NW of WA. Race *assimilis*: across inland Australia.

546 Blue-breasted Fairy-wren *Malurus pulcherrimus*

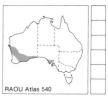

RAOU Atlas 540

Like Variegated Fairy-wren, race *assimilis*, in every respect except: **Male** crown, mantle dark blue with a purplish sheen; ear coverts slightly paler. Breast dark slaty, with a blue to navy blue sheen; no contrast between blue sides of breast and black centre as in 'Purple-backed Fairy-wren'. **Size** 15 cm. **Voice** like Variegated Fairy-wren. **Habitat** sand plains, heath, mallee, mulga-eucalypt and jarrah forests.

547 Red-winged Fairy-wren *Malurus elegans*

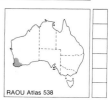

RAOU Atlas 538

Like Blue-breasted Fairy-wren except crown and mantle are pale blue; ear coverts even paler. **Female** dull black bill. **Voice** like Variegated Fairy-wren. **Size** 15 cm. **Habitat** near water; swamps in Darling and Stirling Ranges, SW of WA.

543 Superb Fairy-wren

544 Splendid Fairy-wren

545 Variegated Fairy-wren

Note: Race *amabilis* of 545 Variegated Fairy-wren is now considered to be a full species *Malurus amabilis*, the Lovely Fairy-wren.

545 ♀
Race *rogersi*

♀ 545
Race *amabilis*

♂ 545
Race *amabilis*
Breeding

545 ♀
Race *lamberti*

545 ♂
Race *lamberti*
Non-breeding

545 ♂
Race *lamberti*
Breeding

547 ♀

547 ♂
Breeding

546 ♀

♂ 546
Breeding

N. Day.

548 White-winged Fairy-wren *Malurus leucopterus*

Race *leucopterus* 'Black and White Fairy-wren': **Male breeding** velvety black plumage with white wings; tail deep blue. Note: some have blue in the body plumage. **Male eclipse** patchy black or brown above; tail brown. **Female/Imm.** dull grey-brown above; whitish below; lacks red eye-ring. Race *leuconotus* 'White-winged Fairy-wren': **Male breeding** distinctive bright to deep blue; wings white; tail deep blue. **Male eclipse** like female; bill dark horn. **Female/Imm.** as *leucopterus*. **Size** 11.5-14.5 cm. **Voice** distinctive 'thin' musical trilling, higher than Superb Fairy-wren. **Habitat** race *leucopterus* confined to Dirk Hartog and Barrow Islands, off WA coast; heathlands, saltbush. Race *leuconotus* arid to semi-arid saltbush, spinifex and cane-grass areas.

RAOU Atlas 535

RAOU Atlas 535

A = Race *leucopterus*
B = Race *leuconotus*

♂ Dorsal pattern
Race *leuconotus*

549 Red-backed Fairy-wren *Malurus melanocephalus*

Male breeding black with a crimson to bright orange-red lower back and rump; these feathers are puffed out in display. Short blackish tail. **Male eclipse** like female; traces of red may appear on back. Legs pale pink to fawny-brown. **Female** grey-brown upperparts; *no* red eye-ring; fawnish-white below; tail brown. **Size** 12-13.5 cm. **Voice** drawn out, reedy or chattering songs and notes, similar to White-winged. **Habitat** spinifex, tropical swamps, samphire tidal flats and dense undergrowth. In family parties 'brown birds' predominate. Check female Variegated Fairy-wren.

♂ Dorsal pattern

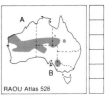
RAOU Atlas 541

550 Rufous-crowned Emu-wren *Stipiturus ruficeps*

Race *ruficeps:* **Male** bright rufous, unstreaked crown. Face, throat blue. Grey-brown to rufous-brown above; feathers streaked black. Six dark filamentous tail feathers. **Female** *lacks* blue colouration of face, throat. Race *mallee* (may be a separate species, 'Mallee Emu-wren'): **Male** chestnut forehead; crown dull brown with slight streaking. Eyebrow, cheek, upper breast light grey-blue. Upperparts darker. **Female** *lacks* blue-grey colouration. Tail filamentous, shorter than race *ruficeps* and Southern Emu-wren. **Size** 14-15.2 cm *ruficeps;* 16.5 cm *mallee.* **Voice** high, trilling, rapid; often softer than fairy-wrens. **Habitat** spinifex, sometimes in associated or adjacent mallee scrub. Flight feeble.

Juv.

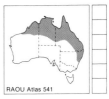
RAOU Atlas 528

A = *S. ruficeps*
B = *S. mallee*

551 Southern Emu-wren *Stipiturus malachurus*

Male crown dark rufous, streaked black. Grey-brown to grey above. Grey-blue eyebrow, throat, upper breast. Orange-brown underparts. Six feathers of tail very long (10 cm). **Female** similar; *lacks* grey-blue and rufous colouring. **Size** 17.5-20 cm. **Imm.** like female; markings less distinct. **Voice** like fairy-wrens, thin, trilling, descending; also soft chirps; short harsh alarm calls. **Habitat** coastal heathlands, tea-tree swamps and dense vegetation. Flight feeble.

Flight

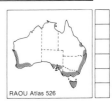
RAOU Atlas 526

Note: Race *mallee* of 550 Rufous-crowned Emu-wren is now considered to be a full species *Stipiturus mallee*, the Mallee Emu-wren.

548 ♀

♂ 548
Race *leucopterus*

548 ♂
Race *leuconotus*

♀ 549

♂ 549

551 ♀

551 ♂

♂ 550
Race *mallee*

♀ 550
Race *ruficeps*

550 ♂
Race *ruficeps*

552 Black Grasswren *Amytornis housei*

Male mostly black; bold white streaks on head, back, breast. **Female** *not* black; light chestnut below; dark undertail coverts. **Size** 21 cm. **Juv.** darker; whitish streaks. **Voice** wren-like; ticking, grating. **Habitat** spinifex in gullies.

RAOU Atlas 518

553 White-throated Grasswren *Amytornis woodwardi*

Male black; white streaks above. Black whisker-mark. White throat, rusty below. **Female** brighter; white lores. Diagnostic rusty underparts. **Size** 22 cm. **Voice** rising and falling trills. **Habitat** spinifex on escarpments.

RAOU Atlas 516

554 Carpentarian Grasswren *Amytornis dorotheae*

Male face, frons black, streaked white. Black whisker-mark. Chestnut lores, lower back. Throat, breast white. Primaries edged reddish-brown. **Female** chestnut flanks, lower belly. **Size** 16-17 cm. **Juv.** duller. **Voice** cricket-like buzz. **Habitat** on spinifex escarpments.

Juv.

RAOU Atlas 517

555 Striated Grasswren *Amytornis striatus*

Race *striatus:* **Male** bold chestnut above (inland WA); brownish above (SE Aust.). All birds are streaked white. Black whisker-mark. Orange-buff eyebrow. White throat. Buff-white below. **Female** chestnut flanks. Other races: *whitei* (NW of WA); *merrotsyi* (Flinders Ranges, SA). **Size** 14.5-17.5 cm. **Juv.** duller; markings indistinct. **Voice** thin squeak. **Habitat** porcupine grass, mallee.

Race *merrotsyi*

Juv.

Race *striatus*

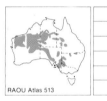

RAOU Atlas 513

556 Eyrean Grasswren *Amytornis goyderi*

Male faint whisker-mark. Crown, nape greyish-brown. Upper back, tail coverts rufous-brown, streaked white. Throat white; greyish below. Flanks pale rufous. **Female** faint whisker-mark; richer rufous flanks. **Size** 15 cm. **Voice** faint two-note whistle. **Habitat** cane grass on high dunes.

RAOU Atlas 515

557 Grey Grasswren *Amytornis barbatus*

Male ginger-brown, streaked white; white below. Black crown streaked white. White facial area. Black eye-stripe. Thin black throat band. Flanks pale buff. **Female** breast streaked. **Size** 18-20 cm. **Voice** high, twittering; two notes. **Habitat** cane grass; lignum clumps. Two races.

Juv.

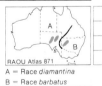

RAOU Atlas 871

A = Race *diamantina*
B = Race *barbatus*

558 Thick-billed Grasswren *Amytornis textilis*

Male stout bill. Head streaks; whisker-mark. Dark amber-brown above; pale brown below. Throat, breast streaked white. **Female** rufous flanks. Race *modestus:* **Male** pale fawn. **Female** chestnut flanks. **Juv.** duller. **Size** 15-20 cm. **Voice** high squeak. **Habitat** saltbush, cane grass.

Race *textilis*

Race *modestus*

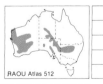

RAOU Atlas 512

559 Dusky Grasswren *Amytornis purnelli*

Race *purnelli:* **Male** reddish-brown; streaked. Slender bill. *No* black whisker-mark. Rich buff below; flanks grey-brown. **Female** rufous flanks. Race *ballarae* (W Qld): **Male** pale below; flanks pale grey. **Female** flanks also rufous. **Size** 16.5-17 cm. **Voice** shrill alarm. **Habitat** tussock grasslands.

Race *purnelli*

Race *ballarae*

RAOU Atlas 511

♂ 552

552 ♀

♀ 553

♂ 553

♂ 554

♀ 554

♂ 556

556 ♀

♂ 555
Race *whitei*

♀ 555
Race *striatus*

555 ♂
Race *striatus*

♂ 557

559 ♂

♀ 558

558 ♂

♀ 559

N.Day.

560 Eastern Bristlebird *Dasyornis brachypterus*

Pale eyebrow, throat, Upperparts and underparts rich to soft browns and grey-browns, tinted olive. Light scaly pattern on breast. **Size** 20-22 cm. **Juv./Imm.** no reliable data. **Voice** loud, penetrating four-part call; harsh, short notes. **Habitat** dense coastal and mountain heaths; taller swamps, stream thickets.

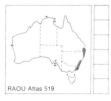

RAOU Atlas 519

561 Western Bristlebird *Dasyornis longirostris*

Bill longer and tail shorter than other bristlebirds. Crown, nape brownish-black, dappled grey. Pale eyebrow. Upperparts and underparts subtle browns and greys tinted olive and rufous. Faint scaly pattern on breast. **Size** 17-20 cm. **Juv./Imm.** no reliable data. **Voice** five-part call, probably male only; three-part call, probably female only. Also 'tink'. Also short, harsh notes. **Habitat** dense coastal heaths; taller swamp and stream thickets.

RAOU Atlas 520

562 Rufous Bristlebird *Dasyornis broadbenti*

Pale eyebrow, lores. Rich rufous crown, nape, ear coverts (less rich from western to eastern areas of range.) Throat, breast pale grey, with dark scaly pattern. Back greyish or darker brown, tinted olive. Centre wing, rump cinnamon-brown. Tail dark-brown. **Female** slightly smaller. Race *littoralis* (WA): Smaller, may be extinct. **Size** 23-27 cm. **Juv./Imm.** no reliable data. **Voice** penetrating, repetitive call and squeaking variations; also short, sharp 'tik'. **Habitat** dense coastal heaths, taller thickets; wet forest (Otway Ranges, Vic.).

RAOU Atlas 521

563 Pilotbird *Pycnoptilus floccosus*

Sturdy; terrestrial. Eye red. Rich reddish-buff from frons to throat, darker, scaly pattern. Upperparts dark-brown; rufous-washed rump. Underparts rufous-brown; centre belly whitish. Chestnut-pink undertail coverts. **Size** 16.5-17 cm. **Voice** sweet, penetrating 'a-guinea-a-week' (male); less distinct call (female). **Habitat** dense, wet forest gullies, all altitudes. Identify from Origma in NSW by rather broad, semi-erect tail flicked up and down.

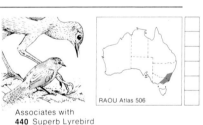

Associates with
440 Superb Lyrebird

RAOU Atlas 506

564 Origma *Origma solitaria*

Frons, front cinnamon-brown. Upperparts dark-brown. Rich rufous underparts, contrast with greyish-white throat. Rump washed rufous. Tail blackish. **Size** 14 cm. **Voice** shrill, melancholy, repeated 'good-bye'; staccato, softer and rasping notes. **Habitat** floors of rocky gullies; caves in sandstone, limestone. Tail flicked sideways.

563

Tail flick

564

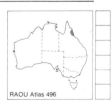

RAOU Atlas 505

565 Australian Fernwren *Crateroscelis gutturalis*

Male white eyebrow and throat. Fairly long bill. Upperparts dark olive-brown, crown darker. Underparts paler. **Female** duller. **Size** 12-14 cm. **Juv.** dark brown without facial markings. **Voice** a scolding note; high-pitched squeaks; strong whistling; chattering. **Habitat** rainforest floors above 650 m. Bows head; flicks short tail.

RAOU Atlas 496

560

561

562

563

564

565
Juv.

565 ♂

566 Atherton Scrubwren *Sericornis keri*

Dark olive-brown; face slightly paler; chin, throat lighter
still. Bill black. Slightly larger, longer-legged, shorter-
winged, more terrestrial than Large-billed Scrubwren.
Size 13.5 cm. **Voice** scolding call. **Habitat** rainforests above
650 m.

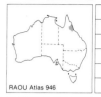

RAOU Atlas 946

567 Large-billed Scrubwren *Sericornis magnirostris*

Dark eye; longish black bill. Face, lores sandy-buff.
Upperparts olive-brown; underparts paler. **Size** 12-13 cm.
Voice soft twitterings, scolding notes and repeated
's-cheer'. **Habitat** dense, wet forests. Rarely on ground;
active to above middle storey.

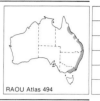

RAOU Atlas 494

568 Yellow-throated Scrubwren
Sericornis citreogularis

Male black face, forehead, ear coverts. White and yellow
eyebrow; bright yellow throat. Outer primary edges
yellowish. Legs longish; cream or pinkish-brown.
Female facial area brownish. **Size** 12.5-15 cm. **Voice** clear,
melodious and mimicry; harsh chatter. **Habitat** dense,
wet forest gullies. Largely terrestrial.

RAOU Atlas 493

569 Tropical Scrubwren *Sericornis beccarii*

Male eye reddish; discontinuous white eye-ring. Forehead,
lores blackish. White mark above lores. Double white
wing bar on dark shoulders. **Female** olive-brown forehead
and lores. Race *dubius* (SE part of range): Plainer markings
less distinct. **Size** 11-11.5 cm. **Voice** soft, musical warble;
harsher notes. **Habitat** rainforests, monsoon forests, dense
riverine scrubs. Active to middle storey.

Race *dubius*

RAOU Atlas 490

570 White-browed Scrubwren *Sericornis frontalis*

Male pale eye; blackish lores; grey ear coverts. White
eyebrow and white stripe well below eye. Throat white
with faint dark streaks. Small white marks on dark
shoulders. Upperparts dark olive-brown; rump rufous.
Underparts dirty yellow, darker at sides. **Female** greyer.
Race *maculatus* 'Spotted Scrubwren' (west of Spencer
Gulf, SA): Spotted black throat, breast. Race *laevigaster*
(Qld): Black ear coverts; tail tipped white; underparts
brighter. Race *humilis* (Tas. and Bass Strait islands):
Plainer face and wing markings; larger and darker.
Size 11-14 cm. **Juv.** duller; browner. **Voice** repeated
'ts-cheer'; harsh scolding notes. **Habitat** dense undergrowth
all altitudes, including urban areas, salt marshes, heaths.

Race *frontalis*

Juv.

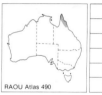

RAOU Atlas 488

571 Scrubtit *Sericornis magnus*

Eye brown. Whitish eye-ring, eyebrow, lores and throat.
Ear coverts grey. White spots near shoulder. White edges
to wing-tips. **Size** 11-11.5 cm. **Voice** 'too-whe-too', like
White-browed Scrubwren (race *humilis*) and Brown
Thornbill. Also whistling. **Habitat** dense, ferny, wet forest
undergrowth. May move higher into trees.

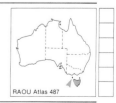

RAOU Atlas 487

567

571

♂ 570
Race *humilis*

♂ 570
Race *frontalis*

570

♂ 570
Race *maculatus*

♂ 570
Race *laevigaster*

566

♂ 568

569 ♀

569 ♂

572 Chestnut-rumped Hylacola
Sericornis pyrrhopygius

Male dull white eyebrow. Upperparts olive-brown; crown
greyer. Greyish-white throat and breast, streaked dark brown.
Chestnut rump. Erect tail; dark band before white tip. Belly
buff; flanks washed yellow. **Female** underparts duller.
Size 13-14 cm. **Voice** varied, lengthy, canary-like song
interwoven with mimicry; also a harsh 'chip'. **Habitat** heaths
of coastal, mountain and hinterland areas; dense
undergrowth of forests and woodlands.

Tail
cocked

RAOU Atlas 498

573 Shy Hylacola *Sericornis cautus*

Male conspicuous white eyebrow. Upperparts olive-brown;
crown greyer. White shoulder spot. White throat and
breast boldly streaked black. Rich rufous rump. Erect dark
tail with white tip. Flanks grey-brown; undertail coverts
rich rufous. **Female** slightly duller. **Size** 12-14 cm.
Voice strong song but less mimicry and vocal range than
Chestnut-rumped Hylacola. Also sharp, harsh notes.
Habitat coastal thickets and sandplain country in
SW Aust., elsewhere in low undergrowth of mallee.

Dorsal pattern

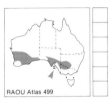

RAOU Atlas 499

574 Redthroat *Sericornis brunneus*

Male pale eyebrow and lores. Throat has chestnut-red
centre. Upperparts grey-brown washed olive on back and
rump. Tail darker; white outer tail feathers and tip.
Underparts greyish. **Female** throat grey; chin white.
Size 11.5-12 cm. **Voice** rich and varied like Clamorous
Reed-Warbler but softer. An accomplished mimic; female
less so. **Habitat** mallee, mulga, saltbush, bluebush, lignum
and spinifex country; coastal areas in western part of its
range.

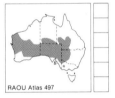

RAOU Atlas 497

575 Striated Calamanthus *Sericornis fuliginosus*

Singing

Rust forehead. Dull white eyebrow. Upperparts dark,
heavily streaked olive-brown. Throat whitish. Underparts
buffy-yellow, streaked blackish-brown. Tail erect; dark
band before white tip. In SW Aust. upperparts greyer;
more reddish in birds of arid areas, but all have whiter
underparts. **Size** 12-14 cm. **Voice** sharp, musical, lengthy,
twittering song. **Habitat** damp heaths of coastal and
mountain areas; sparse, low ground cover; rocky plains of
arid areas. May be recognised as two species: *fuliginosus* (no
races) SE Aust.; *campestris* (three races); arid Vic., SA and WA.

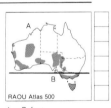

RAOU Atlas 500

A = Rufous
B = Striated

576 Speckled Warbler *Sericornis sagittatus*

Eyebrow, lores and behind ear coverts whitish. A black
line along side of head. Crown brownish, finely streaked
white. Back and wings grey-brown, broadly streaked
darker. Cream underparts, boldly streaked blackish. Tail
has broad dark band before white tip. **Size** 11.5-12.5 cm.
Voice soft, musical, variable song; a harsh grating twitter;
mimicry. **Habitat** open woodlands. Usually on or near
ground litter; often with thornbills.

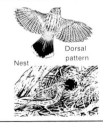

Dorsal
pattern

Nest

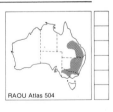

RAOU Atlas 504

Note: Race *campestris* of 575 Striated Calamanthus is now
considered a full species *Sericornis campestris*, the Rufous
Calamanthus.

572

573

575
Rufous Calamanthus

535
Little Grassbird

575
Striated Calamanthus

574 ♂

♀ 574

576 ♀

♂ 576

577 Weebill *Smicrornis brevirostris*

Pale eyebrow. Bill short, pale. Face pale; ear streaked.
Back olive; abdomen yellow. Race *flavescens:* Brighter.
Size 8-9 cm. **Voice** clear, high, sharp, repeated 'tiz'.
Habitat dry forests, woodlands, mallee. Identify from
pardalotes and Yellow Thornbill.

596

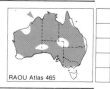
RAOU Atlas 465

578 Brown Gerygone *Gerygone mouki*

Long white eyebrow. Face violet-grey. Eye red-brown.
Olive-brown above. Dark tail band; tail tips white. Race
richmondi: Buff-brown above. **Size** 9.5-10 cm. **Voice** weak,
repetitious. **Habitat** rainforests, open forests.

Undertail pattern

RAOU Atlas 454

579 Large-billed Gerygone *Gerygone magnirostris*

No eyebrow mark. Dark. Thin white eye-ring. Pale buff
flanks. *No* white tail tips. **Size** 10.5-11.5 cm.
Voice downward song. **Habitat** about mangroves, streams.

Undertail pattern

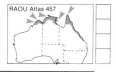
RAOU Atlas 457

580 Dusky Gerygone *Gerygone tenebrosa*

Pale frons, eyebrow; white eye. Plain brown above; dusky
below. *No* tail marks. **Size** 11.5 cm. **Voice** plaintive,
downward. **Habitat** mangroves, creeks, gorges.

Undertail pattern

RAOU Atlas 461

581 Mangrove Gerygone *Gerygone laevigaster*

Bold white eyebrow; reddish eye. Face, upperparts ashy-
brown. Dark tail, tipped white. Race *cantator:* Darker.
Imm. yellowish below. **Size** 11 cm. **Voice** sustained warble.
Habitat mangroves, nearby forests.

Undertail pattern

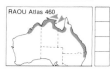
RAOU Atlas 460

582 Western Gerygone *Gerygone fusca*

Dull white eyebrow; red eye. Greyish-brown above. Tail
bold black and white. **Size** 11-11.5 cm. **Imm.** yellowish.
Voice clear rising, falling. **Habitat** open woodlands,
mallee.

Undertail pattern

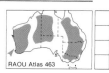
RAOU Atlas 463

583 Green-backed Gerygone *Gerygone chloronota*

Eye red. Dull green above. Light grey below. Grey head.
Tail brown. **Size** 10 cm. **Voice** similar to but lighter than
Western Gerygone. **Habitat** dense edges of paperbark
swamps, estuaries; nearby open forests.

Undertail pattern

RAOU Atlas 458

584 Fairy Gerygone *Gerygone palpebrosa*

Race *personata:* **Male** blackish throat; white cheek stripe.
Brownish-green above; lemon below. Race *flavida:*
Male throat pale lemon; blackish on chin. White tail
marks. **Female** (both races) whitish throat. **Size** 10-11.5 cm.
Imm. (both races) pale yellow throat. **Voice** long warble.
Habitat rainforests, mangroves.

Race *flavida*

RAOU Atlas 456

585 White-throated Gerygone *Gerygone olivacea*

Eye red. Throat white. White forehead spot. Upperparts
grey-brown. Tail dark, white tips. Bright yellow below.
Size 10 cm. **Imm.** all yellow below. **Voice** downward.
Habitat open forests, woodlands.

RAOU Atlas 453

577
ace *flavescens*

577
Race *brevirostris*

585

585
Imm.

♀ **584**

584
Juv.

♂ **584**
Race *personata*

583

578

581
Imm.

582

581

579

580

586 Mountain Thornbill *Acanthiza katherina*

Forehead buff-olive with pale crescents. Eye whitish. Greenish-brown upperparts. Dull rufous rump. Pale to greenish-yellow underparts. **Size** 10 cm. **Voice** not recorded. **Habitat** restricted range in rainforests of NE Aust.

RAOU Atlas 474

587 Brown Thornbill *Acanthiza pusilla*

Juv.

Forehead rufous with pale crescents. Dark red eye. Throat, chest light grey, streaked black. Olive-brown upperparts. Cinnamon-brown rump. **Size** 10 cm. **Voice** short, pleasant warble; harsh alarm call. **Habitat** most forested areas where sufficient undergrowth.

RAOU Atlas 475

588 Inland Thornbill *Acanthiza apicalis*

Tail cocked

Forehead greyish-brown with whitish crescents. Eye red. Dark striations on throat, chest. Upperpart pale olive-brown. Reddish rump. Underparts pale. Races *hamiltoni* and *albiventris* rump rich red; *whitlocki* rump paler; *leeuwinensis*, SW of WA. Minor race is *tanami*, western NT. **Size** 10 cm. **Voice** like Brown Thornbill. **Habitat** dry scrub to coastal heaths. Carries tail cocked.

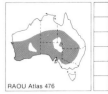

RAOU Atlas 476

589 Tasmanian Thornbill *Acanthiza ewingii*

Faintly marked tawny forehead. Eye red. Throat, breast grey, dappled light and dark. White flanks. Rufous-brown wing patch; darker edge to wing feathers. **Size** 10 cm. **Voice** like Brown Thornbill, except in breeding season. **Habitat** Tas. woodlands and scrub. Identify from Brown Thornbill, Scrubtit and White-browed Scrubwren (race *humilis*).

RAOU Atlas 473

590 Chestnut-rumped Thornbill
  Acanthiza uropygialis

Forehead light brown, speckled white. Eye white. Face pale, freckled. Upperparts dull brown. Rump chestnut. Tail black, tipped white. Underparts white. **Size** 10 cm. **Voice** short, melodious song; also penetrating 'seee-tit-tit-seee'. **Habitat** dry woodlands, mallee, mulga.

Hollow nest

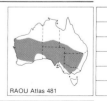

RAOU Atlas 481

591 Slaty-backed Thornbill *Acanthiza robustirostris*

Forehead, crown grey with dark streaks. Eye red-brown. Slaty-grey upperparts. Pale cinnamon rump. Black tail, tipped dull white. Underparts greyish-white. **Size** 9-9.5 cm. **Voice** 'seep-seec'; also harsh 'treeit'. **Habitat** inland scrub-covered plains and mulga.

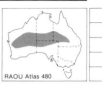

RAOU Atlas 480

592 Western Thornbill *Acanthiza inornata*

Forehead light, freckled brown. Whitish eye. Upperparts grey-brown. Pale olive rump. Tail brown. Underparts pale buff, *no* streaks. **Size** 10 cm. **Voice** soft twittering; good mimic. **Habitat** open woodlands, karri and jarrah forests.

RAOU Atlas 472

Note: 587 Brown Thornbill and 588 Inland Thornbill are now considered to be one species 587 Brown Thornbill.

586

591

591

587

588

570
White-browed Scrubwren

589

588

590

592

587

589

592

590

K. Day.

593 Buff-rumped Thornbill *Acanthiza reguloides*

Forehead, face buff; white feather tips. *No* eyebrow; white eye. Pale buff rump. Underparts pale yellowish; throat speckled grey. Broad black tail band, tipped white. Race *squamata:* Brighter yellow. **Size** 11 cm. **Voice** metallic warble. **Habitat** open forests, lightly timbered ranges.

RAOU Atlas 484

594 Slender-billed Thornbill *Acanthiza iredalei*

Pale speckled forehead, face. Pale eye. Greyish-olive above; pale buff rump. Creamy underparts. Tail dark brown, tipped white. Race *hedleyi:* Darker. **Size** 9 cm. **Voice** musical twitter in flight. **Habitat** samphire near salt pans; semi-desert. Race *hedleyi:* mallee.

Rump variations

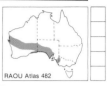

RAOU Atlas 482

595 Yellow-rumped Thornbill
Acanthiza chrysorrhoa

Forehead black, spotted white; crown light brown. White eyebrow. Grey and white cheek spots. Back olive-grey. Rump bright yellow. Underparts pale yellowish. Dark tail, tipped white. **Size** 10-12 cm. **Voice** tinkling. **Habitat** open woods, parklands; often on ground.

Bulky nest

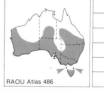

RAOU Atlas 486

596 Yellow (Little) Thornbill *Acanthiza nana*

Crown brown, unmarked. Eye dark; *no* eyebrow. Streaked ear coverts. Dull olive-green upperparts. Underparts yellow. Tail brown; black sub-terminal band. **Size** 10 cm. **Voice** persistent 'tizz tizz'. **Habitat** dry forests; often in acacias.

577

RAOU Atlas 471

597 Striated Thornbill *Acanthiza lineata*

Brown crown, streaked white. Face, ear coverts, throat, breast light with dark striations. Eye grey-brown. Back olive-brown. Abdomen light-yellowish brown. **Size** 10 cm. **Voice** like Yellow Thornbill, but softer. **Habitat** dry forest.

Front view

RAOU Atlas 470

598 Southern Whiteface *Aphelocephala leucopsis*

Face white, bordered black on forehead. Eye white. Upperparts grey-brown. Underparts off-white, with buff flanks. Brown tail, tipped white. Race *castaneiventris,* (WA): Chestnut flanks. **Size** 10 cm. **Voice** tinkling, wistful. **Habitat** open arid country, especially near dead trees.

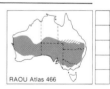

RAOU Atlas 466

599 Chestnut-breasted Whiteface
Aphelocephala pectoralis

Face white, bordered black before grey crown. Eye white. Back rusty-brown. Chestnut band across chest. Rufous flank marks. **Size** 10 cm. **Voice** plaintive bell-like tinkle. **Habitat** gibber plains, semi-desert.

RAOU Atlas 468

600 Banded Whiteface *Aphelocephala nigricincta*

White face, bordered black on forehead. Eye white. Chestnut-brown above. Narrow black breast band. Rufous flank marks. **Size** 10 cm. **Voice** musical, but weaker than Southern Whiteface. **Habitat** stony plains; sandhills with scattered plants.

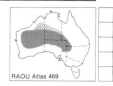

RAOU Atlas 469

596

597

594

594

595

595

593

593

593
Race *squamata*

598
Race *castaneiventris*

599

600

598

N. Day.

601 Varied Sittella *Daphoenositta chrysoptera*

Head white, grey, black or a mixture. Back whitish, grey or brown, streaked black in northern and eastern races. Wing black with broad white bar (northern races) or cinnamon bar (southern). Underparts white, streaked dark in eastern races. **Size** 10-11 cm. **Juv.** white marks on crown and back. Buff wing covert margins. **Voice** incessant 'chip'; upward inflected whistles. **Habitat** sclerophyll forests and woodlands. Very active; in groups up to 20.

Juv. ♂

Juv. ♀

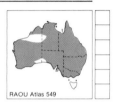

RAOU Atlas 549

602 White-throated Treecreeper *Cormobates leucophaea*

White throat, breast; striped flanks. **Female** orange spot on cheek. Race *minor:* Smaller, darker; mottled belly; grey breast. **Size** 13-15 cm. **Juv.** indistinct white streaks on scapulars; females have orange-chestnut rump. **Voice** repeated piping note; tremulous calls. **Habitat** rainforests (all races); sclerophyll forests and woodlands (*leucophaea* only).

Race *leucophaea* ♂

Race *minor* ♂

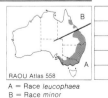

RAOU Atlas 558

A = Race *leucophaea*
B = Race *minor*

603 Red-browed Treecreeper *Climacteris erythrops*

Reddish face, eyebrow. Boldly striped belly. **Male** face brownish-orange. **Female** chestnut face and stripes on chest. **Size** 15 cm. **Juv.** grey face; buffish-grey underparts. **Voice** descending chatter, often answered with two sharp notes. **Habitat** eucalypt forests and sub-alpine woodlands.

RAOU Atlas 560

604 White-browed Treecreeper *Climacteris affinis*

White eyebrow. Bold black and white striped belly. **Female** chestnut line over brow and faint stripes on chest. **Size** 14 cm. **Juv.** brow indistinct. **Voice** weak, insect-like notes and song. **Habitat** acacia woodlands, belar, *Callitris*.

Juv.

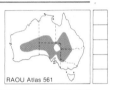

RAOU Atlas 561

605 Brown Treecreeper *Climacteris picumnus*

Broad pale-buff eyebrow, fine buff and black streaked belly. Upperparts brown (race *picumnus*) to almost black (*melanota*). **Male** black marks on chest. **Female** rufous marks on chest (often hidden). **Size** 16-18 cm. **Juv.** darker, more colourful. **Voice** staccato notes, harsh rattle; chuckling songs. **Habitat** open woodlands, forest clearings and edges; eucalypts along watercourses. Often on ground; bobs tail when resting.

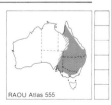

RAOU Atlas 555

606 Rufous Treecreeper *Climacteris rufa*

Cinnamon-rufous face, belly. **Male** black and white streaks on chest. **Female** rufous and white chest streaks. **Size** 15-17 cm. **Voice** like Brown Treecreeper but higher-pitched. **Habitat** eucalypt forests, woodlands. Habits similar to Brown.

♂

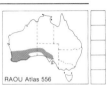

RAOU Atlas 556

607 Black-tailed Treecreeper *Climacteris melanura*

Brownish-black head, upperparts. No eyebrow. Dull rufous belly. **Male** white-streaked black throat. **Female** white throat; chestnut and white chest stripes. **Size** 17-19 cm. **Voice** piping notes like White-throated Treecreeper; song like Brown Treecreeper. **Habitat** similar to Brown. Habits similar to Brown.

♂

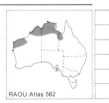

RAOU Atlas 562

601
Race *chrysoptera*

601 ♂
Race *striata*

601 ♀
Race *striata*

601
Race *pileata*

601 ♀
Race *pileata*

601 ♀
Race *leucoptera*

601 ♂

601
Race *chrysoptera*

607 ♀

601
Race *leucocephala*

603 ♂

603
Juv.

603 ♀

♀ 604

♂ 604

♂ 602

♀ 602
Juv.

♀ 605
Race *picumnus*

♂ 605
Race *picumnus*

♀ 606

608 Red Wattlebird *Anthochaera carunculata*

Grey-brown bird streaked with white. Crown almost black; silvery-white face. Dark pink pendulous wattle at ear. Dark red iris. Belly yellow. Legs pinkish. **Female** smaller. Western race *woodwardi* is more heavily streaked than eastern race *carunculata*. **Size** 31-39 cm. **Juv.** browner, especially on crown; smaller wattles. Iris red-brown. **Voice** raucous, harsh, 'tobacco box, tobacco box' and 'chokk'. **Habitat** forests, woodlands, suburbs.

Dorsal flight

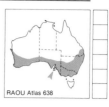
RAOU Atlas 638

609 Yellow Wattlebird *Anthochaera paradoxa*

Grey-brown bird streaked with white. Crown blackish, boldly streaked with white. Face, chin and eyebrow white. Long, pendulous, yellow-orange wattle at ear. Yellow patch on belly. **Female** smaller. **Size** 38-48 cm. **Juv.** paler; smaller wattles; less yellow on abdomen. **Voice** raucous croaks, 'kuk', 'kukuk'. **Habitat** restricted to Tas.; widespread in coastal heaths with emergent eucalypts, forests, suburban gardens.

Imm.

RAOU Atlas 639

610 Little Wattlebird *Anthochaera lunulata*

Dark olive-brown bird finely streaked and spotted with white. Silvery-white wash over face to cheek. Inconspicuous, minute, brown wattle at ear. Rufous wing patch conspicuous in flight. **Female** smaller. Three races: *lunulata* (SW Aust.) has more distinct white face and reddish-brown iris; *tasmanica* (Tas.) is larger and darker than *chrysoptera* (eastern mainland Aust.) which has a khaki iris. **Size** 26-33 cm. **Voice** harsh cackles, 'cockay cock', 'quok'. **Habitat** coastal woodlands, heaths and scrubs, especially in banksia; suburban gardens.

Races

chrysoptera

lunulatus

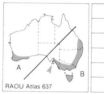
RAOU Atlas 637

A = *A. lunulata*
B = *A. chrysoptera*

611 Spiny-cheeked Honeyeater
Acanthagenys rufogularis

Bill pink with dark tip. Crown grey-brown, lightly scalloped with darker brown. Iris pale blue. White 'spiny' feathers from bill to cheek. Bare pink skin under eye and around gape. Throat and breast cinnamon. Back grey-brown, mottled darker brown. Conspicuous whitish rump. Abdomen creamy-white with brownish spots. Tail tipped white. **Female** smaller. **Size** 22-27 cm. **Juv.** duller; spiny cheek feathers yellow. **Voice** strong melodious warble, not unlike butcherbird; also short 'tock'. **Habitat** desert scrubs, mallee, woodlands, orchards.

Dorsal flight

RAOU Atlas 640

612 Striped Honeyeater *Plectorhyncha lanceolata*

Bill grey-blue. Head and nape streaked black and white. Throat white. Feathers on throat and upper breast are long and thin (lanceolate) with white centre. Back dark grey, mottled with black. Abdomen whitish or buff with scattered fine brown streaks. Legs grey-blue. **Size** 20-23 cm. **Juv.** not boldly streaked. **Voice** melodious 'cherr-cherr cherry-cherry'. **Habitat** woodlands, open forests, mainly inland, occasionally mangroves.

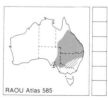
RAOU Atlas 585

Note: 610 Little Wattlebird may now be considered as two species
– 610 Little Wattlebird *Anthochaera lunulata* of SW of WA, and
Brush Wattlebird *Anthochaera chrysoptera* of SE Aust.

608

608
Juv.

609

610

611

612

613 Helmeted Friarbird *Philemon buceroides*

Races

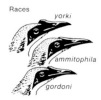

yorki
ammitophila
gordoni

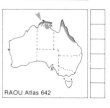

RAOU Atlas 642

Race *yorki:* Silver crown has a frilled whitish nape. Large, gently sloping knob (casque) at forehead. Facial skin bare, dark leaden-grey. Iris red-brown. Back, rump, tail dull grey-brown. Underparts paler, silvery-brown and lightly streaked. **Female** smaller. Race *gordoni* 'Melville Island Friarbird': Smaller; inhabits mangroves. Race *ammitophila* 'Sandstone Friarbird': Large; no knob; inhabits sandstone areas. **Size** 30-37 cm. **Juv.** throat, breast less streaked; smaller knob. **Voice** harsh, metallic whistles or cackles; 'poor devil, poor devil'; 'wach-a-wehre'; 'watch-out'; 'sergeant major'. **Habitat** forests, woodlands, mangroves. Pugnacious, noisy bird.

614 Silver-crowned Friarbird *Philemon argenticeps*

Head: dorsal view

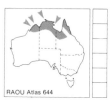

RAOU Atlas 644

Like Helmeted Friarbird but smaller. Forehead, crown, nape silvery-white. Bare facial skin dark leaden-grey. Small, erect knob at forehead is very conspicuous. Iris red-brown. Back, rump, tail dull grey-brown. Underparts paler, silvery-grey. **Female** smaller. **Size** 27-32 cm. **Juv.** duller, smaller knob. **Voice** like Helmeted but softer; also 'more tobacco, uh-more tobacco-uh'. **Habitat** open forests, woodlands, mangroves.

615 Noisy Friarbird *Philemon corniculatus*

Calling

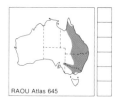

RAOU Atlas 645

Head with bare black skin; buffy eyebrow and silvery chin feathers. Small erect, conspicuous knob on bill at forehead. Long silvery feathers with dark shafts on throat, breast, slightly hackled or tufted. Back, rump, tail dull grey. Underparts pale grey. **Female** smaller. **Size** 31-36 cm. **Juv.** neck, back of head feathered. Small knob. Throat, breast *lack* lanceolated feathers. **Voice** loud, raucous 'four-o-clock', 'chokk chokk'; other squawks. **Habitat** open forests, woodlands.

616 Little Friarbird *Philemon citreogularis*

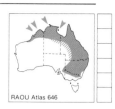

RAOU Atlas 646

Head grey-brown. Darker feathers above and below the bare, bluish-black facial skin. *No* knob on bill. Whitish nape. Fine silky-white feathers on chin. Silvery-white streaks on breast. Back dark grey-brown. Underparts pale grey. **Female** smaller. **Size** 25-29 cm. **Juv.** paler; facial skin lighter; yellowish wash over chin, throat. Yellow spots on side of breast. **Voice** raucous; 'arr-koo', 'rockety krook-shank'. **Habitat** open forests, woodlands.

617 Regent Honeyeater *Xanthomyza phrygia*

Dorsal pattern

RAOU Atlas 603

Bill black. Head, neck black; bare facial skin yellow and warty. Back, breast pale lemon, scaled black. Wings mainly black, with conspicuous yellow patches. Abdomen mainly pale lemon, black margins. Yellow outer-web to black tail feathers. **Size** 20-23 cm. **Juv.** duller; browner; yellow bill. **Voice** bell-like 'tinck tinck-tinck'. **Habitat** open forests, woodlands.

615

613

615
Juv.

614

613
Juv.

617

616

616
Juv.

N. Day.

618 Blue-faced Honeyeater *Entomyzon cyanotis*

Head black. Large patch of light blue bare skin around eye. White line on nape. Chin and throat dark grey. Back olive-yellow; underparts white. Three races: *harteri* smaller with larger face patch than *cyanotis; albipennis* white in wing and with discontinuous line on nape. **Size** 25-32 cm. **Juv.** dark brown on head. Facial skin yellow or green. **Voice** loud 'ki-owt'. **Habitat** open forests.

Race *albipennis*

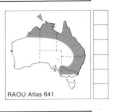

RAOU Atlas 641

619 Bell Miner *Manorina melanophrys*

Head and back olive-green. Bill orange. Forehead and edge of throat black; lores bright yellow; bare skin behind eye bright orange. Legs orange. Underparts olive-green. **Female** smaller. **Size** 17-20 cm. **Juv.** skin around eye paler. **Voice** bell-like 'tink-tink'. **Habitat** forests, woodlands. Colonial species.

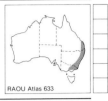

RAOU Atlas 633

620 Noisy Miner *Manorina melanocephala*

Crown, most of face and ear black; rest of head grey. Bare skin behind eye yellow. Bill yellow. Back and rump grey. Underparts pale grey with darker scallops on breast. **Female** smaller. **Size** 24-28 cm. **Juv.** similar. **Voice** harsh calls and piping 'pwee-pwee-pwee'. **Habitat** woodlands, suburbs. Colonial species.

Flight

RAOU Atlas 634

621 Yellow-throated Miner *Manorina flavigula*

Two yellow streaks of bare skin from bill. Like Noisy Miner but rump white, crown grey, forehead and side of neck washed with yellow. **Female** smaller. Several races: *obscura* (SW Aust.) duskier; *lutea* (NW Aust.) smaller and whiter than *flavigula* (central Aust.). **Size** 23-28 cm. **Voice** similar to Noisy Miner. **Habitat** dry woodlands, especially mallee. Usually in flocks.

Flight

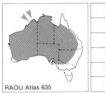

RAOU Atlas 635

622 Black-eared Miner *Manorina melanotis*

Like Yellow-throated Miner but darker-bodied; black ear patch and less yellow on forehead and neck; rump, back grey. **Female** smaller. **Size** 24-27cm. **Voice** similar to Noisy Miner. **Habitat** Mallee.

Flight

RAOU Atlas 967

623 Macleay's Honeyeater *Xanthotis macleayana*

Head and neck brown-black; nape speckled white. Naked skin below eye yellowish. Yellow-orange ear tufts. Back brown, heavily mottled buff-yellow and white. Chin grey. Breast darker, streaked olive-brown and white. **Size** 18-21 cm. **Juv.** duller. **Voice** musical 'to wit, too weeee twit'. **Habitat** rainforests, mangroves, gardens.

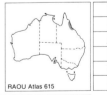

RAOU Atlas 615

624 Tawny-breasted Honeyeater *Xanthotis flaviventer*

Upperparts olive-brown with nape faintly speckled grey. White streak under eye from gape to nape. Small yellow ear tuft. Throat, sides of neck and ear coverts grey. Breast tawny-brown, faintly streaked. **Size** 18-22 cm. **Juv.** similar. **Voice** noisy whistles. **Habitat** mangroves, rainforests, forests.

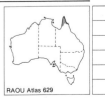

RAOU Atlas 629

Note: 622 Black-eared Miner is now considered a race of 621 Yellow-throated Miner *Manorina flavigula.*

618

618
Juv.

619

623

624

620

622

621

N. Day

625 Lewin's Honeyeater *Meliphaga lewinii*

Dark olive-green, slightly streaked. Darker head, squarish yellow ear tufts. Eye blue. Cream gape extends under eye. **Size** 18-22 cm. **Juv.** less streaked. Base of bill yellow. **Voice** loud staccato chatter. **Habitat** wet forests.

Bill: from above
Bill: from side

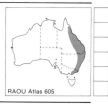

RAOU Atlas 605

626 Yellow-spotted Honeyeater *Meliphaga notata*

Like Lewin's Honeyeater but paler, with yellow gape and rounder ear patch. Eye brown. **Size** 16-19 cm. **Voice** piercing 'ee yeu', 'tchu-chua'. **Habitat** wet forests.

Bill: from above
Bill: from side

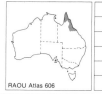

RAOU Atlas 606

627 Graceful Honeyeater *Meliphaga gracilis*

Like Yellow-spotted Honeyeater but smaller, with a longer, thinner bill. Eye brown. **Size** 14-17 cm. **Voice** 'plik'. **Habitat** wet forests.

Bill: from above
Bill: from side

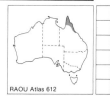

RAOU Atlas 612

628 White-lined Honeyeater *Meliphaga albilineata*

Grey-brown. Whitish line from gape passing under eye to small whitish ear tuft. **Female** smaller. **Size** 17-20 cm. **Voice** loud 'tu-wheer, tuwhit'. **Habitat** wooded gorges.

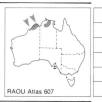

RAOU Atlas 607

629 Eungella Honeyeater *Lichenostomus hindwoodi*

Smaller than Bridled Honeyeater. Short black bill. Stripe below eye whitish. Greyer with white streaks on breast; lacks patch on side of neck. **Size** 16-18 cm. **Voice** laughing whistle; a recorded call is 'pee pee pip-pip-pip-pip-pip-pip', slower at end. **Habitat** Eungella rainforests, Qld. A recently described species.

Facial pattern

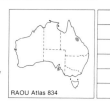

RAOU Atlas 834

630 Yellow-faced Honeyeater *Lichenostomus chrysops*

Grey-brown. Broad yellow stripe under eye which is bordered by black. **Size** 15-18 cm. **Voice** 'chick-up'. **Habitat** forests.

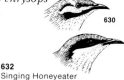

630
632
Singing Honeyeater

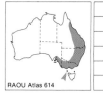

RAOU Atlas 614

631 Bridled Honeyeater *Lichenostomus frenatus*

Dark brown with blackish head. Iris blue. Yellowish streak from gape to nape. Bill black with yellow base. Small whitish area behind eye; thin yellow ear tuft. Silver-buff patch on side of neck. **Size** 18-22 cm. **Juv.** similar. **Voice** loud 'we-arr', 'wachita'. **Habitat** rainforests.

631
630

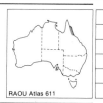

RAOU Atlas 611

627

628

626

629

625

631

630

632 Singing Honeyeater *Lichenostomus virescens*

Grey-brown. Broad black band from bill through eye on to neck. Yellow streak below eye. Ear tuft yellow, tipped white. Breast pale grey, streaked dark grey. **Size** 17-22 cm. **Habitat** arid and coastal shrublands, woodlands, suburbs (WA).

Feeding on fruit

RAOU Atlas 608

633 Varied Honeyeater *Lichenostomus versicolor*

Like Singing Honeyeater but yellower. Underparts yellow, streaked brown. **Size** 18-21 cm. **Habitat** mangroves.

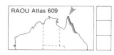

RAOU Atlas 609

634 Mangrove Honeyeater *Lichenostomus fasciogularis*

Like Singing Honeyeater, but darker, especially on breast. Throat yellowish, scalloped brown. Hybridisation occurs between Varied and Mangrove Honeyeaters. **Size** 18-21 cm. **Habitat** mangroves.

RAOU Atlas 610

635 White-gaped Honeyeater *Lichenostomus unicolor*

Dark olive-grey upperparts; greenish wash on wings. Conspicuous white gape. Underparts mid-grey. **Size** 18-22 cm. **Juv.** similar, yellow gape. **Voice** variable loud 'whit-o-weee'. **Habitat** mangroves, riverine forests.

RAOU Atlas 628

636 Yellow Honeyeater *Lichenostomus flavus*

Bright yellow-green. Thin dark line through eye. **Size** 16-19 cm. **Juv.** duller. **Voice** varied loud whistles 'wheee-a'. **Habitat** coastal and riverine forests, mangroves, gardens.

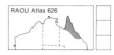

RAOU Atlas 626

637 White-eared Honeyeater *Lichenostomus leucotis*

Crown grey with fine black striations. Face, chin, throat black. Conspicuous white ear patch. Olive-green back and tail. Yellowish green abdomen. **Female** smaller. Two races: *leucotis* (E Aust.) is larger and brighter than *novaenorciae* (WA). **Size** 18-22 cm. **Juv.** duller with olive-green crown; cream ear patch. **Voice** loud 'chock up, chock up' and other softer calls. **Habitat** forests, woodlands, mallee.

Adult ♂

Juv.

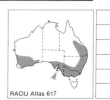

RAOU Atlas 617

638 Yellow-throated Honeyeater *Lichenostomus flavicollis*

Dark grey crown, face, upper breast. Bright yellow chin and throat. Small silvery-grey ear patch, tipped yellowish. Back olive-green. Abdomen grey-yellow. **Female** smaller. **Size** 18-22 cm. **Juv.** paler, particularly on throat. **Voice** loud 'tonk, tonk' often repeated; also 'pick-em-up'. **Habitat** most habitats on Tas. and Bass Strait islands.

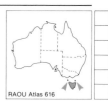

RAOU Atlas 616

639 Yellow-tufted Honeyeater *Lichenostomus melanops*

Forehead, crown, chin, throat yellow. Centre of throat blackish, streaked yellow. Forehead feathers tufted. Black feathers from bill through eye expanding on ear coverts; bright golden ear tuft. Back olive-green; abdomen olive-yellow. **Female** smaller. Four races in SE Aust. that vary in size and darkness of plumage, including *cassidix* ('Helmeted Honeyeater'). **Size** 17-23 cm. **Juv.** similar; duller. **Habitat** eucalypt forests and woodlands with shrub layer, particularly along watercourses.

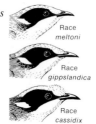

Race *meltoni*

Race *gippslandica*

Race *cassidix*

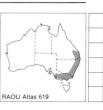

RAOU Atlas 619

Note: 634 Mangrove Honeyeater is now considered a race of 633 Varied Honeyeater *Lichenostomus versicolor*.

634

633

632

636

635

638

637

639
Race *cassidix*

. 639

N. Day.

640 Purple-gaped Honeyeater *Lichenostomus cratitius*

Head grey. Blackish mask through eye. Grey ear coverts; small yellow ear tuft. Line of purple skin from gape to cheek. Side of throat yellow. Back olive-green; abdomen yellow-grey. **Size** 16-20 cm. **Juv.** duller with yellow gape. **Voice** harsh chattering. **Habitat** mallee, woodlands.

640

632
Singing Honeyeater

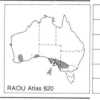

RAOU Atlas 620

641 Grey-headed Honeyeater *Lichenostomus keartlandi*

Pale grey head. Blackish face; dark grey ear coverts. Crescent-shaped yellow ear tuft. Breast pale yellow, faintly streaked darker. Buff-olive back. **Size** 15-17 cm. **Juv.** duller. **Voice** loud 'chee toyt' repeated. **Habitat** mulga, woodlands, rocky hillsides and gorges.

RAOU Atlas 621

642 Yellow-plumed Honeyeater *Lichenostomus ornatus*

Bill black. Greenish-olive crown; darker face. Faint yellow line under eye. Ear coverts tipped dark brown. Yellow neck plume. Olive-brown back. Underparts fawn, heavily streaked olive-brown. **Female** smaller. **Size** 15-18 cm. **Juv.** duller; base of bill and gape orange-yellow. **Voice** loud 'chick-owee', 'chikwididee'. **Habitat** mallee, semi-arid eucalypt woodlands.

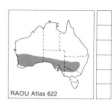

RAOU Atlas 622

643 Grey-fronted Honeyeater *Lichenostomus plumulus*

Bill black. Head yellowish; face darker. Fine black line from bill to below ear. Thin black plume in front of large yellow neck plume. Back olive-green. Underparts buffish-grey, lightly streaked dark brown. **Size** 15-17 cm. **Juv.** base of bill and gape yellowish. **Habitat** open woodlands, mulga, mallee.

Juv.

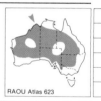

RAOU Atlas 623

644 Fuscous Honeyeater *Lichenostomus fuscus*

Bill black. Dull olive-brown, paler below. Face darker. Dusky ear coverts, tipped yellow. Gape, base of bill and eye-ring yellow or black (breeding). **Size** 14-17 cm. **Juv.** similar; bill brownish. **Voice** loud 'arig rig-a-taw-taw'. **Habitat** open forests and woodlands.

Breeding

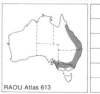

RAOU Atlas 613

645 Yellow-tinted Honeyeater *Lichenostomus flavescens*

Bill black. Forehead and face yellow. Black, crescent-shaped mark at ear. Thin, bright yellow (but inconspicuous) plume. Olive-buff back. Underparts yellow, faintly streaked. **Size** 14-17 cm. **Juv.** similar; brownish bill. **Voice** 'chee-uck-ooo-wee'; 'porra-chu-porra-cheu-cheu-cheu'. **Habitat** woodlands.

Juv.

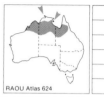

RAOU Atlas 624

646 White-plumed Honeyeater *Lichenostomus penicillatus*

Bill black. Olive-grey bird with yellower head. Faint black line before white neck plume. **Female** smaller. Several races: *carteri* (WA) is yellower and *penicillatus* (southern Aust.) is greener than *leilavalensis* (central Aust.). **Size** 15-19 cm. **Juv.** similar; base of bill orange. **Voice** 'chick-owee'; 'chick-abiddy'. **Habitat** open forests, woodlands, particularly *Eucalyptus camaldulensis* along watercourses.

Display flight

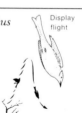

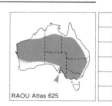

RAOU Atlas 625

Note: 644 Fuscous Honeyeater now considered a race of 645 Yellow-tinted Honeyeater *Lichenostomus flavescens.*

640

641

645

643

644
Non-breeding

642 Juv.

642

646

646
Juv.

647 Black-chinned Honeyeater *Melithreptus gularis*

Race *gularis* (S & E Aust.): Bill black. Head black; white line across nape. Eye-skin pale blue. Centre of chin and throat black; sides of throat whitish. Back olive-grey. Underparts pale grey. Race *laetior* (N & W Aust.): Golden back; green-yellow eye-skin; buffish underparts. **Size** 15-17 cm. **Juv.** similar; crown brown; eye-skin, bill yellow-orange. **Voice** loud churring. **Habitat** woodlands.

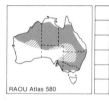

RAOU Atlas 580

648 Strong-billed Honeyeater *Melithreptus validirostris*

Like Black-chinned Honeyeater but back olive-brown; abdomen grey. Two races: *kingi* (King Is.) underparts darker than *validirostris*. **Female** smaller. **Size** 15-17 cm. **Juv.** crown dark brown; eye-skin, base of bill orange. **Voice** loud 'cheep'. **Habitat** forests on Tas. and Bass Strait islands.

Juv.

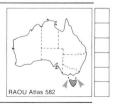

RAOU Atlas 582

649 Brown-headed Honeyeater *Melithreptus brevirostris*

Upperparts olive-brown. Head grey-brown with pale buffish line across nape. Eye-skin dull yellow-orange. Underparts pale grey-buff. Several races: *brevirostris* (E Aust.), *augustus* (SA), and *leucogenus* (W Aust.) with progressively darker heads; *magnirostris* (Kangaroo Is.) has larger bill. **Size** 13-15 cm. **Juv.** similar; eye-skin bluish; gape yellow-orange. **Voice** 'chick'; 'breeet, breeet'. **Habitat** woodlands, mallee.

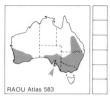

RAOU Atlas 583

650 White-throated Honeyeater *Melithreptus albogularis*

Bill black. Head black, but only above upper bill. Chin white. White line across nape extends to eye. Eye-skin bluish-white. Black shoulder crescent. Back olive-yellow; underparts white. **Size** 13-15 cm. **Juv.** similar; brownish head; gape and bill yellow-orange. **Voice** 'tserp-tserp'; 'pi-pi-pi...'. **Habitat** woodlands.

Head pattern

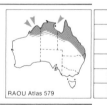

RAOU Atlas 579

651 White-naped Honeyeater *Melithreptus lunatus*

Like White-throated Honeyeater but black on face continues below bill and just on to chin; white nape-line does *not* reach eye. Eye-skin red (race *lunatus*, E Aust.), or whitish (race *chloropsis*, W. Aust.). **Female** smaller. **Size** 13-15 cm. **Juv.** crown brown; base of bill orange. **Voice** 'mjerp, mjerp'. **Habitat** forests.

Head pattern

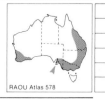

RAOU Atlas 578

652 Black-headed Honeyeater *Melithreptus affinis*

Like White-throated Honeyeater, but chin, throat entirely black; *no* white on nape. **Size** 13-15 cm **Juv.** head dark brown; bill brown. **Voice** sharp whistle. **Habitat** forests, gardens of Tas. and Bass Strait islands.

Juv

RAOU Atlas 584

653 Green-backed Honeyeater *Glycichaera fallax*

Bill dark grey. Upperparts dull greenish-grey. Faint, narrow eye-ring of whitish feathers. Throat whitish; breast, abdomen yellowish. **Size** 11-12 cm. **Juv.** unknown. **Habitat** rainforests of northern C. York Pen. Identify from *Gerygone* species.

RAOU Atlas 604

647
Juv.

647
Race *laetior*

647

648

649

649
Juv.

651

651
Race *chloropsis*

651

651
Juv.

650
Juv.

650

653

652

654 Brown Honeyeater *Lichmera indistincta*

Dull olive-brown with darker face. Wedge of yellow or white behind eye. Western race *indistincta* larger than eastern race *osculans*. **Size** 12-16 cm. **Juv.** yellower; face paler. **Voice** loud penetrating call. **Habitat** mangroves, forests, suburbs, heaths with emergent trees.

Breeding

RAOU Atlas 597

655 White-streaked Honeyeater *Trichodere cockerelli*

Head and back dark brown; yellow ear spot. White specks on shoulder. Golden wash over wings and tail. Underparts grey; breast lightly streaked. **Size** 15-19 cm. **Juv.** duller with yellow chin. **Voice** like Brown. **Habitat** swamps, woodlands.

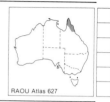

RAOU Atlas 627

656 Tawny-crowned Honeyeater *Phylidonyris melanops*

Crown tawny. Eyebrow and chin white. Dark grey-brown face, ear coverts, and crescent on shoulder. Back grey-brown with darker streaks. Underparts dull white; brown specks on flank. Cinnamon underwing. **Female** smaller. **Size** 15-18 cm. **Juv.** crown grey-brown; streaked; chin pale yellow. **Voice** musical, flute-like. **Habitat** heaths.

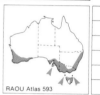

RAOU Atlas 593

657 Crescent Honeyeater *Phylidonyris pyrrhoptera*

Male dark grey with yellow patch in wing. Red-brown eye. Underside paler; broad dark crescent across shoulder and side of breast with whitish line immediately under it. **Female** similar but dull olive-brown; smaller. **Size** 14-17 cm. **Juv.** like adult. **Voice** loud 'egypt' and melodic song. **Habitat** coastal heaths to forests.

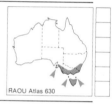

RAOU Atlas 630

658 New Holland Honeyeater *Phylidonyris novaehollandiae*

Streaked black and white with yellow wing patch. White iris. Eyebrow commences at eye; small white ear patch; white 'beard'. White tip to tail. Race *longirostris* (SW Aust.) has longer bill than *novaehollandiae* (SE Aust.). **Female** smaller. **Size** 16-19 cm. **Juv.** yellowish instead of white; rump brown. Iris dark; gape yellow. Yellow edge to alula. **Imm.** eye grey; browner body. **Habitat** coastal heaths to woodlands.

Juv.

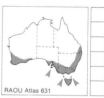

RAOU Atlas 631

659 White-cheeked Honeyeater *Phylidonyris nigra*

Like New Holland but iris is dark brown; eyebrow commences at bill. *No* 'beard' but large white cheek patch. *No* white tip to tail. Western race *gouldii* has longer bill than eastern race *nigra*. **Female** smaller. **Size** 16-19 cm. **Juv.** duller with yellow gape. **Imm.** like adult. **Habitat** coastal heaths to woodlands.

Juv.

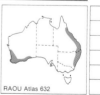

RAOU Atlas 632

660 White-fronted Honeyeater *Phylidonyris albifrons*

Forehead (except centre), lores, eye-ring and moustache white; grey cheek patch. Red spot behind eye. Throat black with specks of white. Back brownish-black; abdomen white. **Female** smaller. **Size** 16-18 cm. **Juv.** browner on head, back and throat. **Voice** melodic eerie song. **Habitat** arid shrublands to woodlands.

Juv.

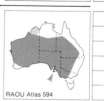

RAOU Atlas 594

655

657 ♂

657 ♀

659

658

660

656

656
Juv.

654

N. Day.

661 Painted Honeyeater *Grantiella picta*

Male pink bill. Black head and back. Yellow wash over wings and tail. Underparts white; black streaks on flank. **Females/Juv.** browner; *no* streaks on flank. **Size** 15-17 cm. **Habitat** open forests, woodlands, particularly where trees are infested with mistletoe.

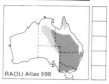

RAOU Atlas 598

662 Brown-backed Honeyeater *Ramsayornis modestus*

Thin whitish line under eye. Drab brown above; dull white below. Breast scalloped pale brown. **Size** 11-12 cm. **Juv.** similar; breast streaked. **Voice** chattering song. **Habitat** near swamps, mangroves.

RAOU Atlas 595

663 Bar-breasted Honeyeater *Ramsayornis fasciatus*

Crown dark brown, scalloped white. Face, chin white. Black line on jaw. Back drab brown with whitish streaks. Breast whitish with bold black bars. **Size** 12-15 cm. **Juv.** streaked breast. **Voice** chattering song. **Habitat** melaleuca swamps, woodlands.

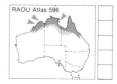

RAOU Atlas 596

664 Rufous-banded Honeyeater *Conopophila albogularis*

Head grey. Chin, throat white. Back brown, lemon-yellow wing patch. Broad rufous breast band. Flanks grey-brown; abdomen white. **Size** 11-13 cm. **Juv.** lacks breast band. **Voice** musical twitter. **Habitat** near swamps, mangroves.

RAOU Atlas 600

665 Rufous-throated Honeyeater *Conopophila rufogularis*

Head, back grey-brown. Chin, throat rufous. Lemon-yellow wing patch. Underparts pale grey-buff. **Size** 11-15 cm. **Juv.** browner; white throat. **Voice** rasping chatter. **Habitat** riverine forests, woodlands.

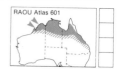

RAOU Atlas 601

666 Grey Honeyeater *Conopophila whitei*

Dull grey-brown above; yellowish-green wash over wings. Underparts dull white; darker throat, breast. **Size** 10-12 cm. **Juv.** similar; pale eye-ring. **Habitat** arid scrub.

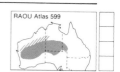

RAOU Atlas 599

667 Eastern Spinebill *Acanthorhynchus tenuirostris*

Male long thin bill. Head glossy black. Red eye. Chin, throat white with rufous centre. Black crescent over shoulder. Back grey-brown; rufous nape. Outer tail tipped white. Underparts cinnamon-brown. **Female** smaller, duller; crown olive-grey. Several colour shades differ in size and colour shades. **Size** 13-16 cm. **Juv.** chin, throat cinnamon. Base of bill orange. Iris brown-red. **Voice** rapid piping. **Habitat** heaths, forests with heath.

Tail pattern

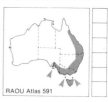

RAOU Atlas 591

668 Western Spinebill *Acanthorhynchus superciliosus*

Dark olive-grey above. Broad chestnut collar over nape extending to chestnut throat and breast. White, then black bands across breast. Abdomen buff. **Female** smaller, duller; lacks breast bands; no chestnut on throat. **Size** 13-16 cm. **Juv.** like female; yellowish base to bill. **Voice** shrill 'kleet-kleet'. **Habitat** heaths, woodlands.

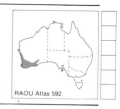

RAOU Atlas 592

♂ 661

663

662

666

665

664

667 ♂

667
Juv.

668 ♂

♀ 668

669 Banded Honeyeater *Certhionyx pectoralis*

Speckles on back
Imm.

Bill black. Face (including eye), crown and back black; nape freckled grey. Lower back grey; rump white. Underparts white. Black band across breast. **Size** 11-14 cm. **Juv.** a yellow patch behind eye. Crown, underparts creamy-white with dusky breast band. **Voice** tinkling twitter. **Habitat** forests, woodlands.

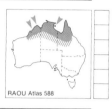

RAOU Atlas 588

670 Black Honeyeater *Certhionyx niger*

Ventral view

Male long, decurved black bill. Head, throat, back, wings, tail, and stripe down centre of belly are all sooty-black; rest white. Legs black. **Female** breast grey-brown speckled; whitish abdomen. Faint, pale buff stripe above eye. **Size** 10-12 cm. **Juv.** like female. **Voice** feeble 'peeee'. **Habitat** arid shrublands.

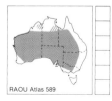

RAOU Atlas 589

671 Pied Honeyeater *Certhionyx variegatus*

Male black head and throat. Small blue wattle below eye. Bill grey-blue. Breast, rump, abdomen white. Broad white streak on black wings. Tail white except for two black central feathers and broad black tip. **Female** mottled grey-brown above; throat, breast slightly streaked grey-brown. Mottled wing-stripe. Abdomen whitish. **Size** 15-18 cm. **Voice** 'tee-titee-tee-tee'. **Habitat** arid savannah.

Display flight

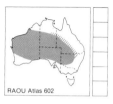

RAOU Atlas 602

672 Dusky Honeyeater *Myzomela obscura*

Uniform dark grey-brown, slightly darker on head; paler on belly. No distinctive markings. Bill black. **Female** smaller. **Size** 12-14 cm. **Juv.** similar; duller with orange-grey lower bill. **Voice** 'chirp chirp chirp'; trills and 'tip-tip-eeee-chip'. **Habitat** rainforests, mangroves, woodlands, near swamps.

Juv.

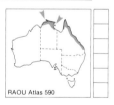

RAOU Atlas 590

673 Red-headed Honeyeater *Myzomela erythrocephala*

Male head, neck, chin, throat and rump scarlet. Lores black. Back, wings, lower breast sooty-brown; abdomen grey-brown. **Female** forehead, throat tinged crimson; crown, back, wings and rump brown. Throat, breast smoky-grey. Abdomen whitish. **Size** 11-13 cm. **Juv.** like female. **Voice** harsh whistles. **Habitat** in and near mangroves.

Ventral view

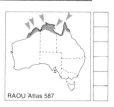

RAOU Atlas 587

674 Scarlet Honeyeater *Myzomela sanguinolenta*

Male like male Red-headed Honeyeater but scarlet on breast, head and rump. Wings black with white edges to feathers. Back black and scarlet. Abdomen light creamy-grey. **Female** very like female Red-headed but more olive-brown. **Size** 10-11 cm. **Juv.** like female. **Voice** tinkling bell-like 'clink-clink-clink'. **Habitat** mangroves, coastal forests and woodlands.

Singing

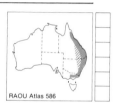

RAOU Atlas 586

242

672

669
Juv.

673 ♂

669

♀ 673

671 ♂

674 ♂

♀ 674

♀ 671

670 ♂

670 ♀

675 Crimson Chat *Ephthianura tricolor*

Male brilliant crimson forehead, crown, breast, flanks, rump. White throat, centre belly, undertail coverts. Eyes creamy-white. Nape, ear coverts, lores blackish-brown. Back dark brown. Note: *all* chats have black or dark bills and legs; short blackish-brown tails, tipped white. **Female** upperparts, head light brown. Throat, belly white. pale red and buff patches on breast, flanks, rump. **Size** 10-12 cm. **Juv.** like female; *lacks* red on breast. **Voice** high 'see-ee-ee'; melodious whistle; short harsh metallic notes. **Habitat** salty areas of inland plains, rocky hills, mallee heath. Flocks of mixed chat species may occur.

Flock in flight

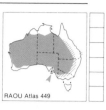

RAOU Atlas 449

676 Orange Chat *Ephthianura aurifrons*

Male head, rump, underparts pale orange-yellow, becoming luminous orange on forehead, breast. Eyes reddish-brown. Throat, lores black. Back fawny-yellow, mottled darker. **Female/Juv.** grey to yellowish-brown above. Whitish eyebrow. Rump yellowish. Pale yellow below; breast washed grey-brown; belly washed lemon. **Size** 10-12 cm. **Voice** metallic 'tang'; 'cheep-cheep' in flight. **Habitat** low shrubs in salty areas, gibber plains where shrubs; coastal swamps in WA.

♂ at nest

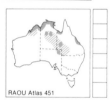

RAOU Atlas 450

677 Yellow Chat *Ephthianura crocea*

Male forehead, face, rump, underparts bright yellow. Narrow blackish breast band. Eyes creamy. Thin dark eye line to bill. Crown, back grey-brown, washed yellow. **Female** paler, *lacks* breast band. **Size** 10.5-12 cm. **Juv.** like female; greyer. **Voice** metallic 'tang'; cricket-like note; musical 'pee-eeep'. **Habitat** coastal and inland swamps, including vegetated bore-drains. Also shrubby saltbush flats. A little-known species.

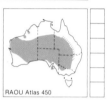

RAOU Atlas 451

678 White-fronted Chat *Ephthianura albifrons*

Male white forehead, face, throat and belly. Black band from back of crown and nape across breast. Eyes pinky-white. Bill black. Back grey. Legs black. **Female** upperparts, including forehead, grey-brown. Pale eyebrow. Underparts white or pale grey; narrow blackish-brown breast band. **Size** 11-12.5 cm. **Juv.** like very pale female; breast band absent or indistinct. **Voice** repeated, soft, finch-like 'tang'. **Habitat** low vegetation in salty coastal and inland areas; crops. High, jerky flight; perches prominently.

Juv.

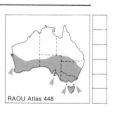

RAOU Atlas 448

679 Gibberbird *Ashbyia lovensis*

Male crown grey-fawn. Yellow eyebrow, lores, face, underparts. Eyes white to yellow. Back, rump grey-brown to buffy-brown. Yellow breast, flanks, washed grey-brown. **Female** browner above; paler below; breast band buffy-brown. **Size** 12-13 cm. **Juv.** bill horn; like female, but brown. **Voice** 'wheet-wheet-wheet' in flight; musical chatter; alarm of 5-6 piercing notes. **Habitat** stony, open inland plains. Upright posture. Resembles chats but 'pipit-like'. Stands on rocks; runs; wags tail like Richard's Pipit.

Tail wag

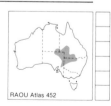

RAOU Atlas 452

677 ♀

677 ♂

676 ♀

676 ♂

679 ♂

675 ♀

♀ 678

678
JUV

675 ♂

♂ 678

Nicolas Day.

680 Yellow-bellied Sunbird *Nectarinia jugularis*

Long, slender, curved black bill. **Male** olive-yellow above; deep yellow below. Chin to upper breast dark metallic purplish-blue. Tail tipped white. **Female** *no* metallic blue bib. **Size** 10-12 cm. **Voice** high-pitched 'dzit-dzit'; hissing whistle; trill. **Habitat** rainforest edges, mangroves, gardens. Also called Olive-backed Sunbird.

Nest

RAOU Atlas 572

681 Mistletoebird *Dicaeum hirundinaceum*

Male head, upperparts glossy blue-black. Throat, breast, undertail coverts scarlet. Bill dark, short. Underparts grey-white; dark central streak on throat, breast. **Female** brownish-grey above; undertail coverts pale scarlet. **Size** 10-11 cm. **Imm.** as female; bill pink. **Voice** high-pitched double note; also warble. **Habitat** varied, wherever mistletoe grows.

Incubating

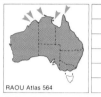

RAOU Atlas 564

682 Spotted Pardalote *Pardalotus punctatus*

Bright crown. Wings, tail black, spotted white. Eyebrow white. Rump chestnut. **Male** throat, undertail coverts bright yellow; back fawn with buff spots; pale underside. **Female** throat cream; crown spots yellow. **Size** 8-9.5 cm. **Imm.** like female; crown paler; unspotted. **Voice** loud or soft double notes. **Habitat** eucalypt forests.

Flight

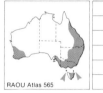

RAOU Atlas 565

683 Yellow-rumped Pardalote
Pardalotus xanthopygus

Like Spotted Pardalote. Rump bright yellow. Back greyer, spotted light grey. **Size** 9-10 cm. **Voice** same as Spotted. **Habitat** dry eucalypt woodlands, especially mallee.

Flight

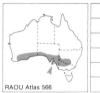

RAOU Atlas 566

684 Forty-spotted Pardalote *Pardalotus quadragintus*

Ear coverts lemon-yellow. Body dull olive-green; pale below. Small white spots on dark wings. Tail dark with white spots. **Size** 9-20 cm. **Voice** soft double note; also repeated single note (hollow and faint). **Habitat** Tas. coastal forest.

RAOU Atlas 571

685 Red-browed Pardalote *Pardalotus rubricatus*

Body pale fawn-grey. Dark crown spotted white. Eyebrow spot orange to red. Orange-buff wing patch. Some yellow on breast. **Size** 10-12 cm. **Voice** five notes, increasing in pitch and speed. **Habitat** inland woodlands.

Red on brow often absent

RAOU Atlas 570

686 Striated Pardalote *Pardalotus striatus*

Differs across Aust. in number of primaries edged white, in crown streaking, wing spot and rump colour.
Male slightly brighter; mostly grey. Yellow throat, eyebrow. Crown black, usually streaked white. White edging, and red or yellow spot on dark wings. Back brown; rump paler. Tail black, tipped white. Underparts pale; flanks yellow. **Size** 9-11.5 cm. **Imm.** dull; *no* crown streaks. **Voice** loud double or triple notes. **Habitat** eucalypt forests, woodlands.

Pardalotes are acrobatic foragers

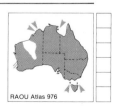

RAOU Atlas 976

Note: 683 Yellow-rumped Pardalote now considered a race of 682 Spotted-Pardalote *Pardalotus punctatus*.

♂ 680

681
Imm.

680 ♀

♀ 681

♂ 681

682 ♀

684

682
Juv.

685
Juv.

682

685

♂ 682

♂ 683

686
Race *melanocephalus*

♀ 683

686
Race *ornatus*

686
Juv.

686
Race *striatus*

686
Race *substriatus*

N. Day.

687 Pale White-eye *Zosterops citrinella*

Conspicuous white eye-ring. Eye brown. Bill dark brown. Olive-yellow above; darker on wings. Throat lemon-yellow. Breast, abdomen off-white. Undertail coverts lemon-yellow. Legs brown. Aust. race is *albiventris*. **Size** 12 cm. **Voice** not recorded. **Habitat** woodlands and forests on islands off NE Qld.

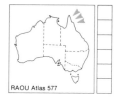

RAOU Atlas 577

688 Yellow White-eye *Zosterops lutea*

Three races recognised. Race *lutea* (east of Wyndham, WA): Conspicuous white eye-ring. Olive-yellow above. Forehead and underparts lemon-yellow. Bill dark brown. Eye brown. Legs brown. Race *balstoni* (west of Wyndham, WA): Colours duller, upperparts slightly greyer. Race *hecla* (intermediate zone). **Size** 10.5 cm. **Voice** rapid, loud warbling song. **Habitat** coastal mangroves and adjacent thickets.

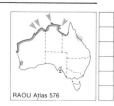

RAOU Atlas 576

689 Silvereye *Zosterops lateralis*

Bill black. Flanks of males darker than in females; all with conspicuous white eye-ring. Seven races in Aust. Race *gouldii* (SW of WA): Whole of upperparts olive-green. Throat greenish-yellow; breast, abdomen pale grey. Flanks pale buff. Undertail coverts yellow. Six races (S to E Aust.) are all grey-backed. Race *halmaturina* (SA and W Vic.): Basically like *lateralis*, but with buff flanks and variable throat colouration from wholly yellow to almost totally lacking yellow. Race *lateralis* (Tas.; large numbers cross Bass Strait to spend winter in SE Aust.): Rufous flanks. Throat grey or white, sometimes yellow near chin. Undertail coverts whitish. Race *familiaris* (E Aust. to Rockhampton, Qld): Yellow-green head, wings and rump. Throat yellow or pale green, breast and abdomen grey. North of Sydney, NSW, undertail coverts are lemon-yellow. Race *ramsayi* (Mackay to Iron Range, N Qld): Similar to, but brighter than *familiaris;* undertail coverts richer yellow. Race *chlorocephala:* Distinct Great Barrier Reef island form. Yellower above, whiter below than mainland birds; similar to Pale White-eye in many respects. **Size** 12 cm. **Voice** repeated high-pitched 'tee-oow'; pleasant warbling song. **Habitat** most natural vegetation types within their range; orchards, gardens. Identify from Large-billed and Green-backed Gerygones. Also called Grey-backed Silvereye. Race *chlorocephala* sometimes called Capricorn Silvereye.

Ventral flight

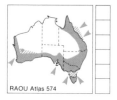

RAOU Atlas 574

Facial pattern

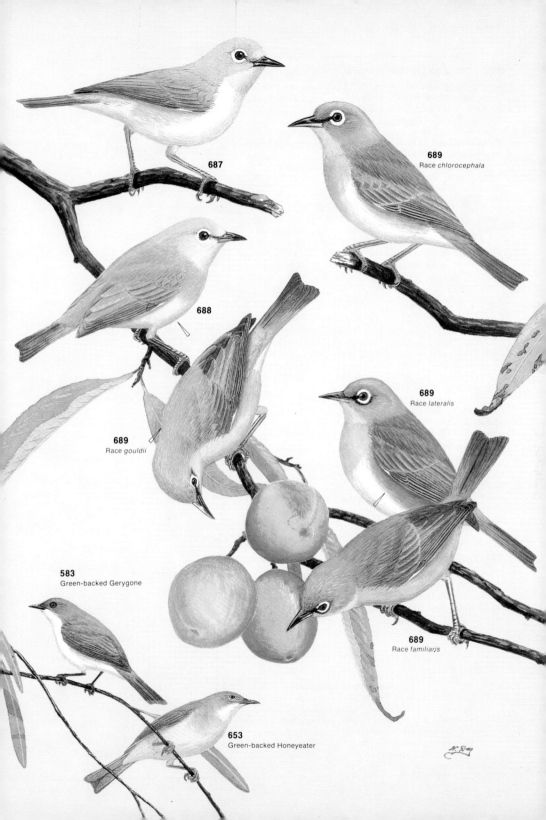

687

689
Race *chlorocephala*

688

689
Race *gouldii*

689
Race *lateralis*

583
Green-backed Gerygone

689
Race *familiaris*

653
Green-backed Honeyeater

690 European Goldfinch *Carduelis carduelis**

Red-faced; white and brown finch with large yellow wing bars conspicuous in flight. Pinkish-white bill. **Male** bright red face; black lores, crown and shoulders. Tail and trailing edge of wing tipped white. Back and flanks tawny-brown. Side of head, rump, abdomen white. **Female** less red on face. **Size** 13 cm. **Juv.** brownish head, streaked plumage. **Voice** liquid 'tu-leep', 'tsi-i-it'; liquid twittering song. **Habitat** settlements and agricultural areas. Undulating flight.

Dorsal flight

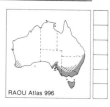

RAOU Atlas 996

691 European Greenfinch *Carduelis chloris**

Stoutly built, dull-green finch with green-yellow streaked wings and side of tail; tail black and forked. **Male** heavy ivory bill; large head. **Female** duller, yellow less obvious. **Size** 15 cm. **Juv.** duller bill and plumage. **Voice** 'chip-chip-chip'; nasal 'twe-e-ee'; song is trill followed by ascending 'zeep'. **Habitat** gardens and parks. In pairs or flocks; flight undulating.

Dorsal flight

RAOU Atlas 997

692 House Sparrow *Passer domesticus**

Male bill black; grey crown. Large black bib and breast. Chestnut nape. Whitish-grey ear coverts, underparts and rump. White bar on shoulder. Tail brownish-grey. **Non-breeding male** bill horn-brown; breast smudged black. **Female** horn-brown bill, no black on face. Pale stripe extends back from eye. Whitish-grey underparts. **Size** 15 cm. **Juv.** paler, yellowish-ivory bill with yellow gape flanges. **Voice** harsh 'cheer-up', and chattering song. **Habitat** human habitation.

Dorsal flight

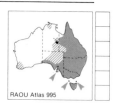

RAOU Atlas 995

693 Tree Sparrow *Passer montanus**

Bill black; chestnut crown. Small crescent-shaped black spot on cheek; black throat. Upperparts streaked brown and . black; grey below. **Non-breeding** bill blackish-brown to yellow at base. **Size** 14 cm. **Juv.** paler bill; pale brown plumage. **Voice** soft 'tek', and twittering song. **Habitat** human habitation.

Dorsal flight

RAOU Atlas 994

694 White-winged Wydah *Euplectes albonotatus**

Male black finch; very long black tail. Blue-grey bill. Upperpart of wings white; shoulder brownish-yellow to yellow. **Female** brown bill; upperparts streaked brown and black; buff, streaked with brown below. **Non-breeding male** as female but white on wings and yellow on shoulder. **Size** 15-18 cm. **Voice** 'cheee-eee'. **Habitat** grassland near rivers.

RAOU Atlas 951

695 Red Bishop *Euplectes orix**

Solid black and scarlet finch. **Male** upperparts and undertail .coverts scarlet. Bill, front half of head and underparts black. Short dark brown tail. **Female/Non-breeding male** buff eyebrow; upperparts streaked brown, buff and black. Underparts buff. Distinguished from female House Sparrow by brown-streaked breast and flanks. **Size** 11 cm. **Voice** 'zik zik zik', and others. **Habitat** reed beds. Not recorded recently; believed extinct.

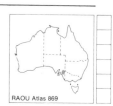

RAOU Atlas 869

* Introduced

693

692 ♀

♂ 692
Non-breeding

♂ 692
Breeding

691

691
Juv.

695 ♀

694 ♀

♂ 694

690
Juv.

690

♂ 695

N. Day

696 Red-browed Firetail *Neochmia temporalis*

Olive-green and grey. Scarlet rump, eyebrow, sides of bill.
Size 11-12 cm. **Juv.** duller; black bill; eyebrow shorter.
Voice high-pitched, almost inaudible, piercing 'seee'.
Habitat varied; usually dense shrubs interspersed with
open grassy areas.

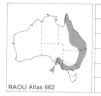

RAOU Atlas 662

697 Beautiful Firetail *Stagonopleura bellum*

Olive-brown. Red bill; black mask. Crimson rump,
uppertail coverts. Bold barring on flanks. **Male** centre
abdomen black. **Size** 11-12 cm. **Juv.** duller; bill black.
Voice mournful, floating whistle; song unknown.
Habitat thick forest and scrub, often near casuarina and
tea-tree thickets.

RAOU Atlas 650

698 Red-eared Firetail *Stagonopleura oculata*

Olive-brown, finely barred in black. Red bill; crimson
rump and uppertail coverts. Small crimson ear patch.
Bold white spots on black flanks. **Breeding female** paler
ear patch, bill. **Size** 11.5-12 cm. **Juv.** duller; bill black.
Voice piercing, floating, single note 'oooee'. **Habitat** dense
coastal forest and scrub.

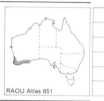

RAOU Atlas 651

699 Painted Firetail *Emblema pictum*

Flight

Male slim, brown-backed. Scarlet face, rump and mid-
belly. Bill long, tapered to fine red-tipped point. Large
white flank spots. **Female** face duller; red bill, lores and
rump; white flanks spots larger. **Size** 10-12 cm. **Juv.** duller
than female; red rump only. **Voice** loud, harsh 'trut'.
Habitat stony hills on spinifex plains.

RAOU Atlas 654

700 Diamond Firetail *Stagonopleura guttata*

Chest
band

Male solid 'upright' finch. Maroon bill; lores black. Grey
above, white below; black chest band. Flanks spotted
white; crimson rump. **Female** bill coral-pink; lores
brownish. **Size** 12 cm. **Juv.** blackish bill; dull, indistinct
chest bar. **Voice** two-syllable plaintive whistle descends,
then ascends. **Habitat** grassy woodland. Hops vigorously.

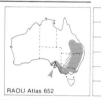

RAOU Atlas 652

701 Star Finch *Neochmia ruficauda*

Male red face. Dark olive above, yellow-olive below.
Chest, flanks, rump and tail spotted white. **Female** duller;
red only on lores and forehead. **Size** 10-12 cm.
Juv. brownish-olive; bill black. **Voice** loud penetrating
'sseet'. **Habitat** tall grass along swamps and rivers.

RAOU Atlas 663

702 Crimson Finch *Neochmia phaeton*

Tail flick

Male slender 'upright' crimson finch with long tapered tail.
Nape and crown grey. Upperparts washed grey. Belly and
undertail coverts black (white on C. York Pen. birds). Fine
white flank spots. **Female** crimson, washed brownish-olive;
centre belly pale creamish-fawn. **Size** 12-14 cm. **Juv.** duller
than female; bill black. **Voice** piercing 'che-che-che'.
Habitat watercourses with tall grass; cane fields. Flicks tail.

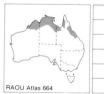

RAOU Atlas 664

702 ♀

702 ♂

702 ♂
Cape York Pen. form

696
Juv.

696

698

697

♀ 699

699 ♂

701
Juv.

♂ 701

700

700
Juv.

N. DAY

703 **Zebra Finch** *Taeniopygia guttata*

Grey body. Wax-red bill; black and white tear stripes.
White rump and zebra-barred tail conspicuous on fleeing.
Male chestnut ear patch, black chest bar; fine black and
white barring on throat. Flanks chestnut, spotted white.
White abdomen. **Female** abdomen buff. **Size** 10 cm.
Juv. as female but bill black. **Voice** nasal twang 'tiaah'; soft
rhythmic song. **Habitat** most open country; not
C. York Pen.

Rump

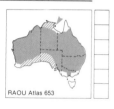

RAOU Atlas 653

704 **Double-barred Finch** *Taeniopygia bichenovii*

Neat owl-faced, brownish-grey finch. Bill greyish-blue;
face white, bordered black. White underparts with two
narrow black bands above and below chest. Black wings
spotted white. Black tail; rump white (black rump, race
annulosa, W of Gulf of Carpentaria). **Size** 10-11 cm.
Juv. duller; chest bars indistinct. **Voice** high pitched,
floating, nasal 'tiaah'. **Habitat** varied; open forests,
grasslands and beside creeks.

Tail flick

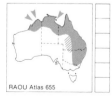

RAOU Atlas 655

705 **Masked Finch** *Poephila personata*

Slender body; red-brown above; buff below. Bill heavy,
waxy-yellow. Black mask and chin. White rump; long
black pointed tail. **Female** smaller mask; less black on
chin. Race *leucotis* (C. York Pen.): Pale on cheeks and
lower flanks. **Size** 12-13.5 cm. **Juv.** duller; bill black.
Voice long, nasal 'tiat'; soft 'tet'; soft, mechanical song.
Habitat open woodland. Flicks tail frequently.

Tail flick

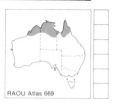

RAOU Atlas 669

706 **Long-tailed Finch** *Poephila acuticauda*

Male fawnish-tan. Blue-grey head; black lores. Large
black bib. Long sharply-tapered black tail; white rump;
orange legs. Bill varies from waxy yellow (W Aust.) to
orange-red (W Qld). **Female** smaller-bib. **Size** 15-16.5 cm.
Juv. duller; bill black. **Voice** soft 'tet', and loud, long pure
whistle; soft musical song. **Habitat** open woodland
near creeks. Jerks head on landing.

Rump

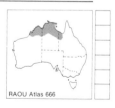

RAOU Atlas 666

707 **Black-throated Finch** *Poephila cincta*

Male stocky pinkish-fawn. Blue-grey head; black bill;
large black bib; short black tail. Black rump on C. York
Pen. birds — race *atropygialis*. White rump to the south
— race *cincta*. **Female** smaller; rounder bib. **Size** 10 cm.
Juv. duller. **Voice** hoarse floating whistle; soft 'tet'; very
soft musical song. **Habitat** open forest, woodland. Jerks
head up and down on landing.

Head jerks

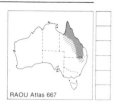

RAOU Atlas 667

708 **Plum-headed Finch** *Neochmia modesta*

Male olive-brown above; spotted white on wings. White
below, barred brown. Forehead, crown, chin deep claret.
Bill, lores and tail black. **Female** no claret chin-spot. Thin
white line above and to rear of eye. **Size** 11-12.5 cm.
Juv. no claret head marks; faint barring on abdomen.
Voice long, drawn out 'ting'. **Habitat** open woodland
bordering watercourses.

Courtship behaviour

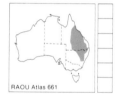

RAOU Atlas 661

704

704
Race *annulosa*

703
Juv.

♀ **703**

703 ♂

706
W Aust. form

705

706
W Qld form

705
Race *leucotis*

706
Juv.

♀ **708**

708 ♂

707

707
Race *atropygialis*

N. Day.

709 Pictorella Mannikin *Heteromunia pectoralis*

Male black-faced grey finch with white breast mottled black. Cinnamon crescent over eye and ear to side of neck. Fine white spots on wings. **Female** face brownish-black, more black on breast. **Size** 11 cm. **Juv.** bill dark; plumage grey-brown. **Voice** loud 'teet'. **Habitat** open grassland.

RAOU Atlas 659

710 Chestnut-breasted Mannikin
Lonchura castaneothorax

Male solid brownish finch with black face, grey crown and heavy grey bill. Chestnut breast divided from white abdomen by heavy black bar. Golden-brown rump and tail. **Female** paler. **Size** 10 cm. **Juv.** dark bill; olive-brown above, buff below. **Voice** bell-like 'teet'. **Habitat** reed beds, rank grass.

Ventral pattern

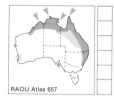

RAOU Atlas 657

711 Yellow-rumped Mannikin *Lonchura flaviprymna*

Solid finch. Pale grey head. Back and wings cinnamon-brown; cream-buff underparts. Straw-brown rump and tail. **Size** 10 cm. **Voice** bell-like 'teet'. **Habitat** reeds and rank grass.

Juv.

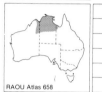

RAOU Atlas 658

712 Black-headed Mannikin *Lonchura malacca**

Stout body; heavy grey bill. Head, nape, throat, undertail coverts and belly black. Remainder underparts white. Upperparts and wings light chestnut with deep chestnut rump. **Size** 11 cm. **Juv.** grey head; paler above, buff below. **Voice** shrill 'peep-peep'. **Habitat** reed beds.

Lonchura singing posture

RAOU Atlas 870

713 Nutmeg Mannikin *Lonchura punctulata**

Bill grey; head and throat chocolate-brown. Upperparts grey-brown. Underparts dull-white, scalloped dark brown. **Size** 11 cm. **Juv.** brownish-yellow below. **Voice** 'ki-ki-te-te'. **Habitat** reeds, rank grass. Flicks tail constantly.

Tail flick

RAOU Atlas 983

714 Blue-faced Finch *Erythrura trichroa*

Male grass-green finch with cobalt-blue face and throat. Black bill. Dull scarlet rump and uppertail coverts. **Female** duller, with less blue. **Size** 12 cm. **Juv.** dull, with pale grey bill. **Voice** high-pitched 'tseet-tseet'. **Habitat** edges of rainforest.

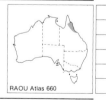

RAOU Atlas 660

715 Gouldian Finch *Erythrura gouldiae*

Male elegant, colourful finch with lilac chest and yellow abdomen. Ivory bill, red tip. Face black in most but crimson in some and yellow-ochre in rare individuals. Grass-green above with cobalt-blue rump. Black tail drawn into fine, thin wisps. **Female** duller. **Size** 14 cm. **Juv.** upper bill blackish, lower bill white; plumage ashy-grey and olive. **Voice** 'ssitt'. **Habitat** open woodland and grassland.

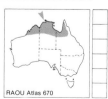

RAOU Atlas 670

* Introduced

♂ 709

♂ 714

712

713

710
Juv.

♂ 715
Yellow-faced form

711

710

♂ 715
Red-faced form

715 ♂

♀ 715

715
Juv.

716 Metallic Starling *Aplonis metallica*

Lustrous black body. Bright red eye. Bill, legs, black.
Size 21-24 cm. **Imm.** eye dark. Brown above; striated below.
Voice harsh, chattering, wheezing. **Habitat** tropical forests,
woodlands, gardens. Conspicuous nest colonies high in
trees. Flocks.

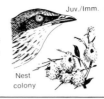

Juv./Imm.

Nest
colony

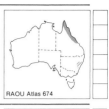

RAOU Atlas 674

717 Common Starling *Sturnus vulgaris**

Glossy black. Bill straw-yellow. After post-breeding moult
body speckled; bill black. **Size** 20-22 cm. **Fledgling/
Juv.** mouse-grey/brown, bill dark. **Voice** chattering
twitters, whistles; mimicry. **Habitat** urban and country
areas. Flocks feed on ground. Roosts colonially.

Flock
in flight

RAOU Atlas 999

718 Common Mynah *Acridotheres tristis**

Cocoa body. Black head, throat. Yellow bill, facial skin,
legs, feet. White wing patches obvious in flight. **Size** 23-
25 cm. **Fledgling/Juv.** like adult; brownish head.
Voice varied, noisy. **Habitat** about urban areas. Mainly on
ground; 'bouncing' walk; 'arrogant'. Roosts colonially.

Dorsal flight

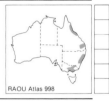

RAOU Atlas 998

719 Yellow Oriole *Oriolus flavocinctus*

Khaki-yellow/green above; lightly streaked below. Bill
orange. Eye red. Wing dark, edged cream. Tail dark,
tipped cream. **Female** paler. **Size** 25-30 cm. **Imm.** duller;
streaked yellow; bill dark. **Voice** melodious roll of repeated
notes; ventriloquial. **Habitat** tropical forested areas;
mangroves.

Imm.

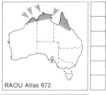

RAOU Atlas 672

720 Olive-backed Oriole *Oriolus sagittatus*

Bill reddish; eye red. Back finely streaked; heavy streaking
below. **Male** greener; wing-feathers edged grey.
Female greyer, wing-feathers edged cinnamon. **Size** 25-
28 cm. **Imm.** duller; rufous on head, upperwing covert edges;
bill dark. Eyebrow conspicuous, creamy. **Voice** rolling
'orry-orry-ole'; ventriloquial. Peaceful Dove call similar.
Habitat wooded areas.

Imm.

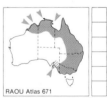

RAOU Atlas 671

721 Figbird *Sphecotheres viridis*

Male facial skin pinkish, red or orange. Back olive-green.
Northern males brilliant yellow below (race *flaviventris*
'Yellow Figbird'). Southern males duller grey-bluish; green
below (race *vieilloti* 'Green Figbird'). **Female** (both races)
upperparts brownish. Face skin bluish. Throat and breast
cream, heavily streaked. **Size** 27-29.5 cm. **Voice** soft musical;
short sharp yelps. **Habitat** tropical rainforest edges, parks.

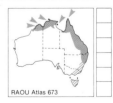

RAOU Atlas 673

722 Spangled Drongo *Dicrurus bracteatus*

Bill heavy, black; bristles at base. Eye red. Body black; breast,
wings, tail glossy black. Flaring tail fork. **Size** M 30-32,
F 28-30 cm. **Imm.** dusky black, speckled below. Eye brown.
Voice varied: rasping, hissing, crackling. Very vocal.
Habitat open forests (wet), urban areas, woodlands. Swift,
erratic flight. Singly; small flocks.

Hawking

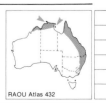

RAOU Atlas 432

* Introduced

719

716

722

720

721
♀

721
♂
Race *flaviventris*

721
♂
Race *vieilloti*

717
Juv.

717
Breeding

717
Post-moult

718

H. Bay

723 Golden Bowerbird *Prionodura newtoniana*

Male underparts, central crown and nape yellow.
Upperparts and central tail feathers golden-olive brown.
Female olive-brown, ash-grey below. **Size** 23-25 cm.
Imm. belly and flanks washed yellow, increasing until
some yellow feathers clearly apparent before moult to
adult. **Voice** rattles, croaks, mimicry. **Habitat** tropical
rainforest above approx. 900 m. Solitary, or imm. male
associations of two to six.

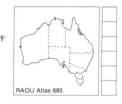

RAOU Atlas 685

724 Satin Bowerbird *Ptilonorhynchus violaceus*

Male glossy blue-black. Bill and legs whitish. Eye blue.
Female dull green; rufous wings and tail. Underparts off-
white, washed greenish, scalloped brown-grey; throat
duller. Bill and legs dark. **Size** 27-33 cm. **Imm.** as female to
fourth year when throat greener, bill paler, then odd blue-
black feathers until seventh year adult moult. **Voice** two-
note whistle, hissing, buzzing, mimicry.
Habitat rainforests and nearby areas.

Mixed flock

RAOU Atlas 679

725 Regent Bowerbird *Sericulus chrysocephalus*

Male black and gold; pale bill. **Female** bill, throat patch
and rear crown black. Wings and tail brown-olive; rest
greyish or fawn, mottled and scalloped brown. **Size** 24-
28 cm. **Imm.** as female; male plumage gradually acquired
after two years. **Voice** infrequent; scolds, chatterings,
mimicry. **Habitat** rainforests and nearby areas; forests,
scrubs, orchards.

Imm. ♂

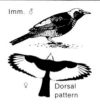

♀　Dorsal
pattern

RAOU Atlas 684

726 Spotted Bowerbird *Chlamydera maculata*

Dusky brown to blackish-brown above, head paler. Body
heavily spotted buff to rufous. Pink nape crest. Throat
and breast finely spotted black. Westen race *guttata* smaller,
darker than *maculata*, and lacking ash-grey hind neck.
Size 25-31 cm. **Voice** harsh grating hissings; mechanical
sounds, mimicry. **Habitat** dry open woodland.

Courtship behaviour:
crest presentation ♂

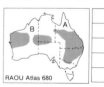

RAOU Atlas 680

A = *C. maculata*
B = *C. guttata*

727 Great Bowerbird *Chlamydera nuchalis*

Grey with brownish-grey back; wings and tail heavily
spotted pale grey. Stout decurved bill. Lilac nape crest
which females and imm. frequently lack. **Size** 32-37.5 cm.
Imm. slight abdomen and flank barring. **Voice** like
Spotted Bowerbird. **Habitat** dryer woodlands, low open
forest, particularly watercourses.

Courtship behaviour:
parade posture ♂

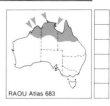

RAOU Atlas 683

728 Fawn-breasted Bowerbird
Chlamydera cerviniventris

Grey-brown with back, wings and tail feathers finely
tipped whitish; contrasting fawn lower breast, abdomen
and flanks. Decurved black bill. More white about face.
Size 25-30.5 cm. **Voice** like other *Chlamydera*.
Habitat coastal vegetation, often near rainforest;
mangroves, watercourses, vine forests, eucalypt-melaleuca
woodlands.

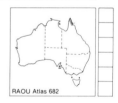

RAOU Atlas 682

Note: Western race *guttata* of 726 Spotted Bowerbird *Chlamydera
maculata* is now considered a full species *Chlamydera guttata*, the
Western Bowerbird.

♂ 723

723 ♀

724 ♂

♀ 724

♂ 725

725 ♀

726
Western Bowerbird

726

727

728

729 Tooth-billed Bowerbird *Scenopoeetes dentirostris*

Singing over court

Stocky. Pale buff cheeks. Stout black bill. Upperparts
dark olive-brown. Dirty white underparts. Legs much
shorter than Green Catbird. **Size** 24-27 cm. **Voice** over
display court: strong varied, predominantly bird mimicry
and 'chuck', otherwise silent save harsh flight alarm.
Habitat tropical rainforest approx. 600 to 1400 m.

RAOU Atlas 678

730 Spotted Catbird *Ailuroedus melanotis*
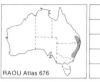
Stout. Bright green; paler below; heavy whitish spotting.
Bill whitish; eye red. Head whitish and buff with
contrasting black markings. Greater coverts, secondaries,
tail finely tipped white. **Size** 26-30 cm. **Voice** cat-like
wailings; single or double high-pitched 'chip' or 'tick'.
Habitat tropical rainforest, more common on highlands.·

RAOU Atlas 677

731 Green Catbird *Ailuroedus crassirostris*
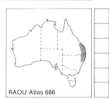
Like Spotted Catbird but more uniform green; no black
markings. White patch each side of lower throat. **Size** 28-
33 cm. **Voice** like Spotted Catbird. **Habitat** temperate
rainforest.

RAOU Atlas 676

732 Paradise Riflebird *Ptiloris paradiseus*
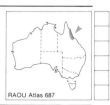
Male velvet black. Long decurved bill. Iridescent blue-
green crown, throat-breast 'shield' and central tail. Lower
breast and abdomen black, broadly scalloped oil-green.
Rustling flight. **Female** dark olive-brown. White eyebrow.
Chestnut wings and tail. Underparts buff-white with brown
chevrons and barring. **Size** 25-30 cm. **Imm. male** like females
until black feathers and flight-rustle develop. **Voice** double,
sometimes single explosive 'yaas'. **Habitat** temperate
rainforest. Riflebirds climb and tear rotten wood.

RAOU Atlas 686

733 Victoria's Riflebird *Ptiloris victoriae*

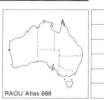
Male as Paradise Riflebird, but broader, more greyish-
velvet black between throat-breast 'shield' and oil-green
abdomen. Central tail feathers iridescent blue-green.
Female as Paradise but rich cinnamon-buff below. **Size** 23-
25 cm. **Imm.** as Paradise. **Voice** single or explosive 'yaas'.
Habitat tropical rainforest.

♂ Displaying

RAOU Atlas 687

734 Magnificent Riflebird *Ptiloris magnificus*

Imm. ♂ moulting

Male velvet black. Iridescent crown. Broad blue-green
throat-breast 'shield'. Central tail feathers iridescent blue-
green. Remaining underparts and filamentous flank
plumes black, suffused purple-red. **Female** like other
riflebirds. More cinnamon above, dull white below, barred
blackish-brown. **Size** M 28-33, F 26-28 cm. **Voice** clear loud
whistle 'wheew-whit'. **Habitat** tropical rainforest.

RAOU Atlas 688

735 Trumpet Manucode *Manucodia keraudrenii*

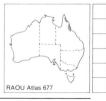
Starling-like. Short bill; red eye; elongated nape plumes.
Glossy black with iridescent sheen; long rounded tail.
Size 27-32 cm. **Voice** powerful, long, trumpet-like blast.
Habitat tropical rainforest.

RAOU Atlas 689

Note: Some authors consider that 730 Spotted Catbird is a race of
731 Green Catbird – we prefer to retain them as separate species.

733 ♂

735

♂ 732

♂ 734

733 ♀

♀ 734

732 ♀

730

731

729

736 White-winged Chough *Corcorax melanorhamphos*

Black, open wings show large white area. Eye red. Long down-curved bill. Long tail. **Imm.** eye brown. **Size** 45 cm. **Voice** descending whistles; harsh gratings. **Habitat** dry woodland. In parties; identify from currawongs, corvids.

Nest

RAOU Atlas 693

737 Apostlebird *Struthidea cinerea*

Grey, pale streaks. Stout bill. Brown wings. **Size** 29-32 cm. **Voice** harsh chattering. **Habitat** open forests, woodlands and scrub. In parties.

RAOU Atlas 675

738 Australian Magpie-lark *Grallina cyanoleuca*

Black and white. White bill, eye. **Male** white eyebrow; black throat. **Female** white face *and* throat. **Imm.** dark bill and eye, white *eyebrow* and *throat*. Slender black legs. **Size** 27 cm. **Voice** 'pee-wee'; also 'pee-o-wit'. **Habitat** open areas, often near water. 'Plover-like' walk.

Imm.

RAOU Atlas 415

739 White-breasted Woodswallow *Artamus leucorhynchus*

White rump, breast and belly, cut-off from uniform dark grey-brown throat, upperparts and all-dark tail. **Size** 17 cm. **Juv.** dark areas mottled. **Voice** 'pert, pert'; chattering. **Habitat** trees near water, including mangroves.

Clumping

RAOU Atlas 543

740 Masked Woodswallow *Artamus personatus*

Male clear-cut black face and throat, edged white. Pale grey below. Mid-bluish grey above. Tail thinly tipped white. **Female** washed dusky. **Size** 19 cm. **Juv.** mottled. **Voice** 'chap, chap'; chattering. **Habitat** open forests to gibber, often with White-browed Woodswallow.

RAOU Atlas 544

741 White-browed Woodswallow *Artamus superciliosus*

Male broad white eyebrow. Upperparts, throat deep blue-grey. Breast, belly rich chestnut. Undertail coverts, tail thinly tipped white. **Female** duller eyebrow; more pastel overall. **Size** 19 cm. **Juv.** mottled. **Voice** and **Habitat** like Masked Woodswallow.

Foliage feeding

RAOU Atlas 545

742 Black-faced Woodswallow *Artamus cinereus*

Smoky-grey overall except black face, rump, vent and broad white tail tip. Underparts paler. Race *albiventris* (NE Qld): White undertail coverts; whitish underparts. **Size** 18 cm. **Juv.** mottled. **Voice** 'chep, chep'; chattering. **Habitat** open forests, gibber.

Forms

Eastern   Intermediate   Central

RAOU Atlas 546

743 Dusky Woodswallow *Artamus cyanopterus*

White leading edge to blue-grey wing; body smoky-brown. Black tail with broad white tip. **Size** 18 cm. **Juv.** mottled. **Voice** 'vut, vut'; chattering. **Habitat** open forests, woodlands.

Artamus
Tail wag

RAOU Atlas 547

744 Little Woodswallow *Artamus minor*

Dark chocolate-brown body. Greyish-blue wings, tail. Broad white tail tip. **Size** 12 cm. **Juv.** speckled cream. **Voice** 'peat-peat'; chattering. **Habitat** open forests, grasslands, gorges.

Juv.

RAOU Atlas 548

745 Black Butcherbird *Cracticus quoyi*

Whole body bluish-black. **Size** 32-45 cm. **Imm.** two phases: one entirely dull blue-black; other (NE Qld) dark brown, streaked rufous above, light cinnamon below. **Voice** musical, yodelling call. **Habitat** tropical rainforest, mangroves, agricultural land. Shy.

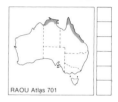

RAOU Atlas 701

746 Grey Butcherbird *Cracticus torquatus*

Black head; prominent white collar; grey back. Black wing has narrow white streak. Underparts white, washed grey. White rump. Tail black, tipped white. Female browner. **Size** 24-30 cm. **Imm.** brown above, crown streaked lighter. Collar, underparts, rump, tail tip are buff. Bill darker. Race *argenteus* 'Silver-backed Butcherbird' (northern NT): Smaller; lighter grey on back; white underparts; more white on tail, wing. Race *latens* (northern WA): Like *argenteus* but partly developed black bib on breast; small black chin patch. **Voice** rich melodious piping. **Habitat** open forest, woodland and mallee; agricultural land. Direct flight.

Calling in flight

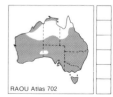

RAOU Atlas 702

747 Black-backed Butcherbird *Cracticus mentalis*

Strikingly black and white, with grey rump. White on shoulder extends down middle of black wing. Underparts white. Terminal white band on black tail. **Size** 25-28 cm. **Imm.** brown *not* black; back greyer. **Voice** melodic song but weaker than Grey. **Habitat** open forest, woodland, agricultural land. May become race of Grey Butcherbird in the near future.

Ventral flight

RAOU Atlas 704

748 Pied Butcherbird *Cracticus nigrogularis*

Strikingly black and white, with white rump. Wide white collar separates black head from back. Black bib. White bar on black wing. Tip of black tail has white corners. **Size** 32 cm. **Imm.** grey-brown *not* black; indistinct collar is lighter brown. **Juv.** bib buff (or absent in very young birds); underparts dirty white. **Voice** beautiful flute-like song. **Habitat** open woodland, scrubland, agricultural land.

748

738 ♂

738
Australian Magpie-lark

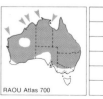

RAOU Atlas 700

749 Australian Magpie *Gymnorhina tibicen*

A variable species; glossy black and white. Race *tibicen* 'Black-backed Magpie': **Male** black head separated from black back by wide white collar. White shoulder, wing band, rump and undertail coverts. White tail has black terminal band. Underparts and wing black. **Female** collar and lower back light grey. **Imm.** like female but grey-brown *not* black. Race *hypoleuca* 'White-backed Magpie': **Male** back entirely white. **Female** back mottled grey. **Imm.** like female; black areas mottled brown-black. Race *dorsalis* 'Western Magpie': **Male** like *hypoleuca*. **Female** central back feathers black, white-edged, giving mottled appearance. **Imm.** back, underparts grey-brown; generally duller bird. **Size** 36-44 cm. **Voice** familiar flute-like carolling. **Habitat** open forest, woodland, agricultural and urban land. Strong direct flight.

Race   Race
hypoleuca   *tibicen*

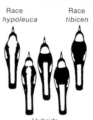

Hybrids

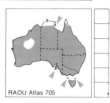

RAOU Atlas 705

746
Race *argenteus*

745 Imm: dark brown form

745

747
Imm.

748
Juv.

747

748

746

746
Juv.

749

♂ **749**
Race *hypoleuca*

749 ♀
Race *dorsalis*

749 ♀
Race *hypoleuca*

749 ♂
Race *tibicen*

749 ♀ Race *tibicen*

749 Juv.
Race *tibicen*

N. Gray

750 Pied Currawong *Strepera graculina*

Bill robust with well-defined hook. Black body; large and
prominent white crescent-shaped patch on wing.
Undertail coverts, base of tail and tip, white. Less white
in birds at SW of their range; can be confused with Grey
Currawong. **Size** 41-51 cm. **Imm.** markings as for adult, but
generally greyer and brownish around throat. **Voice** noisy,
distinctive and ringing, double-call 'curra-wong'.
Habitat open and low open forest, woodland, scrub,
agricultural and urban lands.

Dorsal
flight

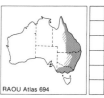

RAOU Atlas 694

751 Black Currawong *Strepera fuliginosa*

Tas. only. Bill more robust than Pied, with well-defined
hook. Black body; white tip to tail and primaries. Tail
significantly shorter than Pied and Grey. Small white
patch on wing. **Size** 46-48 cm. **Imm.** duller. **Voice** usual call
described as musical 'Kar-week week-kar'. **Habitat** open
forest, woodland, scrub, heathland and agricultural lands.
To be identified from Forest Raven.

Dorsal
flight

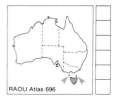

RAOU Atlas 696

752 Grey Currawong *Strepera versicolor*

Variable species; grey with white markings. Bill slender
without well-defined hook. Race *versicolor:* Grey with
darker crown and shading around eye. Large and
prominent white window in wing. Flight and tail feathers
tipped white; white undertail coverts. **Female** smaller.
Imm. duller, brownish. Note that west of Melbourne
(Vic.) plumage becomes progressively darker, and white of
wing patch is reduced; can be confused with Pied. Race
arguta 'Clinking Currawong' (Tas.): Darkest race,
almost black. Race *intermedia* 'Brown Currawong'
(Yorke and Eyre Peninsulas, SA): Darker and browner
than *versicolor*. Race *melanoptera* 'Black-winged
Currawong' (mallee regions): Darkest mainland form;
very dark grey and lacking white wing patch. (Darker
forms of nominate race *versicolor*, *plumbea* of WA, and
centralia of central Aust., are *not* considered to be distinct
races.) **Sizes** 45-53 cm. **Voice** ringing, clinking call.
Habitat open and low open forest; woodland generally,
mallee heath, scrub and agricultural lands. May resemble
Laughing Kookaburra when flying through forest away
from observer.

Race
versicolor

Dorsal
flight

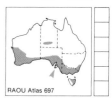

RAOU Atlas 697

Race
arguta

Dorsal
flight

Dorsal
flight

Race
melanoptera

753

751

752 Race *versicolor*

750

750

736

752
Race *versicolor*

752
Race *arguta*

751

752
ce *intermedia*

752
Race *melanoptera*

N. Day

753 Australian Raven *Corvus coronoides*

Black. Plumage glistens in sunlight, as in all Aust.
corvids. Long, floppy throat hackles. White eye. In hand,
feather bases grey; sides of chin unfeathered. **Size** 52 cm.
1st year extensive bare pink skin on sides of chin. Brown eye.
Voice high-pitched, child-like wailing; series of notes
uttered slowly, the last with a strangled dying finish.
Habitat most types except closed forests. When calling,
throat hackles fanned to form long 'beard'.

Throat hackle

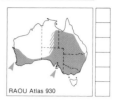

RAOU Atlas 930

754 Forest Raven *Corvus tasmanicus*

Black. White eye. In hand, feather bases grey. Very prominent
bill. Short tail. Isolated northern race *boreus* has a longer
tail. **Size** 52 cm. **1st year** brown eye. **Voice** very deep, harsh,
'rolls its Rs'; notes uttered slowly, the last in a series often
fading away. **Habitat** most types within its range. The only
Tas. corvid. Looks large, heavily built, ponderous in flight.

Throat hackle

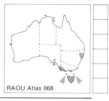

RAOU Atlas 868

755 Little Raven *Corvus mellori*

Black. White eye. In hand, feather bases grey. Slightly
smaller than the other two raven species. **Size** 50 cm.
1st year brown eye. **Voice** a series of rapid-fire, rather deep,
guttural barks, each note abruptly cut off. **Habitat** most
types, except closed forests. When perched, each call-note
often accompanied by a flick of both wings above the back.
Flight more rapid and agile than the two larger ravens.

Throat hackle

RAOU Atlas 954

756 Little Crow *Corvus bennetti*

Black. White eye. Slender bill. In hand, feather bases
white. A small (Australian Magpie-sized) crow when
compared with the other four Aust. corvids. **Male** slightly
larger. **Size** 48 cm. **1st year** brown eye. **Voice** flat, hoarse
and very nasal, rather deep in pitch; a monotonous series
of notes uttered rather rapidly but with each note
prolonged. **Habitat** most types in arid and semi-arid
zones. Remarkably tame around outback towns. Flight
more rapid and agile than Torresian Crow.

Throat hackle

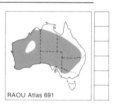

RAOU Atlas 691

757 Torresian Crow *Corvus orru*

Black. White eye. In hand, feather bases white. Slightly
smaller than the two large ravens. **Size** 50 cm.
1st year brown eye. **Voice** high-pitched series of staccato
honking sounds, usually uttered rapidly but sometimes
finishing with one or more longer notes; also a series of
long notes with a harsh, snarling quality, the last note
dying away. In the arid zone, also uses a loud falsetto
stuttering call. **Habitat** most types. After landing on a
perch, often lifts and settles the wings several times. More
heavily built, tail broader and squarer than Little Crow.

Throat hackle

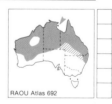

RAOU Atlas 692

758 House Crow *Corvus splendens**

Mostly black; broad grey-brown nape, collar, mantle and
breast. Brown eye. **Size** 43 cm. **Voice** repeated cawing
sounds. **Habitat** urban areas. Ship-assisted colonist from
SE Asia, sometimes arriving at Aust. ports.

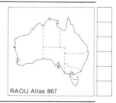

RAOU Atlas 867

* Introduced

The Handbook

In the pages that follow, you will meet the concept of *order* in the natural world. We commence with a summary of some of the major sequences that comprise a bird's life cycle. When you see a bird, any bird, it is going about one aspect of its day, its year, its life. So, for that matter, are you.

Now, having identified your bird from one of the preceding colour plates, you can begin to learn all about its life and requirements.

The life cycle of a bird

Males and females meet for courtship with the intention of breeding. Pair bonds are established, either for life, for one year, or for brief matings which are followed by solitary nesting and/or brooding by one of the sexes. Elaborate courtship ceremonies occur between the sexes in many birds; in others it is an inconspicuous happening.

Availability of the correct nest site, safely located and typical of its species, is vital for successful breeding. Environmental damage affects this aspect of a bird's life cycle probably more severely than anything else. Nesting may be above or below ground. It may be colonial, where only the immediate nest area is defended, or solitary, often in a defended territory of variable size. Site choice usually dictates nest materials. Some birds build no nest, others have elaborate structures.

Nest and territory defence may be by direct physical attacks and vocalising, by distraction displays designed to lead an attacker away, or by skilful camouflage. The number of broods per season varies. One brood is considered normal for most Australian birds, but many species have demonstrated a capacity to breed from two to four times in a season in which optimum environmental conditions prevail.

Eggs of most bird species are plain white or pastel in colour, and may have darker speckles, spots or blotches. A smaller number have camouflaging patterns on them. Eggs of hollow-breeding species may have a high gloss, and those of a burrow-breeding species may have a chalky surface. Shapes vary a little between species.

Often eggs are given minimal care until the entire group (clutch) is laid. Then intensive incubation with covering and heating commences in earnest. The period of incubation depends, to some extent, on external temperatures, and body bulk and egg size ratios, and to a large extent, on the degree of advancement to be achieved at hatching. Incubation does not last long in species which have naked, blind and virtually helpless young. In birds which have advanced (precocious) and largely independent young, incubation may take much longer.

Hatchlings usually have a tiny 'egg tooth'. It is a hard protruberance on the upper-bill tip which helps them chip a hole in the eggshell. Hatching may take from a few minutes to several days, depending on egg size, thickness of shell, external air temperature and degree of parental assistance. Hatchlings must recognise (imprint on) their parents from the moment of hatching and vice versa, so that each knows the other from then on. Cuckoos may be an exception: do hosts and neighbouring birds imprint on them?

Natal covering of nestlings varies from quite naked to lightly or fully clad in fluffy down, depending on egg size, incubation period and future lifestyle.

For nestling or chick maintenance, suitable food must be brought fairly soon after hatching as the yolk reserves of the baby are soon exhausted. Warmth, shading, and protection from predators and territorial neighbours is also required. Education of the baby proceeds by mimicry of adults, observation, and trial and error.

Every bird species undergoes a series of feather moults. These commence as the natal down is lost and continue throughout life. Usually, all the feathers change once a year, either in a pre-breeding or post-breeding moult. However, there are plenty of exceptions to this. Many have a partial moult, changing either body or wing feathers in turn, or moulting the wing feathers in series so that flight capacity is not lost. Penguins have a total body moult over a short period for re-waterproofing purposes. Many migratory birds arrive in or leave Australia in a state of partial or complete moult. They moult into, or out of, a drab, less conspicuous winter or eclipse plumage. As you will appreciate, it is important that you work hard to identify the visiting wader species, gulls and foreign wagtails.

In this book, we use the following terminology for the ages of birds.

Nestling (= Hatchling = Downy) In or about the nest. Naked or downy, i.e. *before* feathers develop.

Fledgling (leaving the nest) Partly or wholly feathered. Flightless or partly flighted, but *before* flight.

Note: These first two categories are dependent on parental care. Exceptions do exist. Both could be called 'chicks'.

Juvenile (= Juvenal) Fledging to free flying birds, with the feathers which *first* replaced the natal down. May or may not be still under parental care.

Immature (= Sub-adult) All plumages which *follow* first moult *until* full breeding capacity and/or plumage is reached.

Adult Birds which breed or are *known to have* breeding capabilities. Adult plumages are those which do not change in appearance in subsequent moults (allowing for alternating eclipse plumages in some species, e.g. waders).

Death may be by mechanical means — killing, accidents, becoming prey, being tossed out by a cuckoo, or by various physiological (systemic) means — diseases, starvation, exposure, overwhelming parasite load, poisons or pollutants, even old age!

Most information incorporated into the breeding bars (pages 284-341) is derived from our interpretation of Gordon Beruldsen's (1980) *A Field Guide to the Nests and Eggs of Australian Birds*, Rigby, Adelaide. Other sources and personal information from many of our own contributors were also used.

Modern avifaunal regions

Three major avifaunal regions are recognised in Australia. Each contains a number of sub-divisions. The Torresian is in the humid tropical and subtropical area. The Eyrean exists right across the semi-arid interior. The Bassian occupies the temperate south-eastern climatic zone. There is a certain amount of overlap between the three regions, for example in the south-west of Western Australia the Bassian overlaps with the Eyrean.

All are areas where much of the endemic fauna form identifiable associations. Each group of birds is broadly discrete from that in the next avifaunal region. However, there is mixing where the overlap zones exist, just as there is in the avifaunal regions of the world (see map below), and there are some that occur across all three regions. Introduced and vagrant birds may occur virtually anywhere.

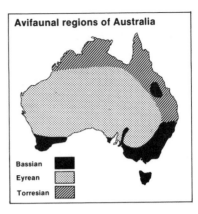

Avifaunal regions of Australia

Bassian
Eyrean
Torresian

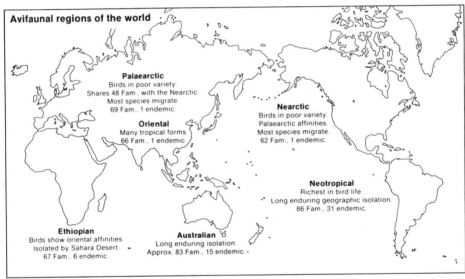

Avifaunal regions of the world

Palaearctic
Birds in poor variety.
Shares 48 Fam., with the Nearctic.
Most species migrate.
69 Fam., 1 endemic.

Nearctic
Birds in poor variety.
Palaearctic affinities.
Most species migrate.
62 Fam., 1 endemic.

Oriental
Many tropical forms.
66 Fam., 1 endemic.

Neotropical
Richest in bird life.
Long enduring geographic isolation.
86 Fam., 31 endemic.

Ethiopian
Birds show oriental affinities.
Isolated by Sahara Desert.
67 Fam., 6 endemic.

Australian
Long enduring isolation.
Approx. 83 Fam., 15 endemic.

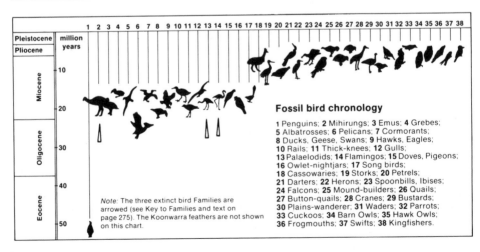

Fossil bird chronology

1 Penguins; **2** Mihirungs; **3** Emus; **4** Grebes; **5** Albatrosses; **6** Pelicans; **7** Cormorants; **8** Ducks, Geese, Swans; **9** Hawks, Eagles; **10** Rails; **11** Thick-knees; **12** Gulls; **13** Palaelodids; **14** Flamingos; **15** Doves, Pigeons; **16** Owlet-nightjars; **17** Song birds; **18** Cassowaries; **19** Storks; **20** Petrels; **21** Darters; **22** Herons; **23** Spoonbills, Ibises; **24** Falcons; **25** Mound-builders; **26** Quails; **27** Button-quails; **28** Cranes; **29** Bustards; **30** Plains-wanderer; **31** Waders; **32** Parrots; **33** Cuckoos; **34** Barn Owls; **35** Hawk Owls; **36** Frogmouths; **37** Swifts; **38** Kingfishers.

Note: The three extinct bird Families are arrowed (see Key to Families and text on page 275). The Koonwarra feathers are not shown on this chart.

Pleistocene
Pliocene
million years
Miocene
Oligocene
Eocene
10
20
30
40
50

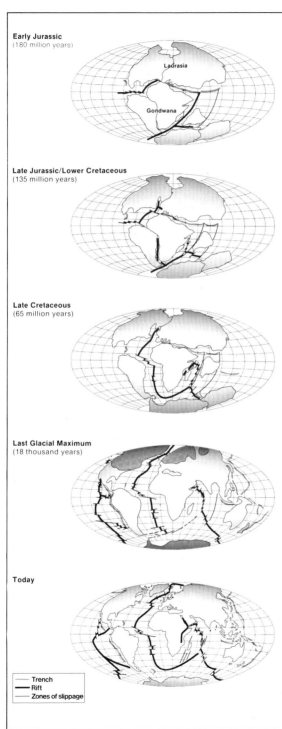

Early Jurassic
(180 million years)

Laurasia

Gondwana

Late Jurassic/Lower Cretaceous
(135 million years)

Late Cretaceous
(65 million years)

Last Glacial Maximum
(18 thousand years)

Today

Trench
Rift
Zones of slippage

Prehistoric birds

Birds evolved from small, running, bipedal reptiles (dinosaurs) which were probably warm-blooded. Their evolution took place in the Late Jurassic period. At that time, the world's land masses were interconnected and vertebrates, including primitive birds and mammals, could probably move across the great northern continent, Laurasia, and the southern continent, Gondwana. It was even possible to move between the two masses on dry land.

After this period, major but very slow rifting and separation began. Seaways widened, breaking the two supercontinents into the fragments that are today's familiar land masses.

The earliest and most primitive bird known is the famous *Archaeopteryx lithographica*. It lay buried for some 140 million years in lime-rich lagoonal rocks that were quarried extensively as lithographic limestone in Bavaria, southern Germany.

In modern Australia, the earliest known evidence of any bird is a series of small feathers from Lower Cretaceous lake sediments, exposed in a road cutting at Koonwarra, Victoria. The feathers are about 110 million years in age.

Birds evidently reached ancestral Australia soon after the origin of their Class. The Orders of birds we know today steadily evolved from Early Cretaceous times onward. Continental separation and drift gave rise to parent stocks, which today characterise the world's avifaunal regions (see map page 274).

Fossils that have been found on each continent indicate the path of evolution and genetic inheritance of today's bird fauna. Thus, it was discovered that giant runners, the dromornithids (mihirungs), existed in Australia but became extinct about 26 000 years ago. Likewise, palaelodids (flamingo-like birds) and flamingos have been found as fossils but are gone from the contemporary fauna. Their evolution and demise is linked to the change in climate from a cool temperate one to a warm one with less moisture. This change in climate happened as Australia broke away from its southern 'dock' some 40-50 million years ago and drifted north towards Asia. Forests of Southern Beech which once were known in central Australia gave way to grasslands; permanent lakes dried or became intermittent.

Much remains to be done in the search for fossil birds in Australia. A gap in our knowledge exists for the period between 135 and 20 million years ago, but we do know that birds did inhabit this continent for *most* of that time. If you would like to assist in fossil research, you can enlist as a volunteer at the museum in your capital city, or at one of the universities.

Where the birds live: vegetation and landform habitats of Australia

Geology and soils, together with latitude, altitude, surface topography and availability of water, determine which groups of plants are found in particular areas. The following pages give a summary of those habitats in which the vegetation is the dominant visible feature, as well as those in which the landform is dominant.

The purpose of these descriptions is to amplify the very brief descriptions of habitat given in the field information section. Space limitations have meant that the precise terms introduced here have not always been used in the field information section.

The sequence of presentation is broadly based on a structural classification proposed by Dr R. L. Specht during the 1970s. The classification looks at identifiable plant community groups as a whole and analyses, not so much what species are present, but how each association exists in terms of spacing, density and heights of all its component species. In addition, the number of horizontal layers that the member species impart to the structure is taken into account (there may be several layers, or just one).

Habitats often merge with each other. Some of the richest bird localities are those where several habitat types meet. You are likely to see the endemic birds of each 'pure' habitat, plus the species which thrive in several habitats or in the fringe zones.

Closed forest
Closed forest (rainforest or monsoon forest) is forest closed in by an umbrella-like canopy of soft-leaved trees. Usually luxuriant, often majestic, it occurs in high rainfall areas and is named tropical or temperate depending on the mean annual temperature. Dense fringes may make physical entry difficult. Once under the canopy, reasonable mobility is possible, but to see and identify birds in the canopy is often a *real* challenge.

Open forest
Open forest (wet or dry sclerophyll; eucalypt forest) consists of trees spaced with *no* continuous canopy. In high rainfall areas, **tall open forest** is often called wet sclerophyll; most open forest is in drier areas and may be called dry sclerophyll; **low open forest** is often in alpine or coastal zones, with stunting caused by severe environments. Eucalypts tend to dominate these forests.

Woodland
Woodland is the dominant forest type of the semi-arid zone of Australia. Conditions here produce relatively widely spaced trees. Various mixed associations occur, e.g. *Acacia*, *Casuarina*, *Callitris*. The different types are classified according to ground cover, hence **grassy woodland** or **shrubby woodland**, or according to height, hence **low woodland**.

Open scrub
Open scrub (mallee) develops in the lower rainfall belt on calcareous or infertile sandy soils. The tree layer is of multi-stemmed shrubs 2 to 8 metres tall, especially the mallee-type *Eucalyptus* species. The understorey varies with aridity and soil type; two broad types are recognised.

(i) **Grassy open scrub** occurs on calcareous soils where an understorey of tussock grasses has developed, but it grades into grassy woodland in higher rainfall areas. Annuals and ephemeral herbs are also typical of the understorey. On deep sandy soils at the arid extremes of its range, the understorey of grassy open scrub is often dominated by the spiny hummock grasses or spinifex (*Triodia*).

(ii) **Shrubby open scrub** has quite a dense understorey of hardy shrubs and develops on stony calcareous soils, particularly coastal dune limestones, and on sandy soils underlain by heavy clays where the broombushes (*Melaleuca* and *Baeckea* species) form dense thickets. Grass and herbs are rare. Prominent areas of bare ground covered with a lichen crust form in undisturbed regions.

The open scrubs were not occupied for agriculture until the 1960s and 1970s. At first there was low intensity sheep grazing on the natural vegetation, then successive years of above-average rainfall encouraged scrub clearance for wheat crops. Since that time, much land of marginal capacity for wheat growing and grazing has been cleared, and a serious erosion problem has developed. Superphosphate used to encourage growth of introduced pastures has stopped natural regeneration in many areas; elsewhere natural vegetation removal has resulted in salting of the surface soil.

Tall shrubland

Tall shrubland occurs in the semi-arid region of Australia where the annual rainfall is less than 25 centimetres. The shrubs are 2 to 8 metres tall and Mulga (*Acacia aneura*), frequently multi-stemmed, is typical. Scattered low shrubs may be present and a herbaceous layer of perennial grasses and seasonal herbs is well developed, although reduced beneath dense canopies. These shrublands occur also on rocky hillsides in semi-arid areas where the characteristic shrub genera include *Cassia*, *Eremophila* and *Acacia*.

Vast areas of this formation are leased for sheep and cattle grazing. Stock there rely heavily on top feed, particularly during droughts, resulting in destruction of many mature Mulga stands. In addition, rabbits have often prevented seedling growth. Many regions of tall shrubland have been severely degraded and are subject to soil erosion.

Tall open shrubland

Shrubs in tall open shrublands are more widely scattered than in tall shrubland. Tall open shrubland occurs widely throughout semi-arid Australia and grades into both tall shrubland and the desert complexes. Shrubs are mainly *Acacia* species with a well developed layer of grasses and ephemeral herbs.

In southern Australia, tall open shrubland develops on sandy soils. Scattered dwarf mallee eucalypts occur in association with a dense assemblage of sclerophyllous shrubs 1 to 2 metres tall. This formation has been called 'mallee-heath' in South Australia and Victoria. In semi-arid regions, severe cattle overstocking, particularly in drought years, has had an adverse effect on the vegetation.

The mallee-heath areas were left untouched for many years until it was found in the late 1940s that the addition of soil trace elements such as molybdenum and copper allowed pasture growth suitable for sheep. Large areas have been cleared since this discovery, often with limited success, but some have been permanently preserved in national parks.

Heath

Heath communities are confined to higher rainfall regions of southern and eastern Australia where the soils are very infertile. They occur in two distinct habitat types, on coastal lowlands and in sub-alpine swamps. Heaths, particularly lowland heaths, are very diverse florally, with representatives of many plant Families including Casuarinaceae, Proteaceae, Mimosaceae, Myrtaceae, Xanthorrhoeaceae, Epacridaceae, etc. Annual herbs and grasses are rare in the ground layer. Heaths occur in a variety of plant densities and are classified as **closed heaths** or **open heaths**. They often extend as an understorey into open forests, woodlands or shrublands at the extremes of their distribution.

Low nutrient levels in heath soils have meant that comparatively little has been cleared for farming, although the addition of fertilisers does render some areas suitable. Main threats to this formation come from coastal and alpine recreational and housing developments and also from the increasing amount of sand mining being carried out in coastal heaths on stabilised dune systems. Fire frequency has increased in heaths since white settlement and is degrading some areas. Fairy-wrens, emu-wrens, scrubwrens and honeyeaters are often well represented in heathland communities.

Low shrubland

Low shrubland, formerly known as Shrub Steppe, is dominated by well separated shrubs up to 2 metres tall of the Family Chenopodiaceae. These plants are semi-succulent with hairy leaves and are well adapted to soils with high clay and salt content, and periodic flooding and drought conditions.

Important species in this formation are bluebush (*Maireana sedifolia*) and the saltbushes (*Atriplex* species). After rains, grasses and ephemeral plants in the Families Compositae, Cruciferae and Leguminosae occur. Gibber plains are often covered with a very open low shrubland (see below). Salt marshes around coastal tide inlets and the salt pans of central Australia are structurally part of this formation but are treated separately (see p. 279).

Low shrublands are important sheep grazing areas. The sheep eat the chenopodiaceous shrubs in times of drought. Over-stocking has led to the destruction of many such areas and its replacement by annual grasses. Often there is little shrub regeneration and all the top soil erodes away.

Parrots, small doves, fairy-wrens, chats and some honeyeaters are seen in low shrubland. Flooding may attract wader species and a variety of waterfowl.

Gibber plains

Gibber plains (stony desert) consist of a sheet of continuous small- to medium-sized stones and rocks which effectively determine how the sparse plants are spaced, and perhaps to what height they will grow. These deserts formed over millions of years as widespread regional erosion of an earlier land surface dumped the most resistant siliceous rocks. A visit to one of the remaining mesa-like flat-topped hills will show you how it came about.

Cattle graze on gibber plains and erosion problems develop about artificial water sources such as stock tanks, bore drains and dams. Emus, chats, birds of prey, Australian Plovers and Pratincoles are likely to be seen on gibber plains.

Closed grassland

Closed grassland is dominated by grasses of short or medium height where masses of individual plants are in close contact at their bases and have interlacing leaf canopies. Smaller herbs are also present. These communities are typical of the flood plains of many rivers draining Australia's north coast where the heavy black soils flood during the monsoon, then dry and crack deeply towards the end of the dry season.

The grazing of cattle, the frequent firings which encourage green grass in the dry season, and destruction by introduced pigs and water buffalo severely damage these grasslands.

Closed grassland is also found in sub-alpine areas of south-eastern Australia where tussocks of *Poa* and *Danthonia* merge to form a closed tussock grassland. These areas are also grazed by sheep and cattle. Alpine grasslands have been severely damaged by summer pasturing of cattle, burning off, and the introduction of exotic weed species.

Closed herbfield

Closed herbfield is an essentially sub-alpine association of herbs and grasses where a continuous low ground cover forms. Snow usually covers it for several months or weeks of each year and sphagnum moss is common in its wetter hollows. Fire and grazing in the alpine areas of Tasmania, Victoria and New South Wales have caused extensive damage — so too has the provision of fire breaks, vehicle access tracks, and the trampling by humans in the summer. Most of the small number of bird species which inhabit the region in the summer, tend to move out (down) in the winter — altitudinal migration or nomadism.

Tussock grassland

Tussock grassland mostly occurs in northern Australia along the southern edges of the high summer rainfall zone (monsoonal influence) on calcareous cracking clay soils. Mitchell Grass (*Astrelba*) dominates these rolling treeless plains where the tussocks occur about one metre apart. Except in drought years, a dense cover of short grasses and herbs occupies the spaces. The tussocks die during the dry season or drought and regenerate from the root stock following rains. In western Victoria, the geologically recent basalt plain sustained a closed tussock grassland dominated by *Themeda* and *Danthonia* species, but most has been destroyed by grazing, improved pastures and land clearance.

Hummock grassland

Hummock grassland exists where large tussocks of spinifex and similarly structured grasses begin to trap wind-blown sand over a period of time, causing mounds (hummocks) to form in and about each tussock. Over many years, these enlarge and begin to overlap each other, forming a complex land terrain in some arid areas. The best example probably exists in the Simpson Desert, where the lower sides of the many parallel dunes have hummock grassland associations. It is noticeable that in this habitat and in the habitat descriptions that follow, the geological component of the land surface becomes more obvious. It is more visual, and is seen to be responsible for controlling the vegetation structure and spacing.

Salt marshes and mangroves

Salt marshes and mangroves are very often found together along the coastline. Mangroves dominate the seaward fringe of many estuaries, more so in the tropics where many species and zones of recognisable mangrove communities exist. Only one mangrove species is found in southern Australia. No single bird species is a specific frequenter of this mangrove (*Avicenna marina*), but in the tropics a number of species may spend virtually all their lives in the mangrove communities — more work on this aspect of ornithology is needed.

Salt marshes often colonise the land directly behind mangrove fringes as the sediments creep outward and fill in the estuaries. Once again, recognisable zones of plants having different salt tolerances are seen in saltmarsh communities, and may be differently utilised by bird species. The salt marsh extends inland as far as the reach of the highest-ever tides — the king tides — and so is inundated briefly once in a while. Salt marshes also occur about inland salt lakes, in basins or hollows in the land from which there is only seepage or evaporative escape for the water, and on land where poor farming practices, over-grazing and tree clearance, have radically altered the soil/water relationships.

Coastal dunes

Coastal dunes are readily recognisable. Low coastal shorelines around Australia are usually backed by a series of coastal dunes formed largely during higher sea levels in the recent geological past. A marked plant succession occurs from the seaward fringe of the frontal dune, inland, resulting in a gradual stabilisation of the sand and the development of a more diverse vegetation. The zones frequently parallel the coast for several kilometres inland.

As the dune stabilises, additional species are able to grow and a dense closed scrub often develops. In northern Australia a different and less well-defined succession occurs.

Coastal dune systems all round Australia are under considerable pressure. Development of coastal resorts has involved destruction of dune vegetation and construction of houses, often just above the high tide mark. As a result, severe beach erosion has occurred. Groynes and sea walls have been built in an attempt to halt sand loss from popular beaches. More recent threats to other major coastal dune systems are sand mining operations for heavy minerals (rutile, illmenite, zircon and monazite) and increasing problems posed by dune buggies, trail bikes and rabbits.

Inland waters

Inland waters across the continent are variable, intermittent, or non-existant, because of low and unreliable rainfall, high evaporation and fairly level topography. Perennial streams are confined to the northern and eastern coasts and along small stretches of the southern coast. The largest river system is the Murray/Darling and its tributaries, but even there, flow is very variable as no permanent snowfields exist to maintain river levels in summer.

Major streams in Australia often change within one year from a peak flow that innundates vast areas of flood plain, to a chain of pools and billabongs with little or no flow between them.

Rivers in more arid regions generally do not flow every year and drainage is towards the extensive playa basin areas rather than towards the coast. The rivers are grouped into basins of drainage.

The most extensive areas of **swamp** (wetland) in Australia are associated with the northern coastal rivers and the Murray/Darling basin. Other smaller swamps are widely scattered through higher rainfall areas where they may occur in natural or man-made depressions. Apart from sub-alpine bogs, most swamps dry out during the summer months.

The only extensive **freshwater lakes** in Australia are those of the Tasmanian central plateau. Here, lakes, lakelets and ponds ranging in depth from less than a metre to more than 200 metres resulted from the last glaciation period. Similar lakes occupy glacial basins in the Australian Alps. The remaining freshwater lakes in Australia are confined to the higher rainfall areas; the majority of these either dry out annually or have been dry a number of times since European settlement.

Saline lakes vary in character in terms of the dissolved salts and the presence or absence of water itself. They include some of the volcanic crater lakes of western Victoria, the mound springs south-west of Lake Eyre which are the natural outlets of the subterranean Great Artesian Basin, and the numerous salt pans of arid Australia. In *most* years these lakes, including the extensive bed of Lake Eyre, consist of extensive areas of white salt crust supporting no vegetation at all, and with surface temperatures reaching 150°C in the summer.

Pollution from mining waste, industrial and household effluents, uncontrolled boating, conversion of lakes into reservoirs for the generation of hydro-electric power or for water storage and the release of cold, de-oxygenated bottom water, land clearance and creeping salinity levels, pose the main threats to the comparatively small number of our natural freshwater lakes, streams and wetland areas.

Obviously, all of Australia's birds are dependent in one way or another on the freshwater complexes of the continent. The nomadic lifestyle of many species reflects their capacity and need to follow the rains, and to breed only if local conditions are right.

Marine habitats

Marine habitats divide into three types, each having their own birds and each sharing some birds with adjacent habitat types. **Estuaries** occur where freshwater streams meet the tide's influence. These 'mixing of the waters' zones could be said to extend seaward as far as the diluting influence of fresh water on the the sea. This will vary with the season, the amount of rainfall or melting snow, the range of normal or king tides, and the width and depth of the embayment into which the fresh water flows. Estuaries are also areas of active sedimentation from the land. Mangroves often fringe the seaward side and salt marshes follow as the land level rises and progresses outward.

Our definition of **coastal seas** includes all of the comparatively shallow seas lying directly on the submerged portions of the continental shelf of the Australian continental plate (see the map inside the front cover for its extent). By definition, Bass Strait, Torres Strait, Gulf of Carpentaria, Timor and Arafura Seas and the Great Barrier Reef, are *all* coastal seas.

The **oceans** include all sea areas beyond the continental plate where the really deep water lies (see the map inside the front cover). The boundary between these pelagic (oceanic) areas and the edge of the continental shelf is proving a very rich area to visit for sea-bird watching — take a fishing boat trip if you possibly can — the results can be fascinating.

Cliffs and exposed rock faces

There are thousands of cliffs and exposed rock faces around Australia. Many contain caves or deep joints, faults, crevices; some have vegetation on them, some are bare. Only a relatively small number of bird species *consistently* breed on rock ledges in Australia. These include the Little Penguin, Fairy Prion, Common Diving-Petrel, gannets and boobies, Great Cormorant, Black-faced Shag, Red-tailed Tropicbird, Osprey, Wedge-tailed Eagle, White-bellied Sea-Eagle, Peregrine Falcon and Australian Kestrel, Feral Pigeon, Rock-Pigeon, Rock Parrot, Barn and Masked Owls, swallows and martins, Grey and Sandstone Shrike-thrushes, Origma, pardalotes, sparrows, Common Starling and Common Mynah.

Individuals of many other species may breed in such sites from time to time. Quarry faces, open-cut mines, ore and mullock heaps, road and railway cuttings and embankments, and the ledges and roofs of large office buildings, factories, silos, aircraft hangars, etc. may be regarded as 'human cliffs and rock faces'.

Islands

Islands vary in extent and geological nature. They may merely be sand or mud banks exposed at low tide in an estuary or bay, or offshore mountain tops or ranges, as are many of the islands of our continental shelf. Sometimes these become enhanced or enlarged by the growth of coral upward from the floor of the shallow seas, or along the edge of the shelf itself, e.g. the Great Barrier Reef. Islands may have no vegetation at all, an individual plant character, or extensions of the flora of the adjacent mainland. Islands usually have fewer land bird species than the nearby land.

Caves

Caves form in many ways in many different geological substrates — by solution in limestone areas, by rifting and jointing in almost every type of rock, by the flowing on of molten lava to form lava tunnels, by plucking or grinding of sea or river in cliffs of coastlines or gorges, by the abrasion of wind-blown sand. Mines, railway- and pipe-line tunnels may be regarded as 'human caves'. Only one bird species, the White-rumped Swiftlet is fully adapted to total blackness and cave-dwelling in Australia. It uses echo-navigating clicks to find its way round in the dark (see page 317). Swallows and martins, the Grey Shrike-thrush, and the Masked Owl, use the twilight zone of caves and mines at times. Take a torch, watch out for snakes, wear a helmet and be very quiet — caves are *extremely* vulnerable to human interference.

Agricultural and pastoral lands

Agricultural and pastoral lands now dominate a huge proportion of the continent. Even those wilderness regions, which remain directly uncontaminated by Europeans and their crops, stock, feral plants and animals, receive indirect pollution from airborne or waterborne chemicals. Direct human interference with the land is the rule, not the exception. We urge all persons interested in any way with natural history, at any level, to increase their efforts in the documenting, not just of individual animals or plants, but of entire communities and associations and their ecological webs, and to the saving of natural vegetation.

Urbanised land

Urbanised land with its endless rows of tightly packed homes, blocks of flats, factories and offices which now obscure the soil for thousands of hectares around every major European settlement, represents for most of the Australian native bird fauna, the end of the road! But some are able to adapt or hang on in gardens and reserves. They, together with the introduced bird species, constitute completely new, although species-impoverished, bird communities which must be studied.

Relief for birds and other fauna must come in the form of massive green belts, selected species plantings, wetland provision, coastal reserves, a ruthless onslaught against feral animal and plant species, and an equally ruthless educational and control programme for humans.

Hints for bird-watchers

It is easy to imagine, looking out at the 28-52 bird species in your garden or neighbourhood, that there cannot possibly be any more to discover about any one of them. But this is not so. Pick one, any one, of the most common birds, and make a point of looking up its entire published literature. With very few exceptions you will find that enormous gaps exist in the printed knowledge of even the most common local species —no matter where you live. So, try it! Observe keenly, report correctly, and write something about one of your local birds.

Take thorough notes on any strange birds that you see — try to do a little sketch and add as many significant details as possible. Include proportions, relative size, colours of plumage and soft parts (eyes, legs and facial skin). Record behaviour, postures, calls and flight mannerisms. Take notes on anything which will help you to identify the bird.

We have mentioned only a small number of the hundreds of books and thousands of journal articles on the many aspects of bird study. Your role as a bird-watcher is to seek them out and read, read, read . . .

Two excellent Australian general bird biology texts exist. These are J.D. Macdonald's (1980) *Birds for Beginners —how birds live and behave*, A. H. & A. W. Reed, Sydney, and Ian Rowley's (1975) *Bird Life*, Collins, Sydney.

Two books on bird-watching are Rosemary Balmford's (1980) *Learning about Australian Birds* Collins, Sydney, and Ted Schurmann's (1977) *Bird Watching in Australia*, Rigby, Adelaide.

If you are enjoying this book, please join either *The Bird Observers Club* or the *Royal Australasian Ornithologists Union* (see addresses in current Telephone Directory). They provide aid and comfort, plus direction, if you still cannot identify *that* bird. They also provide you with an opportunity of taking part in an urgent and crucial national service — maintaining and restoring Australia's native plant and animal ecology.

We repeat (see page 2). Start today. Tick them all off in the little boxes which appear beside the maps on the pages facing the colour plates. No cheating — treat it like a golf score. Make bird-watching your excuse to see Australia first.

Considering that the bird's home environment is of vital importance to its day to day and year to year survival, we have devoted the preceding seven pages to describing Australia's habitats. It is not nearly enough, we know, but you can go on building your knowledge of these habitat categories, and what goes on inside each and between each. The bird and its habitat is a life times' study in itself.

Lastly, The Handbook contains 58 pages of bird Family summaries, some with references, some without. The broad plan for each entry is to mention taxonomic and evolutionary information first, followed by general biology and behavioural information and concluding with breeding information. All of the birds which *breed* in Australia have a diagrammatic representation of their breeding season(s).

Hint, Hint, Hint, Hint . . .

- Keep the sun behind you when observing.
- Build a bird feeding table and/or a bird bath in a safe place.
- Examine dead birds on roads and beaches — send rare ones to the Museum.
- Read the scientific names with close attention. Can you interpret their meanings?
- Learn to read the daily weather map. Try to relate each day's weather to the dispersal of birds.
- Always record locality, date, time of day (state if daylight-saving time) on *all* of your records and notes.
- Look for indirect evidence of birds — scratches, moulted feathers, droppings, pellets, damaged fruits or flowers. Play detective — what did this?
- Keep a notebook in a waterproof cover. Use biro or pencil, *not* felt-tipped pens.
- Use binoculars and/or a small telescope for easier and more satisfying bird-watching.
- Report all banded (ringed) birds to the proper authority. Never remove a band from a living bird.
- Take a camera into the bush and try to photograph a bird or two — then think about buying a telephoto lens!
- Try to map the territory of several different bird species that live near you.
- Try to tape-record some bird songs in the wild.
- Do you have a space in your garden? Plant a shrub known to provide nectar for birds.
- Take a bag of bread to the beach and feed it to the gulls — then try to interpret all their posturings and calls.
- Report people who are behaving suspiciously to land owners, park rangers or to police — safeguard the bush and its inhabitants.
- Take a torch or spotlight into the bush. Which birds are up and about? Where do the rest roost?
- How do the birds react when rain suddenly falls after a dry spell?
- Make up a chart in the kitchen, recording all of the birds which pass before the window and why.

Emus   Family Dromaiidae

Emus belong to the small, ancient and essentially Southern Hemisphere Order Struthioniformes, also called ratites. Ratites cannot fly. They lack a keel on the sternum (breast bone), which anchors the flight muscles, and do not have barbules (minute branches) that hold the web of normal feathers together.

Only one species of Emu survives. Smaller species once occurred on King Island, Tasmania, and Kangaroo Island, South Australia, but were exterminated last century. These are the only Australian bird species *definitely* known to have become extinct in recent times. The Tasmanian race *diemenensis* has also become extinct.

Emus eat mainly vegetables and fruit; sometimes they eat insects. They swallow stones to help mechanically digest (triturate) hard foods in the stomach. In the arid interior of Australia they are nomadic and to some extent migratory. An extensive Emu-proof fence exists in Western Australia to guide Emus away from crop areas.

The males, which do all of the incubating and caring for the young, are smaller and lighter than the females. Up to 20 (usually between nine and 12) large and glossy dark green eggs are laid. Goannas, dingoes and feral pigs are nest predators.

The Emu is Australia's national bird emblem.

The Emu is Australia's national bird emblem. Recent research (1984) shows the extinct Kangaroo Island Emu to be a distinct species *Dromaius baudinianus*, from the King Island Emu D. minor.

Reading
Davies, S. J. J. F. (1968), 'Aspects of a study of Emus in semi-arid Western Australia', *Proc. Ecol. Soc. Aust.* **3**, 160-166.

Breeding season

J	F	M	A	M	J	J	A	S	O	N	D

1 Emu

Cassowaries   *Family Casuariidae*

The Cassowary is a distinctive bird with a vertical helmet (casque) and a large sharp claw on the innermost of its three toes. This large, flightless, dark ratite inhabits tropical rainforests and is considered distantly related to the Emu. It may be dangerous if cornered or provoked, kicking out with its feet. The female lays about four large pale green eggs on forest litter. The male incubates the eggs for about two months. It is considered to be a sedentary species, but it gathers food over a wide 'local' area. It eats fallen fruit from trees and vines as well as dead birds and mammals. Fragmentation and permanent destruction of the rainforests in northern Queensland is reducing the population of the Cassowary in the more southerly portion of its distribution.

The Cassowary has a large claw on its innermost toe.

Breeding season

J	F	M	A	M	J	J	A	S	O	N	D

Southern Cassowary

Ostriches   Family Struthionidae

In Australia, several Ostrich-plume farms were established in the late nineteenth century. Survivors from the original and largest farm are semi-feral, located across several properties near Port Augusta, at the head of Spencer Gulf, South Australia. The massive thighs (drumsticks) of Ostriches are nearly bare of feathers — a cooling mechanism for these fast-running birds (speeds of 55 kilometres per hour have been recorded). Males are polygamous. Unlike Emus, both sexes brood the large white eggs. A few ostriches were sighted near Morgan, South Australia, in 1975 but inbreeding is ruining their chance of survival. Imported black feather dusters are perhaps the best-known Ostrich-derived plume products in Australia today.

The Ostrich has two toes on each foot. Only the large inner toe has a nail.

Breeding season
3 Ostrich (*Insufficient information*)

Grebes   Family Podicipedidae

Grebes fly well but prefer not to in daylight. Migratory or nomadic flights are at night. Birds dive to feed and escape danger.

Breeding plumage *differs* from non-breeding plumage. Both sexes take part in ritual courtship ceremonies and later in nesting activities. In spectacular displays (see page 18), Great Crested Grebe partners face each other in the water, shaking erected head crests and ruffs, apparently preening and offering each other nest material. At the climax of the display, they rise up in the 'penguin posture', colliding breast to breast. Copulation later occurs on the hidden, floating or anchored nest-platform or aquatic vegetation. In general, the grebe's white eggs (three to nine) stain rapidly. When a grebe leaves its eggs, it covers them with weed. Downy young are brightly marked and striped. After hatching they move under the wings into the fur-like back plumage of whichever parent is on the nest. They are fed by parents which carry them in turn on their backs. Older chicks follow parents for food.

The Hoary-headed Grebe has lobed toes.

Reading
O'Donnell, C. F. J. (1981), 'Head, plumage variation and winter plumage of the Southern Crested Grebe', *Notornis* **28**, 212-213.

Breeding seasons

	J	F	M	A	M	J	J	A	S	O	N	D
4 Great Crested Grebe												
5 Hoary-headed Grebe												
6 Australasian Grebe												

Penguins   Family Spheniscidae

Penguins have flattened feather shafts and keep their dense plumage waterproof with oil from a tail gland. Each year, *all* penguins *must* leave the sea briefly to completely moult the worn plumage; they stand quietly in a cloud of feathers. Birds forced to swim at this time may drown. Similarly, sick penguins treated for serious fuel oil contamination *must never* be released to sea until the *next* annual moult is complete.

Most Australian penguin records are either of winter migrants (Fiordland, Rockhopper) or rarer vagrants. The colour plate (see page 21) is arranged accordingly.

The Little Penguin of 'Penguin Parade' fame in Victoria is the only penguin that breeds in Australia. It also breeds in New Zealand. These birds feed on small fish and crustaceans, nest in burrows and have one or two chicks.

Little Penguins come ashore at dusk.

Reading
Reilly, P.N. (1983), *Fairy Penguins and Earthy People*, Lothian, Melbourne.

Breeding season

	J	F	M	A	M	J	J	A	S	O	N	D
17 Little Penguin												

Albatrosses   Family Diomedeidae

Albatrosses are related to the three Families of petrels. All are united in the Order Procellariiformes. Albatrosses have long, slender, hook-tipped bills with small tubular nostrils placed on each side. A shallow groove (nasal sulcus) runs forward. The 'plate' shape at the top of the upperbill base helps identify 'mollymawks' in the hand (see pages 24-7).

Albatrosses are superb long-winged gliders that consistently fly in a wheeling pattern. Into the wind they rise, wings stiff, to a point of stall. They then steeply glide down wind to pick up speed, turn at right angles across wind on reaching sea level, then repeat the process. They rarely flap in a strong wind; effortless and graceful gliding may continue for hours.

Their feet are webbed for swimming, act as air brakes during approach to alight, and act as stabilisers as birds soar around cliff-induced updraft currents on breeding islands.

Albatrosses also rest on the sea where they may be confused with sitting Gannets and white-phase Southern Giant-Petrels.

Observers can look for albatrosses off coastal headlands in temperate or southern regions, usually in winter. Compare their appearance, relative size, flight mannerisms and behaviour with that of other large sea-birds in such coastal areas. The best place to observe albatrosses closely is from boats that go well out to sea. Albatrosses consistently scavenge from ships and fishing boats.

For identification, features like bill colour, and head, underwing and upperwing patterns are useful. The patterns change with maturity from a usually dark plumage to a paler one. There are a number of races and island populations of some species, each with its own minor features. Wandering Albatrosses breed in different plumages, the southern populations are whiter and were once called 'Snowy Albatrosses'. The northern populations can breed even when they are still rather brown. A colony of great albatrosses breeding at New Amsterdam Island (Indian Ocean), was recently described (1983) as a new species, *Diomedea amsterdamensis*. Adults look like immature Wandering Albatrosses but with a black cutting edge and dark bill tip (see pages 26-7).

The sequence of great albatross plumages shown page 22 is thus a *compilation of average stages* of the broad pattern that occurs from fledging to old age. It is *also* a broad summary of the different races of the Wandering and Royal Albatrosses. Treat it as a *general guide* to ages, *not* as a series of *absolutely defined* stages.

Only the nominate race of the Shy Albatross breeds in Australia, on Albatross Island off north-west Tasmania, and on Pedra Branca and The Mewstone, off southern Tasmania. It also breeds in New Zealand. Earth and faecal material forms a raised platform where one large white egg is laid and incubated for several weeks. Dancing courtship displays precede egg-laying. Nestlings are downy and are fed by both parents.

A scene at Albatross Island, Bass Strait — a Shy Albatross adult (middle) with two nestlings.

Breeding season

J	F	M	A	M	J	J	A	S	O	N	D

24 Shy Albatross

Petrels, Shearwaters   Family Procellariidae

The petrels and shearwaters are characterised by nostrils encased in a tube, joined at the top of the bill base. Albatross nostrils are small and separated on the bill sides; diving-petrels also have separated nostrils. Storm-petrels differ in having longer legs and shorter wings than petrels. In flight, petrels have long wings and in strong winds they can appear very graceful, wheeling and gliding up and down, sometimes in huge arcs.

Between 40 and 44 species are on record in Australia. This is a significant proportion of the 66 species occurring world-wide. Only nine species breed in Australia.

Fulmarine petrels have very long nostrils and vary from the giant-petrels *Macronectes* to Snow Petrel *Pagodroma* in size. This group consists of several genera including *Fulmarus* (Fulmars), *Thalassoica* (Antarctic Petrel) and *Daption* (Cape Petrel). All have stiff-winged flight interspersed by quick flapping. 'Gadfly petrels' *Pterodroma*, *Halobaena* and *Bulweria* have short stubby black bills, short heads and long wings. They are perhaps the most graceful of petrels. Blue Petrels are superficially like prions (*Pachyptila*), but bone structure, bill colour and shape suggest they are closer to *Pterodroma*. Recently Bulwer's Petrel *Bulweria bulwerii* has been sighted off Western Australia. It is a small, all dark

The nesting site of a Gould's Petrel at Cabbage Tree Island, off the north coast of New South Wales.

Breeding seasons (*variable)

J	F	M	A	M	J	J	A	S	O	N	D

33 Great-winged Petrel

37 Herald Petrel*

42 Gould's Petrel

petrel with broad pale-brown bars across the long wings and with a long wedge-shaped tail. Its flight mannerism is between *Pterodroma* and storm-petrels, being buoyant and twisting. With wings held forward, it often patters close to the surface like a prion.

Prions are specialised petrels with bluish plumage. Bill shape varies enormously through the range of Broad-billed Prion (width as great as 25 mm), Lesser Broad-billed, Antarctic, to Slender-billed Prion (as narrow as 9 mm). The forms within *this* group (often known as 'whalebirds') are extremely variable and a recent paper by Cox treats all but the Slender-billed as one clinal species. Possibly the Slender-billed Prion should also be placed under *Pachyptila vittata* with the 'whalebirds'. A *second* group, Fairy and Fulmar Prions, were also lumped together by Cox as a single species —*Pachyptila turtur*.

Procellaria, *Calonectris* and *Puffinus* form the other group of petrels, the latter two being known as shearwaters (mutton-birds). The four *Procellaria* are very large, have bulbous, pale bills and range the southern oceans. *Calonectris* are large, pale shearwaters. Australia's representative is the Streaked Shearwater. *Puffinus* are a large, variable group of petrels with long slender bills. They are either all dark, or dark and white. Most have fluttering, sometimes gliding flight; all alight to pick up or dive for food.

Most petrels are wanderers, some are migrants of the highest degree. The Short-tailed Shearwater *Puffinus tenuirostris* or 'Muttonbird' breeds in south-eastern Australia and migrates to the north Pacific every year in millions. Other petrels have similar migratory routes (e.g. Providence, Cook's, Mottled Petrels). Some petrels do almost the opposite, for example the Asian Streaked Shearwater migrates to northern Australia. Fluttering and Hutton's Shearwaters are examples of migrants from New Zealand. Many Antarctic and Sub-Antarctic species wander north in the winter to Australian waters including the Cape Petrel, giant-petrels and White-headed Petrel.

Marine animals of varying sizes from small tuna to micro-organisms are taken. Prions sift food with the help of lamellae (stiff hair-like membranes) along the inside of the upper mandible (very well developed in Broad-billed Prion). Petrels occur solitarily or in extremely large flocks of up to millions as in the Short-tailed Shearwaters. Petrels breed mostly in burrows or crevices. Giant-petrels nest in depressions surrounded by dried vegetation. Other fulmarine petrels breed in raised scrapes on the ground, on hillsides and cliffs. One white egg is laid.

Reading

Cox, J.B. (1980), 'Some remarks on the breeding distribution and taxonomy of the prions (Procellariidae; *Pachyptila*)', *Rec. S. Aust. Museum* **18** (4), 91-121.

Harper, P.C. (1980), 'The field identification and distribution of the prions (genus *Pachyptila*) with particular reference to identification to storm-cast material', *Notornis* **27**, 235-286.

Harper, P.C. & F.C. Kinsky, (1978), *Southern Albatrosses and Petrels*, Price, Milburn and Co. Ltd, Wellington.

Harrison, P. (1983), *Seabirds, an Identification Guide*, A.H. & A.W. Reed Ltd, Wellington.

Serventy, D.L., Serventy V. & J. Warham, (1972), *The Handbook of Australian Seabirds*, A.H. & A.W. Reed Ltd, Sydney.

Serventy, D. L. (1967), 'Aspects of the population ecology of the Short-tailed Shearwater', *Proc. 14th Internat. Ornith. Congress*, 165-190.

Breeding season

J	F	M	A	M	J	J	A	S	O	N	D

52 Fairy Prion

A Fairy Prion nesting in a rock crevice.

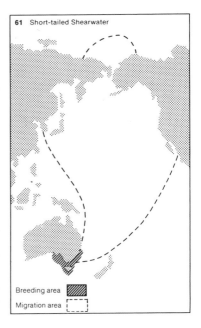

61 Short-tailed Shearwater

Breeding area

Migration area

Breeding seasons

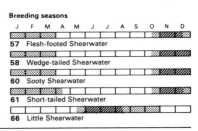

J	F	M	A	M	J	J	A	S	O	N	D

57 Flesh-footed Shearwater

58 Wedge-tailed Shearwater

60 Sooty Shearwater

61 Short-tailed Shearwater

66 Little Shearwater

Storm-Petrels   Family Oceanitidae (Hydrobatidae)

Storm-petrels are closely related to the true petrels (Procellariidae) and differ in having longer legs and shorter wings. The bill is small with raised nostrils. Storm-petrels can be divided into Sub-Families: Oceanitinae which have long legs and short wings, and Hydrobatinae which have shorter legs and longer wings. Storm-petrels are the smallest petrels.

The Wilson's Storm-Petrel *Oceanites oceanicus* is the most wide-ranging storm-petrel, breeding in the southern oceans and moving to the Northern Hemisphere. In deeper Australian waters Wilson's Storm-Petrel is quite common. The White-faced Storm-Petrel *Pelagodroma marina* is the only breeding Australian species and probably migrates northwards in the winter. The Grey-backed Storm-Petrel *Oceanites nereis* breeds on the islands south-east of New Zealand and migrates to south-east Australia. The White-bellied and Black-bellied Storm-Petrels *Fregetta* are two difficult species to identify. The first breeds on Lord Howe Island; the second breeds in the Sub-Antarctic. Of the *Oceanicus* petrels (Hydrobatinae) Leach's Storm-Petrel is a Northern Hemisphere vagrant to Australia and Matsudaira's Storm-Petrel possibly migrates to north-west Australia from Japan annually, but sightings are few due to a lack of observers.

Oceanitinae storm-petrels generally fly by fluttering and bouncing on the water with their legs extended. Hydrobatinae storm-petrels glide more and have tern-like wing beats.

Storm-petrels are usually seen in waters over 100 metres in depth. They feed on micro-organisms, picked off the surface. The White-faced Storm-Petrel breeds in burrows deep in sandy or loose soil. Storm-petrels lay one white egg.

Reading

Flight mannerisms

Wilson's: purposeful, fast, direct; hovers; patters with feet while wings raised in 'V'.

Grey-backed: like moth; skims low; leaps from side to side, pushing off sea with both feet.

White-faced: bounces up and down on sea, dangling long legs; sways from side to side. Long glides.

Black-bellied & White-bellied: both zig-zag low and smack water with breast every few moments.

Matsudaira's: soars; glides very slowly. A little-known species.

Leach's: deep, slow wing beats, swooping flight; sometimes glides. Rarely patters on water.

Breeding season

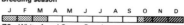

70 White-faced Storm-Petrel

Diving-Petrels   Family Pelecanoididae

Diving-petrels are small, black and white birds. They have short bills with separate nostrils which open upward. They are short, dumpy birds with rounded wings. All species are closely related and difficult to identify, nostrils and bill shape being the main differences. They prefer waters away from the coast but usually not over 100 metres in depth. When disturbed they fly off the water in a quail-like manner. They fly through waves, using their wings to propel themselves under water. Their diet is small fish and crustacea. Most are fairly local, the Georgian has strayed once to Sydney (1958). Common Diving-Petrels nest in tunnels in shallow soil and lay one white egg.

Diving-petrels swim underwater with partly opened wings.

Breeding season

75 Common Diving-Petrel

Pelicans   Family Pelecanidae

Pelicans are very distinctive members of the Order Pelecaniformes, a group characterised by four toes joined by webs, the hind toe directed forward, and sealed nostrils (except in the tropicbirds where it is adapted for diving).

In pelicans the gular region is naked and expanded into a large pouch. In extremely hot weather, pelicans open their bills and rapidly vibrate the soft skin of the pouch. This radiates heat from the numerous blood vessels in the tissue. As a cooling mechanism it must be quite effective, for pelicans are able to breed in hot-arid and hot-humid areas, as well as in more temperate zones. This behaviour is known as 'gular fluttering'. Cormorants and the Darter also do it, but less conspicuously.

Pelicans are affected by pesticides and related chemicals from the food they eat. The result is egg-shell thinning, which leads to egg loss.

Australian Pelicans are nomadic. One to four white eggs are laid in a ground hollow; the young are naked when hatched.

Reading
Vestjens, W. J. M. (1977), 'Breeding behaviour and ecology of the Australian Pelican . . . in NSW', *Aust. Wildl. Res.* **4**, 37-58.

Breeding season (*variable*)

77 Australian Pelican*

Gannets, Boobies   Family Sulidae

Gannets and boobies are straight-billed birds, adapted to plunging into the sea from great heights. Gannets lack the naked gular region and mask of the boobies and have shorter tails. Except when breeding in colonies on land, they are found out at sea. One to two whitish eggs are laid in a mound or on a stick nest. One chick is favoured, the other usually dies. Abbott's Booby of Christmas Island is illustrated on page 43.

Reading
Nelson, J. B. (1978), *The Sulidae, Gannets and Boobies*, OUP, London.

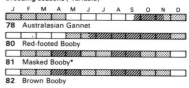

Breeding seasons (*variable*)

78 Australasian Gannet

80 Red-footed Booby

81 Masked Booby*

82 Brown Booby

Darters   Family Anhingidae

Darters are very long-necked cormorant-like birds with sharp, pointed bills. When fishing only their necks are visible. Their habits are similar to the cormorants.

Reading
Vestjens, W. J. M. (1974), 'Breeding behaviour of the Darter at Lake Cowal, NSW', *Emu* **75**, 121-131.

Breeding season (*variable*)

83 Darter*

Shags, Cormorants   Family Phalacrocoracidae

Shags and cormorants are long-necked birds with bills that are hooked at the tip. All Australian species are black or pied. Two groups are defined: the sea-cormorants or shags (*Leucocarbo*) and the other cormorants (*Phalacrocorax*). All catch fish by swimming and diving from the surface. After fishing, cormorants and darters spread their wings, the reason for this is not yet known. One to five whitish eggs are laid in a platform nest in a tree or on the ground.

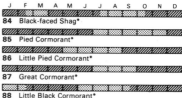

Breeding seasons (*variable*)

84 Black-faced Shag*

85 Pied Cormorant*

86 Little Pied Cormorant*

87 Great Cormorant*

88 Little Black Cormorant*

Frigatebirds   Family Fregatidae

Frigatebirds are black or black and white with long bills that are hooked at the tip. The adult male has a red gular pouch that resembles a balloon when inflated. Their flight is very graceful. They are piratic, mobbing other birds to steal food. Occasionally they catch their own food. One white egg is laid in a nest of sticks, usually on bushes.

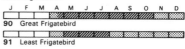

Breeding seasons

90 Great Frigatebird

91 Least Frigatebird

Tropicbirds   Family Phaethontidae

Tropicbirds are white with black markings and straight tern-like bills. Adults have very long central tail streamers which are either red or white. Some populations have pinkish (Red-tailed) or apricot (White-tailed) hues to the feather tips, when plumage is fresh. Tropicbirds breed on cliffs, in crevices, on islands and lay one white egg.

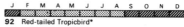

Breeding season (*variable*)

92 Red-tailed Tropicbird*

Herons, Egrets, Bitterns   Family Ardeidae

Accurate field observations, particularly of plumage, soft-part colours, and behaviour changes which occur just before egg laying, are unknown for a surprising number of heron species. Detailed study and reporting by bird-watchers is needed in Australia.

Herons are adapted to capture prey such as insects, crustaceans, frogs and fish in water, and insects on land, using four main feeding techniques: standing and waiting, slow stalk, active pursuit, and (sometimes) hovering and plunging. The first three techniques use modified wing and leg movements to attract, disturb or confuse prey. Some (e.g. Striated Heron, Little Egret) will spread one or both wings, searching for prey in their shadows. This reduces glare but may attract fish as would shade from an overhanging branch. One or both wings may be flicked to startle prey; a foot is treadled to either disturb prey or possibly, as in the case of the Little Egret, to attract it to its yellow sole.

Until the beginning of this century, heron species which acquired spectacular plumes were ruthlessly killed to supply the millinery trade. Populations of many species were severely reduced because breeding adults were shot just as egg laying commenced. Today, with no such hunting, conservation depends on preservation of suitable wetland habitats which *must* be maintained undisturbed.

Colonial nesting species are monogamous, pairing only for the duration of the breeding season. Ornamental plumes and soft-part colour changes are important in establishing the pair bonds. The nest site is vigorously defended; the Australasian Bittern probably does not defend its nest site (it is little studied but closely related to the polygamous European Bittern) because several females nest in its territory. Heron feeding areas are not defended and spectacular concentrations may form when food is abundant. The Eastern Reef Egret is exceptional in that pairs defend the feeding area when it is exposed at low tide.

Breeding seasons (*variable*)

J	F	M	A	M	J	J	A	S	O	N	D

94 Great-billed Heron
95 Pacific Heron
96 White-faced Heron
97 Pied Heron
98 Cattle Egret
99 Great Egret*
100 Little Egret*
101 Intermediate Egret*
102 Eastern Reef Egret
103 Striated Heron
104 Rufous Night Heron
105 Little Bittern
107 Black Bittern
108 Australasian Bittern

Storks   Family Ciconiidae

The Black-necked Stork (formerly known as Jabiru) feeds on small mammals, frogs, lizards, insects and carrion. They are sedentary and remain paired for many years. They only occur in groups of more than four or five when severe drought reduces suitable habitat. Nests are large stick and reed platforms in tall trees, low bushes or on the ground surrounded by water. The birds lay two to four eggs. Rarely do all chicks survive the 100-115 days to nest departure.

Breeding season

J	F	M	A	M	J	J	A	S	O	N	D

109 Black-necked Stork

Ibises, Spoonbills   Family Plataleidae

Ibises and spoonbills chase visible prey; ibises feed on hard ground if crickets or grasshoppers are abundant; both probe in water for invisible prey.

Huge mixed breeding colonies may occur. Ibises' nests are packed close together on reeds, bushes or islands — rarely in trees. Spoonbills may nest low, intermingled with the ibises, or high in outer branches of large trees. Ibises frequently travel 30-40 kilometres from colonies to feed, using thermals to gain height before flying directly to or from the colony. Unlike herons, ibises and spoonbills *always* fly with their necks extended.

Breeding seasons (*variable*)

J	F	M	A	M	J	J	A	S	O	N	D

110 Glossy Ibis*
111 Sacred Ibis*
112 Straw-necked Ibis*
113 Royal Spoonbill*
114 Yellow-billed Spoonbill*

Geese, Swans, Ducks   Family Anatidae

Waterfowl probably evolved from a shorebird-like ancestor about 50 million years ago. The Family Anatidae is large, with three Sub-Families, 13 tribes, 43 genera and about 148 species with world-wide distribution. Australia has birds of all three Sub-Families including the unique Anseranatinae with its single genus and species, the Magpie Goose. We have ten of the tribes, including Stictonettini (containing only the Freckled Duck) and 23 species (19 native, two vagrants and two introduced; one more vagrant, [Lake] Baikal Teal *Anas formosa* from eastern USSR, was identified in the Northern Territory late in 1983 and is not discussed further here).

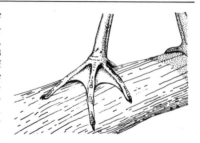

The Magpie Goose has a semi-palmated (partly webbed) foot.

Closely associated with water, most waterfowl possess webbed feet, dense waterproof plumage, and usually rather broad, flat bills with lamellae (a fine series of grooves) which act as sieves or gripping surfaces for feeding. Waterfowl also display great diversity in size (35 cm-long pygmy-geese to the 150 cm-long Mute Swan). Diverse feeding habitats are utilised. Some are mainly terrestrial, grazing on open plains or in shallow billabongs, others utilise rivers, deep lakes, coastal estuaries and the seashore.

Courtship displays vary in Anatidae, ranging from simple 'haughty' posturing in geese to elaborate animated displays by brightly coloured male dabbling ducks. Geese and swans usually mate for life, ducks take a new partner every year.

Waterfowl nest in many habitats, from isolated rocky islands to swamps, among crops, in arctic tundra and flooded woodlands. Nests can be on the ground or high in tree hollows, varying from basic scrapes lined with down (ducks) to large bulky nests of vegetation (swans). Typical clutch sizes are eight or more in ducks, and five to six in swans. Incubation varies from 21-28 days for stiff-tailed and dabbling ducks, and up to 35-40 days for swans.

Black Swans at their nest.

All waterfowl have a covering of thick, waterproof down on hatching and may enter the water almost immediately. The fledging period is from 35 days for teals to 100 days for swans.

The attainment of nuptial plumage may be only six months in dabbling ducks. Some species, however, assume an immature plumage after the juvenal stage and do not reach nuptial plumage until after 12 months.

The flight feathers of most waterfowl are moulted simultaneously, usually after the young have been raised. A flightless and very vulnerable period ensues: from six to eight weeks in swans to three to four weeks in ducks. Only the Magpie Goose moults its flight feathers sequentially so that flight is never lost.

Some male ducks enter an eclipse plumage (a dull non-breeding plumage) after breeding, but others (some tropical species) do not attain this plumage. Eclipse plumages are subject to much speculation and are not fully understood.

The flight feathers of the Black Swan are moulted simultaneously. This leaves the bird flightless for a short period.

Waterfowl migration is very apparent in the Northern Hemisphere where vast numbers leave northern breeding areas, moving south to warmer regions along fairly defined 'flyways'. Southern Hemisphere waterfowl do *not* perform regular seasonal migrations. In Africa and Australia large irruptive, nomadic movements occur in some species due to the widely fluctuating water regimes resulting from irregular rainfall patterns over large areas of these continents.

Twelve of the 19 Australian waterfowl species (63 per cent) are endemic to Australia and New Guinea. Notes on some of the most interesting endemics follow.

Magpie Goose. This goose of the far north plains and swamps of Australia was more widely distributed before 1900. Breeding colonies existed as far south as Westernport Bay, Victoria, and Bool Lagoon, South Australia. In New South Wales it occurred on the Lachlan and Murrumbidgee Rivers. By 1911, it had disappeared from the southern parts of its range because of extensive shooting for food, habitat destruction, and poisoning when flocks invaded crops. Today it only occurs as a vagrant from the north.

Cape Barren Goose. The taxonomy of this strange goose is still confused. Some taxonomists suggest a relationship to the Southern American Kelp Goose *Chloephaga*. Others place it tentatively with the Shelducks *Tadornini*. Affinities with *both* true geese and shelducks are currently accepted and therefore it is placed in a separate tribe Cereopsini.

Freckled Duck. This primitive species is considered to be related to the swans due to the similar plumages, swan-like voice, simple courtship display and grey, downy young. An inhabitant of large, permanent, inland cumbungi swamps and dense coastal tea-tree swamps, it is dispersive and nomadic during droughts, sometimes occurring in large numbers near the coast. This species, classified at present as being of 'indeterminate status' was subject to an Australia-wide census during the 1982-83 drought. The minimum population estimate was 8000, the maximum 18 700.

Chestnut Teal. This species is less common than the Grey Teal and more coastal in distribution. Its population has probably declined since European arrival due to the elimination of its optimum habitat, thought to have been brackish tea-tree swamps. It readily uses nest boxes for breeding, but it is questionable whether this truly benefits the species. Courting males perform attractive communal 'whistling' and 'burp-whistling' displays.

Pink-eared Duck. This aberrant member of the Anatini is well-suited to Australian conditions, utilising extensive, shallow, temporary, inland, floodwater pools at any time of the year. The highly specialised bill is fringed with very fine lamellae to filter out microscopic plants and animals, which are the bulk of the bird's diet.

Musk Duck. This species is named for the musky odour of the males, resulting from secretions of the uropygial gland (a small oil gland at the tail base). The strange lobe of the male's throat varies in size with age and sexual activity. When breeding, the lobe is engorged with blood and is part of the birds' bizarre splashing courtship display.

Conservation of waterfowl could be greatly assisted by research into population fluctuations and their relationship to habitat quality, water regimes, climatic data and hunting pressure. Amateur bird-watchers could provide a lot of the base data on species' abundance and diversity by participating in co-ordinated seasonal counts throughout Australia.

Reading

Delacour, J. (1954-64), *The Waterfowl of the World*, 4 vols, Country Life, London.

Johnsgard, P. A. (1973), *Waterfowl: Their Biology and Natural History*, Univ. of Nebraska Press, Lincoln.

Cowling, S. J. (1978), 'The Status of Endangered Waterfowl and Wetlands in Australia' in *The Status of Endangered Australian Wildlife*, Royal Zool. Soc. SA, Adelaide, pp. 123-131.

Frith, H. J. (1982), *Waterfowl in Australia*, Angus and Robertson, Sydney.

Courting Chestnut Teal males (bottom) attract a female (top) with their communal whistling displays.

Breeding seasons (*variable*)

	J	F	M	A	M	J	J	A	S	O	N	D
115 Magpie Goose												
116 Wandering Whistling-Duck												
117 Plumed Whistling-Duck*												
118 Black Swan*												
119 Mute Swan*												
120 Freckled Duck*												
121 Cape Barren Goose												
122 Australian Shelduck												
123 Radjah Shelduck												
124 Pacific Black Duck*												
125 Mallard												
126 Grey Teal*												
127 Chestnut Teal*												
128 Australasian Shoveler*												
131 Pink-eared Duck*												
132 Hardhead												
133 Maned Duck*												
134 Cotton Pygmy-Goose												
135 Green Pygmy-Goose												
136 Blue-billed Duck*												
137 Musk Duck*												

Birds of Prey   Families Pandionidae, Accipitridae, Falconidae

The Order Accipitriformes, diurnal birds of prey, contains five diverse Families: Cathartidae (New World vultures, condors); Pandionidae (Osprey); Accipitridae (Old World vultures, kites, buzzards, hawks, eagles, harriers etc.); Sagittariidae (Secretary Bird); and Falconidae (falcons, caracaras etc.). However, these Families may *not* share one origin. The Order may consist of unrelated groups resembling each other convergently. Cathartidae and Falconidae may be more closely related to the Procellariiformes-Pelecaniformes, and the Strigiformes, respectively, than to the other diurnal raptors.

In the Order, 'reversed size dimorphism' applies for many species. That is, females are generally larger than males. This has relevance for feeding ecology and breeding behaviour.

The three Families that occur in Australia are listed below.

Osprey   Family Pandionidae

This Family contains only one genus *Pandion*, with one species, the Osprey. Usually coastal dwelling, it is a highly specialised fish catcher. It has some unique (probably adaptive) anatomical features: a reversible outer toe, spicules under the foot, and closable nostril. (See illustrations above right.) It constructs a stick nest in trees, on rocky outcrops, or on the ground. Its nests may be used for many years and may assume massive proportions.

Breeding season

J	F	M	A	M	J	J	A	S	O	N	D

138   Osprey

Kites, Goshawks, Eagles, Harriers   Family Accipitridae

This Family consists of 12 Australian genera and 17 species. The genera are listed below.

Elanus. Australia's two elanid kites are specialist hunters of small rodents. The Letter-winged Kite hunts the nocturnal Long-haired Rat *Rattus villosissimus* in central Australia. When these rats reach plague numbers (often after flooding), Letter-winged Kites breed continuously in colonies — the only Australian raptor to do so. When rat populations subsequently fall, the kites must either leave or starve. Large-scale dispersal to coastal areas may occur. Black-shouldered Kites seem to have increased numerically in coastal areas this century, possibly due to increased populations of the introduced House Mouse. The species hunts from perches and by hovering, mainly at dawn or dusk. The birds build small stick nests in tree canopies, often breeding in spring and again in autumn.

Aviceda. The Pacific Baza is the only local example of its genus. Bazas have a short head crest, a long tail, and relatively weak feet. Largely insectivorous, they crash into tree tops to take phasmids (leaf insects). A small nest of twigs is built high in a forest tree.

Milvus. This genus has two species: one, the Black Kite, occurs in Australia. Tens of thousands of Black Kites occur in northern Australia during the dry season, but six months later they have gone, along with the slightly less numerous Whistling Kites. Many may migrate to inland Australia to breed, others may go north to Asia — only a large-scale banding operation will tell. Ever an opportunist and scavenger, the Black Kite is attracted to bushfire smoke, and is often the first of the predatory birds to take fire victims. It is

These Black Kites are soaring in a thermal.

Breeding seasons (*variable)

J	F	M	A	M	J	J	A	S	O	N	D

139   Black-shouldered Kite*

140   Letter-winged Kite*

141   Pacific Baza*

primarily a carrion feeder, and is often displaced at the carcass by more aggressive species. It breeds in a fairly large stick nest — either newly built or a disused existing one.

Lophoictinia and *Hamirostra*. These genera contain two monotypic Australian endemic species: the Square-tailed Kite and Black-breasted Buzzard respectively. The two are related, but their relationship to other raptors is obscure. Detailed behavioural, anatomical and biochemical studies of both would be invaluable. The Black-breasted Buzzard is more common in northern and central Australia, in contrast to the more coastal Square-tailed Kite. Both feed on nestling birds, and both build large stick nests. Pairs of buzzards share incubation, nest guarding and hunting almost equally — an unusual phenomenon. Even more unusual is their habit of feeding their nestlings and one another, at the same time.

Haliastur. This genus contains two species, both in Australia: the widespread Whistling Kite, and the north coastal Brahminy Kite. The two are similar in important respects: both use a distinctive, slow, wheeling flight to locate carrion (live prey is also taken); both generally nest high in tree forks, lining the stick nests with green leaves (Brahminy Kites sometimes use seaweed).

Accipiter. There are about 50 species in this genus, of which only three occur in Australia. They are the Brown Goshawk, Collared Sparrowhawk and Grey Goshawk. Accipiters have short, rounded wings, long tails and fairly long, yellow legs. Long toes and claws facilitate capture and killing of prey. The three Australian species take birds, small mammals, reptiles and insects. Birds are likely to be the major dietary component of the Collared Sparrowhawk and probably the Grey Goshawk. The introduced rabbit is an important prey species for the Brown Goshawk. All three species generally construct stick nests high in trees, lining these with green leaves. The same nest may be used several times. The two colour morphs of the Grey Goshawk interbreed freely, producing offspring of either colour. On rare occasions Grey Goshawks have interbred with Brown Goshawks.

Erythrotriorchis. The Red Goshawk has been regarded as sufficiently different from the accipiters to warrant its own monotypic genus. It has comparatively long wings and a fairly short tail, together with extremely powerful legs and feet. One of Australia's rarest raptors, it appears restricted to remote woodlands of northern Australia. Historical records suggest its range is shrinking. Red Goshawks use large stick nests placed high in tall trees — few nests have been found in recent years.

Haliaeetus. The White-bellied Sea-Eagle is the only Australian representative of this genus. It has long, broad wings, well suited to soaring, and powerful legs, feet and talons (sharp claw on toes). Spectacular dives to the surface of coastal and inland waters are used to secure fish, while other foods, including mammals, reptiles and birds are often taken as carrion. The species uses a sizeable, flat-topped stick nest lined with green leaves. Sites chosen include tree forks, offshore rock outcrops and cliff ledges. Nests may be used for many successive years.

Aquila. This genus contains very large eagles with long, 'fingered' wings, extremely powerful legs and feet, and deep, sharply hooked bills. The Wedge-tailed Eagle is Australia's only example of the genus. It is predominantly a carrion feeder across the continent, although live prey, rabbits, small macropods and birds are also taken by diving

Sexual dimorphism in the Brown Goshawk: large female (left); small male (right).

Breeding seasons (*variable*)

J F M A M J J A S O N D

142 Black Kite*

143 Square-tailed Kite*

144 Black-breasted Buzzard*

145 Brahminy Kite*

146 Whistling Kite*

147 Brown Goshawk*

148 Collared Sparrowhawk*

149 Grey Goshawk*

150 Red Goshawk* (*not well known*)

151 White-bellied Sea-Eagle

152 Wedge-tailed Eagle

153 Little Eagle

154 Spotted Harrier

155 Swamp (Marsh) Harrier

or by rapid pursuit. Wedge-tails have a long history of human persecution, mainly as a consequence of alleged stock predation. Intensive research has shown the accusation to be largely unfounded. Nevertheless, the species remains unprotected in Western Australia, as does the Brown Goshawk. Wedge-tailed Eagles construct very large stick nests, often low to the ground if there are no sturdy trees. A nest may be used for many years, or several alternative nests in the same vicinity may be used in rotation.

Hieraaetus. Birds in this genus share feathered tarsi (lower legs) with the *Aquila* eagles, but are usually smaller, more slender, and have long toes and powerful claws much like the *Accipiter* hawks. The Little Eagle is Australia's sole example. Rapid, powerful flight secures prey, both birds and mammals (especially rabbits, where available). Little Eagles usually build a platform-type stick nest, lined with green leaves, in a tree fork. The same nest may be used for some years. The abandoned nest of another species may also be used.

Circus. The birds of this genus, the harriers, have long tails and wings, and very long legs. Their prey, small rodents and waterfowl, are sought by a characteristic low quartering flight over grasslands and swamps. An owl-like facial disc promotes acute hearing and thus prey location. In Australia the Swamp Harrier engages in spectacular diving displays above the chosen breeding site — a platform trampled in long grass, crops or swampland. Sometimes the species is polygamous; invariably it is very sensitive to nest disturbance. After breeding, many Tasmanian Swamp Harriers migrate to the mainland. There, at night in long grass or swamps, they roost communally with mainland birds.

Spotted Harriers are the world's only tree-nesting harriers. A nomadic bird of the inland areas, they are monogamous, defending large exclusive territories. Like most raptors, females do most nest building, incubation and guarding of the young; males hunt (females hunt once the chicks have attained two weeks).

The Marsh Harrier's nest is a platform in long grass, crops or swamplands.

The owl-like facial disc of the Spotted Harrier assists hearing and thus prey location.

Falcons   Family Falconidae

Falcons are powerful birds with long, narrow, pointed wings and fairly short tails. Unlike the Accipitridae, they *lack* a spasmodic clutching foot mechanism; prey is generally killed by severing the neck vertebrae with a bite. To this end they have powerful bills, with tomial teeth in the upper mandible, and corresponding notches below.

The Family has one genus in Australia, *Falco*, and six species: Black Falcon, Peregrine Falcon, Australian Hobby, the rare arid zone Grey Falcon, Brown Falcon and Australian Kestrel. While the Black, Grey and Brown Falcons prey on birds and mammals, Peregrines and the Australian Hobby seem to rely largely on birds and insects, often taken in spectacular stoops or by rapid pursuit. Australian Kestrels hover or perch in search of ground-dwelling small vertebrates and insects. Falcons generally nest on cliff ledges, in tree hollows or in disused stick nests of other species. No reliable published reports exist to indicate that any of the Australian falcons build their own nests, despite assertions to the contrary. Falcons are among birds most severely affected by pesticides. DDT affects the shell gland, causing egg-shell thinning, which leads to lowered reproductive success. Thus, falcon populations serve as environmental quality guides.

Peregrine Falcons have powerful bills with tomial teeth in the upper mandible and corresponding notches below.

Breeding seasons

	J	F	M	A	M	J	J	A	S	O	N	D

157 Black Falcon

158 Peregrine Falcon

159 Australian Hobby

160 Grey Falcon

161 Brown Falcon

162 Australian Kestrel

Mound-builders (Megapodes) Family Megapodiidae

Megapodes are considered to be most closely related to pheasants (Phasianidae). These big-footed birds scratch and pile sand, soil and vegetation litter into a large mound. Their eggs are laid in tiers in a deep hole in the mound's top. A combination of the sun's direct heat, and the heat generated by the fermentation of the rotting litter incubates the eggs. In some areas of New Guinea and some Western Pacific islands, incubation of the local Scrubfowl's eggs is assisted by volcanic heat.

Mated for life, a pair inhabits a large territory. Normally only one of the pair operates a mound; the Scrubfowl is an occasional exception. Males usually manage the mounds and control the incubating temperature. The Malleefowl is able to maintain total temperature control; the Australian Brush-turkey and Scrubfowl have less control.

The chicks are quite independent. They dig their own way out of the mound and fly within hours of surfacing. Apart from humans, mound predators include goannas, pythons, carnivorous marsupials and introduced pigs and foxes.

If pressed, megapodes fly well but heavily. They usually roost in trees. All feed on invertebrates and small vertebrates, seeds and fallen native fruits.

The Scrubfowl is widespread from the Philippines across to New Guinea, Australia and Western Pacific islands. The other species are local endemics. Plumage colours suit their varied habitats quite closely. The jungle-dwelling Australian Brush-turkey is very dark; the Scrubfowl is medium brown and lives in a range of dense to lightly vegetated, sometimes rocky, terrains. In the open scrubby country of inland Australia, Malleefowls are camouflaged; the black chest line breaks up the bird's pattern as it stands quietly among small mallee eucalypt boughs.

Fossil skeletal elements of a very much larger megapode (called *Progrura gallinacea*) have been found in Pleistocene deposits of south-east Queensland.

Reading
Frith, H J. (1962), *The Malleefowl*, Angus & Robertson, Sydney.

A diagrammatic cut-away of a Malleefowl mound showing the egg chamber and leaf litter.

Megapode hatchlings

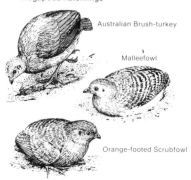

Australian Brush-turkey

Malleefowl

Orange-footed Scrubfowl

Breeding seasons

	J	F	M	A	M	J	J	A	S	O	N	D
163 Orange-footed Scrubfowl												
164 Malleefowl												
165 Australian Brush-turkey												

Quails, Pheasants Family Phasianidae

Two Sub-Families occur in Australia: Phasianinae, native quails and introduced pheasants; Odontophorinae, the introduced California Quail. All introduced species are rare or confined to islands.

Pheasants and quails are dumpy ground birds with long necks, small heads, short bills, strong legs and feet. Quails have short tails. Pheasants are large with long tails that are often decoratively coloured.

Native quails are fairly nomadic, wandering wherever conditions are suitable and breeding in large numbers in some seasons. The Stubble Quail prefers open grassy areas; the King Quail likes rank grasslands, often near swamps; the Brown Quail prefers grassy regions near forests and bracken. Quails hide in grass until nearly walked upon, then flush into a rapid, whirring flight, low to the ground.

Nests are simple, located on the ground under bushes or grass. Between four and 11 eggs are laid. They are pale in colour and darkly spotted. At times, open hunting seasons on these birds are declared.

Breeding seasons (*variable)

	J	F	M	A	M	J	J	A	S	O	N	D
166 Stubble Quail												
167, 168 Swamp and Brown Quails*												
169 King Quail												
170 Peafowl												
171 Feral Chicken*												
172 Common Pheasant (*Insufficient information*)												
173 California Quail												

Button-quails Family Turnicidae

Most button-quail species prefer to live in grassland and appear to be nomadic. The first indication of their presence comes as they 'explode' from near an observer's feet. Button-quails feed on seeds and insects. Females lay about four eggs in a cup-shaped ground nest near a tussock or shrub. Males incubate the eggs for about 14 days and care for the young. Their calls are little known and worthy of further study.

Two species are particularly rare: habitat clearance has diminished the Black-breasted's numbers and the Buff-breasted is locally restricted and rarely reported.

Breeding seasons (*variable)

J	F	M	A	M	J	J	A	S	O	N	D

174 Red-backed Button-quail*
175 Painted Button-quail
176 Chestnut-backed Button-quail
177 Buff-breasted Button-quail
178 Black-breasted Button-quail
179 Little Button-quail*
180 Red-chested Button-quail*

Plains-wanderer Family Pedionomidae

This monotypic Family is confined to Australia. Classification has been disputed since its discovery. It closely resembles the button-quails (Turnicidae) in appearance and in that the female is the brighter and dominant bird, but it has a hind toe like true quails. The quality of its plumage is similar to the bustards, and its eggs and some of its behaviour resemble some waders. Current taxonomy places it near the button-quails but in a Family of its own.

The Plains-wanderer is a cryptically coloured, upright little bird that will 'freeze' or run, rather than fly. In flight, its wings are rounded, slightly drooped and have a weak fluttering action.

The Plains-wanderer inhabits grassy plains; it was once more widely spread (see map, page 82). It is possible that introduced grasses and grazing have had a deleterious effect on the population. The Plains-wanderer is nomadic and a wet-year breeder. Males incubate and care for the young, the females do not participate once eggs are laid. The nest is a ground scrape, lined with grass. The four eggs are pale green-buff blotched and spotted brown, grey and olive.

Reading
Bennett, S. (1983), 'A review of the distribution, status and biology of the Plains Wanderer *Pedionomus torquatus*, Gould', *Emu* **83**, (1), 1-11.

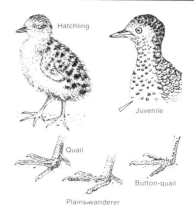

Hatchling

Juvenile

Quail

Button-quail

Plains-wanderer

The Plains-wanderer resembles button-quails in appearance and in that the female is the brighter and dominant bird, but it has a hind toe like true quails.

Breeding season

J	F	M	A	M	J	J	A	S	O	N	D

181 Plains-wanderer

Rails, Crakes, Swamphens, Coots Family Rallidae

The rails, gallinules (swamphens, moorhens) and coots are a large cosmopolitan Family of mainly aquatic birds. Australia is represented by 16 species, two of them vagrants. Rails superficially resemble fowls, but are unrelated. In Australia they range from sparrow-sized (Baillon's Crake) to rooster-sized (Purple Swamphen). All rails are characterised by: short wings; fairly long, powerful legs with long, unwebbed toes; short tails; general shortness and stoutness of body. Bill shape ranges from long and slender in Lewin's Rail to short (majority of rails) and sometimes stout (Purple Swamphen). Swamphens, moorhens and coots have large frontal shields (skin extended from the bill into the frons), ranging through vestigial frontal shields (crakes, bush-hens, water-hens) to none. Coots are characterised by flaps of skin on their toes which help to propel them through water. Their manner of flight varies from rapid fluttering, which is like the quails' but weaker, to flightlessness in some island forms, as in the Tasmanian Native-hen.

Rails have a characteristic habit of flicking their tail up and down when swimming or walking, especially noticeable

Purple Swamphen

Dusky Moorhen

Red-necked Crake

Australian Crake

Spotless Crake

Lewin's Rail

The size and shape of bills and frontal shields varies in the Family Rallidae.

Breeding seasons (*variable)

J	F	M	A	M	J	J	A	S	O	N	D

182 Buff-banded Rail*
183 Lewin's Rail
184 Chestnut Rail

in those with white markings on their tail coverts. The function of this is not quite known. Many rails are notorious for their secretive habits. Except for the coots, moorhens, swamphens and native-hens which feed in the open much of the time, the rest spend their time in dense vegetation, especially reeds and associated habitats. The only way to see some species is to wait by the waterside until one appears.

The voice of rails generally consists of harsh, hoarse squeaking, nasal noises and clicking. Their voices often give away their presence as each species has its own distinctive calls. Rail food varies from small invertebrates and worms to vegetable matter, depending on the species. Australian rails are nomadic. They build up their numbers in wet years and disperse to the coast and remaining waterholes in dry years. Nests are deep, fibrous, well-lined and cup-like. Except for the coots, which have large floating nests anchored to reeds, or nests built on tops of bushes standing in water, all nests are well-concealed in thick vegetation. Egg clutches vary from three to 10. When hatched, nestlings are downy and soon are able to walk and then run.

Breeding seasons (*variable*)

J	F	M	A	M	J	J	A	S	O	N	D

186 Red-necked Crake
188 Baillon's Crake*
189 Australian Crake
190 Spotless Crake
191 White-browed Crake
192 Bush-hen
193 Tasmanian Native-hen
194 Black-tailed Native-hen*
195 Dusky Moorhen*
196 Purple Swamphen*
197 Eurasian Coot*

Cranes   Family Gruidae

Fossil cranes date back 40-60 million years. Four of the world's 15 modern and widespread species are endangered.

The Sarus Crane has two races but only race *sharpii* occurs in Australia. It was first recorded in Queensland in 1967.

Brolgas and Sarus Cranes are alike in behaviour and biology. Their food includes insects, freshwater and saltwater invertebrates, small vertebrates and plant matter. Bulkuru sedge *Eleocharis dulcis* is a preferred Brolga food. Brolgas are considered non-migratory but move long distances for food and water. Both cranes are monogamous, probably forming life pairs and breeding at traditional sites during each year's wettest months. A drought may halt breeding. Nests of coarse grass, sticks and leaves often form a raised mound above water or on dry land. One to three (usually two) eggs are laid. Both sexes incubate for 29-32 days. Brolga hatchlings are grey, Sarus Crane hatchlings tawny. They run and swim hours after emerging but are fed by their parents Families persist for up to 10 months.

An incubating Brolga on a raised nest.

Breeding seasons (*variable*)

J	F	M	A	M	J	J	A	S	O	N	D

198 Brolga*
199 Sarus Crane*

Bustards   Family Otididae

The 11 genera of Old World bustards are all very similar in appearance and biology. Genus *Ardeotis* occurs in Australia, Africa, India and Arabia.

Nomadic omnivores (insects, small vertebrates, plant material), bustards seek areas abundant in food after rain and can survive long periods without drinking.

The onset of breeding is closely allied to the amount and intensity of rain and the number of wet days. Bustards are probably polygamous. Only females incubate and care for the young. Males can breed at five to six years; females at two to three years. One or occasionally two eggs are laid in a ground scrape and incubated for 23-24 days. Young are precocial (mobile very soon after hatching).

Bustards were killed in their thousands after 1860 until fully protected in 1935. Foxes and habitat destruction reduced their range to northern monsoonal Australia where heavy rains prevent human access during breeding. Population recovery is slow. A rehabilitation programme operates in Victoria.

When courting, the male Kori Bustard inflates its throat sac and gives roaring calls.

Breeding season (*variable*)

J	F	M	A	M	J	J	A	S	O	N	D

200 Kori Bustard*

Waders   Families Jacanidae, Burhinidae, Rostratulidae, Haematopodidae, Charadriidae, Recurvirostridae, Scolopacidae, Phalaropodidae, Glareolidae

Introduction

The Royal Australasian Ornithologists Union has been conducting research into the waders of Australia since 1981. In the many investigations run by the RAOU, volunteer bird-watchers get pleasure from gaining, then using, their knowledge of birds to generate information. This information helps to plan for the conservation of Australia's avifauna.

Over 1.7 million waders spend the non-breeding months in Australia. Some 84 per cent of these occur at 19 major sites. Three major regions of Australia account for over 80 per cent of the waders in Australia (*i*) the south-eastern marine embayments, estuaries and lakes of South Australia and Victoria, (*ii*) the Gulf of Carpentaria and (*iii*) the Northern Territory and the north-western coast of Western Australia. The most abundant species are the Red-necked Stint, Curlew Sandpiper, Sharp-tailed Sandpiper and Banded Stilt in southern Australia, and the Great Knot, Red Knot, Bar-tailed Godwit, Large Sand Plover, Mongolian Plover and Grey-tailed Tattler in the north.

A mixed flock of waders roosting at high tide. The flock includes Grey-tailed Tattlers, Bar-tailed Godwits, Terek Sandpipers, Eastern Curlews and Whimbrels (sleeping).

National wader counts are held twice yearly (Summer-February and Winter-July), involving over 300 people counting at over 500 sites, mostly in the more populated southern and eastern parts of Australia. They provide data on the numbers of each species and their important sites within these regions. Over time, these data will provide an index of population fluctuations for many species, enabling those which are declining to be identified and conservation measures to be undertaken.

Aerial surveys are conducted in conjunction with the national wader counts as well as at other times in parts of remote northern Australia. Where ground access is often difficult, aerial surveys have contributed much to knowledge of where there are important wader habitats.

Ground-based expeditions to the remote northern coastline are also organised. More than five expeditions to the Broome-Port Hedland coast, an area which supports over half a million waders, have been held. Counting and banding work has shown that this area is of critical importance to waders migrating into Australia and moving onward to the rest of the continent.

Regular monthly wader counts are held at a selection of sites throughout Australia. They are done by amateurs, usually on weekends. A national overview of these results will reveal when and where the peak migratory passage occurs.

Groups and individuals are conducting wader banding studies in all capital cities and some provincial centres. All such work is undertaken by amateur groups. Over 10 000 waders have been banded in Australia and these have resulted in a small number of recoveries within Australia and a few from overseas. Why don't you join in?

All this information is of great value in planning national conservation priorities for these internationally significant birds, and to provide information in support of the Australia-Japan Migratory Birds Treaty.

The following pages (300-304) summarise the wader Families. Regretfully, for some birds we have omitted regions of their origin in the Northern Hemisphere.

Curlew Sandpipers and Red-necked Stints fly in a mixed flock.

Jacanas (Lotusbirds)   Family Jacanidae

Jacanas appear more akin to rails (Rallidae) than waders, but are considered to be an early wader development. They occur in tropical or subtropical areas of South America, Africa, India, South-East Asia and Australia. Our resident species is possibly locally nomadic or migratory. The Pheasant-tailed Jacana, of South-East Asia, *may* arrive here — unreliable records exist.

Jacanas have small spurs on their wings. Their head bobs back and forth as they walk over floating vegetation. In flight, their long legs and toes trail. They nest during rainy/monsoon periods on a damp pile of floating herbage.

Breeding season (*variable)

J	F	M	A	M	J	J	A	S	O	N	D

201   Comb-crested Jacana*

Thick-knees (Stone Curlews)   Family Burhinidae

Largely crepuscular and nocturnal in habit, the thick-knees' evolutionary relationship to other waders is still not clear. Two sedentary species occur in Australia. The Bush Thick-knee is not uncommon in temperate and tropical mainland Australia, especially in the north, but is becoming rare in settled southern areas. The Beach Thick-knee is uncommon but widespread in the tropics.

Breeding seasons (*variable)

J	F	M	A	M	J	J	A	S	O	N	D

203   Bush Thick-knee*

204   Beach Thick-knee

Painted Snipe   Family Rostratulidae

Egg-white protein analysis shows that the Painted Snipe is fairly closely related to the jacanas. One species is South American; the other occurs through central and southern Africa, southern Asia, to China, Japan and Australia. The local breeding race seems non-migratory but nomadic. It is mainly crepuscular and difficult to find.

Reading
Lowe, V. J. (1963), 'Observations on the Painted Snipe', *Emu* **62**, 221-237.

Breeding season (*variable)

J	F	M	A	M	J	J	A	S	O	N	D

205   Painted Snipe*

Oystercatchers   Family Haematopodidae

The evolutionary development of the oystercatchers is obscure, but they have some affinities with avocets, stilts, and possibly thick-knees. They are non-migratory but locally nomadic. Pied and Sooty Oystercatchers occur widely round Australian coasts. The Pied is a local race of a species spread over the world, including New Zealand (South Island); the Sooty is a native Australian. The Pied is common; the Sooty, which prefers rocky shores, is less so.

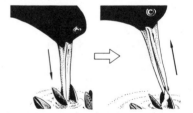

The feeding technique of Oystercatchers is shown here.

Their food is obtained by cutting the adductor muscles closing bivalve mollusc shells, and by prising limpets and other gastropods from rocks, or by dismembering crustaceans.

Oystercatchers are social, possibly due to a relatively long period before maturity and pair formation. Pair bonds are often stable over a long period. Some interbreeding occurs, giving hybrid offspring with mixed characteristics (these may be infertile).

Breeding seasons (*variable)

J	F	M	A	M	J	J	A	S	O	N	D

206   Pied Oystercatcher*

207   Sooty Oystercatcher*

Lapwings, Plovers, Dotterels   Family Charadriidae

Lapwings of the Sub-Family Vanellinae are medium-sized, with bills shorter than head length and wing length greater than 15 cm. Two species are local natives, the Banded and Masked Lapwings. Some of the world's 23 species are migratory but not to Australia.

Banded Lapwings are nomadic, usually occurring in drier lands, preferring areas with little cover. They tend to breed in localised colonies and breeding tends to follow rains. Banded Lapwings are fairly common in suitable habitats, more so in temperate Australia.

Masked Lapwings are common, particularly on cleared grazing lands. Two races occur, one across northern Australia, one across the southern regions ('Spur-winged Plover'). The two races overlap in mid-Queensland where interbreeding occurs. During breeding, solitary pairs are very territorial; at other times non-breeding birds may form large flocks. They are non-migratory but locally nomadic up to 150 kilometres.

Plovers and dotterels are small and included in the Sub-Family Charadriinae. The name 'dotterel', although previously embracing the smaller plovers in Australia, is now preferred only for the Inland and Red-kneed Dotterels which do *not* belong to the genera *Pluvialis* (greater plovers) or *Charadrius* (lesser plovers).

The 38 species of the Sub-Family breed in various climatic conditions, from Arctic Siberia and North America to temperate areas like North America, central Asia, South America, South Africa, Australia and New Zealand. Some are found in tropical-subtropical regions of Central and South America, Africa and Australia. Generally, species breeding farthest north in Arctic areas, then migrate furthest southward to escape the northern winter. Those breeding in temperate to tropical areas migrate lesser distances and include some virtually sedentary or only partially nomadic species.

Of the 13 species recorded, five are native Australian residents; eight migrate here or are vagrants.

The Inland Dotterel (formerly 'Australian Dotterel') is uncommon, nomadic and virtually the only species adapted for inland arid areas. The other residents are common, but the Hooded Plover is becoming less so, possibly due to its habitats of southern open ocean beaches and associated grassy dunes becoming more accessible to humans and more frequently disturbed. The migrant species coming here breed in the Northern Hemisphere, except for the Double-banded Plover which breeds in New Zealand and is the only known east-west migrant wader species.

The larger, moderately common, Lesser Golden and Grey Plovers, both breed in tundra regions of far north Siberia and North America. Those reaching Australia are believed to breed in north-eastern Siberia and Alaska. The birds breeding in North America mostly migrate to South America; other wintering (southern summer) areas are China and India.

Of the other smaller migrant plovers, only the Mongolian, Oriental and Large Sand Plovers are common, mainly around northern Australia. The Large Sand, Oriental and Caspian Plovers breed in central Asia, whereas the Mongolian Plover seen in Australia breeds in isolated pockets in north-eastern Siberia.

Ringed Plovers are vagrants, breeding in arctic Europe and Asia, generally migrating to southern Europe, India, across to Africa and rarely further east.

Reading

Bock, W. (1964), 'The systematic position of the Australian Dotterel', *Emu* **63**, 383-404.

McLean, G. L. (1976), 'A field study of the Australian Dotterel', *Emu* **76**, 207-15.

McLean, G. L. (1977), 'Comparative notes on Black-fronted and Red-kneed Dotterels', *Emu* **77**, 199-207.

van Tets, G. F., D'Andria, A.N. & E. Slater, (1967), 'Nesting distribution of Australian vanelline plovers', *Emu* **67**, 85-93.

Masked Lapwings will vigorously defend their territory and young.

Breeding

Moulting

Non-breeding

Lesser Golden Plover
Puvialis dominica fulva

Many of the migratory plovers have colourful breeding plumage and drab non-breeding plumage. Birds can often be seen with irregular blotches of colour when moulting into or out of their breeding plumage.

Breeding seasons (*variable*)

	J	F	M	A	M	J	J	A	S	O	N	D
208 Masked Lapwing*												
209 Banded Lapwing*												
213 Red-kneed Dotterel*												
214 Hooded Plover												
222 Red-capped Plover*												
223 Black-fronted Plover*												
224 Inland Dotterel*												

Stilts, Avocets

Family Recurvirostridae

Stilts, avocets (and oystercatchers) probably evolved from a common plover-like stock. Australia is the only country with three species (all nomadic). The Black-winged Stilt ranges worldwide; the Banded Stilt and Red-necked Avocet are endemic Australians. Black-winged Stilts are fairly common in suitable habitats and are vagrants to Tasmania. The Banded Stilt is more restricted to parts of the west and south-west of Western Australia, across to South Australia and Victoria, occasionally in New South Wales. Avocets are fairly common in suitable areas but are sparse in eastern Victoria, Cape York Pen., northern Queensland and northern Northern Territory.

The front toes of stilts are partly *or* fully webbed; they are *always* fully webbed in avocets. The Banded Stilt, unlike other stilt species, can swim but feeds in a pecking, stilt-like manner when wading. Avocets mostly feed by sweeping with their bills. Occasionally they swim, up-ending like ducks, for food.

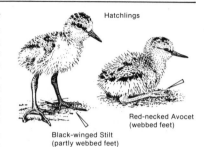

Hatchlings

Red-necked Avocet
(webbed feet)

Black-winged Stilt
(partly webbed feet)

Breeding seasons (*variable*)

J	F	M	A	M	J	J	A	S	O	N	D

225   Black-winged Stilt*

226   Banded Stilt*

227   Red-necked Avocet*

Curlews, Sandpipers, Snipes, Godwits

Family Scolopacidae

This is the largest wader Family. Its species *mostly* breed in northern temperate to Arctic areas. Those migrating to Australia tend to breed in north-eastern Siberia and Alaska rather than western Siberia or Canada. They vary in size from the world's smallest wader, the Red-necked Stint, to the world's largest, the Eastern Curlew. Most are believed to migrate over established species' routes and generally between the same areas each year. Many instances have been recorded of ringed birds being seen in the same locations after one or more overseas migratory flights to breed. Because breeding areas of many different species overlap, there have been occasional Australian sightings of rare vagrant species that normally migrate to Africa or South America.

Juveniles hatch in the northern summer and, arriving from spring to early summer in Australia, do not return to their breeding areas until they are more than a year old. They either stay for the southern summer or migrate relatively small distances northwards. Usually, only juveniles remain in Australia during winter, but very occasionally adults in breeding plumage that have not put on enough body fat for overseas migration may be seen locally during the southern winter.

Abbreviated notes on the species migrating to Australia from the Palaearctic follow:

Ruddy Turnstone. Migrates to S Hem. continents. In Aust. common on rocky coasts; some over-winter.

Eurasian Curlew. Migrates to Europe and Africa. Very rare vagrant here.

Eastern Curlew. Migrates to Taiwan, Philippines, PNG, Aust. Common in suitable areas, especially N, E and SE Aust. coasts.

Whimbrel. Migrates to India, China, SE Asia and S Hem. areas. A race breeding in NE Siberia migrates to Aust. where common around N and E coasts.

Little Curlew. Migrates to NZ, PNG, N Aust.; rare in S of Aust.

Upland Sandpiper. Migrates to S America. Rare vagrant to Aust.

Wood Sandpiper. Migrates to S Africa, S Europe, India, SE Asia, S

China, Japan, PNG and Aust. Reasonably common in N Aust.; uncommon but regular in S Aust. on and near coasts.

Green Sandpiper. Migrates to Africa, SE Asia. Rare vagrant in Aust.

Grey-tailed Tattler. Migrates to China, Taiwan, Australasia. Common N coast of WA, around to NSW.

Wandering Tattler. Migrates to Pacific coasts of America, Pacific islands, Australasia. Rare.

Common Sandpiper. Migrates to S Europe, Africa, S Asia and Aust. where fairly common on N and E Aust. coasts.

Greenshank. Migrates to S Africa, S Europe, Persian Gulf, India, SE Asia, E China and Aust. Common some areas; widespread around our coastline.

Spotted Greenshank. Migrates to SE Asia. Rare vagrant to N Aust.

Redshank. Migrates to Africa, S and SE Asia; occasionally N Aust. coast.

Lesser Yellowlegs. Migrates to Central and S America. Rare vagrant in S of Aust.

Marsh Sandpiper. Migrates to central Asia, Mongolia, Aust. Regular but scarce visitor here.

Terek Sandpiper. Migrates to S Africa, S and SE Asia, Aust. Fairly common to rare here, but widespread.

Latham's Snipe. Migrates to Aust. where common E and SE.

Pin-tailed Snipe. Migrates to S and SE Asia. A *possible* migrant here.

Swinhoe's Snipe. Migrates to India, SE Asia; uncommon in N Aust.

Asian Dowitcher. Migrates to India, SE Asia. Very rare migrant to Aust.

Black-tailed Godwit. Race seen here migrates to SE Asia, Aust. Common on coasts of WA and from N Aust. to NSW.

Bar-tailed Godwit. Migrates to China, Japan, Philippines, PNG; common here except WA.

Hudsonian Godwit. Migrates to Central and S America. Rare vagrant in E Aust.

Red Knot. Migrates to America, Africa, S Europe, Asia, Australasia. Fairly common Aust. coastal areas; some over-winter.

Great Knot. Migrates to India, Burma, Aust. More common N Aust. Some do over-winter, mostly on N coast.

Sharp-tailed Sandpiper. Very common, seldom winters in Aust.

Pectoral Sandpiper. Migrates to S America. Vagrant elsewhere, including Aust.

Cox's Sandpiper *Calidris paramelanotos* appears rare.
Special note: a dispute exists over both identity and variation of characters of this newly recognised and named bird. We have illustrated it as *Calidris paramelanotos* (page 107) and await more details. Some records, previously considered to be of the Dunlin, have been rescinded; the new bird must be identified *also* from the Pectoral Sandpiper, but its behaviour is different — Ken Simpson, Editor.

Baird's Sandpiper. Migrates to S America. Accidental vagrant to Aust.

White-rumped Sandpiper. Migrates to Central and S America. Rare vagrant to Aust.

Western Sandpiper. Migrates to North and Central America. Rare vagrant here.

Little Stint. Migrates to Africa, SE Asia. Uncommon vagrant to Aust.

Red-necked Stint. Migrates to China, Taiwan, Philippines, Australasia. Very common here; many over-winter.

Postures of the Sharp-tailed Sandpiper

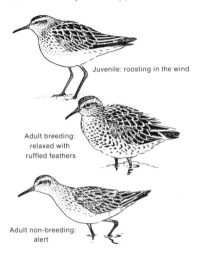

Juvenile: roosting in the wind

Adult breeding: relaxed with ruffled feathers

Adult non-breeding: alert

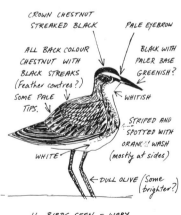

SNAPPER POINT, PORT ADELAIDE.
15/10/83 Light overcast.

CROWN CHESTNUT STREAKED BLACK
PALE EYEBROW

ALL BACK COLOUR CHESTNUT WITH BLACK STREAKS (Feather centres?) SOME PALE TIPS.

BLACK WITH PALER BASE GREENISH?

WHITISH

STRIPED AND SPOTTED WITH ORANGE! WASH (mostly at sides)

WHITE

DULL OLIVE (Some brighter?)

11 BIRDS SEEN - WARY.
(SOME MORE CHESTNUT THAN OTHERS)
IN FLIGHT { PALE WING STRIPE
BLACK STRIPE ON PALE RUMP

One page from a bird observer's notebook.

Long-toed Stint. Migrates to China, India, SE Asia. Rare migrant here.

Curlew Sandpiper. Migrates to Africa, Persian Gulf, India, SE Asia, Australasia. Common; some over-winter here.

Dunlin. Rarely migrates S of equator. Very rare here. Some supposed records of the Dunlin prior to 1981 have been voluntarily rescinded (see Cox's Sandpiper).

Sanderling. Migrates to N and S America, Europe, Africa, India, China, Australasia. Widespread in coastal areas here, especially in N Aust.

Buff-breasted Sandpiper. Migrates to S America. Uncommon vagrant here.

Broad-billed Sandpiper. Migrates to S Europe, India, China, SE Asia, Aust. — a few reach S Aust. annually.

Ruff (Reeve). Migrates to UK, S Europe, S India, SE Asia. Rare but possibly regular migrant to Aust.

Stilt Sandpiper. Migrates to Central and S America. Rare vagrant in Aust.

Phalaropes   Family Phalaropodidae

Phalaropes are small sandpiper-like waders with long necks, long legs and thin, sharp, straight bills. Their toes are not webbed, but lobed.

Red-necked Phalaropes breed in most circumpolar arctic areas and in northern Canada. They migrate mostly to the east of the Pacific Ocean and to seas off the west coast of Africa. Vagrants are occasionally seen in Australia at widespread locations, on lakes or at sea.

Grey Phalaropes breed in arctic Siberia and North America. They migrate to the southern oceans, mainly the eastern Pacific and southern Atlantic. One vagrant has been sighted in Australia.

Wilson's Phalarope breeds in western Canada and northwest USA, normally migrating to coastal and inland waters of South America. Vagrants have been seen occasionally in Australia at widely spread locations, on lakes or at sea.

The Red-necked Phalarope spins around in circles when feeding (below). The lobed foot of the Red-necked Phalarope (above).

Pratincoles   Family Glareolidae

Pratincoles are aberrant waders of drier areas. Sometimes they are *not* included with waders because their evolutionary relationships are uncertain. They fly like terns, feeding on insects caught on the wing or from the ground.

The Oriental Pratincole breeds in central and southern Asia, migrating to the Philippines, Sunda Island and Australia. It is common in the north during October-May; it is rare in the south.

The partly migratory, partly nomadic Australian Pratincole has long legs, long wings and a short tail, somewhat like the foreign coursers. It behaves more like a courser than a pratincole. It breeds sporadically in inland Australia from the Kimberleys (Western Australia) to northern Queensland and south to South Australia, Victoria and inland New South Wales. It visits Australian northern coasts in the winter dry season, also Indonesia and Papua New Guinea. From October to March it may be seen in southeastern, south and west Australia.

Despite temperatures exceeding 45° Celsius, Australian Pratincoles continue to incubate their eggs. They face their backs to the sun and pant.

Hatchling sheltering from the sun.

Reading
McLean, G. L. (1973), 'A review of the biology of Australian desert waders, *Peltohyas, Stiltia*', *Emu* **73**, 61-70.

Breeding season (*variable*)

J	F	M	A	M	J	J	A	S	O	N	D

273 Australian Pratincole*

Skuas, Jaegers

Family Stercorariidae

Of the six world species, five skuas have been recorded in Australia; only the Chilean Skua *Catharacta chilensis* has not.

Skuas are characterised by sheaths covering the base of the upper bill. There are two skua groups: the great skuas *Catharacta*, chunky brown birds with very short central tail feathers, barely longer than the tail; and the jaegers, *Stercorarius*, smaller with specialised long central tail feathers.

Most species probably pass through Australian waters annually, some less than others. The South Polar Skua *Catharacta maccormicki* has only been recorded a few times. The Long-tailed Jaeger is probably much more common than once thought; the sighting off Sydney in December 1982 of flocks of up to 27 supports this. The other skuas are well-known visitors to our shores. The Pomarine, Arctic and Long-tailed Jaegers migrate southward after breeding in the Northern Hemisphere. The Great and South Polar Skuas migrate from the Sub-Antarctic and Antarctic respectively, the South Polar Skua migrating to the northern Pacific in winter.

Both skuas and jaegers are piratic, chasing other sea-birds (e.g. gulls, shearwaters, terns) and forcing them to drop or disgorge their food. Aerobatics with very quick directional changes undertaken in the chase are sometimes quite spectacular.

The jaegers' complicated plumage sequences are still not fully understood: they leave the north as barred juveniles with short tail streamers, moulting into first winter plumage when they arrive in Australia; they slowly acquire adult plumage over three or four years; adults moult their body feathers twice annually and have both breeding and non-breeding plumages; breeding plumage is more uniform and less barred than non-breeding plumage; they only moult the wing feathers once a year. Larger skuas have no well-defined differences in plumages throughout the year.

Skuas are scavengers and readily take refuse from ships. Great Skuas clean up any corpses and take unguarded eggs, as well as young and injured birds from breeding grounds. In the Arctic breeding grounds, jaegers often eat rodents, other small mammals, small birds, insects and even berries. All skuas occasionally catch their own fish and squid.

At sea or at breeding grounds, Great Skuas are solitary or in pairs. In the non-breeding season jaegers, especially the Long-tailed and Arctic, gather in groups of up to 100. At their breeding grounds all skuas pair off. They are strongly territorial, fiercely attacking anything they feel will threaten their young, including man. Great Skuas have occasionally caused people to fall off cliffs because their attacks have been so vicious. Skuas lay one to three, sometimes four eggs, which are stone-coloured and spotted in Great Skuas, and olive to brown and spotted in jaegers. Their nests are scraped-out hollows.

Reading

Cramp, S. (ed.) (1983), *Handbook of the Birds of Europe, the Middle East and North Africa. The Birds of the Western Palearctic, Vol. III, Waders to Gulls*, OUP, London.

Serventy, D. L., Serventy V. & J. Warham, (1971), *The Handbook of Australian Sea-birds*, A. H. & A. W. Reed, Sydney.

Harrison, P. (1983), *Seabirds: an Identification Guide*, A. H. & A. W. Reed, Sydney.

Pomarine Jaeger

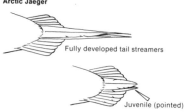

Fully developed tail streamers

Juvenile (blunt)

Arctic Jaeger

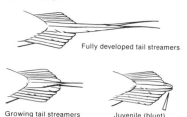

Fully developed tail streamers

Juvenile (pointed)

Long-tailed Jaeger

Fully developed tail streamers

Growing tail streamers

Juvenile (blunt)

Great Skua

Small and pointed tail streamers

Gulls, Terns   Family Laridae

The world has about 42 gull species (Sub-Family Larinae). The Pacific Gull is Australia's only endemic species. Gull relationships are not clearly defined. Some authors emphasise behavioural (ethological) traits, others consider physical (morphological) features more stable and reliable. The darkest in colour of plumage, bill, foot and eye may well be the *least* highly evolved type. In pigmentation and lack of pronounced pattern, these gulls resemble the young of many which later develop highly specialised colours and patterns.

Gulls generally moult completely once a year and have a partial moult of head and body feathers twice a year. (Franklin's Gull moults completely twice a year.) Adults usually undergo the full moult after completing breeding. Northern vagrants have different summer and winter plumages, but local species do not. Relatively long-lived, gulls have, however, a sequence of plumages and moults from dark mottled juveniles to typical adult forms. Smaller gulls attain adult plumage in their second year, but the larger species take three or four years. Variation can occur between fast and slow developing individuals. Unusual plumages may be attributed to moult or feather wear.

Bill and leg colour, shape and size, behaviour and mode of flight are all important characteristics for recognition purposes. The sexes are similar except that females are usually smaller and more finely built.

A Pacific Gull incubating.

Gulls generally are coastal in habitat. They tend to be omnivorous scavengers, mainly along the coast, riverflats and nearby tips. They will feed inland on insects and worms in paddocks, will follow ships a short distance to sea, will feed on the eggs and young of many bird species, and even small adult sea-birds. In turn, gull eggs and chicks are predated by other gulls, skuas, corvids and raptors.

Gulls breed only once a year but if the nest, eggs or young are lost, a new start is often made. Larger gulls tend to breed along shorelines, either by inlets or on offshore islands. Smaller species tend to breed in marshes and swamps. Gulls may nest alone, though most kinds are to a variable extent social breeders. The degree of colony formation usually depends on the local food supply. A series of calls and postures is associated with courtship, nest-building, mating and change-over of incubation, and nest defence. To begin a study of birds, new observers could do no better than to take a bag of bread scraps to a beach and feed the gulls. Observe their behaviour, and try to estimate their ages from the varying plumages.

The behavioural postures of the Silver Gull: (a) upright and aggressive; (b) hunched and ready to pursue; (c) arched and aggressive; (d) forward attitude (often both c and d appear together at the conclusion of other displays); (e) submissive (similar to begging posture of juveniles).

Breeding seasons (*variable*)

J	F	M	A	M	J	J	A	S	O	N	D

279 Silver Gull*

280 Pacific Gull

281 Kelp Gull

Their nests are on the ground and usually are well-formed and constructed of whatever material is locally available. The clutch size is usually two, three or sometimes just one egg; clutches that are laid later in the season are almost always smaller than early ones. Eggs are usually a tapered oval shape, light brown, green or blue in ground (background) colour, and evenly spotted or blotched with black, brown or grey. Incubation varies from 21 days for small gulls to 29 days for large gulls. Newly hatched chicks are heavily covered with down and are capable of leaving the nest within a few days to hide. Older chicks máy take to the water for protection. Both parents care for and feed chicks. They are fed partly digested food, sometimes until they are five to six weeks old and are free-flying.

The downy hatchlings of gulls are grey and/or buff with black blotches: Pacific Gull (upper); Silver Gull in a cryptic posture (lower).

Australia has 22 species of terns and noddies (including the recently added Antarctic Tern *Sterna vittata*) from a world Sub-Family (Sterninae) of 42 species. Terns are related to gulls but have generally straighter, more pointed bills, slender wings, delicate flight and weaker legs. Noddies (*Anous*) are a fairly distinct group of terns, being dark with pale caps. They are gliding birds with broader wings, fluttering less than other terns. Their feet and legs are stronger and their tails are broad, rounded and deeply notched. The Grey Ternlet (*Procelsterna*) is a small, pale noddy with longer legs. It has a distinctive habit of sometimes pattering on the water like a storm-petrel when feeding. The White Tern (*Gygis*) is the only nearly all-white tern. An upturned bill, different nesting habits etc., seem to set it apart from other terns.

The migratory marsh terns (*Chlidonias*) occur mostly in inland waters and sometimes on the coast. All are short-tailed with distinctive breeding and non-breeding plumages. Black and White-winged Terns are blackish in breeding plumage, and grey and white in non-breeding plumage. Whiskered Terns are local breeders, White-winged Terns migrate from east-central Asia, and Black Terns are vagrants (sighted once at Sydney, once at Newcastle).

The genera *Sterna, Hydroprogne* and *Gelochelidon* are all so closely related that recently they were placed in the one genus — *Sterna*. However, *Sterna* types vary from the starling-sized Little Tern to the gull-sized Caspian Tern *Hydroprogne caspia*. Several groupings are clearly identifiable: Caspian Tern *Hydroprogne*; Gull-billed Tern *Gelochelidon*; 'commic' terns — Arctic, Antarctic, Common, White-fronted, Roseate and Black-naped; Bridled and Sooty types, the *small* 'least' terns — Fairy, Little; and crested terns (formerly *Thalasseus*).

Identifying many of the terns is very difficult, none more so than the 'commic' terns. All have blackish bills (sometimes with hints of red) in non-breeding plumage, some attaining red bills in breeding plumage. All are middle-sized terns, white-bellied in non-breeding plumage and grey, white or pinkish in breeding plumage, varying in length from species to species.

Identification relies on a *combination of features* e.g. plumage, size, shape, bill and leg length, primary patterns, amount of translucency in the underwing etc. (see page 118). One characteristic which is useful for separating two notoriously difficult species, Common and Arctic Terns, is the wing-moult sequence. Common Terns moult the inner half of the primaries (inner four to six) twice a year and moult the other primaries once. Therefore, as tern feathers wear (become abraded by use, sunlight etc.) from fresh silver-grey

A flock of roosting terns, including the Crested, Lesser Crested, Common, and the Little.

to worn blackish at certain times of the year, Common Terns show a strong contrast between the inner and outer primaries, the inners being fresh and silvery, the outers old and blackish. Adult Arctic Terns moult primaries once a year in the Southern Hemisphere and usually have uniformly grey upperwings (except when in moult, in which case there are gaps between old and new primaries in the wing).

Care should be taken with this feature because Common Terns undergo a complete wing moult in autumn before migrating. Before they leave for the north they have uniform upperwings. First year birds arriving from the north in the spring *also* have uniform upperwings for some time. Birds remaining for the southern winter can have a complete primary moult as late as August and *again* have uniform upperwings. Subsequently, they follow the same sequence as adults that finish moulting in autumn. As a rule, if a bird is seen before autumn with contrasting grey and blackish primaries *without gaps* between the contrast, then the bird is a Common Tern. Roseate Terns, like Common Terns, moult the inner primaries twice annually and the outer three, once.

Fairy Terns attending to their chicks.

Arctic Terns are perhaps the most travelled birds in the world. They breed in northern Asia, Europe, North America and up into the Arctic Circle, migrating south in August through the tropics to the Antarctic, to wander throughout the southern seas from September to April (immatures remain for winter). Birds banded in northern Europe have been recovered in Australia.

Two main migration routes are known. One population from east Asia and western North America migrates down the west coast of the Americas. The other, from Europe and eastern North America, migrates down the east coast of Africa. It is possible that small numbers of Arctic Terns also migrate via east Asia and eastern Australia as some recent sightings in eastern Australia in spring suggest. Common Terns are also strongly migratory; Australian birds (*Sterna hirundo longipennis*) come from north-east Asia and migrate via east Asia to Australia. It is certain (though hard to prove, even from specimens) that the other north-east Asian race *minussensis* migrates to Australia, because red-billed Common Terns with large amounts of black on the bills and red legs are annually seen in east Australia. Common Terns banded in Europe (race *hirundo*) have on occasions been found dead in Australia. Most White-fronted Terns migrate from New Zealand in the winter, but recently a small population has been found breeding on Battery Island in Bass Strait.

A Whiskered Tern hatchling.

The Antarctic Tern *Sterna vittata* has recently been identified from a specimen in South Australia. It breeds on Sub-Antarctic islands, and some populations migrate north in the winter (the birds breeding closest to Australia do not migrate). It is identified from other 'commic' terns by its pale grey outer tail streamers (dark grey in Common and Arctic) and its short, stout black and red bill in winter (red in summer). In winter it has as much white going onto the crown as the Arctic Tern. It lacks a carpal bar, and is larger and stockier than the Arctic Tern.

Two populations of Little Terns occur in Australia. One population migrates from Asia and is here in non-breeding plumage in summer. The other population breeds in Australia. Gull-billed Terns (race *macrotarsa*) mostly breed here, but there are also a small number of birds from Asia of the race *affinus* (smaller and darker above than the local race). Crested Terns disperse widely throughout Australia; banded

Whiskered Terns at their nest.

South Australian birds have been found as far away as south-east Queensland. Grey Ternlets and White Terns breed in the Pacific and occasionally wander into our waters. The movements of most other Australian terns are poorly understood.

Food is made up of mainly aquatic animal life, the size of the tern correlating with the size of its prey. Some terns occasionally hawk for insects. Unlike gulls, terns rarely eat scraps. Food is gathered by hovering (quick fluttering in smaller terns, slow flapping in large terns) and then either picking from the surface or plunging partly into the water. Most terns are gregarious, breeding and feeding in flocks. Fishermen can often tell whether any fish are about if there are large groups of terns (also shearwaters, skuas, gulls, gannets etc.) congregating and diving in a small area.

Before mating, terns usually have paired flight displays sometimes flying in perfect unison, spiralling, flapping and zig-zagging together. Terns usually breed on islands, often on ground scrapes in sandy regions. These scrapes are sometimes lined with sticks. Some inland breeding terns construct vegetation platforms floating on or near water.

Terns such as the Sooty Terns and Common Noddies often breed communally in thousands. Lesser and Black Noddies breed in trees. White Terns build no nest, but lay an egg on tree branches or palm fronds. Grey Ternlets nest on cliff ledges. Eggs range from dull white to brown, greenish or grey with varying amounts of small blotches and spots. Clutches consist of one or two eggs, sometimes up to three or four. Soon after hatching, tern chicks are downy and fairly mobile.

Black Noddies nest in trees.

Reading: Gulls

Brooke, R. K. (1976), 'Field discrimination of *Larus fuscus* and *L. dominicanus*', *Ibis* **118**, 594.

Carrick, R. & M. D. Murray, (1964), 'Social factors in population regulation of the Silver Gull *Larus novaehollandiae* Stephens', *CSIRO Wildl. Res.* **9**, 189-199.

Grant, P. J. (1981), *Gulls: A Guide to Identification*, T. & A. D. Poyser, Calton, UK.

Kinsky, F. C. (1963), 'The Southern Black-backed Gull (*Larus dominicanus*) Lichtenstein. Measurements, plumage colour and moult cycle', *Rec. of Dominion Mus.* **4**, 149-219 (NZ paper; describes Kelp Gull).

Nelson, J. B. (1980), *Seabirds: Their Biology and Ecology*, Hamlyn Publishing Group, London.

Robertson, B. I. (1977), 'Identification of Pacific and Dominican Gulls', *Aust. Bird Watcher* **7**, 5-10.

Serventy, D. L., Serventy, V. N. & J. Warham, (1971), *The Handbook of Australian Sea-birds*, A. H. & A. W. Reed, Sydney, pp. 191-202.

Watson, G. E. (1975), *Birds of the Antarctic and Sub-Antarctic*, American Geophysical Union, Washington DC.

Wooler, R. D. & J. N. Dunlop, (1979), 'Multiple laying by the Silver Gull *Larus novaehollandiae* Stephens on Carnac Island, Western Australia', *Aust. Wildl. Res.* **6**, 325-335.

Reading: Terns

Hume, R. A. & P. J. Grant, 'Upperwing pattern of adult Common and Arctic Terns', in Sharrock J. T. R. (ed.) (1980), *Frontiers of Bird Identification, a British Birds' Guide to Some Difficult Species*, Macmillan, London, pp. 96-100.

Serventy D. L., Serventy V. & J. Warham, (1971), *The Handbook of Australian Sea-birds*, A. H. & A. W. Reed, Sydney.

Winray, J. S. (1980), 'The Australian breeding record of the White-fronted Tern', *Aust. Bird Watcher* **8**, 137-146.

Harrison, P. (1983), *Seabirds: an Identification Guide*, A. H. & A. W. Reed, Sydney.

Breeding seasons (*variable*)

	J	F	M	A	M	J	J	A	S	O	N	D
286 Whiskered Tern*												
289 Gull-billed Tern*												
290 Caspian Tern*												
294 Roseate Tern*												
295 White-fronted Tern												
296 Black-naped Tern*												
297 Sooty Tern*												
298 Bridled Tern*												
299 Little Tern*												
300 Fairy Tern*												
301 Crested Tern*												
302 Lesser Crested Tern*												
303 Common Noddy*												
304 Lesser Noddy												
305 Black Noddy												

Pigeons, Doves   Family Columbidae

Pigeons and doves belong to the Order Columbiformes, Sub-Order Columbae, Family Columbidae, placing them close to the sand-grouse and the extinct dodos and solitaires. Of the 290-odd species found across the world, 44 occur in the New Guinea region, and New Zealand has one. Australia has 25 recorded species (three are introduced), some of which have evolved to fill the ecological niche occupied by pheasants, grouse and partridges on other continents.

Many Australian species are old endemics that have developed with the changes to the Australian environment. The Wonga Pigeon is one, as is the Topknot — the latter once spread over much more of the continent than it does now. Others, notably the fruit-doves, are recent invaders from the northern islands, and from Asia where many additional species are found.

Although little physical difference exists between pigeons and doves, we tend to use the former name for larger species while 'doves' by popular usage, refers to the smaller birds with generally longer tails.

The need to obtain food has caused many Australian pigeons and doves to become nomads, although the range of their nomadism seems rather restricted. The Superb Fruit-Dove, and to a lesser degree the Rose-crowned, are 'local nomads' with a difference — periodically an individual bird will stray enormous distances down the east coast — both are recorded as vagrants in Victoria and Tasmania. The Flock Bronzewing and Diamond Dove, as inhabitants of a dry, inland environment, are both highly nomadic. The former, in particular, occasionally irrupts into areas far from its generally accepted habitat. By contrast, the Spinifex Pigeon is mostly sedentary, an unusual trait for an inland bird.

The 'big movers' are the migratory Torresian Imperial-Pigeon whose flights into northern Australia from New Guinea are one of Australia's most spectacular ornithological events, and the Topknot Pigeon in its long range search for fruits. Torresian Imperial-Pigeons arrive on Cape York Pen., Queensland, in late July and by late August they appear in Darwin. Their return flight takes place mainly in February and early March. Areas they visit while out of Australia are unknown, although Papua New Guinea and Irian Jaya contain areas frequented by the birds.

Pigeons have long been hunted, first by Aborigines who used nets and throwing sticks, then by the early seamen who made the birds a welcome addition to their diet. As the continent was opened up by settlers, pigeons were hunted more systematically, mainly for food and to a lesser extent for sport. Even now, some species, particularly the Topknot and Wompoo are hunted, but mainly by pot hunters or 'sportsmen'. Small numbers are trapped for aviary use.

Despite casual persecution, the far graver threat is habitat loss. Fruit-doves, as rainforest inhabitants, are greatly at risk, for this irreplaceable resource has been, and still is being, cleared at an alarming rate. In other areas, mining activities, with the incidental problems of hunters and cats that stray from the mining towns, pose a threat to the Squatter and Rock-Pigeons. The Banded Fruit-Dove has a restricted range in Arnhem Land, an area subjected to intense mine exploration work.

Some species are apparently secure. These include the Common Bronzewing and the trio of doves — Bar-shouldered, Peaceful and Diamond.

The Bar-shouldered Dove raises its wings while sun-bathing.

Many pigeons, including this Peaceful Dove, drink by sucking.

An incubating Superb Fruit-Dove — note the very flimsy nest.

The nest site and eggs of a Rock-Pigeon.

Only the Crested Pigeon has gained markedly by European settlement. It has been able to extend its range as grain-growing has become established and waterholes for stock have increased.

Pigeons and doves are either granivorous (grain-eaters) or frugivorous (fruit-eaters) although some are plant-grazers. The Crested Pigeon, for example, feeds extensively on leaves of medicks, plants of the semi-arid plains. Because pigeons can gather large quanities of food in a short time, much less than the time for its digestion, a storage pouch (crop) has evolved on the wall of the oesophagus. The crop is essential, particularly to the Crested Pigeon for its medick leaves and for the Topknot Pigeon which eats the fruit of the bangalow palm. These fruit have large seeds with a comparatively thin layer of flesh around them — little digestible material from such large volumes of food.

The crop has one other vital use, that is in the production of 'pigeon milk'. In breeding adults, a cheese-like secretion fills certain cells on the wall of the crop which are shed but remain in it. The newly-hatched young are fed on regurgitated 'milk', and as they grow, other food is regurgitated with it. By the time they leave the nest, the young are fed almost entirely on normal food.

Many pigeons when drinking are able to suck water up so they do not need to throw back their head to let it run down their throat. This cuts down their vulnerability to predators at drinking places.

Their nests are not elaborate, usually a meagre platform of sticks. The nest site is variable, depending on the species. Some nest on the ground, others on a rock ledge or crevice, but most select the fork of a tree or shrub. One egg, or two, form the clutch and they are white or off-white, often glossy, oval in shape and not large considering the bird's body .

Reading

Frith, H. J. (1982), *Pigeons and Doves of Australia*, Rigby, Adelaide.
Goodwin, D. (1967), *Pigeons and Doves of the World*, Trustees of the British Museum (Nat. Hist.) London.

Breeding seasons (*variable)

J F M A M J J A S O N D

308 Banded Fruit-Dove
309 Superb Fruit-Dove
310 Rose-crowned Fruit-Dove
311 Wompoo Fruit-Dove
312 Torresian Imperial-Pigeon
314 Topknot Pigeon
315 White-headed Pigeon
316 Feral Pigeon
317 Spotted Turtle-Dove
318 Laughing Turtle-Dove
319 Brown Cuckoo-Dove
320 Peaceful Dove*
321 Diamond Dove*
322 Bar-shouldered Dove*
323 Emerald Dove
324 Common Bronzewing
325 Brush Bronzewing*
326 Flock Bronzewing
327 Crested Pigeon*
328 Squatter Pigeon*
329 Partridge Pigeon*
330 Rock-Pigeon
331 Spinifex Pigeon
332 Wonga Pigeon

The bowing displays of the Feral Pigeon (left) and the Crested Pigeon (right).

Cockatoos, Lorikeets, Parrots   Family Psittacidae

The Order Psittaciformes, which embraces the cockatoos and parrots, forms one of the most well-defined groups of birds. They are characterised by: a short, strongly hooked bill, bulging cere, a toe arrangement with two forward and two back; interesting intestinal looping and the lack of an appendix; the presence of a feather aftershaft; a diastatic wing (no secondary feather corresponding to the fifth feather of the greater wing coverts); naked young which are fed by the parent holding the chick's bill inside its own. Their short neck and legs, prominent eye, large head and compact, bulky body, combined with bright plumage dominated by primary colours, give parrots a distinctive and engaging appearance. The ability of many species to mimic human words makes them even more attractive as cage birds.

Parrots form a large, uniform group distributed throughout the intertropical zone as well as the subtropical and colder parts of the Southern Hemisphere. Great diversity and endemism (occurrence of species peculiar to a locality and with the most basic evolutionary traits) occur in Australia and New Guinea. This fact, combined with continental drift evidence, suggests that parrots originated on and radiated from the southern continents.

Within Australia the general direction of evolutionary adaptation has been radiation from Tertiary rainforests through eucalypt woodlands to colonisation of the central deserts. Today, the diversity of species is greatest in the drier eucalypt open forests and woodlands and declines towards both the desert and wetter areas.

Only one Family is now recognised in Australia with three or six Sub-Families, 22 genera and about 54 species. The number of species recognised may soon be reduced because the rosellas with white cheeks (Eastern and Pale-headed) as well as the two ringnecks (Mallee and Port Lincoln), interbreed where they meet. Therefore, the birds in each group are best considered as single variable species. Two species of black-cockatoo occur in south-west Australia; the white-tailed race (*latirostris*) of the Yellow-tailed Black-Cockatoo, and the Long-billed Black-Cockatoo which in recent years has been extensively studied and defined.

Except for lorikeets and the Swift Parrot, most Australian parrots are primarily seed-eaters; fruits, berries, flowers and insects are also eaten to varying extents. It seems incongruous that one of the largest cockatoos, the Red-tailed Black-Cockatoo, is largely dependent on the minute seeds of bloodwood eucalypts and casuarinas. Obviously when the food consists of tiny seeds, large quantities must be consumed. It has been estimated that individual Ground Parrots and Orange-bellied Parrots consume in the order of 10 000 seeds per day to meet their energy and nutrient requirements.

Bill shape variations have resulted from specialisation to particular foods. For example, the straighter, elongated bill of the Long-billed Corella is used to dig up corms; the elongated, down-curved bill of the Red-capped Parrot enables efficient removal of seeds from large-fruited eucalypts, particularly Marri *Eucalyptus calophylla*.

Yellow-tailed Black-Cockatoos have learned to extract insect larvae from tree trunks and roots, from *Banksia* cones and from grasstree flower spikes.

Lorikeets feed on pollen and nectar from flowers; they have specialised brush-tipped tongues and comparatively long, narrow bills. Some also regularly eat fruit. Nectar and pollen

A Yellow-tailed Black-Cockatoo extracts beetle larvae from a tree trunk. Note the foot, bill, cere and tongue anatomy.

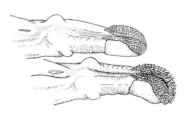

Lorikeets have specialised brush-tipped tongues. This illustration shows a Rainbow Lorikeet's tongue in two positions: normal and relaxed (top); erect for feeding (bottom).

The illegal trapping of highly prized Australian parrots for aviculture is threatening the survival of some species. This nest of the Golden-shouldered Parrot has been excavated by trappers.

are also important in the diet of the brush-tongued Swift Parrot. This species also eats insects and often gleans psyllid plant-bugs which have a sugary coating, from eucalypt foliage.

Most Australian parrots nest in tree hollows, especially those formed in broken limbs of eucalypts. However, Golden-shouldered and Paradise Parrots breed only in tunnels excavated in certain types of termite mounds; Ground and Night Parrots construct nests of coarse grass in dense tussocks; Rock Parrots nest in crannies of boulders on coastal islands. Most hollow-nesting species, with the exception of Galahs which line their hollows with fresh eucalypt leaves, chew woodchips from inside the hollow to form a soft layer on which the eggs are laid.

Parrots' eggs are rounded, white and often lustrous, in common with most species whose eggs are safely concealed in a hollow. The chicks are altricial (naked and helpless at birth) and must be cared for by the parents for an extended period (from 30 days for *Neophema* species to 100 days for black-cockatoos). Chicks of the Ground Parrot, however, are covered in dense blackish down, presumably as protection from cold and damp in their open nests; chicks of black-cockatoos have long yellow down, the function of which is not clear.

In most species, nests are widely spaced; for example the nests of Pink Cockatoos are usually more than two kilometres apart. However, in agricultural districts the uneven dispersion of trees containing suitable hollows may lead to the concentration of breeding birds into habitat remnants. In Western Australia up to seven cockatoo species have been recorded breeding at densities of seven nests per hectare.

In eastern and southern Australia most species breed in spring and summer (August-January) while in the tropical north breeding tends to occur in the dry season (May-August). Species adapted to the arid centre usually have a breeding peak between August and October, but may breed at other times, especially March to June, following rain. When conditions are suitable some species, for example the Budgerigar, may raise several broods in succession.

Most species of Australian parrots are sedentary although in some species, for example the Galah, flocks of non-breeders may travel widely. Several arid country species (Cockatiel, Budgerigar, Night Parrot, Alexandra's Parrot and Scarlet-chested Parrot) are nomadic and are able to exploit sudden availability of food resulting from unpredictable and patchy rainfall. Lorikeets, too, are nomads, their movements determined by the availability of flowers which provide their food.

Migration is undertaken by two species of *Neophema* and the Swift Parrot, all of which breed in summer in Tasmania and spend the winter on the mainland. The Orange-bellied Parrot is a migrant which breeds in coastal south-west Tasmania and winters along the coast of central Victoria and south-eastern South Australia. The Swift Parrot is also a migrant breeding only in Tasmania. Most individuals winter in southern and central Victoria with irregular irruptions to the north and west. Blue-winged Parrots, by contrast, are partial migrants because only the Tasmanian breeding portion of the population migrates. In March and April birds from Tasmania travel north across Bass Strait and Victoria to New South Wales and Queensland, returning in September and October to breed. Blue-winged Parrots breeding in southern Victoria are probably sedentary.

Breeding seasons (*variable*)

	J	F	M	A	M	J	J	A	S	O	N	D
333 Palm Cockatoo												
334 Red-tailed Black-Cockatoo*												
335 Glossy Black-Cockatoo												
336 Yellow-tailed Black-Cockatoo*												
337 Long-billed Black-Cockatoo												
338 Gang-gang Cockatoo												
339 Galah*												
340 Long-billed Corella												
341 Little Corella*												
342 Pink Cockatoo*												
343 Sulphur-crested Cockatoo*												
344 Eclectus Parrot												
345 Red-cheeked Parrot												
346 Rainbow Lorikeet												
347 Red-collared Lorikeet												
348 Scaly-breasted Lorikeet												
349 Varied Lorikeet												
350 Musk Lorikeet												
351 Purple-crowned Lorikeet												
352 Little Lorikeet												
353 Double-eyed Fig-Parrot												
354 Australian King-Parrot												
355 Red-winged Parrot*												
356 Superb Parrot												
357 Regent Parrot												
358 Alexandra's Parrot												
359 Cockatiel*												
360 Ground Parrot												

Threats to the survival of Australian parrots include: (*i*) changes induced by frequent fires and the grazing of stock to the plant species' composition, and hence seed production, of the grassy understorey in eucalypt woodlands; (*ii*) diminishing availability of hollow trees for breeding sites and widespread lack of regeneration of eucalypts to replenish the stock of hollow trees; (*iii*) patchy dispersion of food and nesting sites in the remaining natural vegetation across much of southern Australia; (*iv*) gross destruction of the habitat of specialised species such as those restricted to rainforest (Palm Cockatoo, Eclectus Parrot, Red-cheeked Parrot and Double-eyed Fig-Parrot) or coastal heath and saltmarsh (Ground Parrot, Orange-bellied Parrot); (*v*) constant illegal taking of highly prized species for aviculture.

The first cause may have hastened the Paradise Parrot's decline and is probably contributing to the apparent decline of the Golden-shouldered Parrot. The situation of the Golden-shouldered Parrot has been aggravated by illegal trapping for the avicultural trade. Rapid decline of available nest hollows potentially threatens most species, including seemingly common ones (e.g. Galah) which mainly breed in agricultural districts. A study of a remnant population of Yellow-tailed Black-Cockatoos revealed that patchy food dispersion, due to unsympathetic clearing of native vegetation, meant that the birds could not provide enough food for their young. The result was that the population declined.

Because parrots are often long-lived, continual breeding failure may not become apparent until it is too late to take corrective action. Degradation of coastal salt marshes in Victoria may be a major cause for the decline of the Orange-bellied Parrot to its present critical level of about 200 individuals. Even now, the two most important wintering areas, in Port Phillip Bay, Victoria, are threatened by major land-use changes and the survival of the species is doubtful.

Reading

Forshaw, J. M. & W. T. Cooper, (1981), *Australian Parrots*, 2nd edn. rev. Lansdowne Editions, Melbourne.

Saunders, D. A. (1979), 'Distribution and taxonomy of the White-tailed and Yellow-tailed Black-Cockatoos *Calyptorhynchus* spp.' *Emu* **79**, 215-227.

Breeding seasons (**variable*)

J F M A M J J A S O N D

361 Night Parrot (*Insufficient information*)
362 Budgerigar*
363 Swift Parrot
364 Red-capped Parrot
365 Green Rosella
366 Crimson Rosella
367 Eastern Rosella
368 Pale-headed Rosella*
369 Northern Rosella
370 Western Rosella
371 Mallee Ringneck*
372 Port Lincoln Ringneck*
373 Red-rumped Parrot
374 Mulga Parrot
375 Golden-shouldered Parrot
376 Hooded Parrot
377 Paradise Parrot (*Insufficient information*)
378 Blue Bonnet
379 Bourke's Parrot*
380 Blue-winged Parrot
381 Elegant Parrot
382 Rock Parrot
383 Orange-bellied Parrot
384 Turquoise Parrot
385 Scarlet-chested Parrot

Parasitic Cuckoos, Coucals   Family Cuculidae

Observers will need to learn cuckoo plumages and calls with care; many are difficult to identify. Although much remains to be discovered about breeding behaviour, we are able to include a fraction of what is known.

Parasitic cuckoos often lay small eggs by comparison with their own body weight, for their eggs must resemble their hosts' in size and colouration. Once hatched, the naked baby cuckoo ejects all objects with which it comes in contact in the nest — including the host's eggs and nestlings. By making begging and juvenile calls, even after the cuckoo is fledged, the cuckoo ensures that a constant food supply is brought by the hosts and sometimes by other birds as well.

Cuckoos are vocal when breeding, otherwise they are silent and very difficult to see. They may call by day or night. Oriental Cuckoos and the New Zealand Shining Bronze-Cuckoo (race *lucidus*) do not breed in Australia. All Australian species except the Pheasant Coucal are parasitic on a wide variety of native birds. Most cuckoos are insectivorous. The

The Black-eared Cuckoo's egg (right) closely resembles the chocolate-coloured egg laid by its host, the Speckled Warbler (left).

The Black-eared Cuckoo nestling begs from its foster parent, a Speckled Warbler.

Fan-tailed and bronze-cuckoos *Chrysococcyx* (except Hors-field's) select dome-shaped nests to lay their eggs. The other species may occasionally use dome-shaped nests but normally select open or cup-shaped nests.

The Pallid, Brush, Fan-tailed, Horsfield's Bronze-Cuckoo, Little Bronze-Cuckoo, Channel-billed Cuckoo and the Common Koel all breed in Australia and at least part of their populations migrate north to northern Australia and New Guinea in the winter. The south-east Queensland and northern New South Wales populations of the Little Bronze-Cuckoo (race *barnardi*) migrate to Cape York Pen., northern Queensland, in winter. The New Zealand Shining Bronze-Cuckoo (race *lucidus*) breeds in New Zealand, then winters in eastern Australia and Western Pacific islands. The recent discovery that the Little and Gould's Bronze-Cuckoos actually hybridise, suggests that they may be one species.

The Pheasant Coucal of northern Australia is the only Australian cuckoo which does, in fact, build its own nest, incubate and raise its own family and does not indulge in the parasitic habit. The coucals inhabit areas of very dense vegetation through which they make small tunnels and along which they run in a pheasant-like manner. The presence of observers will cause them to clamber to a vantage-point in a taller tree, from which they may fly heavily away. Their deep hooting calls are very distinctive.

Coucals feed on live insects and small vertebrates. They build open cup-shaped nests and average three to five white, rapidly stained eggs. Their young are covered in a long, white, hairy covering at first.

Reading
Beruldsen, G. R. (1980), *A Field Guide to Nests and Eggs of Australian Birds*, Rigby, Adelaide (see pp. 257-263, also notes on cuckoo parasitism pp. 25-27).

A Pheasant Coucal at its nest.

Breeding seasons (*variable*)

J F M A M J J A S O N D

387 Pallid Cuckoo
388 Brush Cuckoo
389 Chestnut-breasted Cuckoo
390 Fan-tailed Cuckoo
391 Black-eared Cuckoo
392 Horsfield's Bronze-Cuckoo*
393 Shining Bronze-Cuckoo
394 Little Bronze-Cuckoo
395 Gould's Bronze-Cuckoo
396 Common Koel
397 Channel-billed Cuckoo
398 Pheasant Coucal

Hawk Owls   Family Strigidae

This and the next Family (Tytonidae) share many features unique to their Order, Strigiformes. Most authorities now agree that the nightjars and frogmouths (Caprimulgiformes) are the closest relatives of owls and that the two groups share a common ancestor from a time *before* the Paleocene (54-65 million years ago). Owls are linked to nightjars and frog-mouths on the basis of similar egg-white protein distributions, similarities in structures such as intestinal caeca, oil glands, voice boxes, a lack of both the ambiens muscle in the leg and the crop (throat pouch) in which food would normally be stored, and a tendency towards zygodactylous toes (two forward and two back). Other common features such as large eyes, nightly routines, plumage patterns and, in some groups, feather structure, could be a result of the nocturnal tendencies of both groups, rather than of shared evolution.

The hawks (Order Falconiformes) share many traits with owls as a result of similar diets rather than any close relationship. Members of both Orders have strong, hooked bills with ceres, and powerful feet with large talons for catching, killing and ripping prey apart. Both also regurgitate pellets containing indigestible remains of victims. There is a general trend for the females of the two Orders to be larger than their mates in order to reduce competition for food between partners, particularly during the breeding season (see Australian anomaly page 316).

All owls regurgitate pellets containing indigestible remains of victims. These are pellets of the Powerful Owl, showing hair bristles, bones, beetle wings etc.

315

Finally, there are characteristics unique to owls, including an advanced pelvic muscle system. However, the obvious characteristics are adaptations for nocturnal hunting. Large, forward-pointing eyes give fine binocular vision, especially under low light conditions. The size of the eys, though, renders them virtually immovable in the head, but owls overcome this by extraordinarily flexible neck muscles which allow the head to be rotated through a maximum of 270 degrees. In order to hear their prey while flying, most owls have developed near-silent flight. This is made possible by large, broad wings with softened trailing edges to the flight feathers, a comb-like leading edge to the foremost primary, and loose, soft body feathers. Most owls have well developed hearing via large, sometimes asymmetrical, ear openings, and facial discs formed by one or more special types of feathers. The facial discs direct sound waves to the ears as do 'dishes' of radio telescopes. It is the nature of the facial disc which serves most conveniently to distinguish the two Families of owls which have living representatives.

It is clear from the fossil record and the number of extant species (between 100 and 134, depending on the authority) that the Family Strigidae represents the main line of owl evolution. The Family has several structural features which separate it from the barn owls, including shorter, broader skulls, larger eyes and broader pelvic girdles. However, the Australian species, all in the genus *Ninox*, are most distinctive in their behavioural traits. All form pairs which vigorously defend territories with monotonous 'hooting'; all have downy fledglings; all males feed incubating females by calling them *from* the nest. Unique among raptors, Australian hawk owl species display a tendency towards *larger* males.

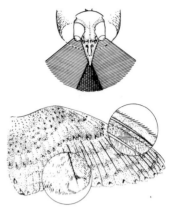

Two adaptations for nocturnal hunting as seen in the Barn Owl: large forward-pointing eyes for binocular vision (above); a comb-like leading edge and softened trailing edge for quiet flight (below).

Breeding seasons

	J	F	M	A	M	J	J	A	S	O	N	D
399 Rufous Owl												
400 Powerful Owl												
401 Southern Boobook												
402 Barking Owl												

Barn Owls   Family Tytonidae

There is no doubt that the two owl Families are much more closely related to each other than they are to any other group. But barn owls have been distinct at least since the Miocene (7-26 million years). The barn owls have the sternum (breast bone) fused to the furcula (wish bone), reduced slotting of the primaries (which are moulted in an irregular sequence), a pectinate (comb-like) middle claw and an inner toe equal in length to the middle toe (see page 155). The general lack of correlation between these features and their functions tends to add weight to separation from the Strigidae.

Tyto is the only Australian genus. Unlike *Ninox* species, barn owls generally defend nest territories not with regular calling but with postures. Some are not territorial at all. The general trend towards opportunistic breeding seems to be correlated to these other tendencies. When they do breed they lay more eggs than *Ninox*; the males feed the females *at* the nest; the fledglings are not downy. They also regurgitate mucous-coated pellets.

Barn Owl talons and detail of middle claw.

Breeding seasons (*variable*)

	J	F	M	A	M	J	J	A	S	O	N	D
404 Barn Owl*												
405 Masked Owl*												
406 Eastern Grass Owl*												
407 Sooty Owl*												
408 Lesser Sooty Owl												

Frogmouths   Family Podargidae

These nocturnal birds capture arthropods, snails and small vertebrates by flying from a vantage perch to the ground. Consequently, they have relatively broad wings, being strong fliers only over short distances. They roost by day on exposed branches, relying on their ability to camouflage themselves as broken branches to avoid predators. They nest in horizontal forks, have two eggs, and their nestlings are downy-white.

Breeding seasons

	J	F	M	A	M	J	J	A	S	O	N	D
409 Tawny Frogmouth												
410 Papuan Frogmouth												
411 Marbled Frogmouth												

Owlet-nightjars   Family Aegothelidae

Australia's very widespread species occurs in many habitat types, but more so in arid regions. It breeds (and roosts by day) in tree hollows or stumps; lays two to four white oval eggs. A fossil is known.

Breeding season (*variable)

J F M A M J J A S O N D
412   Australian Owlet-nightjar*

Nightjars   Family Caprimulgidae

Nightjars hawk evening- and night-flying insects for food. One or two pale eggs are laid in a ground scrape, the superbly camouflaged incubating adults protecting them. Loose concentrations of presumably migrating nightjars may be encountered roosting over a wide area in bushland. Many foreign nightjar species hibernate to escape low temperature periods. This has not yet been proven for Australia's three species.

Breeding seasons

J F M A M J J A S O N D
413   White-throated Nightjar

414   Spotted Nightjar

415   Large-tailed Nightjar

Swiftlets, Swifts   Family Apodidae

The White-rumped Swiftlet breeds in the total darkness of eastern Queensland caves in which tiny, scoop-shaped nests, partly of saliva, are glued to the walls. One egg is laid in each; nestlings are naked. Adults use echo-locating clicks to navigate in the caves.

The two large swifts are annual non-breeding summer migrants to Australia from northern Asia. On arrival, White-throated Needletails slowly disperse along the whole length and on each side of the Eastern Highlands mountain chain, including Tasmania; occasionally some reach New Zealand. Fork-tailed Swifts disperse widely, mainly across the western half of the continent. Both species become nomadic in response to broad-scale weather pattern changes. They rely entirely on aerial insects, especially nuptial swarms of beetles, ants, termites and native bees for food.

Other Asian and Melanesian swiftlets and swifts may be expected as occasional vagrants. Field identification of the Uniform Swiftlet is unreliable.

Part of a White-rumped Swiftlet nesting colony in a cave.

Reading
Crouther, M.M. (1983), 'Observations on White-rumped Swiftlets breeding at Finch Hatton Gorge, 1981-82', *Aust. Bird Watcher* 10, 1-11.

Breeding season

J F M A M J J A S O N D
417   White-rumped Swiftlet

Kingfishers   Family Alcedinidae

Kingfishers perch upright, are large-headed, short-necked, and have long, stout bills. Their flight is swift, strong and direct. Two main groups are recognised: the aquatic kingfishers represented by genus *Ceyx* which feed entirely on aquatic life, and the more terrestrial kingfishers represented by the genera *Dacelo, Halcyon, Syma* and *Tanysiptera*.

Kookaburras are among the largest kingfishers in the world. They feed mostly on the ground for insects and small vertebrates. The Laughing Kookaburra's call is known world-wide.

Halcyon kingfishers are a large, world-wide group with four species in Australia. The Collared Kingfisher is confined to mangroves, feeding on aquatic and terrestrial life. The others are less aquatic; the Red-backed is an arid inland species which moves to the coast in dry years. Sacred Kingfishers nest in Australia, including the south, then migrate to northern Australia, New Guinea, Timor and the Solomon Islands in winter. Many east Australian Forest Kingfishers also migrate to New Guinea. *Syma* kingfishers

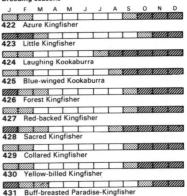

Breeding seasons

J F M A M J J A S O N D
422   Azure Kingfisher

423   Little Kingfisher

424   Laughing Kookaburra

425   Blue-winged Kookaburra

426   Forest Kingfisher

427   Red-backed Kingfisher

428   Sacred Kingfisher

429   Collared Kingfisher

430   Yellow-billed Kingfisher

431   Buff-breasted Paradise-Kingfisher

have distinctive saw-edged bills, but otherwise are similar to *Halcyon* kingfishers.

As adults, paradise-kingfishers *Tanysiptera* have long, thin central tail-feathers, sometimes with racquet-shaped tips. The Buff-breasted breeds in Australia in the wet season, then migrates to New Guinea in the dry. The Common has occurred once at Boigu Island just off the New Guinea coast (a part of Australia).

Kingfishers nest in tree holes (*Dacelo, Halcyon*), termite mounds (*Tanysiptera, Halcyon*), or banks (Red-backed Kingfisher).

Bee-eaters   Family Meropidae

Most Rainbow Bee-eaters breed in southern Australia, moving to northern Australia, New Guinea and East Indonesia in winter. They are insectivorous, sit on exposed perches and with swift and undulating flight, catch insects. They tunnel into sandy banks (or flat ground) to lay four to five white eggs, incubated and tended by both sexes. As many as eight adults have been seen in attendance at one nest hole.

Breeding season

433   Rainbow Bee-eater

Rollers   Family Coraciidae

All rollers perform acrobatic aerial twisting and rolling during their very vocal courtship flights.

The Dollarbird is a regular summer breeding migrant to northern and eastern Australia from southern Asia. During migration they fly at high altitudes. They hunt for insects and even small birds, usually early or late in the day. Dollarbirds hawk from high bare branches. The nest is usually in a hole in a tree; several glossy white eggs are laid.

Breeding season

J	F	M	A	M	J	J	A	S	O	N	D

434   Dollarbird

Pittas   Family Pittidae

The Order Passeriformes, the perching birds (song birds), commences here. It contains *all* the remaining bird species in this book, more than a third of the world's bird Families and more than half of the world's living bird species. The Order is divided into four Sub-Orders and many Families — at present there are 35 Families in Australia.

Passerines have slightly more complex syrinxes (voice boxes) than do the non-passerine Families discussed so far. The song birds sing 'better', although not always pleasingly. An examination of the song birds' toes shows that three point forward and a fourth points backward. The toes are never webbed. All of the song birds have hatchlings which are naked and dependent on one or both parents, although they usually grow quickly.

The brilliantly-plumaged pittas are thrush-like. Stout, longish legs reflect a ground-dwelling existence, but they perch in trees to make territorial calls and to roost. With their body in a crouching attitude parallel to the ground, Pittas sometimes bend their legs and alternately raise and lower their back and head.

A Rainbow Pitta feeds its nestling.

They feed on insects, small invertebrates and reptiles, probably fallen fruit and berries as well. They smash open land snails using a root or stone as an anvil, leaving a tell-tale litter of empty shells.

Pittas' nests are bulky, and normally close to the ground on logs, branch debris or between diverging or emergent tree roots. They are partly or wholly domed, with a large side entrance.

Breeding seasons

J	F	M	A	M	J	J	A	S	O	N	D

435   Red-bellied Pitta

437   Noisy Pitta

438   Rainbow Pitta

Lyrebirds   Family Menuridae

The origins and affinities of lyrebirds are controversial. They were long considered fairly primitive because of their simple vocal organs and were grouped with scrub-birds in the Sub-Order Menurae. However, recent biochemical evidence suggests that they be regarded as true song-birds allied to birds of paradise and bowerbirds.

The name 'lyrebird' stems from the resemblance of the male Superb Lyrebird's tail to a Greek lyre. The tail comprises 16 highly modified tail feathers: two lyrates, two medians and 12 filamentaries which are thrown forward over the head in a drooping fan during courtship display. The Albert's Lyrebird's tail lacks lyrates and consists of 14 feathers.

Lyrebirds rake the forest floor constantly for soil-dwelling invertebrates. The sharp claws on their powerful feet rip away bark, exposing invertebrates living beneath.

The Superb's courtship display takes place on or near earth mounds, the Albert's from vine and twiggy platforms, and both sing loudly. Although the Superb's territorial song contains a short species-specific component (a phrase unique to its species), it is largely a repertoire of mimicked sounds including duetting of other bird species and wing beats and calls of flying parrot flocks. During close pursuit of females, males have a quieter song which contains mimicry of dogs' barking and allegedly sounds produced by inanimate objects.

Male Superb Lyrebirds are polygamous and perform no parental duties. Some females visit more than one male before mating, but male-female association is brief and limited, so that pair-bonding seems to be absent. Breeding commences in winter. The female lays a single egg in the large, side-entranced nest chamber. Incubation takes 50 days, probably because the female deserts the egg for three to six hours each morning during which time embryonic temperature falls to the prevailing low ambient levels and development is interrupted.

Nestling development takes 47 days, the chick being fed about three times hourly. Its weight increases 12-fold to a fledgling weight of 63 per cent of that of the adult female. Estimates of nesting success vary widely (11-20 per cent to 65-79 per cent); the main nest predators are probably native birds, cats, dogs and foxes. Fledglings accompany their mothers and are partly fed by them for up to eight months.

The biology of Albert's Lyrebird is broadly similar to that of the Superb, but is poorly documented. There is an outstanding need for a detailed, long-term study of the ecology and breeding biology of this species.

Reading
Sibley, C. G. (1974), 'The relationships of the lyrebirds', *Emu* **74**, 65-79.

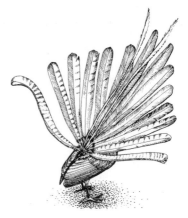

The Superb Lyrebird's tail has 16 tail feathers. The tail feathers of the immature male (shown here) are not fully modified as in the adult.

The Superb Lyrebird builds a large, side-entranced nest chamber.

Breeding seasons

	J	F	M	A	M	J	J	A	S	O	N	D
439 Albert's Lyrebird												
440 Superb Lyrebird												

Scrub-birds   Family Atrichornithidae

The males of the two species, both rare, display rather like immature lyrebirds with elevated and fanned tails, lowered wings, and with the body quivering from the effort of sustained, loud, melodious song and mimicry. Domed nests are close to the ground with side-entrances and are lined with thin, papery wood pulp. One egg is laid (Noisy Scrub-bird); two eggs (Rufous Scrub-bird).

Breeding seasons

	J	F	M	A	M	J	J	A	S	O	N	D
441 Rufous Scrub-bird												
442 Noisy Scrub-bird												

Old World Larks   Family Alaudidae

Larks are widespread in the world and are one of the most clearly defined songbird Families. The Singing Bushlark naturally colonised Australia. The Skylark was introduced in 1857. Both feed on seeds, insects and small molluscs. Both build nests on the ground; cup-shaped (Skylark) or can be fully-domed (Bushlark). Most incubation is by females; the male feeds her at the nest and helps feed the young. The birds may be found in open grassland, crop and saltmarsh areas.

Reading

Mayr, E. & A. R. McEvey, (1960), 'The distribution and variation of *Mirafra javanica* in Australia', *Emu* **60**, 155-192.

Breeding seasons (*variable*)

J	F	M	A	M	J	J	A	S	O	N	D

443 Singing Bushlark*

444 Skylark

Swallows, Martins   Family Hirundinidae

This cosmopolitan Family has six or seven representatives in Australia (the Pacific Swallow *Hirundo tahitica* has yet to be confirmed). They are primitive passerines, shown by features such as the bronchial rings formation. Martins are generally dumpier versions of swallows. Australia's martins have white rumps and square tails; the swallows have deeply forked tails. All have long wings and a graceful flight. Swallows and martins have short, broad bills for insect capture. They superficially resemble swifts (Apodidae) and woodswallows (Artamidae) but are unrelated.

The White-backed Swallow is a nomadic, usually inland species that roosts and nests in tunnels in sandy banks. Welcome Swallows breed in a half-cup mud nest, usually under roof-eaves or bridges in southern and eastern Australia. The Barn Swallow migrates from the Northern Hemisphere to northern Australia — there are no records for Victoria or Tasmania. The Red-rumped Swallow *Hirundo daurica* has occurred once, in a small group on the Daintree River, near Cairns. Fairy Martins build bottle-shaped mud nests, often under bridges. Tree Martins nest in tree- or cliff-holes, lined with mud. All of the Family are very gregarious, often congregating on telegraph wires, and roost as well as breed in their nests. Eggs are pale in colour and sometimes spotted reddish-brown. Two to six eggs are laid.

Reading

Klapste, J. (1977), 'Barn Swallow *Hirundo rustica* in Australia', *Aust. Bird Watcher* **7**, 25-34.

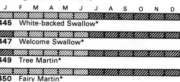

Welcome Swallows breed in a half-cup mud nest, usually under roof-eaves or bridges in southern and eastern Australia.

Breeding seasons (*variable*)

J	F	M	A	M	J	J	A	S	O	N	D

445 White-backed Swallow*

447 Welcome Swallow*

449 Tree Martin*

450 Fairy Martin*

Old World Pipits, Wagtails   Family Motacillidae

Most pipits are grassland birds, a bit like larks, but have different mannerisms, flight and song. Richard's Pipit, Australia's only breeding member of this Family, builds a cup nest of grass in a depression, usually in the shelter of a stone or tussock. It lays three to four finely freckled off-white eggs.

Most wagtails have evolved into a number of well-defined races inhabiting separate parts of their vast breeding range. Wagtails are non-breeding visitors or rare vagrants to Australia from the Northern Hemisphere. Two races of Yellow Wagtail, *simillina* and *taivana* are regular Australian visitors. However, a bird collected in eastern Australia was identified as race *tschutschensis*. These three wintering races *cannot* always be reliably separated in the field.

Reading

Johnstone, R. E. (1982), 'The Yellow Wagtail *Motacilla flava* in Australia', *WA Nat.* **15** (3), 61-66.

Breeding season (*variable*)

J	F	M	A	M	J	J	A	S	O	N	D

451 Richard's Pipit*

Cuckoo-shrikes, Trillers   Family Campephagidae

The campephagids include two genera of Asian 'shrikes' and also the genus *Pericrocotus*, the Asian minivets, none of which are represented in Australia. Cuckoo-shrikes are neither 'cuckoo' or 'shrikes' but superficially resemble the cuckoos in plumage colouration and slender physique and the shrikes in bill appearance.

The flight of cuckoo-shrikes and trillers is undulating. Trillers often sing loudly while flying through the forest canopy and must then be identified from Rufous Songlarks. Many refold their wings as they alight. Members of these genera forage for insects over the outer foliage of trees. Sometimes they flop with outspread wings and tail to grab an insect and to disturb others. They also hawk flying insects from a static perch, or alight on the ground to pick up food. They eat some berries and soft fruits.

Campephagids are mainly arboreal, although the Ground Cuckoo-shrike is more frequently seen on the ground in small social groups. This species is also known to be a co-operative breeder; several adults help at the nest.

Cuckoo-shrikes and trillers build their nests on horizontal branches or forks. They sometimes use the empty nests of other bird species; the mud nest of the Magpie-lark is a favoured choice. The nests of cuckoo-shrikes are so shallow that eggs or young may be lost in strong winds.

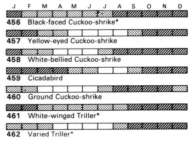

Breeding seasons (*variable)

	J	F	M	A	M	J	J	A	S	O	N	D
456 Black-faced Cuckoo-shrike*												
457 Yellow-eyed Cuckoo-shrike												
458 White-bellied Cuckoo-shrike												
459 Cicadabird												
460 Ground Cuckoo-shrike												
461 White-winged Triller*												
462 Varied Triller*												

Bulbuls   Family Pycnonotidae

Genus *Pycnonotus* contains most species; one in Aust. *P. jocosus*, introduced from China in the early 1900s; a second, Red-vented Bulbul (*P. cafer*) was brought in but may have died out.

Wing size and structure precludes non-migratory bulbuls from being strong fliers, but they are lively, energetic feeders with cheerful, musical calls. Their foods are fruit, insects, buds and young plant shoots.

Research is needed to determine exact status, range, breeding and feeding habits of this little-studied bird.

Breeding season

	J	F	M	A	M	J	J	A	S	O	N	D
463 Red-whiskered Bulbul												

Thrushes, Flycatchers and allies   Family Muscicapidae

This Family contains a widely assorted, loosely related series of song birds, many of which also occur overseas. Years of taxonomic change and revision, consensus and disagreement, have seen the components of this cosmopolitan Family alter frequently. Some birds which previously were held as Sub-Families within a larger Family Muscicapidae are treated in this book as full Families. These are Family Orthonychidae (Chowchillas, Whipbirds, Wedgebills, Quail-thrushes), Family Timaliidae (Babblers), Family Sylviidae (Old World Warblers), Family Maluridae (Fairy-wrens) and Family Acanthizidae (Bristlebirds, Scrubwrens, Gerygones, Thornbills and allies). Even within the genera, species exhibit wide divergence in behaviour and breeding requirements.

Genus *Petroica* includes four red-breasted robins endemic to Australia. Rose Robin, the most arboreal and acrobatic, catches flies in outer canopies of trees. The Red-capped Robin, like other inland birds, may undergo nocturnal torpor; it breeds after good rains. All species build cup-shaped nests, untidily or neatly decorated with grass, lichen etc. Females build the nest and incubate two or three eggs.

All juvenile *Petroica* robins are mottled and streaked brown and buff. The patterns may vary between species. This one is a juvenile Scarlet Robin.

Both parents feed the young and may raise several broods in a season. All are parasitised by cuckoo species. Pairs of 'brown birds' (the male in immature plumage) may successfully rear young. All species show some autumn-winter dispersal or migration. During this migration birds may be seen feeding over open ground.

Future studies (already in progress for Flame Robins) will include banding, and perhaps telemetry, to discover these routes. These studies may prove an annual Bass Strait crossing by Flame and Pink Robins, whether or not several races exist, and determine plumage changes in maturing brown birds. Note: only Flame Robins occur in winter flocks. In the field check throat and abdomen of *coloured* males and look for the company kept by 'brown birds'. Are they *all* females?

Current thought places *all* Australian flycatchers *and* the scrub-robins *Drymodes*, in an Australo-Papuan complex, taxonomically distinct from 'typical' Old World flycatchers. Sometimes they are aligned with pachycephalines (whistlers, shrike-thrushes, Crested Bellbird). Apart from their adaptive flycatcher traits, they have similarities in body proportions (relatively large heads and stout bodies), adult plumages (yellow and green *barely* occurs in monarchs and fantails), and in juvenile plumages. Geographical distributions and presumably regions of origin are also similar. However, such a grouping may be more a reflection of similar ecologies than a phylogenetic relationship. The Crested Shrike-tit is usually included in this robin-flycatcher group but has many differences (see below).

Aside from *Petroica* robins (see above), Australia's members of the robin and flycatcher group comprise six genera and 15 species. These are small, stout, active birds often seen perched on branches or stumps, or clinging vertically to trunks. They show much body, tail and wing movement. They may be located by calls — penetrating monotonous piping or plaintive whistles — which contrast with those of the whistler group, although songs of *Microeca* can be quite melodic. Their diet is mainly insects; robins feed from the ground and surfaces of trunks and branches. Crustaceans form part of the Mangrove Robin's diet.

Microeca flycatchers are nomadic. They are more like 'typical' flycatchers and catch flying insects. They have the smallest nests of any Australian birds, usually on small forks or horizontal branches of fine vegetation and covered with cobwebs, mosses and lichens. The clutch size is one to four. Eggs are shaded green, blue, sometimes cream, buff or white, and are marked brown or grey. They have up to three broods per season. Both parents build nests and rear young. Cuckoos parasitise some species. Adults feign injury if an intruder approaches to distract attention away from their nest or young.

Crested Shrike-tits feed mainly in upper branches, prising invertebrates from bark with their robust bills. They give distinctive chuckling calls or drawn-out plaintive whistles. The female constructs a deep cup-shaped bark nest; two or three white eggs with olive or brown markings are laid.

Whistlers and shrike-thrushes show a close affinity; the Crested Bellbird has features in common with both genera. Recent DNA studies show that whistlers are also close to some monarchines. Grouped together at various levels (often with full Family status), they are robust birds with relatively large heads (hence the name 'thickheads'), and distinctive voices — some are among Australia's most beautiful songsters,

Breeding seasons (*variable*)

	J F M A M J J A S O N D
464 White's Thrush*	
465 Blackbird	
466 Song Thrush	
467 Northern Scrub-robin	
468 Southern Scrub-robin	
469 Rose Robin	
470 Pink Robin	
471 Flame Robin	
472 Scarlet Robin	
473 Red-capped Robin	
474 Hooded Robin*	
475 Dusky Robin	
476 Mangrove Robin*	
477 White-breasted Robin	
478 Eastern Yellow Robin	
479 Western Yellow Robin	
480 Yellow-legged Flycatcher (*Insufficient infor.*)	
481 Lemon-bellied Flycatcher	
482 Kimberley Flycatcher (*Insufficient information*)	
483 Jacky Winter*	
484 Pale-yellow Robin	
485 White-faced Robin	
486 White-browed Robin	
487 Grey-headed Robin	
488 Crested Shrike-tit	
489 Olive Whistler	
490 Red-lored Whistler	
491 Gilbert's Whistler	
492 Golden Whistler	
493 Mangrove Golden Whistler	
494 Grey Whistler*	
495 Rufous Whistler	
496 White-breasted Whistler*	
497 Little Shrike-thrush	
498 Bower's Shrike-thrush	
499 Sandstone Shrike-thrush	
500 Grey Shrike-thrush*	
501 Crested Bellbird*	

with variable repertoires of rich, melodic phrases. Most feed on arboreal and ground-dwelling insects and other invertebrates. Berries are also included. Like its robin counterpart, a large proportion of the food of the White-breasted Whistler is small crabs taken from the muddy substrate of mangroves.

Slightly shorter but stouter, whistlers differ most obviously from shrike-thrushes in their often striking sexual dimorphism. The male appears in contrasting combinations of yellow, black, white, rufous, cinnamon etc. Shrike-thrushes are drab by comparison, with little or no sexual dimorphism. In this respect Crested Bellbirds are most akin to whistlers.

All build open cup-shaped nests of twigs, bark, grasses, roots and leaves. In *Pachycephala* these are shallow, usually low down in small forks and foliage, except for the Grey Whistler which nests high in the canopy, reflecting it. lifestyle. Shrike-thrushes and the Crested Bellbird's nests are deeper, usually in forks of a trunk or large branch, on top of a stump or on an overhanging bank. The Sandstone Shrike-thrush builds on ledges and crevices of sandstone boulders and cliffs among which it lives. The Crested Bellbird habitually places paralysed hairy caterpillars around the nest rim. These are apparently not eaten by the young.

All species have two to three white, cream or buff eggs with brown markings towards the larger end. Some develop breeding territories, become particularly vocal and engage in courtship and territorial displays. Both sexes take part in nest construction and care of young. After breeding some species become nomadic, with small movements north and inland in autumn and winter.

Monarch Flycatchers, Sub-Family Myiagrinae, are a group of forest- and woodland-dwelling insectivorous birds (four genera, 12 Australian species). Bill width varies from the huge, 'boat-shaped' bill of the Yellow-breasted Boatbill to the slender bills of *Arses*, *Monarcha* and the Shining and Restless Flycatchers. Most are black and white with hints of rufous and cream. Some are brightly coloured like the Yellow-breasted Boatbill, Spectacled Monarch, Black-faced Monarch and Black-winged Monarch. All are sexually dimorphic to a varying degree.

Insects are taken either in flight, or in foliage or branches. *Arses* flycatchers have a habit of flitting up tree trunks and probing under bark; they are also distinctive in having erectile frills on their napes. Many species are territorial and may respond immediately to imitations of their calls in the breeding season. All species breed in Australia. Some migrate northwards to north Queensland and New Guinea in winter (Black-faced Monarch, Black-winged Monarch, Spectacled Monarch and Leaden Flycatcher, Satin Flycatcher). All construct cup-shaped nests, have two to three pale, spotted eggs, sometimes with a faint tinge of brown colour.

Fantails, genus *Rhipidura*, are specialised monarchs with long fan-shaped tails that are waved from side to side in an upwards arc with wings held downwards. Four (five or even six) fantails occur in Australia, others occur in New Zealand, Pacific Islands through New Guinea to southern Asia. All are insectivorous. The familiar, misnamed Willie Wagtail is a fantail, not a wagtail (Motacillidae); it occurs throughout Australia (except Tasmania). Grey Fantails are very variable. The Mangrove Fantail is distinct and may be a full species. Two to three eggs, variable in colour and spotted, are laid in cup-shaped nests.

Grey Shrike-thrush nest

Breeding seasons (*variable)

	J	F	M	A	M	J	J	A	S	O	N	D
502 Yellow-breasted Boatbill												
503 Black-faced Monarch												
504 Black-winged Monarch												
505 Spectacled Monarch												
506 White-eared Monarch												
507 Frilled Monarch												
508 Pied Monarch												
509 Broad-billed Flycatcher												
510 Leaden Flycatcher												
511 Satin Flycatcher												
512 Shining Flycatcher												
513 Restless Flycatcher*												
514 Rufous Fantail												
515 Grey Fantail												
516 Northern Fantail												
517 Willie Wagtail*												

Chowchillas, Whipbirds, Wedgebills, Quail-thrushes
Family Orthonychidae

This Family includes a series of ground-dwelling birds from diverse habitats. Genus *Orthonyx* inhabits debris-strewn floors of rainforests: the Chowchilla in northern highlands, the Logrunner in southern coastal and mountain areas. Females build side-entranced domed stick nests. Territories are defended and used annually by these sedentary species. Small groups of Chowchillas call very loudly during the dawn chorus, making them easy to locate.

The two arid country whipbirds (wedgebills) genus *Psophodes* are almost identical in plumage, but are easily identified by their calls. These insectivores run fast, fly low, often with their tail fanned. They perch low in shrubs, especially when singing. They may be solitary or in small flocks. The onset of breeding depends on suitable desert rains; nests are shallow, cup-shaped and low to the ground.

Genus *Cinclosoma*, the quail-thrushes, includes four endemics. Shy, elusive, ground-dwellers, they usually flush away with a quail-like 'whirr'. The cup-shaped nest of leaves and bark is built in a shallow ground scrape. The birds' food includes insects, seeds and probably small reptiles. The Chestnut, Chestnut-breasted, and two races of the Cinnamon Quail-thrush inhabit arid or semi-arid country. They are closely related, and their taxonomy is still debatable. The Spotted Quail-thrush of east and south-east Australian woodlands is declining with encroaching settlements.

Breeding seasons (*variable*)

	J	F	M	A	M	J	J	A	S	O	N	D
518 Logrunner*												
519 Chowchilla*												
520 Eastern Whipbird												
521 Western Whipbird												
522 Chirruping Wedgebill*												
523 Chiming Wedgebill*												
524 Spotted Quail-thrush*												
525 Chestnut Quail-thrush*												
526 Chestnut-breasted Quail-thrush*												
527 Cinnamon Quail-thrush*												

Babblers
Family Timaliidae

Three species of the genus *Pomatostomus* are endemic; one other reaches southern New Guinea. They are omnivorous, live in highly sociable, mainly sedentary, territorial groups, build domed stick nests and erect similar constructions for communal roosting. Very vocal, they typically fly low from cover to cover or 'bounce' away along the ground. The Grey-crowned Babbler has declined alarmingly in some areas.

Breeding seasons (*variable*)

	J	F	M	A	M	J	J	A	S	O	N	D
528 Grey-crowned Babbler*												
529 White-browed Babbler												
530 Hall's Babbler*												
531 Chestnut-crowned Babbler*												

Old World Warblers
Family Sylviidae

The Old World warblers belong to one of the largest passerine Families and are generally small insectivorous birds with pointed bills. All have ten primary feathers; species in many groups resemble each other closely. Relationships between various Family members are not clear, but the closest relatives are thrushes (Turdidae) and Old World flycatchers (Muscicapidae). Many species are migratory.

Most warblers have pleasant and melodic songs from which their Family name is derived. The five genera which breed in Australia are not particularly well known. Observers could contribute to their taxonomy, breeding and behavioural biology, ecological niches and movements about the continent. The recently found Arctic Warbler (genus *Phylloscopus*) is an excellent reminder of the propensity of small birds to move widely about the world's surface.

Reading
McGill, A. R. (1970), *Australian Warblers*, Bird Observers Club, Melbourne, pp. 15–33.

Breeding seasons (*variable*)

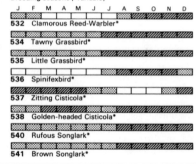

	J	F	M	A	M	J	J	A	S	O	N	D
532 Clamorous Reed-Warbler*												
534 Tawny Grassbird*												
535 Little Grassbird*												
536 Spinifexbird*												
537 Zitting Cisticola*												
538 Golden-headed Cisticola*												
540 Rufous Songlark*												
541 Brown Songlark*												

Fairy-wrens   Family Maluridae

Restricted to Australia and New Guinea, the fairy-wrens' closest affinities are with the Acanthizidae. In Australia they are found in every terrestrial habitat.

Characteristically they keep their tails cocked when hopping on the ground or through bushes. Their bills are short, and their legs long or thick. They usually fly low over the ground or hop. An elaborate distraction display is given if an intruder approaches a nest. The bird scuttles away in a rodent-like display. All are insectivorous, some eat grass seeds. Many of the species rarely drink, taking moisture from their food instead. Their songs are rapid, sometimes complex, reeling and varying in pitch. They also give short contact notes.

The fairy-wrens are well-known for the beauty of the male's plumage, usually consisting of blues (red and black in Red-backed Fairy-wren). The females, immatures and non-breeding males are much duller, usually brown (males always have blue tails).

All fairy-wrens are social, living in groups that maintain their own territory. These co-operative groups consist of a dominant male, one female, subordinate non-breeding birds of both sexes and first year birds. Nests are domed, with a side entrance, usually in a bush or shrub. Two to five eggs, which are pale pink to white and spotted red-brown, are laid; the female broods. Second and third broods in a season are not uncommon, in which case junior males are likely to be left in charge of the earliest brood. With every new brood the female builds a new nest and incubates alone. Snakes are major nest predators.

Emu-wrens are brown and streaked, the males having blue on the face, throat and breast. They have distinctive, filamentous, emu-like tail feathers and are among the smallest of Australian birds — only the Weebill is smaller. Two species are recognised in this book, the inland Rufous-crowned Emu-wren which prefers spinifex, and the heath-dwelling Southern Emu-wren. Recently, however, the Mallee Emu-wren has been treated separately; it is close to the Rufous-crowned in habitat and could be recognised as a separate species. They live in groups like fairy-wrens, are often difficult to see, and will retreat to the undergrowth for protection. Eggs and nests are generally similar to those of fairy-wrens, but 'helpers at the nest' seem to be the exception, not the rule.

Grasswrens include some of the most difficult Australian passerines to see, occurring as they do in remote arid or rocky regions. They can be very shy and will hide in vegetation. They are beautifully streaked brown, rufous, black and white, and vary in size from the starling to the fairy-wren. When escaping from the observer they often run rather than fly; they are very fast runners.

Grasswrens eat seeds as well as insects. Two to three eggs, which are white to pink and spotted brown-red, are laid in a dome-shaped nest hidden in low vegetation. Grasswrens have only one brood per year.

Reading

Rowley, I. (1965), 'The Life History of the Superb Blue Wren *Malurus cyaneus*', *Emu* **64**, 251-297.

Schodde, R. (1982), *The Fairy-Wrens: A Monograph of the Maluridae*, Lansdowne Editions, Melbourne.

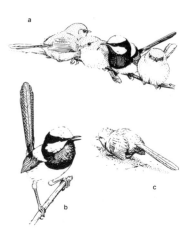

The behavioural postures of the Superb Fairy-wren: (a) clumping and allopreening; (b) territorial singing; (c) rodent-like display.

Breeding seasons (*variable*)

J F M A M J J A S O N D

542 Purple-crowned Fairy-wren*
543 Superb Fairy-wren
544 Splendid Fairy-wren
545 Variegated Fairy-wren
546 Blue-breasted Fairy-wren
547 Red-winged Fairy-wren
548 White-winged Fairy-wren
549 Red-backed Fairy-wren
550 Rufous-crowned Emu-wren
551 Southern Emu-wren
552 Black Grasswren
553 White-throated Grasswren
554 Carpentarian Grasswren
555 Striated Grasswren*
556 Eyrean Grasswren
557 Grey Grasswren
558 Thick-billed Grasswren*
559 Dusky Grasswren*

Bristlebirds, Scrubwrens, Gerygones, Thornbills and allies
Family Acanthizidae

This Australasian Family has a controversial taxonomic history. Different opinions on Family relationships have been published. As late as 1970 the acanthizids, along with the malurids and Australian chats, were often considered Old World warblers (Sylviidae) because of their superficial resemblance and living requirements. Today they are recognised as a distinct Family in an Australo-Papuan passerine assemblage. Acanthizids have thin pointed bills with basal bristles and are mainly insectivorous.

Bristlebirds *Dasyornis* are terrestrial, long-tailed and rufous-brown. They have forward-curving bristles at the bill base and pleasant, squeaky songs. Their nests are domed with a side entrance. They lay two brownish to pinkish eggs, spotted dark brown.

The Pilotbird *Pycnoptilus* is a large, terrestrial scrubwren-like bird with a fairly long tail and a sweet song. It is known to follow foraging lyrebirds and pick out insects that have been flushed out. Three to four pink eggs spotted red to brown are laid in the domed nest with a side entrance.

The Origma or Rock Warbler is confined to sandstone country in the Sydney region. It is also scrubwren-like, but builds a distinctive hanging domed nest with a side entrance in caves. Three white eggs are laid.

The Australian Fernwren *Crateroscelis* of the Atherton Tablelands has New Guinea relatives, previously called mouse-babblers. It is similar in appearance to the genus *Sericornis*. It lays two white eggs in a domed nest with a side entrance.

The genus *Sericornis* is a diverse group of controversial taxonomic interest. Several taxonomists split the genus into: *Sericornis* scrubwrens, *Hylacola*, *Pyrrholaemus* Redthroat, *Calamanthus*, *Chthonicola* Speckled Warbler. However, all are linked in song and display and general patterns, so one genus has been adopted here. At the species level, many forms (races) occur. They range from rainforest to desert and all have domed nests with spotted pale-coloured eggs.

The Weebill *Smicrornis* is the smallest Australian bird. It is thornbill-like but has a small, short bill. A hanging, domed nest contains two to three white to buff-white finely flecked eggs.

Eleven gerygones (fairy-warblers), genus *Gerygone*, occur in Australia. Since many species sing beautiful songs, the generic name is *Gerygone* meaning 'born of sound'. They are dainty birds and actively feed singly or in pairs in the outer foliage of woodland trees. Many occur in mangroves and rainforests. Two to three eggs are laid in a dome-shaped suspended nest. The entrance is protected by a spout.

Twelve thornbills, genus *Acanthiza*, are recognised. Thornbills are smaller and plumper than gerygones and feed in small groups. Identification relies on facial and chest striations, rump colours and calls. The pale-eyed thornbills are mainly terrestrial feeders, while the dark-eyed members are mostly aboreal. All build domed nests and lay two to four eggs. The Yellow-rumped Thornbill constructs an extra cup nest on top of the main domed nesting chamber.

The three whitefaces, genus *Aphelocephala*, are larger than thornbills. They are dumpy, terrestrial feeders with a white face. Whitefaces occur in the dry country of southern Australia where seeds and insects are included in their diet.

Breeding seasons (*variable*)

	J	F	M	A	M	J	J	A	S	O	N	D	
560, 561, 562													Bristlebirds
563													Pilotbird
564													Origma
565													Australian Fernwren
566													Atherton Scrubwren
567													Large-billed Scrubwren
568													Yellow-throated Scrubwren*
569													Tropical Scrubwren*
570													White-browed Scrubwren*
571													Scrubtit
572													Chestnut-rumped Hylacola
573													Shy Hylacola
574													Redthroat
575													Striated Calamanthus*
576													Speckled Warbler
577													Weebill*
578													Brown Gerygone
579													Large-billed Gerygone*
580													Dusky Gerygone*
581													Mangrove Gerygone*
582													Western Gerygone
583													Green-backed Gerygone
584													Fairy Gerygone
585													White-throated Gerygone
586													Mountain Thornbill
587													Brown Thornbill
588													Inland Thornbill
589													Tasmanian Thornbill
590													Chestnut-rumped Thornbill*
591													Slaty-backed Thornbill*
592													Western Thornbill
593													Buff-rumped Thornbill
594													Slender-billed Thornbill*
595, 596, 597													Yellow-rumped, Yellow & Striated Thornbills
598													Southern Whiteface*
599													Chestnut-breasted Whiteface (*Insufficient info.*)
600													Banded Whiteface*

Sittellas   Family Neosittidae

DNA hybridisation studies show sittellas are closely related
to Australo-Papuan flycatchers (Pachycephalinae). Family
similarities exist also in nests, eggs and immature plumages.
The five main Australian sittella forms (races) hybridise
wherever they overlap. They avoid rainforests, but occur in
most other wooded habitats.

   All forms except *leucocephala* are sexually dimorphic in
plumage, females having more black on the face (in *striata*
also on the breast). First year birds seem more dimorphic than
older birds. White spots on the back of the juvenile disappear
at about three months after fledging.

   Average sittella group size is about five; some groups
merge after breeding. Members huddle together when roosting; they sometimes allopreen by day and often forage in the
same tree concurrently. Males have longer bills than females
and forage lower in trees. Sittellas breed communally; young
from early broods attend later broods in the same season.
Only females incubate.

The nest of the Varied Sittella is usually located
in an upright fork of a tree.

Breeding season

	J	F	M	A	M	J	J	A	S	O	N	D

601   Varied Sittella

Treecreepers   Family Climacteridae

The White-throated Treecreeper differs from the other
Australian treecreepers in so many respects that different
ancestry is conceivable. It has shorter legs, the foot's sole has
scaly ridges rather than broad pads. Its bill is thinner,
straighter and has a grey-white lower mandible base; other
climacterids have an all-black bill. Its fore-crown is distinctly
scalloped and the lores have a white line; by contrast, the
other species have a uniform crown and dark lores. Patterns
of sexual dimorphism and juvenile plumage also show a
strong dichotomy. In the White-throated, females have an
orange cheek spot; females of the other species have rufous
chest stripes. White-throated juveniles have black-edged
whitish scapular streaks, and a bright chestnut rump patch
(only in females); nestlings have yellow patches behind the
'knees', on the soles, and the tips of the toenails. These
features are lacking in the other species.

   Other peculiarities of the White-throated probably relate
to its probable rainforest origin. It has a more complex vocal
repertoire including sexually diagnostic calls, an audible tail-
flicking territorial display and an elaborate pre-mating
display, all of which may assist contact in closed habitats with
reduced visual contact. Its little-marked white eggs may
enhance their visibility under such conditions; they differ
strikingly from the heavily marked pinkish eggs of the other
species. The female White-throated builds the nest and
incubates for 22 to 23 days, whereas in the Red-browed and
Brown, both sexes build the nest and the incubation period is
much shorter (16-18 days). Moreover, the White-throated
roosts externally on tree-trunks and sometimes on man-
made constructions, while the other species usually roost
inside hollow dead branches. Parker's (1982) suggestion of
invoking the genus *Cormobates* of Mathews (1922) for the
White-throated is adopted. A new race *intermedia* was
recently described (1983).

   Most *Climacteris* are communal and forage regularly on
the ground. *C. affinis* is apparently non-communal, and *C.
erythrops* rarely feeds on the ground.

   The breeding biology of the Rufous and Black-tailed has
yet to be examined in detail, and their juvenile plumages
described.

The pale wing bars of the White-throated
Treecreeper are exposed in flight (top); a
White-throated Treecreeper's foot (bottom).

Breeding seasons

	J	F	M	A	M	J	J	A	S	O	N	D

602   White-throated Treecreeper

603   Red-browed Treecreeper

604   White-browed Treecreeper

605   Brown Treecreeper

606   Rufous Treecreeper

607   Black-tailed Treecreeper

Honeyeaters   Family Meliphagidae

Honeyeaters are mainly found in Australia and New Guinea but their geographic range extends from Bali to Hawaii and New Zealand. At least one species occurs in every terrestrial habitat in Australia, from tropical rainforests to arid shrublands, from mangroves to suburbia.

The principal and most striking anatomical feature of the Family is the brush-tipped tongue, which functions in the same way as a paint brush, collecting fluids (like nectar) by capillarity. Most honeyeaters can protrude their tongues well beyond their bill tips, enabling nectar collection from the base of long tubular flowers or honeydew extraction from deep, narrow cracks in bark. Most lap up these fluids at rates of 10 or more licks per second and can empty a flower in less than one second.

In Australia, 67 honeyeater species occur. Classification of these into genera and species is still in a state of flux. The degree of variation between species within a genus, varies from genus to genus. For example, *Phylidonyris* with five species shows considerable variation (compare Tawny-crowned with New Holland Honeyeater) but elsewhere in the Family an equivalent (or less) variation results in two genera (e.g. *Acanthagenys* and *Anthochaera*, *Lichenostomus* and *Meliphaga*). Some taxonomists do not consider that *Lichenostomus* is a separate genus from *Meliphaga*. Thus the most recently described species, the Eungella Honeyeater, was described as a species of *Meliphaga*, yet its closest ally is the Bridled Honeyeater *Lichenostomus frenatus*. In the classification followed here, we use *Lichenostomus*.

The distributions shown on the maps need to be explained to avoid misinterpretation. Broadly, they demarcate the regions in which each species has been seen since European settlement. It would be incorrect to assume that a species is equally abundant throughout its range. In fact, many species are unlikely to be seen in the extremities of their geographic range. For example, Regent Honeyeaters are now virtually absent from the Mt Lofty Ranges and Kangaroo Island of South Australia. Mobile species, such as Black, Scarlet, Pied and Painted Honeyeaters, are irregular visitors to southern parts of their range. 'Fuscous' (Yellow-tinted) and Yellow-tufted Honeyeaters are also very infrequent visitors to South Australia. Many of the mobile species could easily appear in the areas *outside* the marked distribution.

Honeyeaters feed mainly on nectar, fruit, and sugary secretions of herbivorous insects (honeydew or lerp), which are rich in carbohydrates (sugars) but low in nutrients. Although they provide most of the food for many honeyeaters, no species feeds entirely on them. All honeyeaters include at least a few insects in their diets to satisfy protein and nutrient requirements.

In southern temperate Australia, honeyeaters may be divided into three groups; 'nectarivorous' genera, such as *Anthochaera*, *Phylidonyris*, *Lichmera* and *Acanthorhynchus*, which feed mainly on nectar; so-called 'insectivorous' genera, such as *Melithreptus*, *Manorina* and many species of *Lichenostomus*, which feed mainly by gleaning foliage or probing bark for honeydew, lerp or insects; 'frugivorous' species, such as Spiny-cheeked and Singing Honeyeaters, which eat large amounts of fruit, at least in some parts of their range.

It should be stressed that these groupings are *not* rigid. In some areas nectarivorous species concentrate on nectar for

The Yellow-tufted Honeyeater feeding: (a) insects; (b) honeydew; (c) blackboy; (d) gum blossom.

The brush-tipped tongue of the White-plumed Honeyeater.

The brush-tipped tongue of a honeyeater functions in the same way as a paint brush.

A male Western Spinebill pollinates a *Grevillea wilsonii*. Note the pollen grains on its crown.

periods of the year, depending on seasonal availability. In fact, almost all species have been observed taking nectar, fruit and honeydew at one time or other.

The groupings, however, highlight the morphological specialisation within the Family. Nectarivorous species are generally longer-beaked, which enables them to probe a greater variety of flowers. The most specialised are the slender-beaked species, such as spinebills. Their long decurved bills match the equally long decurved flowers of many native plants (e.g. the heath *Epacris longiflora*). Short-beaked honeyeaters can extend their tongues to reach nectar at some of these flower bases, but the further the tongue is extended, the less efficient it becomes. Sometimes birds pierce the sides of such tubular flowers, or instead visit the less specialised flowers (e.g. of *Eucalyptus*) where nectar is readily accessible.

Little is known about the ecology of honeyeaters inhabiting the inland areas or the tropical regions of Australia. The long-beaked *Myzomela* and *Certhionyx* are undoubtedly nectarivorous; some shorter-beaked rainforest species are probably frugivorous. The Painted Honeyeater, however, specialises on mistletoe fruits.

Honeyeaters are one of the most successful Australian bird groups. Ten or more species may occur in the one area and sometimes honeyeaters account for more than half of all the individual birds living in an area. In part, this success can be attributed to the abundance and diversity of their carbohydrate food supplies. In some areas sufficient nectar is produced to support more than 20 individuals per hectare. A single ironbark tree, *Eucalyptus leucoxylon*, can support 15 New Holland Honeyeaters (or their equivalent) for a period of one to two months during peak flowering.

Australian meliphagid movements are therefore often associated with the flowering of native plants. In areas with a year-round nectar or honeydew supply, honeyeaters are usually resident, switching from one plant species to another as each blooms. In areas where suitable food is only available for part of the year or where there are large seasonal changes in food supply, honeyeaters show regular seasonal movements. In inland areas where flowering is irregular, nectarivorous honeyeaters are described as 'blossom nomads'. Only Yellow-faced and White-naped Honeyeaters, and perhaps the Red Wattlebird, are considered to be migratory, but their movements are poorly understood. Large, restless flocks of these birds can be seen moving through areas in south-eastern Australia during autumn. Large numbers winter in coastal regions of New South Wales and parts of South Australia. Their origin is not known, but the movements may be altitudinal, birds thus avoiding cold mountain weather in winter.

Honeyeaters are pugnacious and are often seen chasing other birds. This aggression is associated with their food supply defence. Wattlebirds and New Holland Honeyeaters frequently defend nectar sources from members of their own species and other smaller honeyeater species. When two or more nectarivorous species co-occur, nectar sources are usually partitioned. The large wattlebirds, for example, use the richest and most dense nectar sources (*Banksia*, *Eucalyptus*) and aggressively exclude smaller species from these. Smaller species exploit any rich sources not so monopolised and also poorer, more scattered nectar sources (*Lysiana*, *Correa*, *Epacris*). Although less is known about the insectivorous species, they too, probably partition resources along a

An Eastern Spinebill feeding on the heath *Epacris longiflora*.

Breeding seasons (*variable*)

J F M A M J J A S O N D

608 Red Wattlebird*
609 Yellow Wattlebird
610 Little Wattlebird*
611 Spiny-cheeked Honeyeater*
612 Striped Honeyeater*
613 Helmeted Friarbird*
614 Silver-crowned Friarbird*
615 Noisy Friarbird*
616 Little Friarbird*
617 Regent Honeyeater
618 Blue-faced Honeyeater*
619 Bell Miner*
620 Noisy Miner*
621 Yellow-throated Miner*
622 Black-eared Miner
623 Macleay's Honeyeater
624 Tawny-breasted Honeyeater
625 Lewin's Honeyeater
626 Yellow-spotted Honeyeater
627 Graceful Honeyeater
628 White-lined Honeyeater (*Insufficient information*)
629 Eungella Honeyeater (*Insufficient information*)

gradient of food density, with the largest species, *Manorina*, excluding smaller species from the richest sources (e.g. outbreaks of lerp).

Breeding seasons of Australian honeyeaters also depend largely on the availability of carbohydrate food and the locality. Most species breed between late winter (July/August) and early summer (December) but a number of species also breed during autumn and occasionally during winter. Honeyeaters usually moult during summer after spring breeding. Juveniles often have an incomplete post-juvenile moult during summer or autumn.

Female honeyeaters build the cup-shaped nest in either a fork of a shrub or tree, or suspend it in pendulous foliage, often in a eucalypt. Nest location depends on the honeyeater species. Nests are usually constructed of small twigs and strips of bark held together by spiders' webs, and often lined with mammal hair, soft plant material and the occasional feather.

Clutches usually consist of two or three pinkish-buff (sometimes whitish) eggs with darker spots or blotches. Eggs are laid on consecutive days. Incubation normally takes about two weeks. Chicks remain in the nest for a similar period. In nearly all species, only the female incubates but both sexes feed nestlings.

Males of many species give display flights during the breeding season, in which they fly up at an angle into the air, often giving a piping call, then glide back to a perch. Many species breed as monogamous pairs but some species, for example *Manorina* and *Melithreptus*, may breed communally when non-breeding individuals assist the breeding pair by feeding chicks. Miners, in particular, live in distinct colonies and have a complex social system. Some species, notably *Manorina*, but also various *Lichenostomus* and *Phylidonyris*, gather for group displays or 'corroborees'. The purpose of these corroborees is not known.

Honeyeaters have a close mutual association with the Australian flora and are important pollinators and seed dispersers. Among the plants pollinated by honeyeaters are various *Eucalyptus, Banksia, Callistemon, Grevillea, Correa, Eremophila*, mistletoes and epacrids, to name just a few of them. Many of these plants depend on birds for pollination. Planting suitable nectar-producing plants attracts honeyeaters to suburban gardens. Honeyeaters also disperse the seeds of various acacias, chenopods, mistletoes and epacrids.

The nest of a Black Honeyeater is bound to twigs on a fork of a tree. It is not slung beneath a branch. The eggs are buff in colour with grey and dark green speckles.

Breeding seasons (*variable)

	J	F	M	A	M	J	J	A	S	O	N	D
630 Yellow-faced Honeyeater												
631 Bridled Honeyeater												
632 Singing Honeyeater*												
633 Varied Honeyeater*												
634 Mangrove Honeyeater												
635 White-gaped Honeyeater*												
636 Yellow Honeyeater												
637 White-eared Honeyeater												
638 Yellow-throated Honeyeater												
639 Yellow-tufted Honeyeater												
640 Purple-gaped Honeyeater												
641 Grey-headed Honeyeater*												
642 Yellow-plumed Honeyeater*												
643 Grey-fronted Honeyeater*												
644 Fuscous Honeyeater												
645 Yellow-tinted Honeyeater												
646 White-plumed Honeyeater*												
647 Black-chinned Honeyeater*												
648 Strong-billed Honeyeater												
649 Brown-headed Honeyeater												
650 White-throated Honeyeater												
651 White-naped Honeyeater												
652 Black-headed Honeyeater												
653 Green-backed Honeyeater (*Insufficient info.*)												
654 Brown Honeyeater*												
655 White-streaked Honeyeater												
656 Tawny-crowned Honeyeater*												

Reading

Beruldsen, G. R. (1980), *A Field Guide to Nests and Eggs of Australian Birds*, Rigby, Adelaide.

Collins, B. G. & P. Briffa, (1982), 'Seasonal variation of abundance and foraging of three species of Australian honeyeater', *Aust. Wildl. Res.* **9**, 557-570.

Dow, D. D. (1973), 'Flight moult of the Australian honeyeater *Myzantha melanocephala* (Latham)', *Aust. J. Zool.* **21** 519-532.

Dow, D. D. (1979), 'The influence of nests on the social behaviour of males in *Manorina melanocephala*, a communally breeding honeyeater', *Emu* **79**, 71-83.

Ford, H. A. (1976), 'The honeyeaters of Kangaroo Island', *S. Aust. Orn.* **27**, 134-138.

Ford, H. A. & D. C. Paton, (1977), 'The comparative ecology of ten honeyeaters in South Australia', *Aust. J. Ecol.* **2**, 399-408.

Ford, H. A. (1979), 'Interspecific competition in Australian honeyeaters — depletion of common resources', *Aust. J. Ecol.* **4**, 145-164.

Ford, H. A. (1980), 'Breeding and moult in honeyeaters (Aves: Meliphagidae) near Adelaide, South Australia', *Aust. Wildl. Res.* **7**, 453-464.

Ford, H. A. & D. C. Paton, (1982), 'Partitioning of nectar sources in an Australian honeyeater community', *Aust. J. Ecol.* **7**, 149-159.

Ford, H. A. & J. F. Pursey, (1982), 'Status and feeding of the Eastern Spinebill *Acanthorhynchus tenuirostris* at New England National Park, north-eastern NSW', *Emu* **82**, 203-211.

Keast, J. A. (1968), 'Seasonal movements in the Australian honeyeaters (Meliphagidae) and their ecological significance', *Emu* **67**, 159-210.

Keast, J. A. (1968), 'Competitive interactions and the evolution of ecological niches as illustrated by the Australian honeyeater genus *Melithreptus* (Meliphagidae)', *Evolution* **22**, 762-784.

Paton, D. C. (1980), 'The importance of manna, honeydew and lerp in the diets of honeyeaters', *Emu* **80**, 213-226.

Paton, D. C. (1982), 'The diet of the New Holland Honeyeater, *Phylidonyris novaehollandiae*', *Aust. J. Ecol.* **7**, 279-298.

Paton, D. C. (1982), 'The moult of New Holland Honeyeaters *Phylidonyris novaehollandiae* (Aves: Meliphagidae) in Victoria. Part II. Moult of juveniles', *Aust. Wildl. Res.*, **9**, 345-356.

Paton, D. C. & H. A. Ford, (1977), 'Pollination by birds of native plants in South Australia', *Emu* **77**, 73-85.

Pyke, G. H. (1980), 'The foraging behaviour of Australian honeyeaters: a review and some comparisons with humming-birds', *Aust. J. Ecol.* **5**, 343-369.

Recher, H. F. (1971), 'Sharing of habitat by three congeneric honeyeaters', *Emu* **71**, 147-152.

Salomonsen, F. (1967), Chapter on 'Meliphagidae' in Peter's *Check-list of Birds of the World*, Mus. Comp.. Cambridge, Mass.

Schodde, R. (1975), *Interim List of Australian Songbirds — Passerines*, RAOU, Melbourne.

Smith, A. J. & B. I. Robertson, (1978), 'Social organisation of Bell Miners', *Emu* **78**, 169-178.

Breeding seasons (*variable*)

J F M A M J J A S O N D

657 Crescent Honeyeater*
658 New Holland Honeyeater*
659 White-cheeked Honeyeater*
660 White-fronted Honeyeater*
661 Painted Honeyeater*
662 Brown-backed Honeyeater
663 Bar-breasted Honeyeater*
664 Rufous-banded Honeyeater
665 Rufous-throated Honeyeater
666 Grey Honeyeater (*Insufficient information*)
667 Eastern Spinebill
668 Western Spinebill
669 Banded Honeyeater*
670 Black Honeyeater*
671 Pied Honeyeater*
672 Dusky Honeyeater*
673 Red-headed Honeyeater*
674 Scarlet Honeyeater*

Chats   Family Ephthianuridae

This is an endemic Family of brightly coloured species in which the females are similar to but generally duller in plumage than the males. They are among the few small birds which walk and do not hop. While running, they eat insects and seeds gathered on the ground. They have brush-tipped tongues, presumably for feeding on nectar when flowers bloom in the arid inland.

The brush-tipped tongue of the Crimson Chat.

Their nests are cup-shaped, made of fine twigs and grasses, and have a fine lining of vegetable matter and hairs. They are usually placed on a low bush, in a spinifex clump, or on the ground. Some chats breed in loose colonies, but each nest territory is strongly defended. In the non-breeding season small, highly nomadic flocks form, which may consist of mixed chat species. These tend to irrupt and breed after desert rains. Some species appear to have the capacity to go into torpor in response to extreme cold.

Breeding seasons (*variable*)

J F M A M J J A S O N D

675 Crimson Chat*
676 Orange Chat*
677 Yellow Chat*
678 White-fronted Chat*
679 Gibberbird*

Sunbirds   Family Nectariniidae

This Old World insectivorous and nectarivorous Family (about 104 species) extends from Africa to Asia, New Guinea and Australia. Active, pugnacious and noisy, these birds behave rather like honeyeaters. The sexes have different plumages. They build a spectacular suspended nest with a side entrance. Preferred habitat is lush tropical growth of coastal lowlands and offshore islands. They frequent gardens and may enter houses.

Breeding season (*variable*)

J F M A M J J A S O N D

680 Olive-backed Sunbird*

Flowerpeckers   Family Dicaeidae

Now that the pardalotes have their own Family, the Mistletoe-bird is the only Australian representative of the Dicaeidae. The range of the Mistletoebird extends to the Aru Islands and western Papua New Guinea, not to Tasmania. Ripe parasitic mistletoe berries are their main food (insects are eaten when feeding young); the birds are an important agent in the berry's dispersal.

The Mistletoebird does not have a muscular gizzard as do other birds. Its digestive system is an even duct through which large numbers of mistletoe berries quickly pass. The fleshy pericarp is digested and the sticky seed is deposited (bird standing lengthwise) on the branch and soon germinates.

Non-breeding birds are highly nomadic. They are usually in pairs but solitary males are very common. Torpidity has been recorded in cold weather.

The nest is made of plant-down and spiderweb matted to a silken consistency, and hangs from a level twig. It is a neat pear-shaped purse with a slit-like side entrance. The female usually builds it and incubates the eggs alone.

The Mistletoebird perches lengthwise along branches and defecates mistletoe seeds onto them. If the seeds stick to a suitable branch they usually germinate. In this way the Mistletoebird helps the mistletoe plant to spread.

Breeding season (*variable*)

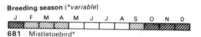

J	F	M	A	M	J	J	A	S	O	N	D

681   Mistletoebird*

Pardalotes   Family Pardalotidae

This small Family (one genus, four to five species) is restricted to Australia. Its nearest relatives are debatable. For a long time pardalotes were placed with the flowerpeckers, Dicaeidae, but recent evidence based on egg-white protein and DNA-hybridisation suggests that their origins lie with an old Australian endemic group which includes the thorn-bills and honeyeaters.

The Yellow-rumped Pardalote is a drier-country representative of the Spotted Pardalote. Where they meet they may interbreed, so may best be considered conspecific. Taxonomic treatment of the Striated Pardalote has also been controversial. Some authors suggest that *Pardalotus striatus* may be divided into four or five species.

Pardalotes are distinctive in appearance — small and colourful with short tails and short blunt beaks. They resemble in size and shape only one other species, the Weebill (*Smicrornis brevirostris*) which is duller, smaller and more active than any mainland pardalote.

All pardalotes glean arthropods from tree foliage, frequently hanging upside down to do so. Many also feed specifically on the sugary lerps exuded by psyllids, small plant-sucking insects living on *Eucalyptus* trees. Clicking sounds made by the bills of these birds when removing lerps is a characteristic of their feeding.

The Red-browed Pardalote inhabits inland and northern Australia mainly in trees lining watercourses. Other species are found in a wide range of eucalypt forests; often two species occur together.

Striated and Spotted Pardalotes may have substantial seasonal movements. Birds travel in winter from wetter (mountain) forests to both inland and more northerly coastal areas. Most Striated Pardalotes from Tasmania leave in autumn and may travel as far north as Queensland. During this dispersal, both species may form very large flocks. Many birds may die. The Forty-spotted Pardalote is restricted to the coastal eucalypt forests of eastern Tasmania and offshore islands; it may have a minor winter dispersal.

A black-headed form of the Striated Pardalote about to enter a nest hole in a dead tree.

All species build characteristic cup or domed nests in tree hollows or burrows drilled in the ground. Like other burrow-nesting birds, their eggs are plain white. The clutch size (about four) is higher than for most other Australian insectivorous birds; incubation and fledging times are relatively long. Both parents work at hole and nest construction. Several other individuals may help to feed the young.

There are, however, interesting differences in the nests each species builds. Spotted Pardalotes nest in loose soil and because each pair defends its feeding territory, nest holes are widely spaced. By contrast, Forty-spotted Pardalotes and Striated Pardalotes nest in hollows in trees and in earth banks. Sites for both these species are often close together — a factor which assists in defending nest sites from other birds. Striated Pardalotes, as a result, nest in large, loose colonies, in sandhills, river banks, road cuttings and old hollow trees. Sometimes they may nest solitarily. But, the Forty-spotted Pardalote, it seems, can only nest successfully in small colonies which it can defend against the more dominant local Striated Pardalotes, competing with it for nesting holes.

No detailed studies exist for the nesting habits of the Red-browed Pardalote — a challenge exists here. To observers, pardalotes are most noticeable when breeding on the ground; they fly to and from the nest hole and may ignore the approach of a bird-watcher. Otherwise, they tend to feed high in eucalypts and may be recognised only through their frequent calling or beak-clicking.

Reading

Noske, R. (1978), 'Comments on some of the scientific names used in the *Interim List of Australian Songbirds*', *Aust. Birds* 13, 27-35.

White-eyes   Family Zosteropidae

These closely related olive-green and yellow birds, usually with white eye-rings, are found in the Old World and in Australia.

Pale White-eyes are restricted to islands off far north-east Queensland and are seen by few ornithologists. Little is known of their habits, or those of the mangrove-dwelling Yellow White-eye of northern Australia.

By contrast, the Silvereyes of eastern and southern Australia have been studied intensively for over two decades. Well over 100 000 individual birds have been banded in an attempt to discover their migratory movements. Once thought to be sedentary or nomadic, it is now known that in autumn some populations undertake lengthy journeys. The Tasmanian race is perhaps most notable; large numbers cross Bass Strait and winter from Adelaide to south Queensland. It appears that the birds travel at night when flocks of hundreds have been heard and observed passing overhead in near continuous streams. During the day their journey is interrupted by feeding activities. The birds search foliage for insects, seeds, nectar (they have a brush-tipped tongue) and fruit (which makes them orchard pests).

Two to four pale blue eggs are laid in a small, neat cup of fine grasses, rootlets, cobwebs etc. Pale White-eyes use leaves — little is known of their breeding.

The series of articles by G. F. Mees and J. Kikkawa ought to be consulted for further information on the genus *Zosterops* in general. Banding studies have been discussed in *The Australian Bird Bander* — read articles by S. G. Lane.

A diagrammatic cut-away showing the lined nest chamber at the end of a Spotted Pardalote's burrow.

Breeding seasons (*variable*)

	J	F	M	A	M	J	J	A	S	O	N	D
682 Spotted Pardalote												
683 Yellow-rumped Pardalote												
684 Forty-spotted Pardalote*												
685 Red-browed Pardalote*												
686 Striated Pardalote*												

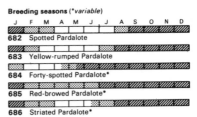

A Silvereye feeding on nectar.

The brush-tipped tongue of the Silvereye.

Breeding seasons

	J	F	M	A	M	J	J	A	S	O	N	D
687 Pale White-eye (*Insufficient information*)												
688 Yellow White-eye												
689 Silvereye												

True Finches   Family Fringillidae

This is a very large, widespread, Northern Hemisphere Family with uncertain relationships. All have 12 tail feathers, nine primaries and a stout conical bill.

The Goldfinch and Greenfinch are the only 'true' finches in Australia and were introduced last century. Both are fairly sedentary and urban-living. The Greenfinch eats seeds, small fruits and buds, but the thinner-billed Goldfinch eats small seeds, especially of Scotch Thistle. Both eat many insects in summer.

In spring, large winter flocks disperse. Breeding males claim territories and sing loud songs from conspicuous perches to attract females. Pair formation involves chases by the male and concludes with the male feeding the female and mating.

Greenfinches lay four to six whitish eggs with brown spots; the Goldfinch lays three to seven pale blue eggs spotted brown. Females incubate for 12 to 14 days; young birds fledge 12 to 14 days after hatching.

The cup-shaped nest of the European Goldfinch in a gorse bush.

Breeding seasons

J	F	M	A	M	J	J	A	S	O	N	D

690 European Goldfinch

691 European Greenfinch

Old World Sparrows   Family Passeridae

Both species were introduced into Australia between 1862 and 1872: House Sparrows released at Sydney, Melbourne, Brisbane and Hobart; Tree Sparrows only in Melbourne. Both eat seeds, grain, flower and leaf buds, insects and food scraps, and are considered to be pest species.

In spring, winter flocks break up as males find territories and nest sites. With loud 'chirrup' songs they attract females, then adopt a stiff head-up, tail-up posture, and hop around bowing before the female.

Bulky spherical grass nests with side entrances and inner cups lined with feathers are built in bushes, hollows and building crevices.

House Sparrows lay three to six grey-white eggs blotched brown. Tree Sparrows lay four to six brown-white eggs with fine brown dots. Incubation by both sexes lasts 14 to 15 days; young birds fledge 15 to 16 days after hatching.

Reading
Summers-Smith, J. D. (1963), *The House Sparrow*, Collins London.

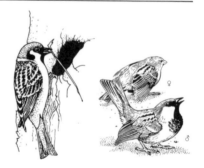

A nest hollow of the Tree Sparrow (left); House Sparrows during courtship (right).

Breeding seasons

J	F	M	A	M	J	J	A	S	O	N	D

692 House Sparrow

693 Tree Sparrow

Weavers, Waxbills, Grass-Finches, Mannikins   Family Ploceidae

The taxonomy of this Family of Old World seed-eaters is frequently rearranged. Groups are often included or excluded depending on current fashion. The 'true weavers' are *always* represented but inclusion of other groups varies.

The Sub-Family Ploceinae (96 species, 11 genera) includes weavers, bishops and wydahs. They weave grass into neat, roofed nests in many beautiful shapes. They have a reduced tenth primary (outer flight feather), strong seed-eating bills and eggs of blues and greens. They are often polygamous.

The genus *Euplectes* (16 species) typically inhabits swampy African grasslands, and eats seeds, grains and insects. Two species were introduced into Australia: the Red Bishop was established on the Murray River at Murray Bridge, South Australia; the White-winged Wydah on the Hawkesbury River, near Windsor, New South Wales. Both were in small loose colonies in reed beds beside the rivers.

A diagrammatic cut-away of a grass-finch nest. Note the structural elements.

Breeding seasons

J	F	M	A	M	J	J	A	S	O	N	D

694 White-winged Wydah

695 Red Bishop

Large winter flocks are formed when males have dull plumage like females. Males then develop bright nuptial plumage and establish territories in which a number of small nests are built. Attempts are made to attract and mate with three to four females, which are chased over the territory by slow, buzzing, circular flights. During this, males fluff out their bright plumage. Three to four bluish-green eggs are laid which hatch in 11 to 14 days. The young birds fledge 13 to 16 days later. Only the female incubates and feeds them.

The Sub-Family Estrildidae (126 species, 28 genera) consists of three tribes: waxbills, grass-finches and mannikins. Smaller than weavers and sparrows, they have only nine primaries, build a roofed, unwoven grass nest and lay pure white eggs. Nestlings beg uniquely with their head down to one side and also have intricate palate and tongue patterns. The estrildid song is very soft and non-territorial in function; females solicit with quivering tails, *not* wings.

Estrildids evolved in Africa, spreading to Asia and Australia. Waxbills remained in Africa but three separate Australian invasions gave rise to the grass-finches and mannikins, our only indigenous seed-eating passerines. The first invasion gave rise to the crimson-rumped grass-finches (*Emblema, Neochmia*), the second to the white-rumped grass-finches (*Poephila*), and the last wave produced the *Lonchura* and the *Erythrura*. The arrangement of Australian finches into genera remains controversial. All eat seeds and, when breeding, eat insects, especially flying termites; all flock throughout the year except the firetails and the Crimson Finch.

All Australian finches are monogamous, probably for life. Most use pre-copulatory courtship for pair formation. The more primitive *Emblema-Neochmia* group use an ancestral 'stem dance' at courtship. The male holds a long grass stem by the thick end and with stiff legs bobs up and down on a branch. Plumage is fluffed and the bill is pointed up in all except the Diamond Firetail which holds its head down. A soft, simple song of repetitive phrases is given. Throughout, both sexes bow and beak-wipe and twist their heads and tail towards one another.

The *Poephila* group have lost the 'stem dance' but waltz together on branches until the female stops. The male in a fluffed upright posture, then sings to her. With tail quivers she invites mating. In the mannikin group, the males sing an extremely soft song with bill wide open and pointed down; both sexes pivot, bow and shake.

Most species are colonial nesters except the Beautiful and Red-eared Firetails, and the Crimson Finch, which establish large individual territories. Males show possible nest sites to the female but she ultimately decides. A nest ceremony confirms the decision. Thick, thorny bushes are the most suitable sites. However, some *Lonchuras* nest in reeds or grass. Red-eared Firetails prefer tree-tops; Painted Firetails, Pictorella Mannikins and Masked Finches nest on the ground. Gouldians nest in tree hollows and termite mounds. Both sexes build; the male carries most of the chosen materials. The domed grass and twig nest is entered by a lateral tunnel. The egg chamber is lined with feathers and plant 'wool'. Nest dimensions vary: Zebras and Beautiful Firetails build the largest; Painted Firetails the smallest.

Normally, four or five pure white eggs are laid. Incubation begins with the fourth egg. Both sexes take turns for one to two hours. Hatching takes 12 to 16 days, depending on the weather. The young are brooded for 12 days and fed by both parents on half-ripe seeds and regurgitated insects. Loud,

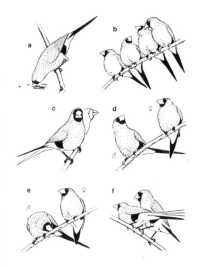

Aspects of grass-finch behaviour: (a) drinking by sucking; (b) clumping and allopreening; (c) singing posture (undirected); (d) waltzing with tails twisted during courtship; (e) bill wiping during courtship; (f) soliciting of male by tail quivering female.

Breeding seasons (*variable*)

	J	F	M	A	M	J	J	A	S	O	N	D
696 Red-browed Firetail												
697 Beautiful Firetail												
698 Red-eared Firetail												
699 Painted Firetail*												
700 Diamond Firetail*												
701 Star Finch*												
702 Crimson Finch*												
703 Zebra Finch*												
704 Double-barred Finch*												
705 Masked Finch*												
706 Long-tailed Finch												
707 Black-throated Finch												
708 Plum-headed Finch												
709 Pictorella Mannikin												
710 Chestnut-breasted Mannikin*												
711 Yellow-rumped Mannikin												
712 Black-headed Mannikin												
713 Nutmeg Mannikin												
714 Blue-faced Finch												
715 Gouldian Finch												

raucous cries accompany the strange begging posture of nestlings in which the wings are *not* quivered. Gouldian nestlings have two large luminous tubercles at each corner of the gape. Nestlings have black patterns of spots or stripes on the mouth and tongue, unique to their own species.

The young fledge about 22 days after hatching, and are independent at 40 days. Zebra and Gouldian Finches and Painted Firetails become sexually mature between 70 and 80 days, which places them among the fastest sexually maturing bird species known. Extensive research has been conducted on physiology and behaviour of Zebra Finches.

All species possess a variety of calls: begging, distress, close contact, nest-attracting, alarm and courtship.

The fledgling of the Gouldian Finch begs for food.

It is believed that the gape markings of a Gouldian Finch nestling stimulate the parent to feed it.

Reading

Goodwin, D. (1982), *Estrildid Finches of the World*, OUP, London.
Immelmann, K. (1982), *Australian Finches in Bush and Aviary*, 2nd edn, Angus & Robertson, Sydney.
Zann, R. (1976), 'Variation in the songs of three species of estrildine grassfinches', *Emu* **76**, 97-108.

Starlings, Mynahs   Family Sturnidae

Metallic Starlings are migratory and fruit-eating. They maintain traditional nest colonies in tall trees, often isolated or taller than the surrounding forest canopy. The Common Starling and Common Mynah are introductions, to some degree commensal with humans, but not completely dependent on them for shelter and food. The Common Starling in particular occurs well away from settlements, and is still extending its range. Both compete with native birds for nesting holes and for food; starlings are significant agricultural pests.

Breeding seasons (*variable*)

J	F	M	A	M	J	J	A	S	O	N	D

716   Metallic Starling
717   Common Starling*
718   Common Mynah*

Orioles, Figbirds   Family Oriolidae

The two orioles are principally forest-dwelling insect- and fruit-eaters, and are migratory or nomadic, perhaps responding to seasonal food supplies. The Figbird, confined to Australasia, is very dependent on figs and other fruit. It eats fewer insects and is unusual among the Oriolidae in being very gregarious.

Orioles and figbirds build strong, deep, cup-shaped, suspended nests; the Yellow Oriole's nest is often placed over a stream or pool. The Oriolidae are thought to be comparatively recent colonists in Australia.

An Olive-backed Oriole at its cup-shaped suspended nest.

Reading

Crouch, H. W. (1970), 'Olive-backed Oriole in South Australia', *S. Aust. Orn.* **25**, 195-200.
Ford, J. (1975), 'Systematics and hybridization of figbirds *Sphecotheres*', *Emu* **75**, 163-171.
Liddy, J. (1982), 'The Olive-backed Oriole: an occasional disseminator of Mistletoe', *Corella* **6**, 93.

Breeding seasons (*variable*)

J	F	M	A	M	J	J	A	S	O	N	D

719   Yellow Oriole
720   Olive-backed Oriole*
721   Figbird

Drongos   Family Dicruridae

Drongos form a fairly uniform group — mainly glossy black, often with ornamental curved tail feathers. Their evolutionary position is uncertain. The migratory Spangled Drongo eats insects, fruit and nectar. Occasionally one is recorded well outside its accepted coastal tropical range. Detailed records of movements, ecology and behaviour are needed.

Breeding season

J	F	M	A	M	J	J	A	S	O	N	D

722   Spangled Drongo

Bowerbirds   Family Ptilonorhynchidae

Bowerbirds are considered by some to be the most advanced of *all* birds because of their remarkable bower building and associated behaviour. Although they are very closely related to the birds of paradise, they definitely constitute a distinct Family. Contemporary field studies of wild bird behaviour by various workers in New Guinea and Australia support this, and the two Families have been considered most closely affiliated to the Australian scrub-birds and lyrebirds (a view strongly supported by very recent DNA studies), starlings, New Zealand wattlebirds and the corvine (crow) assemblage.

The spectacular behaviour of most male bowerbirds has attracted much attention, resulting in considerable scientific and popular literature. The Fawn-breasted Bowerbird, relative to other species in Australia, has lacked study in the field.

Bowerbirds are predominantly local-living forest birds that actively feed when not calling or perched at bowers. Promiscuous males of all Australian bowerbirds (except the Spotted Catbird and Tooth-billed Bowerbird) build bowers or clear a court, decorated in various ways to impress many females. Bower- or court-owning males call much of the day at their display site to attract females and deter rival males. Some have call notes given almost exclusively at the bower, which helps potential mates (and bird-watchers) locate them. A hide (a concealed observatory) is invaluable at a bower if you are to observe male behaviour and the elusive female-plumaged visitors. Females perform all nest building, egg incubation and feeding of young without male help. Most of the avenue bower-building species form often large, locally mobile winter flocks whereas other species remain sedentary and relatively solitary.

Male catbirds do not build bowers and are not promiscuous. They pair with one female, defend an all-purpose territory and assist in feeding their offspring.

Bowerbirds are predominantly frugivorous but their young are fed various percentages of animal items. Catbirds frequently kill other birds' nestlings to feed their own young. Figs are particularly important, notably to the catbirds. Buds, flowers, fresh succulent stems and leaves are also eaten, more so in winter by some species (Satin, Tooth-billed Bowerbird). The latter bird becomes quite folivorous (foliage-eating) in winter, using its peculiar bill to tear and masticate leaves and shoots, while perching inconspicuously.

Nests are bulk cups of twigs, leaves and tendrils usually placed in a shrub or tree fork, a vine, or in a low tree. Eggs usually number one or two but catbirds sometimes lay three. Incubation takes approximately 19 to 25 days, nestlings fledge at about 18 to 22 days and may become independent of parents at between 60 and 80 days after fledging.

Reading

Cooper, W. T. & J. M. Forshaw, (1977), *The Birds of Paradise and Bower Birds*, Collins, Sydney.

Diamond, J. M. (1982), 'Evolution of bowerbirds' bowers: animal origins of the aesthetic sense', *Nature* (UK) **297**, 99-102.

Gilliard, E. T. (1969), *Birds of Paradise and Bower Birds*, Weidenfeld & Nicolson, London.

Vellenga, R. E. (1980a), 'Moults of the Satin Bowerbird *Ptilonorhynchus violaceus*', *Emu* **80**, 49-54.

Vellenga, R. E. (1980b), 'Distribution of the Satin Bowerbird at Leura, NSW, with notes on parental care, development and independence of the young', *Emu* **80**, 97-102.

A bower of the Great Bowerbird.

A very well-established bower of the Golden Bowerbird.

The court of the Tooth-billed Bowerbird.

Breeding seasons

	J	F	M	A	M	J	J	A	S	O	N	D
723 Golden Bowerbird												
724 Satin Bowerbird												
725 Regent Bowerbird												
726 Spotted Bowerbird												
727 Great Bowerbird												
728 Fawn-breasted Bowerbird												
729 Tooth-billed Bowerbird												
730 Spotted Catbird												
731 Green Catbird												

Birds of Paradise   Family Paradisaeidae

Forty-three birds of paradise species form 18 genera through the Moluccas, New Guinea and Australia. Australia's four species are members of two genera. *Manucodia keraudrenii* of northern Cape York Pen., Queensland, also occurs in New Guinea, and three *Ptiloris* species (riflebirds) form a 'super-species' of broken distribution along the central and northern sections of the east Australian coast. The Magnificent Riflebird of northern Cape York Pen. is also in New Guinea; the two smaller riflebirds are endemic to Australia. Unlike the Manucode, which is somewhat drab and a monogamous breeder, the males of the three riflebirds are splendidly plumaged and like so many birds of paradise are promiscuous. Each adult male displays alone on defended dead branches and mates with many females.

The Australian birds of paradise are medium to large sized. The whole Family includes some which are only starling-sized, and some about 25 per cent larger than our Magnificent Riflebird.

Riflebirds are typical of their Family and very closely related to the genera *Lophorina*, *Epimachus* and *Astrapia* of New Guinea. The larger Magnificent Riflebird is clearly a race of the New Guinea species and is distinctly different from the Victoria's and Paradise Riflebird. These two smaller birds are very similar and are considered by some ornithologists as forms of a single species.

Often described as the most beautiful or spectacular group of birds on earth, the birds of paradise have long been admired and studied. Most species are more colourful and ornately plumaged than the Australian representatives although the plumage and courtship displays of our male riflebirds are an impressive indication of what awaits the more adventurous bird-watcher in New Guinea.

Birds of paradise are strong-footed and vocal forest birds with typically, cryptically coloured, often ventrally barred females. Brightly plumaged adult males exhibit much iridescent and metallic colouration. Bill shape is extremely varied relative to the feeding ecology of each species. Most are predominantly frugivorous, and like the Trumpet Manucode, have an all-purpose starling- or crow-like bill. Some, like the riflebirds, are mainly insectivorous and have long decurved bills for probing into dead wood and beneath moss and tree bark of large tree boughs and trunks.

Males of some species display solitarily, like the riflebirds. Other New Guinea species congregate in groups or 'clans' at 'leks' and there display communally in one or several tree tops, providing a fine avian spectacle. At such noisy and colourful leks, visiting females are attracted to the one or two dominant, often central, males who may perform most or all of the matings.

Apart from the harsh advertising calls of male riflebirds given at their display area, these birds may be located as they actually display, or as they fly through the forest, because the oddly modified outer primary feathers produce a strange loud rustling sound during these activities.

The trumpet-like blast of the Trumpet Manucode call is greatly enhanced by a peculiar elongation of the trachea. It is modified to a greatly convoluted structure just beneath the breast skin and over the pectoral muscles.

Riflebirds sometimes add cast snake-skins to the rims of their nests, perhaps for decoration or to deter predators.

The Magnificent Riflebird waves its head during its courtship display.

The cup-shaped nest of the Paradise Riflebird is decorated with cast snake-skins.

Breeding seasons

	J	F	M	A	M	J	J	A	S	O	N	D
732 Paradise Riflebird												
733 Victoria's Riflebird												
734 Magnificent Riflebird												
735 Trumpet Manucode												

Australian Mud-nesters Family Corcoracidae

The Australian Mud-nesters are most notable for their communal way of life, which is perhaps more complex than any other Australian birds'. Basic to their social structure is a close-knit family party, usually numbering about seven in the White-winged Chough, ten in the Apostlebird. The groups consist of a 'breeding unit' which includes a dominant male and several mature females, and a number of immature birds (progeny from previous seasons). Group activities are performed, mostly in the breeding season when nest construction, brooding and feeding of the young are shared more or less equally among all members. Egg incubation, however, appears to be left solely to adults.

An Apostlebird on its mud nest.

The nest, a distinctive bowl of mud and plant fibre, is placed on a limb that is horizontal or nearly so. Construction is in several distinct stages (see diagram). A solid base platform of mud is formed over the branch, and pieces of grass stem or bark liberally coated in mud form the walls. Even first year birds involve themselves in this process, but they lack the dexterity of adults.

The normal clutch size is three to five pale, lustrous eggs. Clutches that are double this number are not uncommon and form when more than one female lays in the same nest. However, only four chicks reach the fledgling stage. The size and rigidity of the nest is an obvious physical restriction. Usually only one Chough brood is raised in a season; with the Apostlebird two broods *may* occur. During breeding a territory is vigilantly defended, but after breeding the birds do not defend it and wander within a 'home range' of several square kilometres.

The construction of the bowl-shaped mud nest of the White-winged Chough is in several stages. (Modification of Ian Rowley's sketches.)

Much time is spent foraging on the ground for insects or other invertebrates and sometimes small vertebrates, such as frogs. In autumn and winter the birds move to more open country and seeds become a significant part of their diet. Large congregations (up to 100 individuals) may occur where food is abundant (e.g. grain fields). Such groupings, however, are merely the result of a rich food source and have no social unity — each family party goes its own way when there is a disturbance or when the food supply is exhausted.

Breeding seasons

J F M A M J J A S O N D

736 White-winged Chough

737 Apostlebird

Magpie-larks Family Grallinidae

One of Australia's most widespread birds, the distinctively patterned black and white Magpie-lark builds cup-shaped mud nests as do the Corcoracidae and was once placed in the same Family. However, plumage, social and anatomical differences now place it in a new Family with the New Guinea Torrent-lark. Three to five pink eggs, blotched purple and brown, are laid. Pairs sing antiphonally.

Note: In the future, the Magpie-larks may be included with the Monarchs and Flycatchers.

Breeding season (*variable*)

J F M A M J J A S O N D

738 Australian Magpie-lark*

Woodswallows Family Artamidae

Although woodswallows have bifurcate (divided) tongues and are often observed taking nectar and pollen, they are considered most closely related to butcherbirds. Both groups have a similar skull structure and black-tipped blue bills.

There is a clear relationship between the nature of the movements of the Australian woodswallows and their geographical races. At one end of the scale, nomadic movements of the Little, Masked and White-browed Woodswallows

A female White-browed Woodswallow on its nest.

339

facilitated gene flow which in turn accounts for the lack of variation. At the other end, the very sedentary Black-faced Woodswallow has developed two markedly different races, while the migratory Dusky and White-breasted Woodswallows are intermediate in their development of minor races.

Woodswallows' movements are in response to the availability of their main food item, namely, flying insects. They also eat terrestrial arthropods. They build flimsy nests in tree-forks, etc.

In line with their gregarious tendencies, they rear their young co-operatively, mob predators, and may roost in tight clusters. This last activity may occur occasionally in the daytime. Other distinctive features include tail-swivelling, and plumages which are soft in colour and texture due to the presence of powder-down.

Breeding seasons (*variable)

	J	F	M	A	M	J	J	A	S	O	N	D
739 White-breasted Woodswallow*												
740 Masked Woodswallow*												
741 White-browed Woodswallow												
742 Black-faced Woodswallow												
743 Dusky Woodswallow												
744 Little Woodswallow												

Butcherbirds, Currawongs   Family Cracticidae

Recent evidence based on egg-white protein and DNA-hybridisation suggests that cracticids are closely related to the woodswallows. Three distinct species of Australian Magpie were once recognised but are now considered races because they interbreed where their ranges overlap.

The Black Currawong, considered a race of the Pied by some, now has full species status based on differing plumage and call. The Silver-backed Butcherbird of the north is now considered a race of the Grey Butcherbird; the Black-backed Butcherbird of Cape York Pen., Queensland, may also be one.

As a Family, cracticids are omnivorous as well as partial scavengers, feeding on invertebrates, small birds, mammals, reptiles, fruits and seeds, utilising many aspects of their territories, and sometimes caching food.

The Australian Magpie has been intensely studied and its behaviour of living in mixed groups and aggressively defending territory is well known. Five different kinds of groups are formed for breeding and feeding activities. Butcherbirds form only family groups, although they do defend their territory.

The butcherbirds and magpies are mostly sedentary and partly nomadic. However, currawongs are annual altitudinal migrants. After breeding as pairs in highland forests, they migrate to more open lowland country in winter, forming large, noisy foraging flocks.

Breeding occurs throughout the distribution range of the cracticids. Nests, mainly of sticks and twigs lined with dry grasses and rootlets are usually placed in tree-forks. Two to five oval-shaped eggs are laid (currawongs' more tapered). Egg colouring varies considerably. Magpie eggs are mostly bluish-green, butcherbird eggs are greenish-grey, and currawong eggs are brownish. All eggs have darker streaks and spots.

Butcherbirds cache food in forks of trees. This nestling will be eaten later.

Reading

Burton, T. C. and A. A. Martin, (1976), 'Analysis of hybridization between Black-backed and White-backed Magpies in south-eastern Australia', *Emu* **76**, 30-36.

Carrick (1963), 'Ecological significance of territory in the Australian Magpie *Gymnorhina tibicen*', *Proc. XIII Internat. Ornith. Congr.*, 740-753.

Ford, J. (1979), 'A new subspecies of Grey Butcherbird from the Kimberley, Western Australia', *Emu* **79**, 191-194.

Wimbush, D. J. (1969), 'Studies on the Pied Currawong *Strepera graculina* in the Snowy Mountains', *Emu* **69**, 72-80.

Breeding seasons

	J	F	M	A	M	J	J	A	S	O	N	D
745 Black Butcherbird												
746 Grey Butcherbird												
747 Black-backed Butcherbird												
748 Pied Butcherbird												
749 Australian Magpie												
750 Pied Currawong												
751 Black Currawong												
752 Grey Currawong												

Ravens, Crows   Family Corvidae

Adaptable, intelligent and considered to be among the most highly evolved birds, the Corvidae may have originated in Asia before the mid-Miocene (20-25 million years ago).

The almost world-wide genus *Corvus* (typical crows) contains five Australian sibling species recently diverged from a common stock. The foreign House Crow has occasionally been recorded as well.

Look for corvids near rubbish tips, country roads and (different species) in lambing paddocks, newly-sown or ripening crops, and orchards in fruit.

The best clue to a corvid's identity is the pitch, tone and tempo of its territorial advertisement calls, and characteristic behaviour patterns. The three large territorial species call from high perches or during a high advertisement flight, which has exaggerated, jerky wing beats. The two small nomads soar and perform aerobatics in large flocks. The two crows have a dipping 'currawong flight' aerial display. Knowledge of corvid ecology is also useful in identification. Usually, at least two species live together. They avoid competition by differences in ecology and social organisation. Usually one is a large resident species, the other a small nomad. Inspect feather base colour (grey or white) and throat hackles to identify dead birds.

Corvids are omnivorous, eating carrion and also caching surplus food. To some extent they specialise: flesh (Australian, Forest Ravens), insects (Little Raven), grain (Torresian Crow). The desert-dwelling Little Crow has a broad diet, exploiting food sources not available to the larger species. The two large ravens may finish off sick lambs or sheep, but *cannot* kill healthy lambs. Regurgitated pellets under perches or nests can provide diet information. Check these at weekly intervals.

The Little Raven and Little Crow move in large nomadic flocks except when breeding. In south-east and south-west Australia they move from inland to coastal areas for summer. Little Ravens breeding in alpine areas move to lower altitudes in autumn and winter.

The Forest Raven is the least studied, yet its mainland populations may be declining. Where it occurs alone it adapts well to man-induced landscape changes but where mainland forest is cleared for agriculture, the Australian Raven moves in, displacing it.

Corvids build a large, bowl-shaped stick nest in a tree or man-made structure. The Little Crow's nest contains a layer of mud or clay under the lining. Corvids are monogamous. Females incubate eggs and tend chicks; males supply food.

The Little Raven and Little Crow are flexible in choice of nest sites and breeding season, have a shorter breeding cycle, and forage in areas unsuitable for nesting. They breed semi-colonially in habitats unsuitable for the large territorial species. In courtship displays a pale nictitating membrane is drawn over the eyes. The courtship of the Australian Raven involves aerial pursuit of the female by the male; that of the Little Raven involves a 'promenade' on the ground by the male; those of the other species have not been described.

Reading

Goodwin, D. (1976), *Crows of the World*, Queensland University Press, Brisbane.

Rowley, I., et al. (1973), 'The comparative ecology of the Australian corvids', *CSIRO Wildl. Res.*, **18**, 1-169.

Little Crows, like other corvids, build large nests of sticks.

Breeding seasons

	J	F	M	A	M	J	J	A	S	O	N	D
753 Australian Raven												
754 Forest Raven												
755 Little Raven												
756 Little Crow												
757 Torresian Crow												

Glossary

Abrasion Wearing down of the feathers.

Adult Birds which breed or are known to have breeding capabilities. Adult plumages are those which do not change in appearance in subsequent moults (allowing for alternating eclipse plumages in some species, e.g. waders).

Allopreening Preening by one bird of another.

Alula Four small feathers found on a bird's 'thumb'. These control airflow over the leading edge of the wing — the 'bastard wing'.

Axilla The area where the underwing joins the body. The feathers in this area are known as axillaries or the 'arm-pit', e.g. Grey Plover.

Bar A fine, transverse mark.

Carpal joint (flexure) The joint found between the 'arm' and the 'hand' of the wing.

Casque A helmet-like structure on the skull or bill, e.g. Helmeted Friarbird, Cassowary.

Cere Bare, wax-like or fleshy structure at the base of the upper beak. containing the nostrils, e.g. Peregrine Falcon, Cape Barren Goose.

Chevrons V-shaped stripes, usually on breast, e.g. Powerful Owl.

Cline A graded series of changes in the character of a bird across a geographic area, e.g. Varied Sittella, Figbird.

Colour morph Different colouring within a single interbreeding population, unrelated to season, age or sex, e.g. Eastern Reef Egret.

Coverts Small feathers hiding the bases of larger ones.

Crepuscular Appearing or flying at dusk, e.g. nightjars, frogmouths.

Cryptic Having protective colouring or camouflage, e.g. Bush Thick-knee, Australasian Bittern.

Culmen The ridge along the whole length or top of the upper mandible.

Diagnostic Having value in a description for the puspose of classification or identification.

Dimorphism (sexual) The occurrence of two distinct types of plumage colour between the sexes of the same species, also shape and size.

Dorsal Pertaining to the upper surface of the body.

Eclipse (plumage) Dull, seasonal plumage assumed by many bird species during late summer, autumn or winter, e.g. ducks, waders, malurid wrens.

Egg tooth A tiny scale-like protrusion on the upper bills of many baby birds to help them chip through the egg shell.

Endemic Native to or peculiar to a particular or defined area.

Extinct Gone forever; no longer extant.

Facial disc A bird's face, disc-like in form, being well-defined and comparatively flat, e.g. owls, harriers.

Family The division of classification into which an Order is divided and which has one or more genera, i.e. the next taxonomic rank below Order.

Feral Having returned to the wild after domestication.

Fingers Term used when a bird spreads its primary feathers in flight, e.g. Little Eagle, corvids.

Flank Area on the bird's side, found directly below the forepart of the closed wing, e.g. Tasmanian race of Silvereye.

Fledgling (leaving the nest) Partly or wholly feathered. Flightless or partly flighted, but *before* flight.

Foreneck The front section of the neck.

Frons The forehead or feathered front of the crown, immediately above the base of the upper bill, e.g. Common Bronzewing.

Frontal shield Distinctive, unfeathered, horny or fleshy forehead which extends down to the base of the upper bill. Does not include nostril.

Gape The fleshy corner of the beak which is often yellow in young birds.

Genus (plural Genera) The division of classification into which a Family is divided and which has one or more species, i.e. the next taxonomic rank below Family.

Gular Of the throat. A gular pouch is distendible skin in the central area of the throat, e.g. Great Cormorant.

Hackles Neck feathers which are longer than normal, e.g. Trumpet Manucode.

Hatchling See Nestling.

Hood Colour mass covering the head, e.g. Hooded Robin, Australian Hobby.

Hybridisation Interbreeding of different species, the offspring of which are infertile and known as 'hybrids', e.g. offspring of Pacific Black Duck and Mallard.

Immature (= Sub-Adult). All plumages which *follow* first moult *until* full breeding capacity and/or plumage is reached. Birds are usually independent of adults.

Juvenile (= Juvenal) Fledging to free flying birds, with the feathers which *first* replaced the natal down. May or may not be still under parental care.

Lamella A small layer of stiff hairs (membranes) on the inner edge of the bill, used to sieve food particles from water, e.g. prions, ducks.

Lanceolate Spear-like in shape. Usually used in describing feather shapes.

Leading edge The front edge of a wing or flipper.

Lobe Roundish projection, e.g. Musk Duck.

Lores Area between the bill and the eye, e.g. Little Tern.

Mandible The upper or lower half of the bird's bill.

Mantle Feathers forming a covering of the upper back and the base of the wings, e.g. Paradise Riflebird.

Mask Black or dark area which encloses the eyes and part of the face, e.g. Masked Woodswallow.

Migratory Of regular geographical movement.

Mirror White circles (spots) in the primary feathers of gulls, e.g. Silver Gull.

Nail The hooked tip of the upper mandibles of albatrosses and petrels, also of waterfowl (*sensu stricta*).

Nape The back of the bird's neck. Nuchal means 'of the nape', e.g. Spotted Bowerbird's nuchal crest.

Nestling (= Hatchling = Downy) In or about the nest. Naked or downy, i.e. *before* feathers develop.

Nomadic Of variable, often erratic movement with regard to time and area.

Nominate If there are more than one race in a species, the race that takes the sub-specific name identical to the specific name of that species is known as the nominate race and should always be named first.

Nuptial Of or pertaining to breeding.

Orbital ring A circular colour patch, fleshy or feathered, surrounding the eye, e.g. Silvereye.

Order The division of classification into which a Class is divided and which has one or more Families, i.e. the next taxonomic rank below Class.

Pelagic Oceanic. Living far from land except when nesting.

Pellet The regurgitated and indigestible remains of prey —usually feathers, hair, bone, scales, etc., e.g. Little Crow, owls.

Piratic Stealing food from other species.

Plumage The whole layer of feathers and down covering a bird's body.

Plume A long, showy, display feather, e.g. egrets.

Primaries The main or outer flight feathers which control the manoeuvrability of the bird — an old term is 'quills'.

Race A group sharing common characteristics that distinguish them from other members of the same species. Often they form a geographically isolated group. In this book, the term is used instead of 'subspecies'.

Rictal bristles Stiff whisker-like protrusions about the base of the bill, e.g. Australian Owlet-nightjar.

Roost A resting or sleeping place/perch for birds.

Rump The squarish area between the lower back and base of the tail, e.g. Yellow-rumped Thornbill.

Scapular Feathers which lie along the dorsal shoulder (base of the wing) of a bird.

Secondaries The inner flight feathers attached to the forearm.

Sedentary Locally living, not travelling far.

Shaft The main stem (rachis) of any feather.

Shoulder General term for upperwing coverts.

Soft parts Unfeathered areas of the body — bill, eyes, legs, feet and any bare skin.

Species The division of classification into which a genus is divided, the members of which can interbreed among themselves, i.e. next taxonomic rank below genus.

Speculum Iridescent dorsal patch on a duck's wing which contrasts with the rest of the wing.

Spur Sharp bony projection on the wing or leg.

Striated (striations) Streaked. Lines along head to tail.

Sub-Adult See Immature.

Sub-terminal Near the end, e.g. dark tail band of Scrubtit, Pacific Gull.

Superciliary The eyebrow stripe of some birds, e.g. Pacific Black Duck.

Talon Sharply hooked claw used for holding and killing prey, e.g. birds of prey.

Tarsus The lower leg of birds; may be feathered, partly so, or not at all.

Terminal At the end, e.g. white tail-tips of Spiny-cheeked Honeyeater.

Tertiary (feather) One of the inner flight feathers on a bird's 'upper arm'.

Trailing edge The back or hind edge of a wing or flipper, e.g. Hardhead, Little Penguin.

Underparts The chin, throat, breast, belly, wing flank and tail, i.e. the ventral surface.

Upperparts The upper areas of the bird's body —the mantle, back, rump and base of tail, i.e. the dorsal surface.

Vagrant A bird found in an area which is not its usual habitat, having strayed there due to disorientation, adverse winds, etc.

Vent The cloaca — includes anus and oviduct openings.

Ventral Pertaining to the under surface of the body.

Vermiculated Densely patterned with fine winding or wavy lines, e.g. Wandering Albatross.

Wattle A fleshy lobe or appendage, often brightly coloured, hanging from the throat or neck of certain birds, e.g. Masked Lapwing.

Wingspan The shortest distance between the wing-tips.

Index of Scientific Names

Common Names

Writers and their contributions

Tom Aumann, B.Sc., B.Ed.
Species 147-150.
Families Pandionidae, Accipitridae, Falconidae.

Australasian Wader Study Group
Principal contributors: Angela Jessop, B.Sc. (Hons), Brett Lane, B.A., Clive Minton, Ph.D., Mick Murliss.
Contributing members: John Bransbury, Peter Curry, Peter Dann, Berrice Forest, Stephen Garnett, David Henderson, Marilyn Hewish, Roger Jaensch, Tom Lowe, Alan McBride, Jim McNamara, Mike Newman, Danny Rogers, Ken Rogers.
Species 201-274.
Families Jacanidae, Burhinidae, Rostratulidae, Haematopodidae, Charadriidae, Recurvirostridae, Scolopacidae, Phalaropodidae, Glareolidae.

David Baker-Gabb, B.Ag., Dip.Sc., M.Sc., Ph. D.
Species 139-140, 142-146, 154-156.
Families Pandionidae, Accipitridae, Falconidae.

Kevin Bartram
Species 20-32, 47-52, 63-93, 166-173, 182-197, 275-307, 386-398, 416-421, 464-468, 502-517.
Families Procellariidae, Oceanitidae, Pelecanoididae, Pelecanidae, Sulidae, Anhingidae, Phalacrocoracidae, Fregatidae, Phaethontidae, Phasianidae, Pedionomidae, Rallidae, Stercorariidae, Laridae, Cuculidae, Muscicapidae (genera *Machaerirhynchus, Monarcha*).

Simon Bennett, B. Appl. Sc.
Species 174-180.
Family Turnicidae.

Ron Brown
Species 115-137.
Family Anatidae.

Margaret Cameron, B.A.
Species 68-76.
Families Oceanitidae, Pelecanoididae.

Mike Carter, C. Eng.
Species 18-19.

Andrew Corrick, B. Sc. (Hons).
Species 94-114.
Families Ardeidae, Ciconiidae, Plataleidae.

Stephen Debus, B.A., Dip. Nat. Resources, Dip. Ed.
Species 138, 141, 151-153, 157-162, 753-758.
Families Pandionidae, Accipitridae, Falconidae, Corvidae.

Denise Deerson
Species 115-137.
Family Anatidae.

Xenia Dennett, B.Sc., Ph.D.
Species 469-473.
Family Muscicapidae (genus *Petroica*).

Peter Fell, B.Sc.
Species 608-674.

Kate Fitzherbert, B.Sc. (Hons).
Species 198-200.
Families Gruidae, Otididae.

Cliff Frith
Species 723-735.
Families Ptilonorhynchidae, Paradisaeidae.

Geoff Gayner
Species 545-559.
Family Maluridae.

Belinda Gillies, B.A., Dip. Ed.
Species 745-752.
Families Grallinidae, Cracticidae.

Marc Gottsch
Species 163-165, 399-403, 409-415, 680-681.

Murray Grant
Species 518-531.
Families Orthonychidae, Timaliidae.

John Hatch, B.A., Ph.D.
Species 44-46, 53-56.

Victor Hurley, B.Sc.
Families Dromaiidae, Casuariidae, Struthionidae, Megapodiidae, Orthonychidae, Maluridae, Ephthianuridae, Dicaeidae.

Jack Hyett, T.P.T.C.
Species 181.
Family Pedionomidae.

Andrew Isles, B.Sc.
Species 333-385.
Family Psittacidae.

Jaroslav Klapste
Species 4-6, 422-434, 443-455, 532-541.
Families Podicipedidae, Alcedinidae, Alaudidae, Motacillidae, Hirundinidae, Sylviidae.

Peter Klapste
Species 4-6, 422-434, 443-455, 532-551.
Families Podicipedidae, Alcedinidae, Alaudidae, Motacillidae, Hirundinidae, Sylviidae.

Tess Kloot
Species 463, 716-722.
Families Pycnonotidae, Sturnidae, Oriolidae, Dicruridae.

Alan Lill, B.Sc., Ph.D.
Species 439-440.
Family Menuridae.

Gordon McCarthy
Species 577-600.
Family Acanthizidae.

Ellen McCulloch
Species 456-462, 716-722.
Families Campephagidae, Sturnidae, Oriolidae, Dicruridae.

Peter Mason, B.Ed., Dip.T.
Species 1-3, 456-462.
Families Dromaiidae, Casuariidae, Struthionidae, Campephagidae.

Peter Menkhorst, B.Sc.
Species 333-385.
Family Psittacidae.

Richard Noske, Ph.D.
Species 601-607.
Families Neosittidae, Climacteridae.

Ian Norman, Ph.D.
Species 115-137.
Family Anatidae.

David Paton, B.Sc. (Hons), Ph.D.
Species 608-674.
Family Meliphagidae.

Paul Peake, B.Sc.
Species 399-415, 739-744.
Families Strigidae, Tytonidae, Podargidae, Artamidae.

Trevor Pescott, M.Sc. (*Honoris Causa*), **Dip. Civ. Eng.**
Species 308-332.
Family Columbidae.

Des Quinn
Species 399-415, 560-576, 675-679.

Pat Rich, Ph.D.
Modern avifaunal regions (page 274), Prehistoric birds (page 275).

Bruce Robertson, B.Sc., B.V.Sc.
Species 280-286.
Family Laridae.

Len Robinson
Species 392-398, 435-438.
Family Pittidae.

Tony Robinson, B.Sc. (Hons), Ph.D.
Where the birds live: vegetation and landform habitats of Australia (page 276).

Ken Simpson, M.Sc. (*Honoris Causa*).
Species 4-17, 33-43, 89-93, 275-279, 392-398, 416-421, 441-450, 464-468, 514-517, Chukar, Common Turkey, Helmeted Guinea Fowl. Families Podicipedidae, Spheniscidae, Diomedeidae, Cuculidae, Aegothelidae, Caprimulgidae, Apodidae, Atrichornithidae, Muscicapidae, Nectariniidae.

Lance Williams, B.Sc.
Species 474-501, 687-689, 736-738.
Families Muscicapidae, Zosteropidae, Corcoracidae.

John Woinarski, B.Sc. (Hons).
Species 682-686.
Family Pardalotidae.

Richard Zann, B.Sc., Dip.Ed., Ph.D.,
Species 690-715.
Families Fringillidae, Passeridae, Ploceidae.

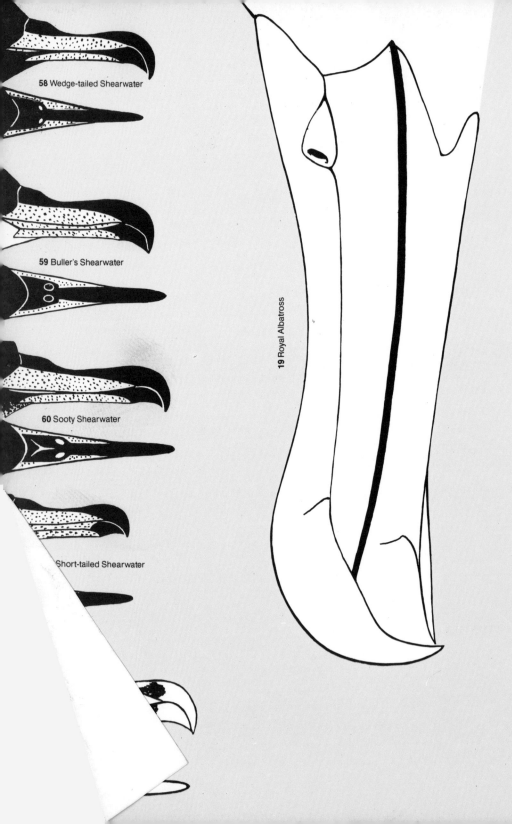

58 Wedge-tailed Shearwater

59 Buller's Shearwater

60 Sooty Shearwater

Short-tailed Shearwater

19 Royal Albatross